To Australian friends and colleagues

Australian External Policy under Labor

Content, Process and
The National Debate

HENRY S. ALBINSKI

University of British Columbia Press
Vancouver

© University of Queensland Press, St Lucia, Queensland, 1977

Published 1977 by University of British Columbia Press
For sale only in North America

Canadian Cataloguing in Publication Data

Albinski, Henry S.
    Australian external policy under Labor

    Bibliography: p.
    Includes index.
    ISBN 0-7748-0070-4

    1. Australia—Foreign relations—1945- 2. Labor Party
(Australia). 3. Australia—Politics and government—1945-
I. Title.
DL 117.A42   327.94   C77-002093-3

Contents

Preface

This book is an analysis of Australian external policy under the first Labor Party government elected to federal office in nearly a quarter of a century. The choice of the term "external policy" is deliberate, in that the study deals with defence and international economic dimensions as well as with more conventionally construed "foreign policy". The object is to link policy outputs with policy process. In addition to emphasizing what policies were evolved, the book is concerned with such themes as the assumptions and perceptions underlying policy movements, the weight of historical and party traditions, the contributions of key élites, the various sources of advice and pressures that sought to influence policies, the environment in which dialogue between the government and its critics was conducted, and party political and electoral implications.

The principal research was carried out in 1974–75, during the author's appointment as a Senior Fulbright–Hays Scholar and Visiting Professor at the University of Sydney and the Flinders University of South Australia, and during a lateral visit to New Zealand. The materials consulted included official documents, newspaper and secondary sources, party and interest group publications, and survey and electoral data. The book's preparation has been greatly assisted by factual and interpretative comment supplied by scores of individuals, a number of whom were interviewed more than once. The respondents were predominantly Australians, but included a number of New Zealanders and Americans who were interviewed at various times in Australia, New Zealand and in the United States. Among the Australians interviewed were parliamentarians of various parties, including former and present ministers and backbenchers. Also interviewed were official and diplomatic personnel, ministerial advisers, party organization figures, interest group spokesmen, journalists and academics. The author is deeply indebted to these many individuals. Conversations with them were, however, conducted on the understanding of non-attribution of their remarks. It is therefore the author's responsibility to introduce such internal evidence without disclosing sources, while offering reasoned judgements as to their relative value. This involves criteria such as the credibility and the position of interviewees, and the cumulative weight of cross-checked information and opinion.

A considerable debt is acknowledged to various Australian and New Zealand universities, and to Australian Institute of International Affairs and New Zealand Institute of International Affairs branches, where seminar and lecture appearances elicited helpful criticisms of the ideas presented there. A similar acknowledgement applies to members of the Australian foreign policy class taught at Flinders University.

Funding for the research project was provided from several sources, notably the Australian–American Educational Foundation. Other sources included the New Zealand–United States Educational Foundation, the University of Sydney, Flinders University and the Department of Political Science and the Central Fund for Research of The Pennsylvania State University.

The author wishes to express his appreciation to a number of individuals and bodies who facilitated the project. Professors Henry Mayer of Sydney and David Corbett of Flinders, and their colleagues, provided sponsorship for the Australian visit and were generous hosts. Considerable gratitude is owed to Messrs H.F. Willcock, B. Farrer and G.C. Weinman of the Australian–American Educational Foundation. Exceptional source material assistance was provided by Mr Ian Hamilton and his associates at the Australian Information Service, Canberra, and by information officers at the Australian Embassy, Washington.

Much valuable material was obtained from certain specialized collections and bibliographic services. Among these were the federal secretariats of the Labor, Liberal and (National) Country Parties, as well as the ALP and Liberal state branches in New South Wales. Included were the offices of the Prime Minister and of the Foreign Minister, the Departments of Foreign Affairs and of Defence, and the legislative research service of the Parliamentary Library. Considerable assistance was provided through the facilities of the Department of Political Science, the Department of International Relations, and the Strategic and Defence Studies Centre, at the Institute of Advanced Studies, Australian National University.

Finally, some special notes of thanks to friends and facilitators: To Dr Peter Boyce, for permission to draw on material published in the August 1974 issue of *Australian Outlook*, a publication of the Australian Institute of International Affairs and of which Dr (now Professor)

Boyce was editor. To Ms Merril Yule and her associates at the University of Queensland Press. To Ms Wanita Askey, for her *par excellence* typing of manuscript. To the author's wife, Dr Ethel Bisbicos Albinski, for her many supportive expressions during the period of research and manuscript preparation.

Henry S. Albinski

University Park, Pennsylvania

1 The Liberal Inheritance: I

At the December 1949 Australian House of Representatives election, the Chifley Australian Labor Party (ALP) government was defeated by a Liberal and Country Party (L–CP) coalition led by R.G. Menzies.* The L–CP won nine consecutive elections and governed for twenty-three years. Finally, at the election of 2 December 1972, Labor was returned to office, where it remained for almost exactly three years.

Inescapably, this inordinately long tenure in office enabled the Liberals to leave an indelible stamp on Australia's foreign and domestic affairs. In early 1966, when he stepped down after fifteen years as Prime Minister, Menzies maintained that the most momentous step during his era had been in foreign policy, specifically, the negotiation of the ANZUS Treaty with the United States and New Zealand.[1] Looking back on the success of his party in the 1972 election, Labor Prime Minister E. G. Whitlam wrote that "The foreign policy of the 1950s which served the previous government politically into the 1970s was clearly exhausted. The Liberal Party itself had ceased to defend or justify it." However, Whitlam speculated that "even if there had been no change of government, there would have been a change of policy; and I am not so churlish as to suggest that it would not have changed for the better."[2] Plainly, the foreign policy legacy of the Liberal years conditioned what Labor set out to do, why and how it did it, and the resulting international and domestic reception.

L–CP foreign policy, like the foreign policy of other governments, derived from a *mélange* of factors. These included perceptions of the character and requirements of the nation itself, the constellation of

* In 1975, the Australian Country Party changed its name to the Australian National Country Party. Reference in this study will be to the Country Party and its CP form of abbreviation.

forces operating within the international environment, the timing and sequence of events abroad, the temperamental and political orientations of those who governed and other miscellaneous considerations. The Liberals entered office against a background of exceptional security anxiety in Australia. The Second World War had finished only four years earlier. The swift Japanese thrust down South-East Asia and into New Guinea, the bombing of Darwin and other points in northern Australia, the belief that an invasion of the Australian mainland had barely been averted had traumatized many Australians. Fears of a Japanese military revival persisted well into the 1950s. Rather than bringing settled conditions in Asia, the war's aftermath was seen to have released new and ominously destabilizing forces. Familiar, friendly colonial powers in the region were being challenged by indigenous, often insurrectionist movements, and replaced by unfamiliar, at times erratic and radical local régimes. A communist régime ·was declared in China only two months prior to the 1949 Australian election. The communist-related "Emergency" in Malaya had begun well before the Liberals entered government. Half a year after taking office they had to contend with the opening of the Korean War.[3] Other international crises followed rapidly: French Indo-China, the Chinese off-shore islands, Indonesian pressures against the Dutch in West New Guinea. There was the Sino-Indian border war, Indonesia's "Confrontation" of Malaysia and, of course, Vietnam and its associated reverberations in Laos and Cambodia. L–CP governments came to interpret the chain of international conflicts and internal upheavals in Asia as interconnected. In one degree or another, Australian governments attributed communist inspiration to nearly all such disturbances. Moreover, in the pithy phrase of former External Affairs (Foreign Affairs) Minister Paul Hasluck, "at the end of the road there is always China".[4]

In other words, L–CP governments came to office and then governed in an atmosphere of what they saw as interminable, often violent and largely communist-directed turbulence in Asia. We should also remember that L–CP governments represented the principal conservative strain within the Australian political party system. They were temperamentally bitterly hostile to communism as such, real or suspected. Domestically, they tried, but failed, in 1951 to outlaw the Communist Party of Australia; overseas, they saw communism as an especially pernicious force.[5] As J. D. Β. Miller summarized it in 1963, they were "anti-Communist for basic reasons of belief, sentiment and social condition. They would be anti-Communist if the Australian Communist Party was the only one in the world. The fact that Communism is a world movement hostile to the kind of institutions we have in Australia and to the countries with whom our associations are closest, fortifies their natural inclinations."[6] Indeed, the L–CP's preoccupation with a communist menace was not basically inconsistent with widespread, historically conditioned popular conceptions of threats and of communism. Postwar L–CP governments may have fed anti-communist sentiment and exploited it electorally, but they did not invent it. Australians on various sides have often treated communism in rather simplistic, categorical terms. This phenomenon has been widely noticed by students of Australian foreign policy. Harry Gelber has written on the way in which, since the nineteenth century, Australia's isolation "encouraged ideological or emotional or liturgical approaches to foreign problems", among them anti-communism.[7] In their understanding of the Australian ethos, Camilleri and Teichmann have argued that "Ideology has not played an important role overall—hedonistic materialism being the governing theme. Anti-communism is probably the nearest approach Australians have had to a fully-blown ideology," starting with the Russian Revolution and proceeding through the cold-war period.[8] In late 1948, when Labor was still governing, opinion surveys in ten nations, including the United States, Britain and Italy, indicated that Australians had the highest expectation that another world war would occur within ten years.[9]

Serious dislocation in Asia, coupled with a sense of communist conspiracy, bore directly on the classical image of Australian security definitions. The foundations were set in the nineteenth century, before Federation, and relative to the rise of Russian and then Japanese power, and of colonial rivalries in the Pacific. The theme is familiar. Australia was, and is, a very affluent, western, basically white society, placed on the rim of Asia, far removed from either Europe or North America. Its relatively small population (currently 13.5 million) is mostly nestled in the south-east corner of an island-continent of nearly 7 million 7 hundred thousand square kilometres and of 19000 kilometres of coastline. The integrity of its communications and access to far-removed friends in time of crisis have been felt to require reasonable tranquility in the Asia–Pacific region and neighbours neither aggressive themselves nor subject to control by unfriendly powers. Hence the joining of historically-fixed security concerns with putatively communist-inspired disorder gave rise to the essential rationale of L–CP foreign policy: "We are a small nation. We are a non-Communist nation. We are a nation possessing many things that others more powerful must envy. There is no small country in the world to whom the protection against external aggression is more important, is more utterly vital, than Australia."[10]

From these general perceptions of what was happening in the

Asian neighbourhood, and what was implied for Australia, L–CP governments drew several interlocked conclusions. Firstly, and most broadly, it was necessary to deter, and if required, to defeat, those movements or nations that might wish to sow discord or undertake actual aggression. In South-East Asia, the weakening or absorption of a particular nation would encourage more provocation by China or other interested parties, demoralize and outflank other smaller states and restrict the strategic elasticity of non-communist nations. In particular, it would denigrate the credibility of the American security shield, the single most important source of deterrence in the region. L–CP governments were therefore quick to condemn threat responses that were, or could be, construed as being tardy or irresolute.

Since Australia's own power and resources were limited, L–CP governments placed much emphasis on the presence/commitment in Asia and the Pacific of friendly major powers. Expressions of such interest would, depending on circumstances, provide a mix of military, diplomatic and economic dimensions. The notion of a major regional "protector" for Australia was itself of very old lineage. For decades, the protector had been Britain. But the quick victories of Japan against British forces in and around Malaya and Singapore at the start of the Pacific war caused Australia, under a Labor government, to look to America. It was American forces that won the battles of the Coral and Bismarck Seas and primarily American forces that carried the war towards Japan during the subsequent Pacific campaigns. After the war, though Britain retained a presence in Asia, Australia pre–eminently viewed the United States as the great power guarantor in the area. Under Liberal governments, the United States was not simply believed to be the most powerful and attractable protector, but there also was the lustre of recent history. When faced with the prospect of a Japanese attack, Australia had found a saviour. That image, though weakened over the years, has continued to colour the debate over the US–Australian alliance and over relations between the two nations generally. The American memorial, built in thanks for US assistance during the Second World War, is the only monument of its kind in the city of Canberra. It is symbolic that, on its perch on Russell Hill, it is surrounded by the complex of Australian Defence Department buildings.

L–CP governments further concluded that Australia must itself pursue policies contributory to the stabilization of conditions to its north. At minimum, it had to *appear* to be interested, active, helpful, and so on, in the employment of policy instruments. The rationale was in three parts. In the first place, though modest, Australia's own contributions in men, *matériel*, development assistance, or whatever, could be of some tangible value. Secondly, as a member of the Asian–

Pacific region, Australia could by example bolster the resolve of Asian nations against aggression or subversion. An Australian "cop-out" was thought in Canberra to be disproportionately debilitating to the cause. Thirdly, and most important, L–CP governments felt that an appropriate, supportive Australian demeanour was vital to the encouragement of great power roles in the region. L–CP governments reasoned that it would be politically, diplomatically and militarily easier for great powers, such as the United States, to become and to stay involved: in Hasluck's words, to alleviate the feelings of the "loneliness of a great power" from which an already widely committed nation might suffer.[11] But "impressing" Washington, or London, was not simply conceived as serving to maintain their interest in Asia. It had two subsidiary motives. One was to widen Australia's entrée into major power councils, to exert an influence over their policy movements, which might otherwise be unavailable. Also a supporting, at large Australian role was regarded as an opportunity to attract great power attention in controversies of special *Australian* concern, but which would normally be secondary in the calculations of great powers.

Calculations of Australian interest, threat perceptions and preferred responses imposed by the L–CP did not, of course, go unchallenged. Bruce Grant, for instance, cautioned against the temptation "to try to involve our protector more and more in the region, so that we can demonstrate our loyalty by dispatching small military units in support. We have become crisis-prone."[12] This was a reasoned criticism. But positions sometimes became polarized. As Donald Horne remarked, "Different security-diagnoses were needed for these opposite faiths: for the vassals, the world had to be threatening; for the individualists, there had to be a diagnosis of no threat. There was no provision for more muddled situations."[13]

Security-related policies were among the most conspicuous steps undertaken by L–CP governments to implement the objectives outlined above. Security treaties were regarded as the cornerstones of the security system. The notion of engaging other powers in the region, and linking them to Australia's security requirements, was not new. It had been broached by the Lyons government in the late 1930s and Labor's External Affairs Minister, Dr H. V. Evatt, pursued such possibilities quite earnestly in the late 1940s. But it was under L–CP governments that first, ANZUS was launched in 1951, and then SEATO three years later. Australia was very energetic in its quest for an alliance with the United States. The tripartite ANZUS Treaty came to be regarded as the fulcrum of Australia's security protection. As we saw, Menzies defied it as the greatest ahcievement of his prime ministership. ANZUS was thought to represent good value for three reasons. Firstly, it was an extension of American security alliances in Asia to the Pacific, and to Australia specifically. It promised that "each Party recognizes that an armed attack in the Pacific area on any of the Parties would be dangerous to its own peace and safety and declares that it would act to meet the common danger in accordance with its constitutional process."[14] While the language of this obligation was softer than NATO's, it was accurately construed by Australia as equally strong in intent. Secondly, as a pact among a very few and very friendly nations, ANZUS facilitated Australian access to the United States for consultation and for planning among the armed services of the three participants. Finally, it was visualized as a stepping-stone to a more inclusive Asian alliance system.

A broader alliance was produced in 1954. Canberra did not find SEATO ideal. Among SEATO's eight original members only three—Thailand, the Philippines and Pakistan—were truly "Asian" and the United States was firmly opposed to organizing any form of standing SEATO force. All the same, Britain and France joined the ANZUS partners in their broader security arrangement. Thailand was brought under a security shield and the Indo-Chinese states were made eligible for assistance. Military consultations, planning and exercises were to be carried out under SEATO's aegis and defence-related economic assistance to Asian states could be jointly arranged. In time, even after SEATO's stature had declined, Pakistan had withdrawn and French involvement had became nominal, L–CP governments in Australia refused to deprecate it. They found some continuing material value in it. They did not wish to "demoralize" Asian states by tampering with it. They took seriously American admonitions in the early 1970s that if the security guarantees available to Thailand under the Manila Pact (an adjunct of SEATO) were dismantled, the viability of ANZUS would probably decline.

L–CP governments believed that Australian contributions to the deterrence or defeat of what they understood to be aggressive, communist-inspired activities in Asia were a natural complement to the security treaty system. Until the election of the Whitlam government, Australia had continously since the Second World War maintained an active military presence in Asia. The post-war Labor government contributed occupation forces in Japan, assisted the British counter-insurgency effort in Malaya with arms and munitions, and contributed warships to voyages up the Yangtze River to provision and otherwise relieve Nanking during the Chinese civil war. When the Liberals came to power, they increased the level of military support in Malaya. Two Australian battalions, plus supporting forces, were eventually committed to Korea. *Matériel* was supplied to the

French in Indo-China. A battalion was garrisoned in Malaya in 1955. First non-combat units and then in 1965 an infantry battalion saw service in Malaysian Borneo during Confrontation. Advisers were first dispatched to Vietnam in 1962. The first combat troops were posted there in 1965 and at their peak Australian forces in Vietnam exceeded 8000 of all services. The cost in Australian casualties in Vietnam was nearly 500 dead and 3000 wounded. When the Liberal government fell in December 1972, combat troops had already been withdrawn from Vietnam, though advisers remained. At that time, the major force remaining overseas was in Malaysia/Singapore. In 1971, Australia had entered a "Five Power Agreement" with Malaysia, Singapore, Britain and New Zealand. This agreement pledged common defence co-operation in the Malaysia/Singapore region and immediate consultation among the signatories regarding responses to actual or threatened attack. Australia volunteered assistance to the integrated British–New Zealand–Australian (ANZUK) force in the region. The Australian contribution of about 4000 represented almost half of the ground force, all of the air defence capability, some naval support and the bulk of the logistical back-up and of a special communications monitoring facility.

None of the overseas troop commitments undertaken by L–CP governments was especially large, and some were token. Separately and collectively, however, they were designed to fulfil broad policy objectives, which in turn related to official perceptions of the meaning for Australia of what was happening to its north. The Korean and Vietnamese commitments, for instance, were designed to check what was defined as overt communist aggression. They were to provide a test of collective will for anti-communist forces in the region. They were supposed to serve, especially in the later stages of the two conflicts, as psychological tonics for the principal contributor, the United States, when the wars had begun to drag out and were subjected to increasing criticism in America. In both cases, Australia was looking for something special for itself. Its early and enthusiastic Korean War commitment was partially aimed at raising American sympathy for a security alliance with Australia. Canberra's original combat contribution to Vietnam was partially aimed at making Washington more sensitive towards Australia's very special concern over Indonesia's Confrontation of Malaysia. The placement of a battalion in Malaya in 1955 was, in part, aimed at stationing troops that, however informally, could be linked and give content to the emergent SEATO alliance.

Australia's security role in Malaysia/Singapore during the late 1960s and early 1970s posed an unusual dilemma. By 1968, Britain had expressed its intention to disengage from a fixed military presence in the region by 1971. This seemed to denigrate a basic

Australian strategic tenet. Prime Minister John Gorton admitted that

> The concept of forward defence by troops stationed outside Australia—
> valid when based on participation with other forces and forces of a major
> Power—needed minute examination when the forces of that Power were
> to be withdrawn and the circumstances of their re-entry were not know.[15]

Although Britain's continuing presence seemed improbable,
Gorton eventually decided to maintain troops in Malaysia/Singapore
after 1971. While a number of factors, including domestic political
argument, impelled the decision, it nevertheless was a decision consis-
tent with underlying Australian assumptions and objectives. In part,
the decision related to shifting American, and more gradually
Australian, perceptions of Asia's security requirements in the 1970s.
A retracted US presence, but a call for Australia and other Asian–
Pacific nations to shoulder a larger share of burdens, was forecast.
More of this later. Additionally, however,

> The Australian–New Zealand military presence was very distinctly an an-
> nouncement to the major powers. Such a physical presence would
> facilitate a British return, albeit from a distance, should a great emergency
> arise in future. The Australian gesture was designed to be, and was, highly
> appreciated in Washington. Although the British departure was regretted,
> there was no political taste or possibility that the US could replace the
> British in the Malaysia–Singapore area. The Australian decision to stay on
> was therefore welcome. Australia could also hope to capitalize on a
> swifter US response should difficulties arise. The Australian.gesture, taken
> as it was in the context of there being no immediately assisting great
> power, was believed in Canberra to enhance Australian entrée into
> American decision-making, either on matters of mutual concern or where
> Australian interests were manifestly involved.[16]

There were other forms in which Australian contributions were expressed towards resisting dislocative forces, engaging great power interest and support, seeking "reassurance" for Australia's special concerns and gaining improved entrée into great power councils. We
specifically refer to Australian–American intelligence linkages and to
the presence of defence-related American facilities on Australian territory.

Some features of Australia's intelligence activity can most appropriately be treated in other contexts. Here we emphasize aspects
that particularly touched on Canberra's willing relationship with
great powers, especially the United States.[17] A general but important
point is that until very late in the L–CP's tenure of office, the early
1970s, Australian intelligence assessments were inordinately dependent on foreign, and especially American, data and analyses. The
situation developed in part because of the limited data-collecting
resources of a nation such as Australia, a certain amount of lethargy
and because the routines of the time made it fairly natural to receive

and depend upon American data and assessments. There is no evidence that the United States actively discouraged a more energetic Australian intelligence-gathering or intelligence-assessing role, although the largely American filter through which intelligence passed indirectly made it easier for Washington to get Australian-based appraisals, and ultimately policy decision, that coincided with American positions. The reconstruction of the principal Australian intelligence-assessing body into the Joint Intelligence Organization (JIO) in 1970 finally gave Australia a competent agency for such purposes. All the same, before and after Australia undertook more independent intelligence assessment, the flow of US and British materials remained constant. There was a great deal of it, and much of it was of very high grade. Foreign intelligence personnel were attached on liaison to JIO, fully sharing in its work, apart from the actual formulation of assessments. In late 1974, two years after the change of government, this group included 'two or three' Americans, 'one or two' Britons and a New Zealander, a junior military officer.

The intelligence-sharing practices were based on an arrangement concluded in the early 1950s among the United States, Britain, Australia, New Zealand and Canada. We say "sharing", because a great deal of Australian-collected data, and assessments, were made available to the partners. Some of the Australian capability was excellent, notably the signal surveillance and interception, cypher and, to an extent, interpretative work performed under the Defence Signals Division (DSD). The American National Security Agency highly appreciated data passed to it from DSD operations. A DSD unit in Singapore, first disclosed by Whitlam in 1973, had for some years been monitoring civilian and military radio traffic in Asia.

Less valuable was ASIS, the Australian Secret (or Security) Intelligency Service. Originally established by Menzies in the deepest secrecy, ASIS was nominally placed under the aegis of the Department of External Affairs (later Foreign Affairs). It evolved under British intelligence auspices, but later became much more American-associated. Its members developed contacts with the Central Intelligence Agency (CIA) and other branches of the US intelligence community, both for training and for bilateral liaison work.

ASIS personnel, who in their field work were concentrated on Asia, operated under cover. In years past, most of this cover was on the familiar pattern of overseas mission members (but excluding chiefs of mission) having ASIS as well as more conventional duties. More recently, persons outside of diplomatic/consular establishments were recruited as well. By far the greatest part of work performed by ASIS personnel was in data gathering, sometimes but apparently infrequently in tandem with friendly American or British counterparts.

ASIS-collected data were fed into Canberra and became part of the Australian intelligence take. Because of its modest scope, because Australia for years took exceptional notice of non-Australian intelligence, ASIS's contribution was limited. All the same, piecing the picture together as well as one can in a very sensitive field, the impression emerges that ASIS-supplied intelligence had some value, but not evenly over time.

There were innuendoes that, to obtain results, ASIS operatives became engaged in "dirty tricks" operations such as bribery, blackmail, perhaps even more formidable escapades. The author's investigations into how this might have worked under the Liberals produced the following inferences: 1. There was not much, but apparently some of a classical "dirty tricks" and espionage component in ASIS operations. 2. What there was of "dirty tricks" operations was roundly condemned, including by professionals in the Australian intelligence community. The objection was pragmatic. Australia lacked the resources and expertise needed to carry out serious cloak-and-dagger work. Worse, if cover should be blown during such operations, Australia stood to lose a great deal of diplomatic credit, especially in countries with which it tried to stay on side. If there had to be dirty trick operations, leave them to those, such as the Americans or the British, who could do the job professionally. Their governments, at all events, passed many of their discoveries to Australia. 3. Under L–CP governments, ministerial control over ASIS was virtually non-existent, a point we need to follow in some detail.

The "blame" did not really rest with the ostensibly responsible senior ministers but with the nature of ASIS itself. Menzies had succeeded in making it so secretive that a succession of Liberal ministers barely knew what was happening, or even that such a clandestine organization had acquired a personality of its own. William McMahon became Foreign Minister in November 1969 and Prime Minister in March 1971. Astonishingly, he apparently did not acquire a reasonably clear picture of ASIS until the later stages of his prime ministership, i.e. the second half of 1972.[18] McMahon seemingly wished to have the country's intelligence/security community brought under systematic examination and, if needed, correction, but the 1972 election was too close at hand to launch an inquiry. Parenthetically, it might be mentioned that from 1970, the Secretary of the Department of Foreign Affairs (FA) was Sir Keith Waller, a person of considerable administrative talent and a man who won Labor's respect following its translation to government. Yet it is possible that even this top public servant in the department to which ASIS was outwardly responsible was himself not fully cognizant of what was transpiring.

These observations are background for an appraisal of two particular involvements imputed to Australian intelligence during the later stages of L–CP government. One American-inspired report argued that ASIS had taken over some surveillance "eyes and ears" work for the CIA after the election of President Allende in Chile. The United States itself was said to be poorly placed to perform the task, because of its known hostility towards the régime. The Australian effort was reputed to have continued to the end of 1972, when the incoming Whitlam government discontinued it.[19] McMahon, by then a member of the opposition, publicly denied knowledge of any Australian intelligence operations in Chile, whether to overthrow the Allende régime or just to spy on it.[20] It is possible, though with an unknown degree of likelihood, that *both* parts of the story may have been correct. An Australian agent or agents *may* have kept a "watching brief" on Chilean developments, though it is unlikely that this could have been the CIA's substitute for its own potential efforts. According to internal evidence from one highly reputable source, there apparently was an ASIS agent in Chile, but his role was not tantamount to any particular "involvement" on behalf of the Americans. In the meantime, even the Australian Prime Minister may honestly have been ignorant of what was transpiring, given the secretiveness of ASIS's operations.

Another report, also from American sources, charged that in the late 1960s, after the closure of the US embassy in Cambodia, Australian intelligence assumed responsibility on behalf of the CIA for surveillance of the Sihanouk government, and that various covert and electronic methods were used.[21] The ostensible purpose was to incriminate the Sihanouk government. Peter Young, a former Australian army major with intelligence service in Indo-China, severely disputed this account. The United States had its own surveillance methods, Australia lacked the facilities or the personnel in the places attributed etc. What Young did argue, however, was that

> Australians work hand-in-glove with their American counterparts ... [and] it is a one-sided co-operation, heavily exploited by the Americans and capable of affording them the opportunity of feeding in slanted information which in turn could produce policies favourable to the originators.[22]

Other sources consulted by the author were considerably less convinced that Australia had been receiving cooked intelligence.

More of the US–Australian intelligence nexus in other connections. We now call attention to another L–CP effort to build a security shield for the region, and for Australia itself. Over time, some thirty American facilities were established in Australia, most under L–CP governments. Most were jointly operated in conjunction with

Australians. Some had only marginal defence applications, but rather were concerned with scientific research and operations, especially in aerospace. None were "bases" in the ordinary sense of housing gar- risons or weapons systems. A few were stood down after their tasks had been fulfilled. But within the network were some extremely im- portant and sensitive facilities. These included the US naval com- munication station at the North-West Cape, Exmouth Gulf, Western Australia, whose ultra-low frequency transmissions were beamed to American submarines. Two other key facilities remained highly clas- sified, even as to their basic functions. They were Pine Gap, at Alice Springs, Northern Territory, and Nurrungar, near Woomera, South Australia. They elicited considerable speculation as to their nature. It is sufficient in present context to state that they were part of a monitoring system of Soviet and Chinese nuclear missile launchings, systems and tests.

Taken together, this network of American facilities fully com- plemented Australia's foreign policy/security objectives, as visualized by Liberal governments. Firstly, they served to enhance the military capability of the United States and of the anti-communist nations, Australia included, in their deterrent as well as their retaliatory or conflict-conduct aspects. Secondly, the emplacement of a large number of expensive and sophisticated facilities in Australia, some of them critical to global strategic objectives, was believed to commit the United States to a physical and psychological presence, the net ef- fect of which would be to enmesh America with Australia on a long- term basis. This was a variation on the theme of the "great power presence". Finally, Australia hoped that, by being hospitable, a manifestly good ANZUS partner, it could persuade the United States to continue to improve upon provision of intelligence data, security planning and acceptance of Australian counsel on assorted issues.

From the foregoing, how close to the mark were the frequent accusa- tions that L–CP governments were mesmerized by military responses to problems, addicted to conservative values, hopelessly unoriginal and willingly bound to American direction? "The task of Australian diplomacy was not so much to influence in any particular direction the policies of these outside powers," Joseph Camilleri argued, "but rather to ensure their continued economic and military presence ... Australian policies were almost wholly derivative, expressing little more than Australia's dependent relationship with one or other of her 'great and powerful friends'."[23]

Even in brief compass, a look at the evidence is worthwhile. In pre- sent context, our concentration is on the early and middle periods of L–CP government. Firstly, were L–CP governments simply imitative of great power, and especially American, preferences? In the large sense, yes, but with qualifications on whose meaningfulness people were and continue to be divided. Australia condemned the North Korean and Chinese roles in the Korean War, contributed troops to the United Nations effort and argued that the allies should not lose resolve when a costly stalemate developed. But, both privately and in public, the Menzies government made representations against steps that could enlarge the conflict with China, against General MacArthur's impetuousness and against "unleashing" Chiang Kai-shek from Taiwan against the mainland.[24] During and between the Chinese off-shore island disputes of 1955 and 1958, Australia carefully avoided any commitment to help defend the islands (the United States had thrown a protective mantle over them through its 1954 security treaty with the Nationalists) and was especially reluctant to be sucked in via its ANZUS obligations. The islands were felt to carry no strategic value and they were felt to be, as the Nationalists were utilizing them, provocations to Peking. Exacerbation of conditions could only upset the tranquil conditions desired by Canberra; in Menzies' words, the islands were not "worth another great war".[25] Australia did not want Taiwan abandoned, nor a precipitous abandonment of the off-shore islands at an inopportune moment. However, "During the three-year lull between the crises ... [Australia] worked for a complete disengagement at an internationally suitable moment. When the second crisis arrived and nothing had been done, Australia told Washington of its displeasure in no uncertain terms."[26]

Australia was not a formal participant at the 1954 Geneva conference on Indo-China, but was active there. The Australian government was distressed about the prospect of a communist victory over the French. It grudgingly accepted the partition of Vietnam. As a reassurance for itself, and for the region, it favoured what came to be the Manila Treaty and SEATO. But the internal evidence is very substantial that Australia firmly opposed US feelers for an allied military intervention. Such intervention would have been wrong because, in former External Affairs Minister R. G. Casey's words,

> It would not have the backing of the United Nations. It would put us in wrong with world opinion, particularly in Asia. It would probably embroil us with Communist China. It would wreck the Geneva conference, and it was most unlikely to stop the fall of Dien Bien Phu. These were the views that I expressed on behalf of the Australian Government to Mr Dulles, Mr Eden, and other leaders at Geneva.[27]

Australia's approach to prosecuting the Vietnamese conflict was, in most important respects, sturdily pro-American. Australia was eager to include its forces in the military effort and generally opposed a "negotiation from weakness" posture. But even here there were some exceptions, however slight. There was a period when, shading off from US policy, Australia favoured more flexibility in approaching negotiations with the other side and was not averse to the participation of the National Liberation Front. L–CP governments did not accede to all American pressures for troop contributions, beyond what Australia eventually supplied. For a time, even after combat troops had been committed to Vietnam, Australia allowed trade with North Vietnam to continue. Although Australian passports were marked "Not Valid for Travel in North Vietnam", Australians travelling there in contravention of this prohibition were not subject to legal disabilities upon returning home.[28] Australia's approach to China itself carried two prongs. Diplomatically, Australia accorded full support to Washington's position of non-recognition and resistance to seating of Peking at the United Nations, especially at Taiwan's expense. But Australia pursued a vigorous trade with China at a time when America had prohibited it entirely and numerous Australians, among them some official persons, visited China.

Our final illustration of Australian divergence from American policy refers to Bangladesh. For a variety of reasons, at the time of the East Bengali revolt against Pakistan and of Indo–Pakistani fighting, US policy carried a decided tilt in favour of Pakistan. The McMahon government, however, not only was the first Commonwealth nation to recognize Bangladesh, but with salutary results, "scored a remarkable success when it orchestrated the recognition of Bangladesh by a small consortium of Asian and Pacific nations".[29]

The above examples span a variety of situations. They include instances of relations with great as well as with smaller powers, of circumstances in which Australia both did and did not have a military stake, of unilateral and multilateral settings, and so on. Of course, detractors of L–CP policy said that any "divergencies" from an American lead were highly exceptional or only marginally important. Viewing the bigger picture, on the big issues, Australia was seen as clinging to America.

What of the related charge that L–CP governments were preoccupied with the security aspects of the Asian neighbourhood and subscribed more to military than to socio-economic policy responses? L–CP governments sought and obviously valued security treaty connections and on numerous occasions committed troops and arranged military assistance programmes. One additional measure of this question was the scope of Australia's investment in its own military establishment. During the 1950s and early 1960s, L–CP governments constantly warned of threats and of the need to defend against them. They did post troops abroad, but in small numbers. Indeed, not much more could have been done, given the state of the country's forces. In the late 1950s, total regular service strength averaged about 47000. By 1961, the army had reached a ten-year low of under 20000. Capital military expenditures were neglected and the proportion of national income spent on defence declined for some years after the peak of the Korean War, from 6.1 per cent in 1952–53 to half of that in the early 1960s. For many years, Australia could not have mustered more than two infantry battalions for simultaneous overseas duty.

By the mid-1960s, the pattern changed. Conscription for unlimited overseas service was introduced in 1964. From its effective start in 1965 to the fall of the McMahon government in late 1972, some 64000 men were conscripted and over 15000 saw service in Vietnam. The regular armed forces reached a peak of nearly 87000 in 1970. The defence budget was increased, to meet both personnel and capital costs. It rose to its peak of 4.6 per cent of Gross National Product at the crest of the Vietnam conflict and then gradually declined.

The inconsistency between dire professions of threats at Australia's doorstep and of very meagre military preparedness could be interpreted in several ways. It could be seen as an exercise in hypocrisy and lack of real conviction that there indeed was an overriding requirement to stand up to communism. Or it could be seen, as L–CP governments themselves explained it, as an effort by Australia to divert most of its resources into domestic Australian economic development, in itself a long-term, militarily-related capability, both for Australia and for its allies. Or it could be seen as a case of having cake and eating it too. There were modest defence costs, but a continuous, symbolic Australian military presence in Asia, demonstrating co-operativeness towards powerful friends and reassuring ostensibly threatened nations in the region—a form of defence on the cheap. Or, taken in perspective, a mixed conclusion is possible. One such interpretation was that

> the Menzies policy of defence through national development was a brilliant success—where would our living standards be today if we had consistently spent say 10 per cent of G.N.P. on defence in the past twenty-five years rather than 3 per cent? However, and here is the rub, we have thereby become as conditioned to the luxury of cheap defence as developed nations have to cheap oil.[30]

What of Australia's approach to nuclear weapons? L–CP governments never made it a matter of policy to move towards the acquisition of an Australian nuclear capability. Could their handling of the nuclear non-proliferation treaty (NPT) have been indicative of hypothetical options to go nuclear at some point? The NPT obligated signatories to refrain from developing, controlling or otherwise acquiring nuclear explosive devices and prohibited provision of second parties with militarily applicable nuclear technology or weapons.

After considerable procrastination, the L–CP signed the NPT in early 1970. It had offered various arguments for its reluctance to embrace the treaty, including presumed hardships imposed on peaceful nuclear development, scepticism over the inspection system and the extended failure of other nations to sign. The United States encouraged Australia to sign, and there was anxiety that continued dragging of feet would not only offend Washington but hamper civilian, nuclear-related assistance from various countries. All the same, although Australia signed, it failed to ratify the NPT throughout the remainder of Liberal government, a period of nearly three years. There is intimation that perhaps two or three L–CP ministers wished to stall on the NPT because they thought it prudent for Australia to retain a nuclear option. New Zealand informants suggested to the author that they sensed a certain nuclear option sentiment in the outgoing L–CP government, though here we are dealing with impression rather than evidence, and the author's overall inquiries suggested that the "open" nuclear option played a very small part in government calculations.[31]

Australia's attitude towards nuclear testing is germane. Australia made direct representations to Paris in criticism of France's atmospheric testing in the Pacific. Late in 1972, together with New Zealand, it helped to organize and then co-chaired a meeting of sixteen Pacific nations, to declare opposition to French tests and to plan appropriate strategy at the United Nations. It co-sponsored a resolution that condemned nuclear tests generally, and French tests in particular. Although Foreign Minister Nigel Bowen took considerable pride in Australia's efforts at mobilizing international opinion in favour of his government's "declared policy" of opposing nuclear tests, he was sceptical about the feasibility of applying economic sanctions against France. At that time, about 11 per cent of France's uranium came from Australia.[32]

We now consider how L–CP governments utilized non-military instruments of foreign policy, notably foreign economic and technical assistance. In 1950, the new L–CP government was a moving force in organizing the Colombo Plan, one of the earliest multinational aid consortia. Foreign-aid spending stood at $74 million in 1962–63. At the close of L–CP government, spending for 1972–73 was projected at nearly three times that figure, $220 million, with $216 million actually spent. By 1971 and 1972, Australian overseas aid ranked amongst the four highest in the world, measured by proportion of GNP. Moreover, L–CP governments followed some practices, or initiated foreign policy schemes, the special value of which was widely broadcast. Australian aid was provided interest-free. The government entered into an export certificate scheme, which enabled Indonesia to purchase Australian goods without hard currency. The government introduced, and then expanded, a system of reduced or fully removed tariffs on various goods, within stated quantitative quotas, that could enter Australia from less-developed countries. L–CP aid programmes did not, of course, escape criticism. If the Papua New Guinea (PNG) share of some 70 per cent were excluded, not all that much remained for others. There was excessive reliance on bilateral assistance, not enough on multilateral. Too much stress was said to be placed on Australian grants requiring use or purchase of Australian goods. All the same, Australia's foreign aid programme under the L–CP was not, at large, either inconspicuous or unimaginative.[33]

How did the aid effort relate to broader foreign policy considerations? To be sure, there was a humanitarian feature in it, but more accurately it was conceived as enlightened self-interest. Apart from any economic spin-offs for Australia, the programme was justified as helping to shore up recipient nations economically so that they could become more immune to destabilizing domestic or external pressures. Harold Holt, Menzies' successor, was particularly impressed by the salience of economic considerations in stabilizing new and poor nations. Australia felt that, like its frequent military contributions in Asia, its aid contributions would also serve as incentives to other donor nations. The L–CP's concentration on South-East Asia as Australia's principal security/strategic concern was complemented by the direction of foreign assistance. For a time India was, apart from Papua New Guinea, the single most generously treated nation. This shifted to Indonesia by the mid-1960s, and the concentration of aid shifted to South-East Asia generally. We should also mention certain L–CP aid programme characteristics that implied a close aid/-politics/security nexus, though such reasoning can be easily exaggerated. For instance, Australia provided some defence co-operation assistance to nations in the region. But, in relative as well as absolute terms, this was not a major programme. In 1972–73, $33 million was spent on defence aid, compared to the $216 million spent on civillian economic assistance. It can be calculated that, with Papua New Guinea aid excluded from the equation, foreign-aid spending, as a proportion of *defence* expenditure, actually declined in the late 1960s, compared to the early part of the decade—to below 5 per cent of the defence allocation. But it should be remembered that defence spending was inordinately low before the mid-1960s, that economic-assistance spending continued to rise (in absolute terms) over each financial year and that Australia's comparative international standing was strong. It can also be shown that, by the time of its exit from office, the L–CP was, within South-East Asia, concentrating its economic assistance on politically safe, distinctly anti-communist régimes, such as Indonesia, Thailand, South Vietnam and Malaysia. The anti-communist colour of these régimes was an incentive for the Australian government. However, given the L–CP's understandable aid focus on South-East Asia, there simply were very few neutralist nations in the region to which to grant aid. When, in 1965, President Johnson expressed a wish for a massive development assistance programme in South-East Asia, Hasluck quickly agreed. Though there was no chance to carry this through before the L–CP left office, Hasluck emphasized that Johnson's offer was not limited to anti- or even non-communist countries, but to "North Vietnam no less than South Vietnam".[34] Despite its position outside the South-East Asian region, and its non-aligned foreign policy, India remained the second most generously treated nation, next to Indonesia. On a *per·capita* basis, of course, India received very little.

Particularly heavy Australian aid started to flow to Indonesia after President Sukarno had lost his power, the Indonesian Communist party (PKI) was rooted out and an anti-communist military régime was installed. Prior to this time, the PKI had been influential in Indonesian politics, Jakarta was on close terms with Peking and Australia had sent an infantry battalion to Malaysian Borneo to help resist Indonesia's Confrontation efforts. In these circumstances, many felt that Australian diplomacy realized one of its finest hours. Gordon Greenwood recounted the Australian reaction as follows:

> Australian diplomats in Indonesia, who had been cast in the difficult role of combining expressions of firm opposition to confrontation with the maintenance of as friendly relations as possible, performed their task with calmness, patience and adroitness ... The extent of their success may be judged from the fact that more or less normal relations were continued in quite abnormal circumstances. It must be rare indeed for two countries to face one another over a vital conflict of policy, with troops not only in the field but actually fighting one another, and at the same time not only maintain unbroken diplomatic relations, but participate in joint educational schemes and in other aid programmes requiring mutual co-operation.[35]

During the Confrontation crisis, a trade treaty was negotiated. A gift of rice was made. Australian medical and technical personnel continued to work in Indonesia. Equipment and other materials under the Colombo Plan were delivered. Indonesian students continued to arrive and study in Australia.

Australian behaviour during the Confrontation dispute actually had two faces. It included a very graduated military response, dextrous diplomacy and a continuation of aid programmes. This is what the Indonesians saw. There also was something else. As recounted elsewhere, based on impeccable sources,

Australia pressed the U.S. very hard to use economic aid to Indonesia as leverage in the hope of bringing Sukarno to his senses. This was done with full appreciation of the possibility that unwanted ricochet effects would result, but the sanctions policy was urged nonetheless. Chinese Communism could not be allowed to have its way in disrupting the Malaysian experiment, and Australia was responding accordingly.[36]

On the matter of the tone of policy under L–CP governments, one more sub-theme needs to be covered. Critics went beyond charging that Australia was being slavish towards the United States and enamoured of military solutions. Asia was that part of the world where L–CP governments acknowledged Australia's vital interests to lie, and where there was greatest need to exercise influence. Yet it was alleged that the image of Australia projected under the Liberals was of a nation that was callous, opposed to currents of national aspiration and even racist. This was characterized as a narrowness, a conservatism that complemented other features of a stubborn L–CP foreign policy. To illustrate the subject, we focus on the L–CP approach to non-European migration and to colonial/racial questions, especially in the context of the United Nations.

L–CP governments did not, of course, invent the restrictive Asian exclusion, frequently called "White Australia" policy. Its roots reached to the nineteenth century and became a form of settled national policy virtually from the start of Australian Federation. In the late 1940s, while Evatt on behalf of the Labor government was beginning to build bridges towards emerging nations in Asia, Immigration Minister Arthur Calwell was enforcing White Australia with implacable single-mindedness of purpose. The succeeding L–CP governments proved themselves less crude, more "small l liberal" in administering the general exclusionist policy. By the late 1950s, the government rescinded the notorious dictation test from the country's migration regulations. It then, gradually, proceeded to ease, but not to erase, restrictions on the entry of non-Europeans. The basic reforms were introduced in 1966, shortly after Holt had become Prime Minister. No explicit numerical quota was ever devised, though the net effect of the government's approach was to limit the number and character of non-European migrants. Individuals were screened according to such criteria as potential for integration into Australian society and their ability to render "positively useful" contributions. Their families were allowed to accompany them. Rules governing non-permanent entry into Australia were considerably simplified and liberalized. Those who originally arrived on temporary visas were not precluded from applying for permanent residence. Gradually, the period required for Australian naturalization was equalized between non-Europeans and Europeans. By the early 1970s, about 4000 non-Europeans and some 6000 persons of mixed racial ancestry were entering Australia annually. Basically, what remained of a discriminatory policy was that standards for non-Europeans remained more stringent than for Europeans, and assisted passage was virtually unavailable to non-Europeans.

Various factors influenced the erosion of the White Australia policy. During the many years of L–CP rule, Australia generally became less defensive about having its social fabric torn and its economic standards reduced by unfamiliar migrants. The post-war economy held up and grew. The influx of great numbers of white, but not Anglo-Saxon, migrants accustomed the nation to a new flavour of population. The presence of thousands of Asian students at Australian universities and the movement of Asian businessmen, journalists and official persons made Asians more familiar and less suspect. Australia's own opening up in foreign policy, with its emphasis on Asia, conditioned acceptance of Asian migrants. An effective Immigration Reform Group campaign helped to publicize the cause of lowered migration barriers against non-Europeans, though for most of the L–CP period of office the ALP actually remained behind the L–CP in reconstructing its own approach.[37]

The general impression is that L–CP governments liberalized the Asian migration policy largely for the reasons suggested above—there was less ostensible "need" for stringency and the climate of reform had spread. To some extent, change was spurred by foreign policy considerations. One consideration was to avert untoward incidents with Asian nations and to enlarge Australia's credit in the region. However, apart from sporadic difficulties, primarily with the Philippines, there was little hard evidence that the L–CP's pursuit of Australian interests was being damaged by restrictive migration practices. The 1966 reforms were, at all events, welcomed in Asia.[38] Relatedly, as the 1960s progressed, the government in Canberra found that pressures against racially discriminating régimes, such as in South Africa and in Rhodesia, were rising at the United Nations, as well as in such bodies as the now much expanded and thoroughly multi-racial Commonwealth of Nations. Thus to forestall possible attacks upon its migration policy, or its treatment of the native Aboriginal population, Australia was given an additional incentive to mend its approach. ·

Overall, the L–CP attitude towards the United Nations was sympathetic but restrained. The coalition parties were less attracted by idealistic conceptions of the value of a world body as a venue for dealing with the really hard problems of international life than Labor was. This attitude was strengthened by the high security threat that was perceived to exist in Asia and the Pacific region. The belief was that such threats could best be countered by non-UN-derived arrangements such as a great power presence, a network of alliances and flexible military responses. Scepticism about the United Nations was compounded by the UN's inability to deal appropriately, or at all, with problems that were seen by the L–CP as intimately connected to Australia's interests. Hence the United Nations was seen as valueless in persuading Sukarno to call off his Confrontation of Malaysia. Earlier, the United Nations had acceded to a settlement of Indonesia's claims to Dutch New Guinea (West Irian), which Australia interpreted as acquiescence in Indonesian bully tactics.

Such predisposing factors made it even more difficult for L–CP governments to welcome the consequences indicated for colonial and racial issues by the proliferation of assertive Afro–Asian members at the United Nations. Throughout the decade of the 1950s, Australia at the United Nations voted a distinctively conservative line on most colonially related questions such as self-determination, independence or equal rights. As Geoffrey Sawer put it, the Australian instinct was to say one of two things.

> Relying on a broad interpretation of what constitutes "domestic jurisdiction" under Article 2 (7), Australia voted against United Nations consideration of such issues unless there was a clear element of danger to the peace or unless a Trusteeship Agreement under Chapter XII of the Charter itself brought the matter within the sphere of international competence as interpreted by Australian conservative governments. Even when not relying on Article 2 (7), Australian delegations tended to resist United Nations intervention in such matters on broader political grounds, such as the unlikelihood of the intervention being for the benefit of the colonial or oppressed peoples concerned, and the likelihood of discussions being dominated by mischief-makers more interested in weakening the western powers than in benefiting Africans, Arabs, etc.[39]

Australian's reaction was in part dictated by the conviction that much that was being advocated before the United Nations was either unrealistic or actually dangerous to world order, in itself a high-priority Australian concern. The L–CP's posture also reflected a reluctance to encourage undesired, internationally sponsored interference in Australia's management of Papua New Guinea, or its migration policy, or its treatment of Aborigines. The peak, as well as the turning-point, in Australian policy was reached in the 1960–61 crisis over the Sharpeville shootings in South Africa and that nation's membership in the Commonwealth. Australia had previously been a strict constructionist of the UN Charter, denying that the United Nations enjoyed jurisdiction over South Africa's domestic policies. At the 1960 and 1961 Commonwealth Prime Ministers' Conferences, Menzies was the staunchest white Commonwealth exponent of the view that it was impermissible for the Commonwealth to delve into the internal concerns of a fellow member. At the 1961 conference, he did what he could to forestall pressures that proved so intense that South Africa was *de facto* pushed out of the Commonwealth. But in April 1961, Australia abandoned its earlier approach at the United Nations and supported a resolution highly condemnatory of South Africa. Menzies himself concluded that Australia could no longer afford to be isolated: "What would have happened to Australia if we had been the only country holding out? We would have been misunderstood all over Asia about our attitude, and we were not going to be misunderstood. We had had enough."[40]

Henceforth Australian voting at the United Nations on South African apartheid, and on South-West African, Portuguese and kindred colonial questions, became less legalistic and more inclined to stand with anti-colonial opinion. It was not, however, by any means a 180 degree turnabout. L–CP governments continued to disapprove of actual sanctions such as economic or diplomatic boycotts against offenders. The government did agree to support sanctions against Rhodesia, though it did so with "profound distaste" and was not punctilious in enforcing them.

At all events, Australia's reorientation on colonial/racial issues was impelled by essentially the same considerations that had led it to assume a much firmer posture in the 1950s. Australia now not only wished to avoid the general penalty of becoming isolated, especially among Asian nations. More particularly, it wished to temper Third World nation temptations to pry into Australia's own affairs, racial and colonial. W.J. Hudson, one of the most assiduous students of Australia's relations with the United Nations, has written that "There seems to be at least a *prima facie* case for assuming that Canberra, in the early sixties, finally decided that Papua and New Guinea were not worth the diplomatic price that Portugal, South Africa and perhaps Spain were prepared to pay. In such an event, it was, of course, essential also to dissociate from South Africa and Portugal."[41] Regarding the L–CP's tack on Rhodesia, another observer wrote that "While New Guinea and Rhodesia bear no comparison, the fact remains that Australia is being pressured in the UN, however irrationally, over its administration of the Territory in a way that makes it quite impossible to support Rhodesia."[42]

Indeed, apart from trying to build a more attractive image for itself among potential international critics, Australia proceeded to institute substantive reforms in the handling of its own colonial/racial policies. By the late 1960s, more forceful attention was being given to improving the condition of Australian Aborigines. As seen earlier, 1966 marked an important liberalizing departure from previous approaches towards non-European migration. Liberalization of the government's policy towards Papua New Guinea was a more complex undertaking. For generations, serious attention had been paid to the security implications of the territory's position to Australia's near north, and anxiety was heightened by Japan's invasion of it during the Second World War. The eastern portion of the island technically had two parts: Papua was Australian territory and New Guinea proper, first a League of Nations mandate, later became the only surviving United Nations non-strategic trust territory. Since 1949, the two portions were administratively connected and subject to common policy. The western half of New Guinea was Dutch, until its acquisition by Indonesia as West Irian in the early 1960s. Australia's concern with forcing the pace of New Guinea independence was, *inter alia*, coloured by security considerations. An extremely economically backward, socially fragile and administratively inexperienced Papua New Guinea would be a potential source of instability, and possibly an inviting target for an externally sponsored radical takeover. With the PKI carrying strong influence in Sukarno's Indonesia, with Indonesia courting China and expressing militancy in its foreign policy, the prospect of West New Guinea falling under Indonesian control further constrained Canberra's willingness to allow Papua New Guinea to slip out of Australian control.

By the mid-1960s, however, conditions had changed. Sukarno was out of power, the PKI was in disarray and Indonesia's foreign policy became much more accommodative. Furthermore, L–CP perceptions of the actual security importance of Papua New Guinea to Australia were lowered. Such factors, combined with steady UN pressure on Australia to expedite the decolonization process in Papua New Guinea, influenced Canberra's approach. L–CP governments believed that criticism laid against Australian administration in Papua New Guinea was sometimes tendentious or otherwise wholly unhelpful. But Canberra admitted that much of what was recommended was sensible, and it found that among Asian (as opposed to most African, Middle Eastern and communist nations) there was understanding of the magnitude of the political and economic tasks involved in Papua New Guinea. There is internal evidence of private assurances to Australia by Asian spokesmen that their votes or occasional critical remarks at the United Nations reflected more a need to impress particular sectors of domestic or international opinion than a revulsion against Australian policy. There was no particular diplomatic fall-out when, in 1969, Australia resigned from the UN Special Committee on the Situation with Regard to the Implementation of the Declaration on the Granting of Independence to Colonial Countries and Peoples (briefly Committee on Decolonization, or "Committee of Twenty-Four"). The committee had been organized in 1961 to help implement the General Assembly's declaration on terminating colonialism. From

1964, the committee had been concerned with Papua New Guinea. Australia consistently rebuffed what it regarded as its dogmatic criticisms and refused to allow it to send its own delegates to Papua New Guinea, on grounds that Australia was answerable to the Trusteeship Council alone.

Australia eventually committed itself to the principle of self-determination for Papua New Guinea, though it resisted the imposition of target dates. A new, primarily elected Papua New Guinea House of Assembly first met in 1964. Responsibilities for self-administration began to be transferred to the embryonic Papua New Guinea government. Rapid progress was made towards indigenizing the territory's public service and socio-economic assistance generally was conspicuously stepped up. Momentum was especially noticeable from 1970. It became extremely rapid from early 1972, coinciding with the appointment of Andrew Peacock as Minister for External Territories under the McMahon government. Peacock laid the final foundations for what, a year after the departure of the Liberals from office, was to become the acquisition of self-government by Papua New Guinea. Formal independence did not arrive until 1975. Peacock's contributions were later acknowledged by the succeeding Labor government. Whitlam was pleased to "pay tribute to him and his work". Among other things, "Andrew Peacock did go a long way towards restoring the [interparty] consensus—a genuine, progressive, concerned consensus, not the phoney consensus of the 60s."[43]

In the formal sense, what was done for Papua New Guinea in 1972 was authoritative government policy. In another sense, however, it was a bit different. It was very largely a Peacock initiative, carried out within nine or ten months in a very personal manner. The Prime Minister's role was essentially one of concurrence. Cabinet was hardly consulted in advance, and it only in general, sporadic and after-the-fact fashion acknowledged the policy. In its way, it was an episode indicative of the rather disjointed state of affairs in which the L–CP government was approaching external policy in its last years of office.

On New Guinea, the result of such an approach proved salutary. In other instances, including on colonial and racial issues, results were less salutary. In 1971, a South African Rugby Union football team was scheduled to play in Australia. Opinion on the advisability of the visit divided sharply. In some quarters, it was argued that, by allowing the visit, Australia would be according *de facto* acceptance to South Africa's practice of racially segregated sport and to its apartheid policies generally. In other quarters, including within the government, the view was that political considerations should not intrude into sport. People who wished to attend matches should have the option to do so. Sincere anti-racialist people were found on both sides of the controversy. But, to the mortification of some of his ministers, when trade-unionist, student and other elements threatened to disrupt the matches if the South Africans came, McMahon pushed the issue into very sharp political relief. He said that RAAF aircraft would, if needed, be placed at the disposal of the travelling South African team and warned that he would not be averse to calling a snap election on a "law and order" issue. In effect, his theme was who governed Australia—the government or agitators?[44]

In the following chapter, we will concentrate on the final stages of L–CP government. We will examine in some detail the conceptual, political and policy process problems that increasingly affected foreign policy movements and that contributed to Labor's ascent to power.

NOTES

1. *New York Times*, 21 January 1966.
2. E.G. Whitlam, "Foreword", in *Australian Foreign Policy: Towards a Reassessment*, ed. C. Clark (Melbourne: Cassell, 1973), p. vii.
3. For background material on the postwar period, see W. Levi, *Australia's Outlook on Asia* (Sydney: Angus and Robertson, 1958), pp. 68ff.; R.N. Rosecrance, *Australian Diplomacy and Japan, 1945–1951* (Melbourne: Melbourne University Press, 1962), *passim*; T.R. Reese, *Australia, New Zealand, and the United States: A Survey of International Relations, 1941–1968* (London: Oxford University Press, 1969), esp. pp. 49–125; A. Watt, *The Evolution of Australian Foreign Policy, 1938–1965* (London: Cambridge University Press, 1967), esp. pp. 69–105; and G. Greenwood, ed., *Approaches to Asia: Australian Postwar Policies and Attitudes* (Sydney: McGraw-Hill, 1974).
4. *Current Notes on International Affairs (CNIA)* 35 (November 1965): 174.
5. For a good general discussion of the problem, see L. Webb, *Communism and Democracy in Australia* (Melbourne: Cheshire, 1954).
6. "Party Traditions", in *Australia and Foreign Policy*, J.D.B. Miller, ABC Commission, Boyer Lectures (Sydney: Australian Broadcasting Commission, 1963), p. 49.
7. H.G. Gelber, "Australia and the Great Powers" (Australian Institute of International Affairs (AIIA) conference paper, Adelaide, June 1974), p. 6.
8. J. Camilleri and M. Teichmann, *Security and Survival: The New Era in International Relations* (Melbourne: Heinemann Educational, 1973), pp. 47–48. For the present author's own elaboration of political culture factors in external affairs, see H.S. Albinski, *Politics and Foreign Policy in Australia: The Impact of Vietnam and Conscription* (Durham, N.C.: Duke University Press, 1970), pp. 3–30. Also see T.B. Millar, *Foreign Policy: Some Australian Reflections* (Melbourne: Georgian House, 1972), pp. 1–13.
9. *Australian Gallup Polls*, nos. 548–58 (October–November 1948).
10. J. McEwen, *Commonwealth [Australian] Parliamentary Debates (APD)*, House of Representatives (HR) (5 November 1968), p. 2438.
11. *Sydney Morning Herald*, 21 September 1964.
12. B. Grant, "Australia's Defence: Two Views, 1968: I. A Regional Role", *Australia's Neighbours*, 4th series, nos. 52–53 (January–February 1968), p. 2.
13. D. Horne, "Options in Australian Foreign Policy in the South-East Asia Region (2): The Domestic Dimension" (AIIA conference paper, Melbourne, May 1975), p. 8.
14. Article IV. For full text, see *CNIA* 22 (September 1951): 499–500. On Australia and ANZUS generally, see J.G. Starke, *The ANZUS Treaty Alliance* (Melbourne: Melbourne University Press, 1965). On SEATO, see L.C. Webb, "Australia and SEATO", in *SEATO: Six Studies*, ed. G. Modelski (Melbourne: Cheshire, 1962), pp. 49–83.

15. *Sydney Morning Herald*, 21 June 1968.
16. H.S. Albinski, *Australia in Southeast Asia: Interests, Capacity and Acceptability* (McLean, Virginia: Research Analysis Corp., 1970), p. 14.
17. For general descriptions of Australia's overseas-directed intelligence services, see M. Suich's articles, *Australian Financial Review*, 3 November 1972 and *National Times*, 2 April 1973; his articles with T. Hayes, *National Times*, 30 September and 7 October 1974; R. Schneider, *Australian*, 25 June 1974 and G. Clarke, *Australian*, 6 July 1974; and M. Walsh, *Australian Financial Review*, 4 September 1973 and B. Toohey, *Australian Financial Review*, 24 June 1974.
18. For an approximate view of this position, see McMahon's remarks, *Australian*, 24 June 1974 and *Sydney Morning Herald*, 24 and 27 June 1974.
19. I. Frykberg, *Sydney Morning Herald*, 7 October 1974.
20. Sydney *Daily Telegraph* and *Australian*, 8 October 1974.
21. T. Hayes and M. Suich, *National Times*, 30 September 1974.
22. P. Young, *Bulletin*, 19 October 1974.
23. J.A. Camilleri, *An Introduction to Australian Foreign Policy* (Brisbane: Jacaranda, 1973), p. 64.
24. See H.S. Albinski, *Australian Policies and Attitudes Toward China* (Princeton: Princeton University Press, 1965), pp. 80–85
25. *CNIA* 26 (February 1955): 117.
26. Albinski, *Australian Policies and Attitudes Toward China*, p. 168.
27. R.G. Casey, *APD*, HR (10 August 1954), p. 97.
28. For treatments of Australia's military involvement in Vietnam, see the Department of Foreign Affairs study *Australia's Military Commitment to Vietnam* (June 1975); and the series by E. Whitton in *National Times*, 28 April, 5 May and 12 May 1975. For some early nuances of policy, see H.S. Albinski, "Australia's Foreign Policy: The Lessons of Vietnam", in *Contemporary Australia*, ed. R. Preston (Durham, N.C.: Duke University Press, 1969), pp. 357–80. For a broad view, see A. Watt, *Vietnam: An Australian Analysis* (Melbourne: Cheshire, 1968), *passim*. For a sharply dissenting view, see University Study Group on Vietnam, *Vietnam and Australia: History. Documents. Interpretations* (Gladesville, NSW: University Study Group on Vietnam, 1966), esp. pp. 80–90.
29. B. Juddery, *At the Centre: The Australian Bureaucracy in the 1970s*, (Melbourne: Cheshire, 1974), p. 104. Also see B. Male, "Australia and Pakistan", *Australia's Neighbours*, 4th series, no. 86 (July–August 1973), p. 7.
30. R. O'Neill, "Foreign Policy and Defence" (AIIA conference paper, Adelaide: June 1974), pp. 1–2. Also see the discussion in T.B. Millar, *Australia's Defence* (Melbourne: Melbourne University Press, 2nd edn, 1969), pp. 100–56.
31. In particular, see J.R. Richardson's writings on the NPT: *Australia and the Non-Proliferation Treaty*, Canberra Papers on Strategy and Defence, no. 3 (Canberra: Australian National University Press, 1968); "Australia Signs the Non-Proliferation Treaty", *Australia's Neighbours*, 4th series, no. 69 (March–April 1970), pp. 1–4; and "Australian Strategic and Defence Policies", in *Australia in World Affairs, 1966–1970*, eds. G. Greenwood and N. Harper (Melbourne: Cheshire, 1974), pp. 249–53. Also see H. Bull, "The Non-Proliferation Treaty and Its Implications for Australia", *Australian Outlook*, 22 (August 1968): 162–75. For a broadly ranging discussion of nuclear affairs, see A. Clunies-Ross and P. King, *Australia and Nuclear Weapons* (Sydney: Sydney University Press, 1966).
32. See the account in *Australian*, 18 November 1972. Also see the comments in Perth *West Australian* 16 October 1972.
33. On foreign aid, see Parliament of Australia, Joint Committee on Foreign Affairs, *Report on Australia's Foreign Aid* (Canberra: 1972), *passim*; A. Clunies-Ross, "Foreign Aid", in *Australia in World Affairs, 1966–1970*, eds. Greenwood and Harper, pp. 160–70; and Albinski, *Australia in Southeast Asia*, pp. 37–63.
34. *CNIA* (November 1965): 716.
35. G. Greenwood, "Australian Foreign Policy in Action", in *Australia in World Affairs, 1961–1965*, eds. G. Greenwood and N. Harper (Melbourne: Cheshire, 1968), pp. 109–10.
36. Albinski, *Australian Policies and Attitudes Toward China*, p. 204.
37. On migration, see H. Opperman, "Australia's Immigration Policy on the Admission of Non-Europeans", *Migrant News* 16 (January–February 1967): 6–11; C. Price, "Im-

migration: 1949–1970", in *Australia in World Affairs, 1966–1970*, eds. Greenwood and Harper pp. 194–202; Anon., "White Australia—Reform?", *Current Affairs Bulletin* 34 (6 July 1964); K. Rivett, "Non-White Migration: A Turning Point?", *Australia's Neighbours*, 4h series, no. 87 (September–October 1973), pp. 1–4; and T.B. Millar, *Australia's Foreign Policy* (Sydney: Angus and Robertson, 1968), pp. 224–35.

38. For some appraisals of Asian reactions to the exclusionist policy, see R.G. Neale, "Australia's Changing Relations with India", in *India, Japan, Australia: Partners in Asia?*, ed. J.D.B. Miller (Canberra: Australian National University Press, 1968), pp. 75–77; A.C. Palfreeman, *The Administration of the White Australia Policy* (Melbourne: Melbourne University Press, 1967), pp. 132–33; Millar, *Australia's Foreign Policy*, pp. 101–102; and G.W. Jones and M. Jones, "Australia's Immigration Policy: Some Malaysian Attitudes", *Australian Outlook* 19 (December 1965): 272–86.

39. G. Sawer, "The United Nations", in *Australia in World Affairs, 1956–1960*, eds. G. Greenwood and N. Harper (Melbourne: Cheshire, 1963), p. 158. For general studies of Australia at the United Nations, see N. Harper and D. Sissons, eds., *Australia and the United Nations* (New York: Manhattan, 1959); and A.C. Castles, *Australia and the United Nations* (Melbourne: Longman, 1973).

40. *The Times* (London), 1 May 1961.

41. W.J. Hudson, "Australian Diplomacy and South Africa", in *Racism: The Australian Experience. A Study of Race Prejudice in Australia*, vol. 3, *Colonialism*, ed. F.S. Stevens (Sydney: Australia and New Zealand Book Company, 1972), p. 173. For commentaries on Australia and the United Nations relative to colonial/racial issues, see Hudson's full comments in "Australian Diplomacy and South Africa", pp. 165–74; and, in the same volume, R. Hall, "Australia and Rhodesia: Black Interests and White Lies", pp. 175–86, and J. Skuse, "Australia's Voting Patterns at the United Nations", pp. 213–218; W.J. Hudson, *Australia and the Colonial Question at the United Nations* (Sydney: Sydney University Press, 1970); G. Sawer and W.J. Hudson, "The United Nations", in *Australia in World Affairs, 1961–1965*, eds. Greenwood and Harper, esp. pp. 234–50; W.J. Hudson, "The United Nations", in *Australia in World Affairs, 1966–1970*, eds. Greenwood and Harper, esp. pp. 213–21; and T.B. Millar, "Australian Voting at the United Nations on Issues Concerning South Africa", *Australia's Neighbours*, 4th series, nos. 13–14 (March–April 1964), pp. 1–4.

42. P. Hastings, *Australian*, 13 September 1968.

43. *Australian Foreign Affairs Record* (*AFAR*), 44 (February 1973): 104. For a general review of policy movements under the L-CP, see J. Griffin, "Australian Attitudes to Papua New Guinea", ed. J. Griffin, *A Foreign Policy for an Independent New Guinea* (Sydney: Angus and Robertson, 1974), pp. 13–22; and various essays in J. Wilkes, ed. *New Guinea ... Future Indefinite?* (Sydney: Angus and Robertson, 1968). On UN activity, see W.J. Hudson, "The United Nations", in *Australia in World Affairs 1966–1970*, eds. Greenwood and Harper, pp. 213–217. A variety of themes, some of them historically oriented, are dealt with in W.J. Hudson, ed. *New Guinea Empire: Australia's Colonial Experience* (Melbourne: Cassell, 1974).

44. This is the light in which the incident was interpreted by Bruce Grant. See his *The Crisis of Loyalty: A Study of Australian Foreign Policy* (Sydney: Angus and Robertson, 2nd edn, 1973), p. 30. For a summary of the events, see C.A. Hughes, "Australian Political Chronicle, May–August 1971", *Australian Journal of Politics and History* 7 (December 1971): 417.

2 The Liberal Inheritance: II

In the preceding chapter, the approach of L–CP governments to external affairs was characterized according to governing perceptions of the international order, the assumptions they drew as to what Australia's interests required and the policy instruments they employed. In general, the L–CP saw the region to Australia's north as distressingly volatile. It ascribed much of this to communist influence and especially to China's machinations. It saw such developments as inimical to Australia's interests and sought the presence of major non-communist powers in the region as a counter to dislocation and aggression. Australia needed to devise a foreign policy that would encourage and complement a great-power checking role. L–CP policy displayed a strong "security" component, a posture that placed Australia solidly at the side of great and powerful friends, and a reticence about embracing the aspirations of nations within the Third World community. We now consider to what extent, why and with what consequences these patterns may have been reconsidered towards the close of Liberal government.

By the late 1960s, and then more expressly into the early 1970s, a reordering appeared to be taking form in the international balance. The world became less polarized between communist and anti-communist camps. The super-powers were less able to dictate to clients or to dispose of international disputes as they saw fit. New clusters of important national and regional influence became more apparent, including China, Japan and the West European region. World politics became affected by the Sino–Soviet dispute. Many saw these phenomena as the emergence of a new balance of forces, more complex than in the past and requiring adjusted policy responses. While the United States and the USSR remained intense rivals and maintained formidable nuclear and conventional military capabilities, they began to move towards a guarded yet mutually interested accommodation· or *détente*. China itself expressed interest in adjusting its diplomatic relations with non-communist states. The United States and a number of other anti-communist nations moved away from fixed confrontational postures.

Official American thinking more explicitly steered away from settings that might require such uncomfortably polar responses as capitulation or massive retaliation. A standing-down in Vietnam and closer relations with China were started. In Richard Nixon's "Guam Doctrine" and in other contexts, the United States expressed reluctance to maintain a large-scale American military presence in Asia. As corollary, America's interests were felt not to require, nor Asian conditions permit, extreme Asian–Pacific dependence on and conformity to the United States. Washington wished nations in the region to assume more self-responsibility for security and economic development, especially within the framework of intra-regional co-operation. Australia and Japan were regarded as two of the region's members most suited to contribute towards such goals. Before it left office, the Johnson administration counselled Australia against an approach of simply clinging to America. Uncreativeness would not only detract from South-East Asian regionalism and could depreciate Australia's chances of having America "on call" in invoking ANZUS or otherwise satisfy Canberra's unique international requirements. Donald Horne said it succinctly: in "varying degrees of politeness or bluntness the American attitude is that something more positive is to be expected of Australia than the role of loyal hanger-on and urger ... One of the paradoxes of the position is that what is most likely to impress the Americans is not 'loyalty' but independent initiative."[1] Nixon was apparently able to transmit some of this sentiment to Australia even before his inauguration.[2] Nor could Britain's declining interest in sustaining a serious presence east of Suez be overlooked by Australia.

Our interest in present context is to recapture the extent to which, in their later years, L–CP governments themselves may have reconceptualized the international scene and Australia's place in it. We can then more profitably proceed to examine the variety of incentives and disincentives that may have influenced actual policy decisions and their management.

Australian academic observers did not themselves agree on what was happening within L–CP government circles. Hedley Bull, for example, felt that Australian policy-makers had been slow to perceive change and that their conversion was not complete by December 1972. He did, however, think that they had recognized that while the United States remained an essential element in an Asian great-power equilibrium, the Soviets, Japanese and Chinese could also contribute to it by providing a check to the ambitions of others. Also he thought he saw a L–CP realization that American power would in the future

be less available, and indeed less necessary, for the region's security.[3]
Fred Mediansky was less persuaded. He thought that old assumptions
about continued reliance and shared interest *vis-à-vis* the United States
had hardly been reconsidered, with the danger that "Australian
diplomacy will seek to continue paying 'dues' for an insurance contract where the terms of coverage have radically changed."[4]

Official pronouncements during the late stages of Gorton's prime
ministership, and then during McMahon's, do not settle the point.
The documentary record, plus the present author's inquiries among
senior ministers of the period, leave a picture of ambivalence and
even contradiction in what L–CP governments really thought. There
are indications that a "new balance" in Asia was recognized, but there
was much uncertainty as to what the range of implications was. In a
strategic assessment completed in early 1971, the government's advisers suggested that there was no serious likelihood of a major threat
to Australia's integrity that could develop within the region for
perhaps up to ten years. However, one former minister told the
author that in this respect the advisers' frame of reference was
narrow—simply the lack of *direct* foreseeable threat to Australia. Conditions in the neighbourhood, which could *indirectly* yet seriously impinge on Australia's safety, were not believed to have changed
measurably. Another former minister said that the government
proceeded within a three- or four-year forecast period, not ten years.
Yet another former minister tended to dismiss this feature of the
strategic assessment entirely. The assessment had mainly been an exercise, while *he*, in his position of responsibility, had needed to react
to the world as it "really" was.

The *Defence Report* for 1972 itself pointed in more than one direction. It acknowledged an evolving *détente* among the great powers and
their concern to maintain a strategic balance, this being a basis for the
tension-relaxing hopes that had been stimulated in many capitals.
Serious great-power competition was, however, expected to continue.
Within South-East Asia, communist states persisted in exacerbating
conditions by abetting insurgency and subversion. North Vietnam
"undeniably" held "expansionist designs", while China had expressed
"no meaningful undertaking" to "work with established governments
in the region and not against them". While the report took notice of
no "immediate" situations that could create a "high probability" of
involvement by Australian forces, it cautioned that "circumstances
could change quickly because of the latent forces of instability in
South-East Asia"[5]

McMahon wrote in late 1972 that there were signs of eased tensions, but the *causes* of tension remained. It was vital for Australia and
its friends to keep in being, not dismantle, security alliances and

military preparedness; "just when they have proved their effectiveness in bringing Peking and Moscow to the conference table", the guard must not be let down.[6]

What emerged was an ambivalent, hesitating L–CP reaction to changes in the international climate and to implications for Australia. Such reaction was not, of course, a necessary sign of "confusion" or of "weakness" on the part of the government. But conceptual tentativeness was only one element affecting L–CP policy at this time. Australian Liberal governments, like governments elsewhere, were subject to a host of historical, intra-party, electoral, personality and other influences over their behaviour. Before looking at actual policy outputs and management, it is therefore helpful to catalogue the dominant incentives, and inhibitions, that intruded upon any decisions to reorient policy.

We begin by discussing the incentives for moving away from orthodox positions. In the first place, there was the goad of great and friendly nation behaviour and advice. The United States and Britain were, after all, Australia's trusted friends and partners. The United States in particular was active in rescaling its approach to the great communist powers, in itself suggesting a more relaxed international atmosphere. There were first-stage strategic arms limitation agreements with the Soviets and other signs of coexistence. Washington's diplomatic and economic isolation of Peking was prominently reduced. The United States was turning down its ground presence in Asia and urging Australia and others to be less passive, more original in their regional roles. Although the original British threat to disengage from South-East Asia by 1971 was retracted, the remaining British presence was slight and insecure. While reducing its obligations in Asia, Britain was increasingly turning towards Europe. Japan itself was searching for a more personally distinctive role in Asia. In other words, if Australia's major friends and allies were no longer construing the world as they once did, were making policy adjustments and to an extent were inviting Australia to cast another look at its own policies, this should have served as incentive for L–CP governments.

Another factor in the equation, which can also be viewed as an incentive for change, was the movement in Australian political life. The Liberal and Country Parties enjoyed their longevity as parties of government. Between 1949 and 1966, their presence in office had been electorally seriously threatened only once. The reason for their near-defeat in 1961 had been their handling of the economy, not external policy problems. The L–CP won handsomely in 1966. It acquired a 10 per cent first-preference popular vote lead and a huge 40-

seat (81-41) representational advantage over Labor in the House. Foreign policy was widely and bitterly argued in the 1966 campaign, and an exceptionally large proportion of swinging voters believed that Australia's Vietnamese commitment and conscription were salient in making their own electoral choice. Such voters dominantly opted for the L–CP—or, perhaps more exactly, against the ALP and its then leader, Arthur Calwell. His reproaches against the Holt government's Vietnamese policy were filled with expletives. He demanded the unceremonious withdrawal of Australian forces from Vietnam and the immediate termination of conscription.[7] A number of the L–CP's critics did more than regret that Labor had been defeated in 1966. Discussing the Australian public mood at that time, Blazey and Campbell approvingly refer to the remarks of Graham Freudenberg, a former Calwell press secretary. Freudenberg

> described Calwell as one of the three "guilty men" responsible for the deepening war in Vietnam [Menzies and Holt being the other two] ... Calwell, because ... he had caused an electoral catastrophe. The loss of Labor seats after this single-cause campaign, persuaded the Liberals they had a mandate to significantly increase the commitment of troops in Vietnam. "Arthur has blood on his hands. He is directly responsible for that commitment," Freudenber said.[8]

The L–CP's inflated 1966 majority, the ostensible popular support for its policies and various self-wounding tendencies within the Labour Party initially created an atmosphere that served as a disincentive for the government to reappraise Vietnam policy or foreign policies more broadly. Within a few years, however, changes began to appear in the configuration of international politics and within American thinking. A massive deflation of the government's earlier complacence can be regarded as incentive to undertake review of older assumptions. Whitlam replaced Calwell as ALP leader in early 1967. He was by far a more electorally attractive and marketable personality than Calwell. He was more politically agile and pragmatic in his outlook on foreign and defence policies and otherwise. Calwell had helped to polarize opinion on Vietnam and related external issues. Whitlam, being more temperate and persuasive, made himself, and the party he led, appear increasingly reasonable and appealing as an electoral option. Calwell excoriated Whitlam for selling out on Labor's principles and for having undermined him during the 1966 campaign over foreign and defence issues.[9] In style and to a degree in substantive terms Whitlam dissociated himself from Calwell. He kept a safe distance between himself and the more strident manifestations of the anti-Vietnam and anti-conscription protest movement. He deplored what he regarded as the sycophancy of professions such as Holt's "All the Way with LBJ" slogan, but conveyed the impression that he was acceptable to Australia's traditional friends. On a visit to America in 1967, he met with some of the most influential foreign policy figures in the country. He scored handsomely in Australia when Johnson described him as the "young and brilliant leader of the Australian Labor Party".[10] Thus when Whitlam called for reappraisals in Australia's foreign policy, he was seen as reputable and taken seriously. The impression was more striking than if Calwell had not, under his leadership, helped to create such a wide gulf between Labor and the L–CP.

Several other political/electoral developments during the late 1960s and early 1970s brought concern to L–CP governments and could likewise be construed as incentives for reordering their foreign policy directions. Whitlam and others worked hard to refurbish Labor's image and the quality of its programme. The party had in the past been reviled for being tied to irresponsible, outside (especially trade-union) dictation. It had been charged with taking decisions in camera and without even allowing its parliamentary leadership to have seats in conference or on the Federal Executive. The conference was portrayed as "36 faceless men" and the Federal Executive as "12 witless men". As of the 1967 Adelaide Federal Conference, a number of such liabilities were removed. Although the party continued to wash much of its dirty linen in public, Whitlam usually managed to be on the side of "respectability", as when he differed with the party's left-wing Victorian branch, with Calwell and with Dr J. F. Cairns, who in 1968 came close to dislodging Whitlam from the ALP leadership. On that occasion, the burden of charges against Whitlam was that he had substituted expediency for party principles and observance of collegially taken decisions.

When engaged in electoral politics, Whitlam earned a reputation for energy, articulateness and, above all, success. The first general election fought by Whitlam as ALP leader was in 1969. Labor failed to gain control of government, but won in most other respects. What helped to make it appear to be such an impressive Labor electoral performance was the inordinately low level to which the party had slumped in the 1966 débacle. In 1969, there was a resounding 7 per cent popular swing to Labor and the government's margin in the House over Labor was cut from 40 to 7. The ALP's come-back was construed by many observers as a prelude to the election that was to follow. Labor now needed only a modest push to gain office. This it accomplished in 1972, with a favourable swing of only 2.6 per cent.

There were various reasons why Labor's fortunes improved from 1967 onwards, and some dealt with foreign policy. Whitlam himself, as we have seen, assumed positions and exhibited a style on foreign policy issues that were electorally profitable. In the public image, his personal leadership qualities were fully competitive with Gorton's, and well ahead of McMahon's. In the late 1960s and early 1970s, public support for specific L–CP external policies began to wane. In 1969, as in 1966, key, potentially swinging voters continued to place high salience on the Vietnam issue. This time, their disposition was to start bringing Australian troops home, rather than keeping the commitment intact, which had been the main disposition among Vietnam-interested swinging voters in 1966.[11]

Various reasons affected decline in public support for standard L–CP external policy approaches. These included perceived weaknesses in the substance of government policies, the government's problem of explaining its policies credibly and the appearance of a credible ALP alternative government. The ALP under Whitlam helped to make alternative policies more palatable. The protest movement of the period, though widely suspect among the public, did serve as a kind of politico-cultural solvent. It attracted a number of "respectable" middle-class people, including churchmen. Out of this period also sprang the Liberal Reform Movement, later called the Australia Party. It originated among progressively minded members of the middle and upper-middle class, whose sympathies would otherwise have been with the Liberals. Among other life-quality and civil libertarian issues that it publicized, the Australia Party proffered ideas about fundamental reorientation in foreign policy, which in some respects were even more radical than Labor was urging. The Australian public was becoming more sensitized to foreign policy concerns, socialized into considering less-conventional and categorical impressions of the world and of Australia's place in it. Denis Murphy's conclusion was that

> the opening of Australians' visions of the rest of the world through the war, the changed emphasis and scope of education and the necessity for so many Australians to think out their positions on the Vietnam war, produced stirrings within those concerned about foreign affairs for something more positive, more tolerant, less radically based and more international in its orientation.[12]

To summarize: Towards what came to be the close of their reign, L–CP governments were subjected to an assortment of incentives to redirect their traditional foreign policy assumptions. These incentives included reconfigurations in the international environment, shifts in the postures of classical great-power allies, the appearance of an effectively challenging Labor Party, declining popular enthusiasm for a number of L–CP policies and a generally more questioning public mood. Running counter, however, were circumstances that constrained the governments of the time.

A very important obstacle to policy reorientation was the internal state of L–CP governments, especially after Holt. Firstly, there was the problem of continuity. Menzies had served as Prime Minister for over fifteen years. Less than seven years separated his retirement in early 1966 and the defeat of the L–CP government in late 1972. During that period there were three Prime Ministers. There also were five Foreign Ministers, and all served during the fewer than five years of the combined period of the Gorton and McMahon governments. Gordon Freeth served only nine months and Leslie Bury only five. In and of itself, turnover at this rate was prejudicial to long-range attempts at basic re-evaluations and to the implementation of sustained policies. The problem was compounded by the circumstances under which ministerial leadership changed. There was little to suggest smooth transitions. Gorton became Prime Minister upon Holt's sudden accidental death. McMahon succeeded Gorton when the latter was dumped in a Liberal caucus leadership spill. Among the Foreign Ministers of the period, two (Hasluck and Bury) surrendered their portfolios in circumstances of poor *rapport* with Prime Ministers. McMahon was diverted to the portfolio after he had the first time, unsuccessfully, contested the leadership against Gorton.

Gorton and McMahon, the last two Liberal Prime Ministers, both suffered from certain disabilities that reflected adversely on their ability to deal systematically with Australia's external affairs. Gorton was disposed to rethink the underlying communist threat and forward defence postulates of the Menzies–Holt era. But the manner in which it was done may have done more to retard than to advance a genuine re-evaluation. Gorton had a proclivity for personalizing policy in a way that others saw as graceless, even tactless. He sometimes showed an innocence of basic facts and was inclined to speak off the cuff. Not only was he inclined to overlook advice from officials, but he manifested a certain insensitivity in handling his colleagues. Menzies had created a Foreign and Defence Committee within Cabinet. It considered issues in some detail and passed the more important ones upwards for full Cabinet consideration. The committee met infrequently under Gorton and eventually was abandoned. Cabinet at large was not given adequate opportunity to consider forthcoming policy announcements. When they came, they were sometimes resented for their impetuosity, sometimes for their substance, sometimes for both. A number of Gorton's senior, more conservatively minded colleagues such as Hasluck, Defence Minister David Fairhall and the powerful CP leader and Deputy Prime Minister, John McEwen, resisted his essays into a new diplomacy.

Gorton's problems were partially temperamental. Sir Alan Watt has suggested that they were also attributable to under-preparation for the role. Previously, to be sure, as a Senator, Gorton had deputized for the Minister for External Affairs and had served as chairman of the Joint Parliamentary Committee on Foreign Affairs. However, "Australian hesitations and uncertainties were enhanced, during the period of re-appraisal, by the fact that ... Gorton ... had not been a member of inner Cabinet circles which, over the years, had dealt regularly with problems of foreign policy and defence."[13]

Another factor was Gorton's political weakness generally. This weakness partially derived from his stylistic shortcomings. It also came from intra-L–CP opposition to his external and domestic policies, for instance his approach to federalism and to the states. It was exacerbated by the fact that with the overshadowing figure of Menzies gone from the Liberal headship, the party began to break out, to feel its way and simply to be more critical of lesser leaders. Gorton's intra-party political weakness was also attributable to the putatively cardinal flaw of politicians—electoral failure. It was in 1969, with Gorton leading the L–CP, that Labor scored a great political recovery. All these factors precipitated two attempts at a leadership spill against Gorton, the second of which succeeded. All told, it was not surprising that, during the Gorton years, a serious and above all orderly re-examination of foreign policy directions was both distracted and obfuscated.

Personality and intra-Cabinet problems during McMahon's prime ministership also constrained effective foreign policy remodelling. Unlike Gorton, McMahon entered the leadership with almost ideal paper credentials. He had been a senior minister for many years and his most recent assignment had been as Minister for Foreign Affairs. He enjoyed a well-deserved reputation for listening carefully to his advisers and for mastering his briefs. He had been a first-rate Treasurer. As Foreign Minister, he had been instrumental in reorganizing the department. Partially because of official advice, he had shifted his own thinking on several subjects. For instance, he acquired a more flexible attitude towards China.

The McMahon government had a poor press during its period in office and criticism of it did not mellow with time. The criticism included the conduct of foreign policy. There were difficulties, some outside McMahon's reach, which in their way continued to inhibit a serious L–CP reappraisal of conventional policies.

Part of the problem lay with McMahon. His talents apparently were more ministerial than prime ministerial. He was short on the skills needed to lead, co-ordinate and accommodate an array of ministerial colleagues and departments. In foreign policy, the old Menzies Cabinet committee system was not revived. Cabinet-level policy discussion and planning was sporadic, exasperating some ministers who had just passed out of the trying Gorton period. The earlier example of Peacock's dealings with Papua New Guinea suggested how casual were aspects of the policy process. McMahon tried to do both too much and too little. The result, testified to by ministers who sat in his government, was tangle and, at times, incoherence.

In defence of McMahon, suggestions have been made that he faced exceptional burdens, the impingement of which prevented clear and decisive approaches to foreign policy. These were said to include an insufficiency of expert personal aides, obstructionism from sectors of the public service establishment, a very busy personal schedule, difficulties with the partner Country Party, and various distractions associated with the forthcoming election.

The political/electoral picture is most worth exploring. McMahon became Prime Minister of a L–CP government at a deplorably inauspicious time. The Liberal Party was restless. It had just toppled Gorton. It saw its grip on office in Canberra slipping, as Labor's fortunes brightened. It wanted a leader who could accomplish marvels— give it resolute leadership, resuscitate its image and polish its policies without offending more traditional party elements, allow the party, and its élites, freedom of spokesmanship and, above all, counter Whitlam and forestall a Labor government. It would have been an unenviable assignment for any person.

McMahon was distracted by running controversy between himself and the Country Party, especially the CP leader and Deputy Prime Minister, J. D. Anthony. While the CP was a "sister" coalition party to the Liberals, it had its own mind and a tradition of decisive leaders. It could not be controlled by a Liberal Prime Minister, especially one operating under a multitude of other pressures. McMahon was reluctant to launch major foreign policy reviews, in part because he felt the Liberals needed a period of peace and healing in the aftermath of Gorton. But, stylistically, he was not a good consensus leader. Nor did he enjoy a good platform presence, which prevented him from stating clearly and attractively what his government's foreign policy really was all about: Was it old? New? A blend? His position was not helped by some unexpected turns in American foreign policy, which on occasion made the L–CP look sluggish and uncreative.

As 1972 wore on and an election approached, Whitlam's public image stood vastly ahead of McMahon's and the polls were showing little encouragement for a Liberal return to office. In the foreign policy area, McMahon found himself stuck on the horns of a dilemma. He could try to "freshen" Australia's foreign policy, bring it closer to Labor's and thereby neutralize Labor's self-professed appeal as a party of creativity and accurate assessment of world conditions. Or he could largely resist this temptation, partially to avert divisive outcries among more traditional L–CP figures, partially to escape the charge of conceding that Labor had somehow been right all the way along and the L–CP wrong. He chose the latter course.

The McMahon government's foreign policy initiatives were constrained by another factor, the Democratic Labor Party. The DLP grew out of the great ALP schism of 1954–55. Its influence on successive L–CP governments was expressed in two related ways. One influence was as a publicist. It took a consistently hard line on foreign policy and defence. It asserted that the communist danger to Australia's interests was real and obvious, and that the nation had to maintain a stiff guard in its military, diplomatic and economic policies towards this threat. It promoted this argument assiduously during and between electoral campaigns, and in various settings, including the forum of the Australian Senate, where it was consistently represented. Most of its partisan diatribes were directed against the ALP, whom it accused of unfitness to govern. Labor was said to harbour radical elements and to foster sell-out foreign and defence policies. This suited L–CP governments well. The DLP was doing them a favour. As a result, the turgid external policy discourse engendered by the DLP made L–CP governments less resilient, less inclined to "give way" to the "street politics" of the protest movement, less disposed to re-examine or realign their own foreign policy directions.

The other side of DLP influence on L–CP governments was more explicitly electoral. While the DLP was not uncritical of L–CP external policies, it found L–CP government much preferable to the prospects of Labor government. It therefore urged its electors to cast their second preferences for government party candidates in House of Representatives elections. DLP voters responded with remarkable faithfulness: 80 per cent and more of DLP second preferences went to the L–CP. The result was striking. Although the DLP never elected one of its own to the House, and its national popular vote varied from a high of 9.4 per cent in 1958 to 6 per cent by 1969, it had a major effect on who did form a government or by what margin. In 1958, 1963 and 1966, the L–CP could have won government outright, without DLP preferences, though less conclusively. Without DLP help, it would have lost the 1961 and 1969 elections. The 1961 election was won by the L–CP by only two seats. In seven seats, the distribution of DLP preferences reversed the lead of candidates who had topped the ballot on first preferences. In 1969, the L–CP won by seven seats; DLP preferences reversed the first preference vote in twelve seats. With the approach of an election in 1972, the McMahon government could not overlook the DLP factor. The prospects for a L–CP victory were bleak enough. The government would almost surely be defeated should a reorientation of its foreign policy cause the DLP to sit on its hands, or to withhold preferences from L–CP candidates, or should DLP voters simply no longer find the L–CP far preferable to Labor.[14]

On balance, both Gorton and McMahon were interested in re-examining and possibly redressing conventional L–CP approaches to external policy. During both prime ministerships, there were incentives as well as inhibitions that coloured the actual outcomes. We will now try to recapture some of the spirit of what *did* eventuate, tying together through examples the substantive and policy process dimensions of external policy in the closing stages of L–CP government.

Events in late 1968 and in 1969 illustrated how Gorton's interest in reconsidering conventional external policy approaches were caught in the cross-fire of personality and political forces previously alluded to. The issues related to Australia's military contributions to Malaysia/Singapore and to its reactions to the Nixon Doctrine and the Soviet naval presence in the Indian Ocean.

We have seen that, when Britain announced its intention to retract its forces from Malaysia/Singapore, the Gorton government faced a difficult choice. Should it, once the British had gone, continue its own troop presence there, contrary to the well-established Australian doctrine of standing in support, but not independent of, a great-power presence? It was a logical question to raise. Gorton wrestled with it for some time. Gorton's way was not eased by some of his earlier vague, or impromptu, references to the prospect of "fortress Australia" and of an "Israeli-type" defence orientation. To many, a "forward defence" posture remained sacrosanct. The DLP's assessment was that Gorton had become a

> man of drift ... [who] does nothing to adapt Australia to changing international circumstances. He wants to avoid responsibility for the defence of Malaysia and Singapore. He put a financial ceiling on defence spending, limiting the contribution Australia can make to any collective American–Australian military operation. And he does nothing positive by way of initiative to help build the regional structure we need for self-defence in South-East Asia.[15]

About that time (late 1968) there was a prospect that Gorton would call an early election. The DLP threatened to withhold preferences in selected seats if an election did take place without proper clarification of the government's intentions on Malaysian and Singapore defence. The DLP reasoned that this would jarr the government into mending its position. If the government still went ahead with an election without having satisfied the DLP, the reprisal of selective DLP preference denial would mean an L–CP government with a reduced

majority. The new but weakened government would then, in fear of
future DLP reprisals, correct improvident policies. In the event, no
early election was called. Gorton promised to continue an Australian
presence in Malaysia/Singapore, but denied that the DLP had influenced his behaviour.[16] But there had been discussion in Liberal
Party circles and within the government about the DLP threat. A
former Liberal parliamentarian has suggested that intra-party pressures may have contributed to the eventual decision to convey the
security commitment.[17]

In August 1969, External Affairs Minister Gordon Freeth made
what proved to be a most controversial statement in the House. It
was an attempt to place recent international developments into
perspective; it was a sign of movement. There was no contemplated
turnabout in policy as such, but some ideas about new realities
generated by the Nixon Doctrine and by polycentrism in the communist world. It played down alleged dangers of a Soviet presence in
the Indian Ocean, questioned implacable ostracism of China and intimated that Australia might wish to review its orthodox approach of
forward defence in concert with great powers.[18] Criticism flowed
from several directions. Some of the criticism was on procedural
grounds, but nonetheless biting. The speech had been drafted in the
Department of External Affairs, then reworked in Freeth's office.
Freeth and Gorton were the only ministers to have perused it. It had
not been seen by Cabinet, or even the Defence Minister or Deputy
Prime Minister and CP leader McEwen. Thus there was resentment at
having been taken by surprise. There also was resentment over the
content of the speech, which was construed by some senior ministers,
by a number of conservative backbenchers and by the DLP as a
shameful document. As Liberal and Country Party rafters shook, the
DLP returned to its tactic of electoral blackmail. An election had to
take place within a few months, and selective withdrawal of
preferences was in store unless the Freeth speech and other disturbing Gortonisms were repudiated. Gorton capitulated by the time an
election occurred in October.

> An Australian "forward defence" presence in South-East Asia was essen-
> tially confirmed; the Soviet Indian Ocean presence was given more
> ominous interpretation; adequate defence expenditures were promised, as
> was a naval base at Cockburn Sound in Western Australia (that is, on the
> Indian Ocean); doubts were raised about the advisability of Australian ac-
> cession to the nuclear non-proliferation treaty. All this gratified the DLP,
> and the threat of second preference allocation was lifted. The DLP had in-
> timidated the government and in so doing slowed Australia's movement
> away from standard but in some minds increasingly frayed cold war
> rhetoric, assumptions and policy.[19]

In policy process terms, the Malaysia/Singapore troop commitment and Freeth speech controversies underlined more than the conservatizing leverage available to the DLP. They illustrated how Gorton's style of hasty expression and lack of consultative care weakened him, and thereby the value of his ideas. The controversies exposed the fractures that had surfaced after Menzies's departure and the willingness of L–CP ministers and backbenchers alike to put pressure on a Prime Minister. The events not only dampened enthusiasm in the Gorton and then McMahon governments for fundamental policy reappraisal but made the L–CP appear confused and susceptible to arm-twisting. This widened the L–CP's public credibility gap and enhanced Labor's electoral position.

Some security matters, and then the China question, comprise our remaining illustrations of the effects on policy outcomes and presentation brought on by the interplay of incentives and disincentives to reorient established approaches.

Australian combat troops underwent phased withdrawal from Vietnam, starting in 1970. Australia followed American leads in the disengagement process. The Gorton and McMahon governments had been unwilling to pull troops out precipitously, to counteract an otherwise over-rapid American withdrawal. It also had been politically imprudent to start moving out troops before the 1969 election, given the DLP's posture. However, as the withdrawal began, no longer could the government charge that withdrawal's champions were simply a noisy, unrepresentative minority in the country and its dupes in the Labor Party. By 1970, military disengagement from Vietnam had actually become politically judicious for the L–CP. General public opinion had swung in that direction by late 1969. By the time Labor entered office, only military advisers remained. This lessened political pressures that might otherwise have been imposed on the L–CP during the 1972 electoral campaign. In a way, so did the announcement that a negotiated settlement had apparently been reached by the United States and the other side. It was, however, a surprise announcement and further undercut the credibility of L–CP claims about the intimately collective nature of the allied effort in the region.

When, however, the United States launched its military intervention into Cambodia in April 1970, Australia's response was very cautious. The American action carried a stated limited purpose: to clear away North Vietnamese sanctuaries and base-camps on the South Vietnamese border, in the hope that this would shorten the conflict at large. To be sure, the United States had not called for an allied effort in Cambodia, Australian military resources were already stretched in South-East Asia and there was little Australia could meaningfully contribute. But there was a genuine reluctance to plunge into a "new war" and to escalate the regional conflict at large. When Australia did make a gesture to assist the new Lon Nol régime in Cambodia, it did so tardily and with modest paramilitary equipment aid.

Perhaps the controlling motive behind Australia's low-key reaction was to exploit opportunities opened by the Asian-Pacific conference on Cambodia, then in process of being organized and which convened in Jakarta in May. Australia's approach to the conference was an instructive example of the nature and extent to which the L–CP was prepared to adjust to shifting conditions. An active Australian role would make possible a demonstration of willingness to assume a more positive and broadly acceptable position within the Asian-Pacific community. It would be a gesture of reassurance to Washington, to show that the entire burden for managing conflict in the area did not fall on American shoulders. It was stimulated by a wish to engage both Japan and Indonesia in more active and influential roles in Asia. This was in keeping with Australia's already established role, together with Japan, in the Asian and Pacific Council (ASPAC) and its general encouragement for the regionally co-operative activities of the Association of South-East Asian Nations ASEAN), of which Indonesia was the key member. Australia took care to eschew an anti-communist complexion within the Jakarta conference, to avoid prejudice to any brokerage opportunities for the conference. This had been a major reason for Australia not to become directly involved in the American military intervention in Cambodia. All the same, Australia was privately never hopeful about the conference's eventual success. Its interest in a genuinely neutral Cambodia, free of any foreign troops, was consistent with American objectives, though of course the American intervention was regarded by detractors as an aggravating rather than a pacifying measure. McMahon was Foreign Minister during these events. At Jakarta, where he was advised by some of Australia's most senior and experienced officials, his performance was skilful.[20]

This L–CP approach to the Cambodian problem gave the Labor opposition little ammunition with which to attack the government. The government's commitment to Malaysia/Singapore through its participation in the ANZUK force was another matter. Remarks made in early 1972 by McMahon and by spokesmen of the Malaysian government created an impression either that Canberra and Kuala Lumpur were not in harmony on security issues or, if they were, that McMahon had confused and misrepresented the position. The intrinsic L–CP view was that Australia was willing to retain armed forces in Malaysia/Singapore as long as those governments thought they were serving a useful purpose, either to help during the build-up of local defences or to provide a form of security reassurance *per se.* McMahon at one point said there was no real necessity for the Five Power Agreement, though he did not mean that in its literal interpretation. He was embarrassed when a Malaysian official said much the same thing, and clarifications from Malaysia had to be sought. The McMahon government in principle accepted, as a long-term proposition, the 1971 Malaysian initiative for a zone of neutralization in South-East Asia. But to the puzzlement of Malaysia, it implied that Australian forces could continue to be stationed in Malaysia and Singapore once such a zone had been declared into being. Although Australian forces in Malaysia/Singapore were clearly not there to suppress disputes between Malaysia and Singapore, that, again to Malaysia's chagrin, is the impression McMahon left.

McMahon's tendency while he was Prime Minister to speak inexactly on complex and sensitive issues such as these made Australian policies themselves appear less coherent and self-assured. It further reduced McMahon's stature as an advocate of prevailing policies and as a political match for Whitlam. Most of the domestic political value McMahon had hoped to harvest from his mid-1972 visit to South-East Asia was dissipated. Labor was able to allege that the L–CP's forward defence strategy had become nonsense. Either the government itself, or recipients of Australian protection, such as Malaysia, or both, were portrayed as caring little for it. The L–CP's keystone proposition of Australia sustaining or partially substituting for a great-power presence in Asia was brought under further question. Labor's own policies, which called for a removal of Australian troops from South-East Asia, became more palatable.[21]

Australia continued to garrison troops overseas in 1972, but the disengagement from Vietnam lowered the numbers. What was to be done about the armed forces generally? We have seen that the government conceded that Australia needed to be more self-reliant. It accepted that prospects for sending troops abroad had been reduced, though it by no means discounted the possibility. The proportion of GNP devoted to defence had fallen to 3.5 per cent from its 1967–68 peak of 4.6 per cent, and the size of the armed forces fell by a few thousand. Labor promised to maintain the level of defence spending at more or less the 3.5 per cent figure, but would have made some further reductions in manpower. The army, for instance, was projected to decline from 40000 to about 36000. The government retorted that Labor could not be trusted with Australia's defences. Labor's figures for the army were argued to be dangerously low and would prevent the overseas recommitment, if ever necessary, of a major task force. Also Labor was charged with refusing to give the

services the tools with which to do their job: "Past history has warned
... that when pressures come from the Labor Party for increased
payments in other fields it usually expects Defence spending to bear
the brunt of reduced costs."[22]

Politically, the government's arguments about defence
preparedness were eroded by the ostensible decline of visible threats
in the region, the spreading mood of great power *détente*, the winding-
down of the combat commitment in Vietnam and the confusion over
whether, and in what role, Australian armed forces were required in
Malaysia/Singapore. The government's persuasiveness was rendered
even more difficult by the conscription issue. The principal rationale
on which conscription had earlier been applied was now missing.
Conscription, which had had a contentious history in Australian
politics, had become an especially acrimonious public issue, tied as it
was to the use of conscripts in Vietnam.[23] The government conceded
some change in circumstances by reducing the period of service from
two years to eighteen months. Towards the close of its time in office,
it was insisting that conscription foreseeably had to continue if army
strength levels were to be upheld. The most the government was
prepared to concede was that, as justified, efforts would be made to
reduce reliance on conscription.[24] On its part, Labor was on record
favouring the immediate abolition of National Service.

Various members of the L–CP government were not unmindful of
the political value of doing away with conscription. Such sentiment
was found among both Liberals and CP ministers. Apart from
shortening the period of service, however, Cabinet rejected other
attempts to tamper with the system. Then came an alleged episode
the authenticity on which senior ministers of the period are
themselves divided, but the outward importance of which bears
mention. According to one tangent of internal evidence, supported in
its essentials by two former ministers, McMahon inserted a pledge of
outright abolition of National Service into an early draft of his 1972
policy speech. If so, this could be construed either as a bold initiative
by the Prime Minister or as another example of impetuous
government. When McMahon's idea came to Anthony's attention,
the account continues, he reacted vehemently and threatened, if
necessary, to carry his protest into the open. McMahon is then said to
have relented, being unwilling to create further division in the
already bruised coalition or to allow Labor to turn the "unfitness to
govern" accusation on to the then government parties. It must be
emphasized that some ministerial recollections give no credence to
this story. If true, however, the episode was only one among several
external policy differences on which the Liberal and Country Parties
made their joint electoral tasks more difficult.

Australian policy towards China in the last stages of L–CP government further illuminates our policy process/output theme. Australia had for years been conducting lucrative trade with China. Wheat, Australia's principal export commodity to China, earned an average of $100 million annually, and the two-way trade balance tipped heavily in Australia's favour. Australia continued to recognize Taiwan only and to oppose giving the Chinese UN seat to Peking, but insisted that trade and politics could be neatly separated.

Australia concluded a major wheat deal with China in December 1969, and in 1969–70, China ranked sixth among Australia's customers. But in 1970–71 and again in 1971–72, no new wheat contracts were negotiated with the Chinese and China became a negligible Australian customer. It was then, in the very late 1960s and the early 1970s, that China began to emerge from its diplomatic hibernation. Various Western governments, including Canada and other NATO members, opened diplomatic relations with Peking. Evidence began to accumulate that the Chinese were staying away from the Australian wheat market because they disapproved of Canberra's diplomacy towards China. This was corroborated by a Labor Party mission that Whitlam led to China in mid-1971. The Chinese said that they were not buying Australian wheat because its sale was in the hands of the Australian Wheat Board, technically an Australian government instrumentality. A senior Canadian mission to Peking was told that Canada would receive special preference for its wheat sales to China, and "If the Australian Government changes its policy toward China, we will give you the same consideration as we have given to Canada."[25]

There definitely had been wheat negotiations between China and the Wheat Board in 1971. The price difference between the negotiating parties was apparently slight and an informant claimed that the government at one point instructed the Wheat Board to lower its asking price. Ministerial informants indicated that the deal collapsed for commercial reasons. On balance, the author is inclined to believe that Chinese political considerations could not be discounted. In September 1972, less than three months before the L–CP lost office, the Chinese finally placed a wheat order with Australia, but virtually as a last resort. They had first made sizeable purchases from Canada, the United States and France, in that order. Their return to the Australian market had not been inspired by changes in Canberra's diplomatic policy. In terms of actual policy movement, the McMahon government had done relatively little. In May 1971, it finally abolished the "China differential" on the sale of strategic materials to China. In the same month, informal exchanges of views between Australian and Chinese officials were undertaken in third nation capitals. These continued sporadically into the next year, without any tangible results. When in late 1971 Peking was awarded China's UN seat, Australia had co-sponsored an alternative, 'two-China' resolution, the terms of which were of course entirely unaccept-able to Peking and its supporters. In 1972, Australian Foreign Minister Bowen did have conversations in New York with the new Chinese UN delegates and Australia encountered no Chinese interference with its election to the Security Council in that year.

At the level of rhetoric and gesture, the McMahon government's handling of Chinese issues left an impression of confusion and misadventure. When the ALP delegation went to China, McMahon denounced it in the strongest terms, calling it an exercise in "instant-coffee diplomacy" and worse than naive, since the ALP had gone to China to play politics with wheat, when trade and politics did not in fact mix. He charged that it had been Labor's fault that Australia's wheat sales to China had been forfeited. He further remarked that the China issue had been·a "political asset" for his party in the past, and was likely to remain so in the future.[26]

The Labor Party mission to China was neither a disaster for Australia nor for the ALP. Indeed, the visit gave the party a substan-tial political boost. This was attributable to the sense of initiative shown by Labor and the manner in which Whitlam and his delega-tion comported themselves. It also owed much to the government's own appearance of having been left behind. The most striking exam-ple of this came almost immediately after McMahon had so strenuously denounced the ALP's China trip and had attacked it for betraying Australia's bonds with America. It is understood that Mc-Mahon first cleared these remarks with Washington, and no objec-tions were offered. McMahon had barely finished delivering his remarks when, in a joint Sino–American announcement, it was revealed that Henry Kissinger had just paid a secret call to Peking and a visit to China by Nixon had been arranged. Laurie Oakes' summary speaks volumes: "McMahon, shaken and embarrassed, issued a state-ment claiming: 'The President's purpose of normalising relations with China has been the publicly announced policy of the Australian Government for some time.' Reporters were forbidden to ask him any questions."[27]

Not only was McMahon himself tangled by these developments, but he and his then Foreign Minister, Leslie Bury, appeared to be operating on separate wavelengths.

> The Prime Minister had taken over the role of making policy statements on China and when Mr Bury was questioned about Australian policy towards China on television on 27 June, he appeared unaware both that the government had started a dialogue with China and that Mr McMahon

had announced that the Chinese were responding. Despite the Prime Minister's welcome of the news of President Nixon's Peking visit, Mr Bury stated publicly that he had "profound misgivings about the process involved" and that he hated to see Australian interests "dragged by the chariot wheels of American political processes and perhaps scattered by an overall deal between two men who may not even be aware of them".[28]

Suddenly, or so it seemed, the ALP's approach to China was more harmonious with US policy than was the L–CP's. In 1973, after becoming Prime Minister, Whitlam openly acknowledged that "if it had not been for President Nixon's initiative, my own Peking visit would, given the Australian climate of the time, have been no political advantage to me, even as late as last December [i.e. during the 1972 election]."[29]

In the second half of 1971, potential opportunity arose for the L–CP to redress some of its political injury over relations with China. Andrew Peacock, at the time Minister for the Army, was called from Hong Kong by James Kibel, an acquaintance with Chinese business connections. Kibel said that the Chinese government wanted Peacock to come for a visit. This was confirmed by the Foreign Affairs Department through Chinese agents in Hong Kong. No conditions were imposed on Peacock. It was clearly established that the Chinese *did not* require Peacock to resign his portfolio to undertake the trip. Not only did the Foreign Affairs Department and its Secretary, Sir Keith Waller, endorse the visit, but apparently so did Foreign Minister Bowen. McMahon considered the matter, and so did the L–CP "inner" Cabinet, which did not include Peacock. Permission for the trip was refused. It may have had something to do with an erroneous belief by McMahon that Peacock would need to surrender his portfolio. It may also have been related to an intrusion by Anthony. He and the CP were then quite concerned about China's refusal to buy Australian wheat. Anthony wished to be the minister who would go to China and as head of a trade mission. For their own reasons, this was something the Chinese would not accept.

Towards the end of 1972, with an election approaching, McMahon volunteered that he would be pleased to send Bowen to China, if there were an invitation. But he was quick to add that recognition of China was not fundamentally important to Australia, and in no circumstances would Australia "capitulate" to Chinese terms, i.e. the abandonment of Taiwan.[30] McMahon preferred that Australia's relationship with China "go along carefully, methodically".[31] A few months earlier, an official Liberal Party foreign policy document had described Labor's approach to China as "sycophantic".[32] Enter the Country Party. The Chinese had resumed buying Australian wheat in September, but the CP was plainly worried about the future. For some time, Anthony had been implacable on the subject of the Chinese menace and on recognition. He had been saying that he would not sell his conscience "just to try to do a trade deal" with China.[33] But in the concluding weeks of the 1972 campaign, with the L–CP running behind in the opinion polls, he indicated that the CP regarded recognition of China as "in the best interests, not just of the trade and political considerations, but of the Australian people and the Chinese people".[34] The CP's deputy leader, Ian Sinclair, though cautioning against rushing into recognition of Peking, openly disagreed with McMahon's formulation that recognition was "not fundamental" to Australia's interests.[35]

The China issue illustrated many of the difficulties endemic to the McMahon government and the obstacles that faced those who might have wished to refurbish Australian foreign policy. There was real difficulty in breaking new ground, simply because of deeply ingrained habits and formulas. When American policy unexpectedly jumped ahead on China, the Australian government was unable to cope and had much political credit shot out from under it. McMahon succeeded to the prime ministership in a period of severe party unrest and was constrained from launching serious policy departures that more pronouncedly could have divided the Liberals and presumably hampered prospects for re-election. Within two months of succeeding Gorton, he did adjust the government's policy towards China in modest ways. But when the ALP trip to China came up, his political instinct was to take a very hard critical line, in the hope of solidifying his own authority and bolstering party fortunes at the expense of a reviving Labor Party. In the general disorientation characteristic of the government's workings at that time, any opportunity that may have been available in a Peacock visit to China was aborted. In this instance, McMahon disregarded official advice. The start of an informal dialogue with China brought McMahon closer to official advice, but short of basic reorientation. One document summarized the general situation as follows: Official advice "could not induce the Government to break radically with its past ideological framework, unless there were compelling reasons for it to do so on independent political grounds."[36] While he was Prime Minister, McMahon's receptivity to official advice on China was diminished by his growing disenchantment with much of the Foreign Affairs Department generally.

On more than one occasion, as we have seen, the expressions of Liberal and Country Party coalition partners were at variance, or the CP was able to impose its own stamp on policy. This further limited the government's manoeuvreability and complicated its already severe credibility problem. When the 1972 electoral campaign was launched, McMahon on Chinese policy seemed to project flexibility in form but firmness in content. He could still not overlook the recent

past, when the DLP had extracted foreign and defence policy concessions from the Gorton government yet contributed to the return of
the L–CP to office in the 1969 election. Hence in an October 1972 interview, when asked whether DLP preferences would be an element
in his judgement on China, he replied "Some, yes—but not decisive."[37]

Had the L–CP been returned to government in 1972, would it have
proceeded to recognize Peking, essentially on Peking's terms? The
question is not entirely idle, because a search for its hypothetical
answer might further illuminate the circumstances under which the
McMahon government was operating in 1971 and 1972. The author is
inclined to answer affirmatively. The new Liberal leader, B. M. Snedden, and Bowen, addressing themselves to this question in 1973, both
said that this would have happened, but without undue haste, and
without automatically granting the Chinese every demand they
might impose. The point is that neither man said that Australia under
another L–CP government would have held out for any "two-China"
formula.[38] The author's own inquiries among former ministers bear
out this conclusion. It should be remembered that, by the end of 1972,
the CP was already, and publicly, disposed towards recognition.
Moreover, the circumstantial evidence is strong. A L–CP victory
would have placed McMahon in a more secure position than he occupied before December 1972 and, at all events, his personal instincts
on China were not hidebound. The DLP, whose decline continued in
1972, would have been taken less seriously, and especially so if there
was some time before the next scheduled House election. Furthermore, the continuing trend toward US–Chinese *détente* and the closing
of the US and allied side of the war in Vietnam would have supplied a
more congenial international climate for such a step. There would
also have been incentive from across the Tasman. The Labour government elected in New Zealand in late November 1972 quickly moved
to recognize Peking. There is very persuasive evidence that if a
National Party government had instead been returned in Wellington,
within a year and probably less it too would have recognized Peking,
after a few preliminary but not too convincing gestures to work out
some kind of two-China formula. The incentive for Australia to follow the New Zealand lead, or even to move alongside it, would have
been considerable.

L–CP governments developed certain stylistic patterns in their handling of foreign and defence issues. We have noticed some of the results
that followed for policy outcomes. Also affected was the mood in
which external matters were dealt with *vis-à-vis* the general public,
and the Labor opposition more specifically. Probably rather more
than most governments in parliamentary systems, L–CP governments
became suspicious and secretive.

We first consider the penchant for secretiveness, a theme to which Jim Spigelman, a personal aide to Whitlam, devoted an entire book.[39] L–CP governments were culpable for having gone too far too often. But special Australian circumstances should not be overlooked. Probably any party or coalition that remains entrenched in office as long as the L–CP, tends towards self-righteousness and smugness. Layers of authority within the system acquire an autonomy of their own. The system becomes less open, less penetrable, less fathomable. Predisposition towards this tendency was also probably contributed to by governing parties that were based far more on downward than on upward linkages of authority and by traditions of bureaucratic power. In Australia, the partisan foreign policy debate had been pungent, even doctrinal. This was heightened by the bitterness of party conflict over Vietnam and conscription. It was hardly mitigated by the little-love-lost personal relations between party leaders, notably Holt and Calwell and McMahon and Whitlam. Also the floridness with which the L–CP, spurred by the DLP, often invested its electoral presentations on external policy inhibited a more sensitive, trusting approach towards the parliamentary opposition between elections. Labor's disposition to reply in kind did not ease the situation.

Our illustrations here are brief, but representative. A Joint (House and Senate) Parliamentary Committee on Foreign Affairs was originally authorized in 1951. Until 1967, the ALP refused to participate, for among other reasons because it felt the committee was a ministerial handmaiden. It was neither a watchdog nor a critic of the government, nor a platform for the presentation of reasoned alternative policy options. Labor relented after the government had made some modifications in committee procedures. Further amendments moved by Labor in 1970 to permit Parliament itself to refer topics for study to the committee, or to meet in public for the most part without ministerial consent, were refused. The L–CP had a natural desire to preserve the Executive's authority in foreign policy. It also harboured suspicions about the advisability of investing much strength in a committee on which Labor was represented, despite the fact that once the ALP had joined, virtually all of its committee members were moderates.[40] The disclosure of the Pentagon Papers in 1971 suggested that Australia's original combat commitment in Vietnam had not, contrary to the Menzies government's exposition, been made on Saigon's initiative. The ALP was incensed by what it believed to have been sheer government duplicity. It was further disturbed by what it regarded as the government's lame explanation of these events and by its disallowance of full access to relevant papers. Labor members insisted on at least a predominantly open hearing on this matter by the joint committee. The request was refused and the Labor members temporarily withdrew in protest from the committee's work.[41]

When the L–CP accepted American defence facilities such as Pine Gap and Nurrungar, it at first refused even to acknowledge that they had defence applications. The government later did make this acknowledgement, but categorically refused to provide any information whatsoever as to what the facilities were about. The confidentiality claim was made on grounds of security. The government also obstructed selected access to the facilities by the ALP leadership, in effect the alternative Australian government. As we will notice later, when Labor came to office and learned about the facilities, it too refused to divulge their function. However, the L–CP's handling of the US facilities was excessively rigid. There is some internal evidence that, while portraying blanket secrecy as an American-imposed requirement, Canberra imposed stricter restrictions on Labor's access to them than Washington itself thought necessary. A partial exception to this generalization may be needed. It is based on a remark of a former minister, but is short on detail and could not be confirmed through other sources. The claim is that before his complete falling out with the L–CP over Vietnam, Calwell, as Leader of the Opposition, was given a confidential briefing on American defence-related facilities as they were then constituted. Calwell, in turn, advised the government *not* to share such information with his deputy Whitlam, calling him untrustworthy. The claim is plausible. Not only was Calwell reasonably well regarded by his opponents until 1966 or so, but Calwell's enmity towards Whitlam had begun before that time. The offer to Whitlam was not made. The "guided tour" of Pine Gap accorded to Whitlam by the Americans in 1971 was courteous, but quite uninformative.[42]

The government's treatment of Australia's intelligence organizations is consistent with the tenor of secretiveness. We have seen that ASIS was never officially acknowledged to exist, let alone identified by function. In 1973, Whitlam admitted the existence of the DSD electronic monitoring unit in Singapore. It was a revelation to most Australians. Four reasons suggest themselves for the L–CP's secretiveness about the nation's intelligence services. Firstly, secretiveness was fostered by ASIS's British-oriented origins and early staffing. The British intelligence tradition was and continues to be considerably more closeted than the American. Secondly, there was the overall secretive ethos of L–CP governments. Thirdly, there was the lack of confidence extended towards the Labor opposition, with whom foreign policy differences were often sharply drawn. Fourthly, there was a feeling that Australian opinion might not have been well disposed to accept "spy" organizations. At all events, we have already noticed how this secretiveness promoted lack of firm authority over and even ministerial information about ASIS. Once again, Calwell may have been an exception to the rule of secretiveness. The account, taken from a source other than the one who commented on Calwell's US defence-facility briefings, was that Calwell was at one time apprised of ASIS's existence. The account continues that Whitlam may have surmised that Calwell had been made privy to something. Late in the life of the L–CP government, he is said to have approached McMahon for access to whatever Calwell may have had. McMahon is said to have thought the request too broad and asked Whitlam to be more specific. In the end, nothing was disclosed.

Prior to the 1972 election, contingency plans for a Labor victory were drawn up in the Foreign Affairs and Defence Departments, including on means for winding down conscription. Although there had been some reports to the contrary, Lloyd and Reid correctly conclude that "The McMahon Government was aware that contingency planning of this sort was going on in a number of departments but no attempt was made to interfere."[43] Lloyd and Reid do, however, also mention that Labor shadow ministers failed to receive the cooperation of the incumbent McMahon government in gaining access to various departments. Lloyd and Reid remind us that, basically, "It was perhaps too much to expect an electorally besieged Prime Minister to introduce procedures scorned by his predecessors in much more propitious electoral circumstances. The entrenchment of a government for an excessively long period prevents the development of rational conventions to regulate the transfer of political power."[44]

Another aspect of the L–CP government's style relates to its politically defensive posture. Specific policy questions aside, the McMahon government was eager not only to maintain good credentials in Washington but to cast Labor in the worst-possible light with the Americans. This was being done at a time when US policy was itself being adjusted and when Labor's electoral fortunes were improving.

For instance, during November 1971 conversations between McMahon and Nixon in the United States, the establishment of a Canberra–Washington "hot line" was agreed upon. The idea had not specifically been broached by himself, McMahon later said, but had "evolved"—though it clearly did not "evolve" on American instigation. The facility was a closed telex machine to which, in Australia, only McMahon, his private secretary and Waller had access.[45] It was used several times on important business. But the enthusiasm for the link-up was far more with McMahon than with Nixon. There was a symbolic need to demonstrate a special relationship between Australia and the United States, and perhaps need to forestall such embarrassments to Australia as were caused by the July 1971

Sino–American communiqué. Indeed, it is really not clear why ordinary communications facilities, such as a telephone with a scrambling mechanism, were thought insufficient. Also illuminating is that the existence of the telex link-up was not publicly disclosed until August 1974, by McMahon himself. Although the "hot line" was an innocuous arrangement, the secretiveness involved seemed to complement other aspects of L–CP government procedures. If secretiveness should be discounted, then at minimum, pettiness remains. An explanation given for keeping the facility secret was that it represented an Australian pipeline to Washington not enjoyed by other US allies, such as Britain, whom Australia did not wish to offend. The link-up was discontinued when Labor became the government.

Less innocuous were remarks by Australian ministers. One of the more notable was by Bowen in October 1971. Speaking in the United States, he warned that certain American policies affecting Australia could abet the ALP's electoral fortunes. This would work against American interests, because of Labor's anti-Americanism and communist control over sections of the trade-union movement, which supported Labor.[46] Such admonitions were unlikely to cause the United States to slow the pace of *détente* with China, or whatever. They indirectly may, however, have added to American disquiet about Labor as an Australian party of government.

It is this effect that also may have flowed from some of the activities of ASIO, the Australian Security Intelligence Organization. ASIO's existence and general range of work was publicly known. ASIO did, however, acquire considerable latitude in conducting its operations. One of its projects—usual, to be sure, for an agency of this type—was to compile dossiers on politically suspect personalities. These came to include parliamentarians, among them Cairns, on whom a report was prepared in 1971, when he was active in the protest movement. Among the conclusions reached was that his advocacy and behaviour could bring about "anarchy and, in due course, left-wing fascism."[47] Materials of this nature found their way to American sources, given the wealth of intelligence exchange between the two countries. Once again, because of biases introduced from Australian sources, an inference is possible of further suspicion of the ALP being stimulated in America.

Concluding our survey of the period, we turn to uses of external affairs themes in the 1972 electoral campaign.[48] We will look first at the L–CP and then the ALP approaches, and then make some effort at appraising outcomes. The government's campaign, especially as projected by McMahon, did not devote undue attention to external is-

sues. Rather, they seemed to pop in and out. In part, this was symptomatic of what at large was not a particularly well-synchronized
campaign effort. In part, it resulted from the L–CP's rising distur-
bance over the prospect of losing, which caused patchwork efforts as
the campaign moved on. For instance, McMahon hastily introduced a
prominent law and order, anti-permissiveness ingredient into his
presentations. Also the L–CP was ambivalent about the value of external issues. It sensed that their electoral salience had declined among
the public and that the L–CP's image as manager of the nation's
foreign policy had not been the best. On the other hand, the government parties could not forget that foreign policy attacks on the ALP
had, as a whole, been electorally serviceable in the past. When the
L–CP did hit external subjects, it tended to assert their primacy.
Hence McMahon's comment towards the close of the campaign that
"of all the issues facing the Australian people at this election, the
defence and foreign policies of the major Parties were undoubtedly
the most critical."[49]

Much of the L–CP external policy portrayal was stark and reminis-
cent of anti-Labor attacks of earlier times; if implemented, ALP
policies were predicted to be catastrophic for Australia. Liberal
Speakers' Notes advised that, unmistakeably, "The defence and
foreign policies of the Government and the Labor Party differ on
almost every issue."[50] McMahon insisted that Labor's policies were a
"recipe for an isolationist, friendless and ultimately defenceless
Australia."[51] For McMahon, the essence was that "Labor's policies are
left-wing madness".[52] Much of the media publicity issued on behalf of
the government parties was colourful. One fairly typical newspaper
advertisement showed an artillery piece pointed towards a body of
water, and asked "Mr Whitlam—after two world wars, you still
haven't got the message?"—Whitlam's defence policies antagonize
South-East Asia and the United States, destroy security systems and
"leave the region with a door open for any aggressor to walk in".[53]

In 1972, Labor consciously played down external affairs. This
strategy was partly based on the belief that the public was not overly
susceptible to making voting choices on external themes. The other
side of the coin was that Labor was afraid to invite a major debate on
a subject that, in the immediate past, had been employed by the L–CP
to Labor's electoral detriment. Some ALP figures felt that the L–CP
had survived the 1969 election because Gorton had stepped up his
foreign and defence policy attack against Labor in the late stages of
the campaign.

When Labor spoke on external affairs, it was not reluctant to
repeat its established positions, such as diplomatic recognition of
China, downgrading SEATO, pulling Australian combat troops out of

the ANZUK force and abolishing conscription. The presentation usually was such as to avoid exposing differences among the party's own wings and personalities, and the tone tended to be subdued.[54] Wherein the government's media advertisements accused Labor of harbouring policies that threatened Australia's security, Labor's own presentations were more likely to allege staleness and confusion in government foreign policy and to portray McMahon as unsuited to his role. For instance, a Labor advertisement proclaimed that "You would have to be worried"—McMahon's leadership was "not good enough for Australia". As an example of McMahon as an inter national figure, it cited his remark that "Our attitude is a clear one. As yet we have not made up our minds definitely as to what our policy should be."[55] Labor criticized the L–CP for failing to regulate the massive flow of foreign investment into Australia and imputed political panic to McMahon's tardy introduction of anti-takeover legislation. But the party couched its policy on foreign investment controls in appeals to Australian pride, maturity and self-respect.[56]

In line with its controlling campaign theme of "It's Time", Labor argued that world events had outrun conventional thinking. It was now time for a change of government to deal with changed realities. It was now the L–CP that was divided and disoriented, Labor maintained, thus turning the argument of the 1960s back on the Liberals. Summing up the campaign, Whitlam said that his party had been "vindicated on all the great matters of foreign affairs for the last twenty years", and that *it* was the party of rebuilding and healing for a national community that had been abraded by Vietnam, conscription, and so on: "Unity and co-operation between all sections of the community must once again become the Australian way."[57]

Which of the two contending party groups observed the more electorally profitable approach to foreign and defence issues? What was the net impact of such issues on the election? We must work from inference, even with the availability of survey data.

Throughout 1972 and extending into the campaign, foreign/defence policy ranked far down the list of national issues regarded as personally important by the electorate. External policy was identified by some 6 or 7 per cent of the electorate, well below the two previous House elections. Moreover, in mid-1972, among those who felt that a change of government would make a big difference in some aspect of public policy, only 17 per cent identified defence as the potentially most affected area. Isolating for the moment this factor of low external policy ranking, the inference is that Labor was right in not expending its oratory on the subject, and the L–CP less sensible in giving it moderate weight.

Elections can, however, be won or lost by very slight electoral movements, and in 1972, Labor won a nine-seat majority on a favourable swing of well under 3 per cent. In other words, a very small fraction of the electorate, if properly sensitized, decides the outcome. The data for 1972 are quite clear that Liberal and DLP supporters were much more inclined to identify foreign/defence policy as personally significant that were Labor supporters. Hence in mid-1972, while the general population figure was 6 per cent, the proportion among Liberal followers was 10 per cent, but only 3 per cent among Labor voters. In November, the party breakdown was 8 per cent and 4 per cent, respectively.[58] In a sample drawn immediately following balloting in six swinging electorates in Sydney, foreign/defence policy as the principal voting inducement was mentioned by 7 per cent of Liberals and 4 per cent of Labor votes.[59] It is plausible to infer that these differences were mostly attributable to differences in the socio-economic make-up of the two party group clienteles. The Liberal electorate at large, better educated and more highly socio-economically placed than its Labor counterpart, would be expected to take a stronger interest in non-bread and butter issues. But the poll just cited also found that there was no exact or nearly exact correspondence between party preference and preference for the foreign policy of a particular party. Overall, some 51 per cent preferred Liberal external policy and 38 per cent chose Labor's. Liberal voters chose Liberal Party foreign policy over Labor's by 92 per cent to 1 per cent, but Labor voters preferred Labor's over the Liberals' policy by only 67 per cent to 19 per cent. Analytically, an inference can be taken that in the 1972 campaign, (i) the government's moderately strong emphasis on foreign policy helped to avert more defections among normal Liberal voters to Labor's side than might otherwise have happened; and (ii) since the content of the government's foreign policy was not wholly unattractive to Labor voters, the Labor campaign may have given insufficient focus to foreign policy, so as to dispel doubts about it among its own followers.

The Sydney six-electorate survey found that the great majority of persons who swung to a party other than the one previously adhered to, went Labor. In a population sample of 345, 76 switched to the ALP. Of these three (or 4 per cent) listed defence policy as their basic reason. This of course was a very small sample from which firm conclusions could be teased. However swinging and new voters are the real targets of political campaigners, especially in marginal seats.

We can now try to reconstruct our various data. Foreign and defence issues, *qua* issues as handled by the parties, probably had the following instrumental effect on electoral outcomes: In very marginal terms, they persuaded some persons to switch to Labor. To a greater extent, among people who already were non-Labor in sentiment, temptations to change to Labor were dampened. In both instances, therefore, external issues can be seen to have impinged essentially on established L–CP rather than on Labor voters. Standing alone, however, this interpretation is definitely, but to an unquantifiable degree, inadequate. There is extremely persuasive evidence, empirical and otherwise, that the electoral swing that enabled Labor to capture office in 1972 was attributable to public acceptance of the "It's Time" exhortation. The L–CP *looked* tired, overcome by events and without effective leadership. Labor *looked* fresh, reasonably clear and self-confident, and effectively led. These impressions were moulded in many ways, including by the images cast by the two parties in their treatment of external affairs. It is quite reasonable to suppose that if the government's stylistic *image* on external policy had been decidedly more attractive, and Labor's image worse, fewer people would have been captivated by the "It's Time" slogan and less tempted to vote Gough Whitlam into office.

Discussing foreign policy in 1972, Bruce Grant, himself a Labor supporter, had made a simple but astute observation. The reason for a change to Labor that appealed to him most was that "both Government and Opposition have become, in different ways, irresponsible". After twenty-three years, the L–CP no longer understood the role of an opposition, while Labor had lost sight of the obligations of power. It was time to reverse roles.[60]

NOTES

1. D. Horne, *Bulletin*, 23 November 1968. Also see C. Burns, *Sydney Morning Herald*, 15 October 1968; and B. Grant, Melbourne *Age*, 13 November 1968.
2. *Bulletin*, 19 January 1969.
3. H. Bull, "Australia and the Great Powers in Asia", in *Australia in World Affairs, 196-6–1970*, eds. G. Greenwood and N. Harper (Melbourne: Cheshire, 1974), p. 326.
4. F.A. Mediansky, "Now Here is Our Foreign Policy", *Current Affairs Bulletin* 49 (1 September 1972): 112.
5. Department of Defence, *Defence Report 1972* (Canberra: 1972), pp. 3–4. Also see the remarks of D.E. Fairbairn, Minister for Defence, *Commonwealth [Australian] Parliamentary Debates (APD)*, House of Representatives (HR) (28 March 1972), pp. 1247–55.
6. Brisbane *Courier-Mail*, 27 November 1972.
7. For the electorate's outlook on Vietnam and conscription and the salience of issues in the election, see H.S. Albinski, *Politics and Foreign Policy in Australia: The Impact of Vietnam and Conscription* (Durham, N.C.: Duke University Press, 1970), pp. 191–209. Also see Albinski, "Vietnamese Protest and the Australian Political Process", *Polity* 1 (Spring 1969): 359–75.
8. P. Blazey and A. Campbell, *The Political Dice Men* (Melbourne: Outback Press, 1974), p. 30.
9. See his *Be Just and Fear Not* (Melbourne: O'Neil, 1972), esp. pp. 230–35.
10. Melbourne *Age*, 16 June 1967. For a political biography of Whitlam, see L. Oakes, *Whitlam PM* (Sydney: Angus and Robertson, 1973).
11. *Australian Gallup Polls*, no. 206 (October 1969).

12. D. Murphy, "New Nationalism or New Internationalism: Australian Foreign Policy, 1973–74", *World Review* 13 (October 1974): 16–17.
13. A. Watt, "Australian Defence Policy in South-East Asia after 1971", *Pacific Community* 1, no. 1 (1969): 15. On the Gorton period generally, see A. Reid, *The Gorton Experiment* (Sydney: Shakespeare Head Press, 1971).
14. For a general review of the DLP, see P.L. Reynolds, *The Democratic Labor Party* (Brisbane: Jacaranda, 1974); and P.J. Duffy, "The DLP in the Seventies", in *Australian Politics: A Third Reader*, eds. H. Mayer and H. Nelson (Melbourne: Cheshire, 1973), pp. 435–45. On the DLP vote, see in particular L.F. Crisp, "The DLP Vote, 1958–69", *Politics* 5 (May 1970): 62–66.
15. Senator V.C. Gair, *Sydney Morning Herald*, 20 January 1969.
16. For accounts, see E. Walsh, *Nation*, 26 October 1968; A. Reid, *Bulletin*, 12 October 1968; and A. Reid *Bulletin*, 19 and 26 October, 9 November 1968 and 1 February 1969.
17. E. St John, *A Time to Speak* (Melbourne: Sun Books, 1969), pp. 127–30.
18. G. Freeth, *APD*, HR (14 August 1969), pp. 310–17.
19. H.S. Albinski, "Foreign Policy", in *Public Policy in Australia*, ed. R. Forward (Melbourne: Cheshire, 1974), pp. 35–36. For an approving view of the retreat forced upon the government, see B.A. Santamaria, "Struggle on Two Fronts: The DLP and the 1969 Election", *Australian Quarterly* 41 (December 1969): 33–42. For a disappointed view, see A. Farran, "'The Freeth Experiment'", *Australian Outlook* 26 (April 1972): 46–58.
20. On Cambodia, see H.S. Albinski, "Problems in Australian Foreign Policy, January–June 1970", *Australian Journal of Politics and History* 16 (December 1970): 313–16.
21. On aspects of the 1972 arguments, see A. Barnes, Melbourne *Age*, 17 June, 5 and 10 October 1972; H. Armfield, Melbourne *Age* 14 June 1972; M. Richardson, Melbourne *Age* 24 November 1972; F. Brenchley, *Australian Financial Review*, 11 August 1974; and P. Browning, *Far Eastern Economic Review*, 28 October 1972.
22. *Australian Defence: The Liberal Party's Objectives* (Canberra: Liberal Party Federal Secretariat, 1972), p. 5. For a summary of defence policy differences between the parties, see *Sydney Morning Herald*, 30 October 1972; and P. Samuel, *Bulletin*, 2 September 1972.
23. On Australia's conscription experience, see R. Forward and R. Reece, eds., *Conscription in Australia* (St. Lucia: University of Queensland Press, 1968); J.M. Main, *Conscription: The Australian Debate, 1901–1970* (Melbourne: Cassell, 1970); and G. Wither, *Conscription: Necessity and Justice* (Sydney: Angus and Robertson, 1972), esp. pp. 1–22.
24. For instance, see Fairbairn, *Sydney Morning Herald*, 15 August 1972; and Melbourne *Age*, 4 September 1972.
25. Cited in S. FitzGerald, *Talking with China: The Australian Labor Party Visit and Peking's Foreign Policy*, Contemporary China Papers, no. 4 (Canberra: Australian National University Press, 1972), p. 29. FitzGerald's piece is very useful reading for Sino–Australian relations generally. Also, especially on the trade side, see H.S. Albinski, "Foreign Policy Considerations Affecting Trade with the People's Republic of China: Canadian and Australian Experience", *Law and Policy in International Business*, 5, no. 3 (1973) 805–35.
26. *Australian*, 16 and 17 July 1971.
27. Oakes, *Whitlam PM*, p. 225.
28. R. O'Neill, "Problems in Australian Foreign Policy, July to December 1971", *Australian Journal of Politics and History* 18 (April 1972): 2–3.
29. *Australian Foreign Affairs Record (AFAR)* 44 (August 1973): 528.
30. *Australian*, 23 November 1972.
31. *Sydney Morning Herald*, 7 November 1972.
32. *Australian Foreign Policy* (Canberra: Liberal Party Federal Secretariat, 1972), p. 5.
33. *Australian*, 7 April 1971.
34. *Australian*, 21 November 1972.
35. Melbourne *Age*, 24 November 1972.
36. Derived from non-attributable source.
37. Television broadcast interview, 9 October 1972, transcript.
38. On Snedden, see *Press Statement*, no. 73/36 (address of 9 March 1973); and his remarks in *APD*, HR (31 May 1973), p. 3017. On Bowen, see *APD*, HR (31 May 1973), p. 2993.

39. J. Spigelman, *Secrecy: Political Censorship in Australia* (Sydney: Angus and Robertson, 1972).
40. For an early account, see H.B. Turner, "The Foreign Affairs Committee of the Australian Parliament", *Australian Outlook* 20 (April 1966): 18–27.
41. See *Australian*, 19 June and 3 July 1971.
42. For summaries, see Spigelman, *Secrecy*, pp. 146–50; and R. Aitchison, *Thanks to the Yanks?* (Melbourne: Sun Books, 1972), pp. 135–36.
43. C.J. Lloyd and G.S. Reid, *Out of the Wilderness: The Return of Labor* (Melbourne: Cassell, 1974), p. 11.
44. ibid., p. 10.
45. See *Australian*, 13 August 1974.
46. *Australian*, 7 October 1971. For a highly critical analysis, see B. Grant, *The Crisis of Loyalty: A Study of Australian Foreign Policy* (Sydney: Angus and Robertson, 2nd ed., 1973), pp. 31–32.
47. The dossier is summarized by P. Samuel, *Bulletin* 22 June 1974.
48. For treatments of the role of external issues in Australian elections generally, see C.A. Hughes, "The Rational Voter and Australian Foreign Policy, 1961–69", *Australian Outlook* 24 (April 1970): 5–16; N.S. Roberts, "Foreign Policy and Australian General Elections", *World Review* 12 (July 1973): 22–30; Albinski, *Politics and Foreign Policy in Australia*, pp. 24–30; and J. Dalton, "Foreign Policy and Domestic Politics in Australia", *Dyason House Papers* 2 (October 1975): 1–4. The principal account of external policy in the 1972 campaign is by C. Clark, "Foreign Policy and the 1972 Elections", in C. Clark, ed., *Australian Foreign Policy: Towards a Reassessment* (Melbourne: Cassell, 1973), pp. 3–16. For the 1972 campaign in perspective, see L. Oakes and D. Solomon, *The Making of an Australian Prime Minister* (Melbourne: Cheshire, 1973); and H. Mayer, ed., *Labor to Power: Australia's 1972 Election* (Sydney: Angus and Robertson, 1973).
49. Statement of 27 November 1972, Office of the Prime Minister *Release*.
50. Liberal Party of Australia, Federal Secretariat, *Speakers; Notes* (Canberra: 1972), p. 11. The details of Liberal Party positions were expounded earlier in *Australian Foreign Policy* and in *Australian Defence*, both issued by the Federal Secretariat.
51. Melbourne *Age*, 31 October 1972.
52. Statement of 27 November 1972, Office of the Prime Minister *Release*.
53. *Sydney Morning Herald*, 28 November 1972.
54. For major delineations of Labor's position, see Australian Labor Party, *Defence and Foreign Policies*, 16 pp. booklet in the *It's Time* series (Canberra: 1972); and Lance Barnard's address to the National Executive of the RSL, 14 August 1972. Labor's programme generally can be taken from a reading of the various selections in J. McLaren, ed., *Towards a New Australia* (Melbourne: Cheshire, 1972).
55. Melbourne *Age*, 18 November 1972.
56. See especially, Australian Labor Party, *It's Time—Foreign Investment*, in *It's Time* series (Canberra: 1972) and, as a representative advertising vehicle, "Grand Australian Land Sale".
57. *Sydney Morning Herald*, 1 December 1972.
58. See ASRB (Australian Sales Research Bureau) polls in Melbourne *Age*, 4 and 10 July and 15 November 1972. For related data, see *Australian Gallup Polls*, no. 234 (September 1972).
59. *McNair Poll*, 2 December 1972.
60. B. Grant, "Labor and the World", in *Labor in Power: What is the Difference?*, Victorian Fabian Society pamphlet no. 22 (Melbourne: 1972), esp. pp. 11–13.

3 Australia and the International Scene

We open our treatment of Labor's period in government with some ground-laying material, on which subsequent discussion of policy outputs, processes and criticisms can more securely be placed. We wish to identify those factors that produced assumptions about the international scene, and Australia's role in it, within Labor as a party and as government, within the parliamentary opposition and among other sectors of opinion. In a sense, we are talking about the "conceptual frameworks" that ordered the thinking of personalities, parties and movements. Nevertheless, the notion of a "conceptual framework" is both too grand and too limiting. It is wrong to assume that even those involved or expert in external policy shaped for themselves pictures of world forces that were full, clear and logically consistent in all major respects. Moreover, it is a misplaced view of reality that assumes that people arrive at their conceptions simply by building logical systems. They are also affected by such factors as their temperaments, their own roles and experiences, the traditional milieu of the parties or movements to which they belong and their appreciation of political constraints.

While searching for patterns or tendencies, we will need to avoid the temptation to superimpose an over-rationalized, and therefore characaturized, model of spokesmen and parties. While it is possible to piece together a coherent account, a good deal of it is based on reasoned inference. Fairly extensive use will be made of interview data, much of it representing the impressions by persons of both themselves and of others.

Our fullest attention will be given to Labor, as the party of government. Labor has its wings and factions, but for the moment we concentrate on the party's more characteristic, or authoritatively enunciated, foreign policy perceptions and formulations. Between his election as ALP leader in 1967 and his accession to the prime ministership, Whitlam was Labor's principal foreign policy spokesman. He travelled widely and acquired a wealth of contacts overseas. He was therefore able to build up an elaborately thought-out set of ideas on external affairs by the time he came to office. Once in government, he took on the Foreign Affairs portfolio. When he relinquished it late in 1973, it was to Senator Don Willesee. Willesee had until then been government foreign affairs spokesman in the Senate and had been involved on the administrative side of foreign policy in his role as Special Minister of State. After Whitlam surrendered the Foreign Affairs portfolio, he continued to exercise a prominent role in the field and was acting Foreign Minister during Willesee's absences from Australia. Lance Barnard had been deputy ALP leader under Whitlam from 1967 to 1972 and the party's shadow Defence Minister. When Labor came to office, Barnard became Deputy Prime Minister and Minister for Defence and held his deputy's position until mid-1974. When in mid-1975, Bernard resigned his portfolio and his seat in Parliament, he was succeeded as Defence Minister by William Morrison. Morrison had at one time been a career External Affairs officer. Before coming to Defence, his ministerial responsibilities had included assisting Willesee on Papua New Guinea matters, and assisting Barnard more generally. These lieutenants were, in political temper and general approach, close to Whitlam.

The meaning of all this is that foreign and defence policy under Labor featured continuity, experience and general compatibility of outlook among the central figures. But the limelight fell on the Prime Minister. When Whitlam decided to resign the Foreign Affairs portfolio, the job would normally have gone to Barnard, to whom it had been previously promised and who wished to undertake it. But Barnard had not yet completed the task of reorganizing the Defence Department, one of the new government's major objectives. At all events, Whitlam reconsidered his opinion that Barnard was fully suited for the role of Foreign Minister. Whitlam's willingness to renege on a pledge to a trusted friend and political ally could be construed as another sign of the importance the Prime Minister personally attached to foreign policy.

Labor's perceptions of the world were brightly coloured by the political circumstances in which the party entered office. The fact of its inordinately long period in opposition was central. The party's reaction was an impatience to attack Australia's foreign policy concerns head on, both to give exposition to what *Labor* believed to be the realities of international life, and more particularly, to launch remedial policies. The urgency to "set things right" was prompted by what Labor thought to have been unconscionable L–CP preoccupations with such symbols as the Chinese threat and the American alliance. With the L–CP at last out of office, Whitlam remarked, "the foreign policy debate and foreign policy decisions can never again be so limited, so restricted, so distorted. In that liberation, I find the chief distinction of my Government's foreign policies—and the greatest challenges and opportunities for the future."[1] Relatedly, as we saw before, Labor felt that on key international problems such as China and Vietnam, its *own* position had been vindicated by events. This introduced an additional spur for Labor as a party of government to challenge orthodoxies and it instilled self-confidence. Labor's incentive to reconsider what it identified as misplaced L–CP tenets also was personal to the party. The ALP was distressed by what it thought to have been the shameless insinuations that Liberal spokesmen had levelled against it for political gain. As Whitlam had previously expressed this sentiment,

> There is no English-speaking democracy in which the ruling party has for so long, so cynically, used the great matters of foreign policy for domestic political purposes. ... It is incredible that in 1971 an Australian Prime Minister should seek to gain political mileage out of kicking the Communist can in respect of China. The tactics of the past are as futile as the policies of the past.[2]

So, when Labor was elected, Whitlam and his colleagues, more than they would have had preceding circumstances been different, construed their victory as a clear mandate for change, an instruction to get on with corrective surgery. Whitlam acknowledged that, in the earlier stages of his government, the primary need was to stress "those aspects of its policies which emphasised its independence from its predecessors". All the same, whether in earlier or later stages of its tenure, Labor continued to underscore its vision and sense of confidence: "We are not merely repairing the past; we are preparing for the future."[3]

This takes us up to Labor's actual dispositions. These were shaped by its qualities as a social democratic party, a party that, though perhaps belatedly in comparison with sister socialist and Labor parties, had evolved a streak that was not only reformist but idealistic. This does not necessarily imply that Labor simply substituted naive idealism for a sober Australian national-interest assessment of international problems. But various people close to the foreign policy centre remarked to the author upon the sense of "principle" they noticed in men such as Whitlam and Willesee, and from which much of Labor's anti-racialist and anti-colonialist foreign policy followed. The "benefit" element in the cost-benefit equation was a better world and the reorientation of Australian society towards deeper sensibility and tolerance.

The author asked Senator Willesee what, after about two years in office, Labor's one or two most significant foreign policy contributions had been. The answer was building towards a structure of anti-racialism and anti-colonialism, and the achievement of world-class standing by Australia, predominantly among Third World nations. In a paper delivered in mid-1974, Willesee argued that his government still believed "in the rather old-fashioned and optimistic notion of the possibility of progress: in the idea that by co-operative effort men and nations can bring about a betterment in their circumstances and hence a more just and equitable world." To Willesee, counter-arguments about the need to replace principles with "realism" were simply masks for selfishness.[4] We recall that Menzies, on his part, had identified the ANZUS alliance as the greatest achievement of his prime ministership.

Labor's outlook on the world and Australia's place in it was also conditioned by the disposition towards a "new nationalism" philosophy. The fullest symbolic exposition of this notion was delivered by Whitlam in Ballarat, Victoria, on the 119th anniversary of the Eureka uprising. The speech was circulated to all Australian overseas posts. Its new nationalism qualities were depicted by a Foreign Affairs Department public information officer as a "mainspring of the Government's political philosophy and hence a motivating force in its actions and reactions on foreign affairs".[5] For Whitlam, the new nationalism was a movement to restore and envigorate .Australia's authentic traditions, especially egalitarianism, fair play and independence. These, he said, were values with long and deep meaning for the Australian Labor Party. The new nationalism was not to be confused either with isolationalism or xenophobia. Labor abjured these values. The link between constructive and mature national pride and international politics was plain. Imitative and unself-critical societies found little respect abroad and made few contributions. "Echoes and shadows, satellites and vassals are not forces for peace and co-operation; they are more likely to be the first victims when peace and co-operation are overthrown."[6] Again, therefore, we find Labor eager to break old and confining moulds, to set new parameters of conduct, or at least to revive those that were dissipated under the Liberals, to see the world more as plural rather than as ranged into blocs and—with special emphasis—to portray Australia as a distinctive and unintimidatable nation.

The new nationalist image of Australia was associated with certain Labor Party predispositions about the international environment, which we will examine more closely later. Here we wish to say that these predispositions included misgivings about great-power regulation of world affairs and about resort to *force majeure* or extortive methods generally as appropriate means to settle international disputes. Excessive followership of the United States was especially unwelcome. It was nationally demeaning. It had led to flagrant distortions of policy under the L–CP and to nauseating political abuse of Labor. It was associated with America's far-flung economic interests and capacity to exert damaging and debasing influence. We should remember that the ALP was not and is not Marxist, but that it has stood in the social democratic tradition of mistrusting various features of capitalism. When capitalism entrenched itself internationally, when, as in Australia, it took the form of extensive foreign ownership and elaborate multi-national company operations, it had to be reigned in. Although it has not subscribed to economic determinism as an animating principle, Labor's attention to the economic dimensions of the play of international life has in this way been heightened. We will see in other contexts how Labor reacted, in word and deed, to international capitalism. For emphasis, we should point out here that at least the rhetoric was frequent and heavy, including invocations by Whitlam of dangers posed by foreign investment to Australia's very birthright.[7]

One other extremely important element contributed to the way in which the Labor government saw and reacted to the international environment. By late 1972, international conditions were somewhat different from what they had been when Menzies was taking pride in having promoted ANZUS, or when his successors were shipping troops to fight in Vietnam. Whitlam himself acknowledged that his government's task of taking a fresh tack in foreign affairs had been simplified by shifts towards great-power accommodation and by the defusing of acerbic issues such as Vietnam within Australian politics: "many changes we are making occur within the context of even more far-reaching changes being made by and between powers far greater than Australia, and principally by the United States herself."[8] Taken in this light, whether or not one subscribes to Labor's rhetoric or policy movements, it should not be overlooked that "re-examination" was ongoing throughout most world capitals by the end of 1972. It is worth considering James Richardson's conclusion that Whitlam was a man of the Kissinger era, not a throwback to some previous period. His foreign policy projections were "unusual only in the Australian context" and reflected "Australia's return to the mainstream of world politics after a long period aground in Vietnam".[9]

We now turn to Labor's perceptions of the world scene; first to its views of general tendencies, then to prescribed guidelines for Australian policy. Australian Labor saw the international politics of the 1950s and 1960s as having been dominated by super-power con-frontations, directly or through surrogates. Then, together with other observers, it sensed the emergence of new international parameters. It took particular notice of pluralization among communist nations, Britain's progressive disengagement and the retraction of a major American military presence from Asia, and the various steps towards great-power *détente*. The ALP was encouraged by these trends. They seemed to lower the risk of conflict, to pave the way towards more durable efforts at building a structure of international co-operation. They also freed Australia from constantly feeling it had to take sides in great-power or communist versus anti-communist disputes. This met Labor's conception of Australian national interests and also complemented the party's broader sense of values. Henry Kissinger, as the prime Western architect of *détente*, was at least selectively adopted as a kind of Labor Party hero. While Kissinger's initiatives would not always be successful, Whitlam remarked, "log-jams are broken, stale habits of mind are abandoned, and movement is often preferable to a dogged preseverance" with an outmoded *status quo*.[10]

The Labor government was especially relieved that a more relaxed climate in Soviet–American relations had diminished the prospect of critical and possibly nuclear confrontation. It especially deprecated others' denigrations of *détente*, since its essential meaning was the avoidance of nuclear mass destruction. This was "the highest goal a nation could ever set for itself".[11]

Another equally important yet sometimes overlooked Labor government reaction must be noted. The government was temperamentally ill-disposed towards fostering international stability by military means. It devoted itself to disarmament and the propagation of regional zones of peace objectives. It encouraged such tension-relaxing measures as were concluded between Moscow and Washington under SALT, the Strategic Arms Limitation Treaty. Without excessive fanfare, however, it committed itself to what it saw as the corollary proposition that existing nuclear balance restrained the super-powers and therefore enhanced the survival of *détente*. This can be read in some snatches of ministerial remarks and was widely confirmed from internal evidence.[12] What it meant in practice was that Labor accepted an effective American nuclear deterrent capability. Instrumentally, as we will show later, this view carried great importance for government policy towards American defence installations on Australian soil.

As with Soviet–American (and Sino–American) accommodation, the Labor government generally welcomed tendencies towards multipolarity, though its conceptualization of this phenomenon was not as crisply articulated as it might have been. In the first place, it noticed the concurrent tendencies of super-power reduction of influence and the emergence of other centres or clusters of regional or world influence, such as China, Japan and the European community. The diffusion of world power was a "good thing", insofar as it encouraged an international buffering effect to confrontational relations and gave Australia and other smaller nations improved room for manoeuvre. Nevertheless, the dispersion of power in the contemporary world was seen to have another facet, with a potential for engendering *instability*, especially within the international economic order: "The consequence of ... [such developments] as the 'energy crisis', the growing world shortage of food, and efforts to regulate the environment and use of the sea, is that foreign elements will have an increased capacity to influence or substantially determine domestic and foreign policies."[13]

The Labor government was seriously concerned about international difficulties that such claims and rivalries could stimulate. Concern with them served to strengthen the ALP's tendency to think that international tensions carried a prominent underlying economic component. It also tended to reinforce the party's predilection to downgrade the notion of contemporary international relations as a contest between communist and anti-communist forces, and to downgrade communism *per se* as a fearsome phenomenon. The world competition for scarce resources was much more connected to Arab oil, Japan's raw material and trading requirements, African and South Asian famine, the pressures of under-development, etc. than to communist conspiracies. For instance, Whitlam openly said in April 1975 that "Who rules in Saigon is not, and never has been, an ingredient in Australia's security."[14]

Also through the prism that it used to view the world, Labor pulled in the party's anti-racialist and anti-colonialist sentiments. Resource imbalances and scramble for economic advantage tended to get identified with the legacies of colonialism and the exploitation of the weak by the strong. There are various sources from which corroboration can be suggested. For instance, in his 1973 study of the attitudes of parliamentarians, Oliver Mendelsohn found that Laborites were far less inclined than Liberals or CP members to take an "antagonistic and fearful view of communist movements and régimes". Only 8 per cent of ALP respondents identified communist and terrorist movements as a prime or fairly important cause of continuing under-development, as against 62 per cent of Liberal and 81 per cent of CP respondents. Two-thirds of Labor respondents viewed communism in Asia as posing *no* threat to Australia, but *no* opposition respondents took this view.[15] Or we can turn to Whitlam himself. Speaking to a group of journalists in August 1973, he remarked that disparities in the rates of national economic development were directly tied to whether a country had been a colony. Colour and colonialism were the two principal internationally destabilizing tendencies—"All this garbage about communism or the threat of China is nothing compared with these two issues which will be around for a long time."[16]

Everything considered, what were Labor's assessments of potential threats to Australia? Its conclusions generally harmonized with both the theoretical assumptions and the party dispositions already recounted. Throughout most of its time in office the government relied heavily on a "strategic basis" assessment that, together with other sources of official advice, was prepared in the first half of 1973 by the Defence Committee, composed of senior military and civilian public service personnel. This strategic basis remained classified, though selections were alluded to by the government, especially Barnard. The government noted with approval the strategic assessment's apparent overall optimism. Circumstances under which Australia could be drawn into great-power, perhaps nuclear conflicts were unlikely, since the prospect of great-power armed confrontation had receded. Also the risk of endangered supplies of raw materials and resources had made the major industrial nations more cautious about resorting to military force. At all events, only the Soviet Union and the United States possessed a capability to launch an invasion of Australia, and neither could realistically be expected to do so. Respecting Australia's own geo-political environment, the strategic basis did not discount frictions. It felt that in South-East Asia there had been movement towards a great-power disengagement, lessening chances that countries in the region could fall victim to great-power competition. Any foreseeable localized conflicts in South-East Asia were not construed as directly or indirectly threatening to Australia's integrity. The security contingencies, it was pointed out, were quite different from those of a decade earlier. The framers of the strategic basis speculated that Australia could reasonably expect to live in a low-threat environment from ten to up to fifteen years, though with decreasing certitude towards the outer end of that time-scale. At all events, enough lead time would probably be available to allow Australia to react appropriately if tremors in the neighbourhood threatened to cloud the security outlook.[17]

In late 1975, during his brief period as Defence Minister, Morrison backed away from the earlier projection of a likely period of up to fifteen years free of threat, and he otherwise seemed to pull in his predecessor's relative optimism.[18] We will see later that, all the same, throughout its tenure, the government continued to be seriously disputed in various quarters for its acceptance of allegedly "sanguine" evaluations. The critics might have been even more severe had they been aware of an unannounced feature of the strategic basis. The assessment apparently hedged its overall optimism somewhat by speculating on possible Australian security difficulties with Indonesia and Japan. Within the Defence Department, planners eventually drew up papers and scenarios that stressed how a resource-hungry Japan might, in a decade or two, try to enforce its writ by military means.[19] On its part, the government might have been spared some criticism of projecting for up to fifteen years in advance were it not for a quirk of events. Among those who helped draft the strategic assessment there came to be some retrospective feeling that it had been injudicious to have probed as far ahead as fifteen years. Why then had it been done? The assessment's drafters had recalled an earlier Barnard remark in which a period of "the next fifteen years" had been promised for evaluation,[20] so they rather casually elected to adopt that time frame.

What policy guidelines were subsumed under Labor's assumptions about the international environment of the 1970s? In the broadest sense, Labor said that it wanted Australia to contribute towards the verification of assumptions about the world heading in rational, less threat-surrounded directions. This included great-power accommodation, normalization of relations among Asian and Pacific countries and further efforts at extirpating racialism and colonialism. For Australia itself, Whitlam insisted, "It is not just a matter of blithely accepting our advisers' view that there is no foreseeable major threat to Australia for fifteen years; it is a matter of actively, consciously, pursuing policies to make the prediction come true."[21] Labor felt there had been too many lost opportunities for international reconciliation in the past, as in the aftermath of the 1954 Indo-China settlement. After the change of régimes in South Vietnam and Cambodia in 1975, Labor was especially eager that all nations should think of these events as an opportunity, as "the beginning of a new era of widened regional co-operation and progress in the entire South-East Asian area".[22]

Labor reasoned that Australia's external policies would not only need to disencumber themselves of the fetishes of the past but to widen their ambit. Labor construed L–CP foreign policy as having suffered from preoccupation with South-East Asia as a security shield and with the United States as patron and protector. Diplomatic diversification of virtually global proportions was called for. Such diversification could in and of itself suppress repetition of what were regarded as earlier distortions and obsessions. The world's parts had become interlocked. External policies needed to take on an orientation that was less bilateral and more functionally framed. Australia had to demonstrate its internationalist credentials and scope for influence.

The ALP government was persuaded that independence was to be the linchpin of Australia's overseas policies, "the idea of a more assertive, purposeful, self-reliant and distinctively Australian policy".[23] The idea of "independence" in foreign policy was a "good thing" to embrace because it conformed to Labor's ideological and sentimental predispositions, and it was a gratifying drum to beat in reaction to L–CP years. It was an objectively good thing, since it enlarged the range of Australia's options and could facilitate the achievement of perceived national interest objectives. It was a pragmatically good thing, since it was believed to leave the right appearances among those whom Australia wished to influence. Whitlam declared that the aim of Labor's early policy decisions, and of future decisions, was to "establish a *reputation* for Australia as a nation with an independent and distinctive foreign policy. We want to be *regarded* as a friendly, tolerant and co-operative neighbour."[24] Independence was, moreover, a good thing because of a combination of the breakdown of great-power domination and Australia's special capabilities as an international actor. Again to Whitlam:

> We are far and away the richest nation in the neighbourhood. We have a gross national product equal to that of all the countries between the Bay of Bengal and the South China Sea. Those countries have 20 times our population. We are an island continent with one of the most formidable natural defences in the world. We have no serious conflict of interests with any of our neighbours and there are no foreseeable conflicts likely to arise well beyond the decade.[25]

The foreign policy net was to be cast more ambitiously than before, and its hallmark was to be "independence". What, however, was to be done, or avoided? In the first instance, Labor wished to de-emphasize military instruments of policy. The party believed that L–CP governments had subordinated foreign policy to defence policy, a relationship that the government felt it had to redress, in fact, invert. It also made certain assumptions about the international scene. Military responses were thought to be less relevant—indeed, often counter-productive—when the emerging global theme was *détente*, not confrontation. It believed that prospects of a threat to Australia itself, and which would require a military response, were low. It looked back on Vietnam and defined it as a classical example of a foolish brandishing and squandering of military resources. It was eager to persuade many nations that Australia was not only peace-loving but its own master. "Independence" in foreign policy meant, *inter alia*, removing some of the trappings of a follower nation, and followership under the L–CP had prominently been displayed by military support at the elbow of great powers.

Australia would not dismantle its military forces, but would adjust them to new circumstances. It would contribute military advice and *matériel* to neighbouring states still in process of building up their own security. But, in striking contrast to the L–CP's forward defence strategy, Whitlam pointedly pledged that "Australia shall *never* again send troops to fight in Asian mainland wars. Australia shall *never* again garrison troops abroad as part of a military commitment to involve this country in Asian wars."[26] Australian intervention in Asia's internal conflicts was precluded, Barnard added, because it was both "repugnant" and "ultimately ineffective".[27] Labor's general philosophy was clear. But, as will be seen later, there was some reason to believe that its self-denying ordinance on intervention overseas may have been tempered by the special case of Papua New Guinea.

The alliance system with the United States, especially through ANZUS, was to be retained. The Labor government made no bones about Australia being an "aligned" country. Defence liaison with and actual security assistance from the United States under some contingencies made the connection worthwhile. So did the opportunities for access to, and therefore possible enhanced influence over, American policy-makers. And, as we have seen, the Labor government concluded that, since the nuclear balance was an important underpinning for *détente*, American defence-related facilities in Australia were foreseeably to be retained. But security alliances, and the American connection especially, were to have their profile lowered. Labor wished to "move away from the narrow view that Anzus is the only significant factor in our relations with the U.S., and the equally narrow view that our relations with the United States are the only significant factor in Australia's foreign relations."[28] At least symbolic importance can be attached to Willesee's lack of any direct mention of the US alliance, or ANZUS, during his major foreign policy exposition to an Australian Institute of International Affairs conference in June 1974.

Diplomacy rather than military responses was Labor's preferred external policy instrument. Consistent with its dispositions, there was to be a distinctive anti-colonialist and anti-racialist ingredient in such diplomatic pursuits. This was regarded as complementary to helping things along, in the context of decelerating great-power confrontation and promoting nation-building efforts, in Asia particularly: "The present Government's policies are directed towards encouraging the militarily and economically dominant powers to cease disruptive intervention in the region, so as to let social and political conflicts work themselves out in truly national solutions."[29] Indeed, on a point we will need to amplify considerably later, the ALP government defined the promotion of regional co-operation as a keystone of its foreign policy efforts in the 1970s. This objective was not simply aimed at politically stabilizing or, in some security sense, immunizing nations in the region, but at constructing more systematic mechanisms for attacking poverty, ignorance, disease and other ills. Such an approach would bring into play Labor's conviction that multi-lateral, functionally oriented diplomacy was increasingly overshadowing traditional bilateral relationships. It also was a natural outgrowth of the party's attraction to socio-economic explanations of international forces and of the belief that Australia enjoyed a wide economic, as well as moral and political, resource base from which to exercise a meaningful role. From this followed another tangent of Labor's concerns—resource policy. This is a complex theme, full of offshoots. In the very simplest sense, it meant synchronizing the exploitation and merchandizing of the nation's natural mineral and energy resources in ways that would contribute towards various external economic and diplomatic objectives, as well as to commercial gain.

The Labor government's approach to constructing a foreign policy for Australia was challenged in various quarters. Some of the more cutting criticism emanated from persons and groups who found the government too timid rather than over-zealous, too conservative rather than too leftish. In numbers, these "radical" critics represented a distinct minority within the party and among the general population. But their presentations were widely ventilated in political, academic and other circles, and affected the mood within which the government–opposition dialogue was itself conducted. Later we will need to examine the influence of the "left" upon policy processes and outputs under Labor. Here, continuing the general theme of our narrative, we focus on general assumptions and policy guidelines, as critiques of the Labor government *per se* and as proffered alternatives.

Our undertaking is difficult. It is plainly not possible to speak of a single "radical" or "left" phenomenon. We are dealing with a number of persons, factions and organizations, of assorted vintage, size, membership, audience, inspiration and inflection of outlook. For instance, we can identify several communist parties and movements, including pro-Moscow, pro-Peking and Trotskyite. Much of the thrust of the radical movement in Australia was not, however, communist in inspiration or direction, and indeed often condemned communists as old-fashioned or as committed to national political systems, such as the Soviet Union, which were taken to be imperialist, repressive, or whatever.

Even within the "new" as opposed to the more traditional and largely communist based "old" left, there were considerable differences. One generalization that seemed to fit was that the newer left arose in part from circumstances symptomatic of protest movements in contemporary Western societies generally. In part, it arose from somewhat distinctive Australian circumstances. Among Western societies, Australia was for a long period more sheltered, inward-turning and not given to a vigorous intellectual climate. When change did occur, about from the decade of the late 1950s, it came rapidly. Australia experienced an infusion of new migrant types, rapid economic diversification, rapid extension of higher education, rapid exposure to newer values and a rapid scramble to establish an Australian personality in foreign affairs and towards Asia especially. Within such an environment, doubt, estrangement and protest were more easily induced.

Also important was the character of Australian politics. Many came to regard the L–CP not just as political parties with occasional turns at government but as virtually synonymous with national government. The stylistic and substantive shortcomings of the L–CP thereby reflected on the *system*. Since L–CP governments were depending on perspective, cautious or reactionary, the system was more likely to be impugned by people interested in a redistribution of domestic and foreign policy priorities. The Labor Party was not itself a fully appropriate vehicle for change. For a long time it projected a clumsy, rather cloth cap and anti-intellectual, and often internally disputatious image. Indeed, its consistent inability to win federal office persuaded some people that it was more sensible, and personally stimulating, to work around rather than within the conventional party system. Moreover, inordinately long periods of continuous government and opposition for the L–CP and Labor, respectively, made both groups less responsible in their behaviour. There was a tendency towards exaggeration, polemicism and perhaps most importantly, especially on the L–CP's part, to politicize values and methods in foreign policy. As we saw earlier, this grew worse during the closing years of Liberal government.

There also were particular areas of public controversy that sparked radical thinking. Australia's position in and focus upon Asia stimulated concern about under-development and political change among new or Third World nations. Australia's own affluence, residual colonial responsibilities and heritage of racism suggested a contrast with the Asian environment and prompted demands for radical reorientations. Issues such as Vietnam and conscription acquired a special emotive quality in Australia, and thereby nurtured radicalism. For some, L–CP policies on Vietnam and conscription were not simply unprofitable in cost-accounting terms, or contrary to national interests, or even broadly immoral. They were policies that were interpreted as being cynically exploited by the governments of the day, governments that relied on fear as a standard technique of political self-service. They were policies that were interpreted as degrading illustrations of the abnegation of national independence to the cause of "follow the American leader". As Australian society was becoming more self-critical and outward-looking, this facet of already unpopular policies further strengthened the impulses for radical challenge. As the Australian anti-Vietnam and anti-conscription protest movement evolved, it enrolled a multiplicity of people and interests who thereby contributed an element of legitimacy to the movement at large. There were young people as well as older people, churchmen as well as secularists, middle-class professionals as well as some worker members, advocates of peaceful change as well as some professed revolutionaries, ALP parliamentarians as well as persons who had never been active in party politics.[30]

Once the L–CP had been replaced by Labor, some earlier incentives for radical expression on foreign policy disappeared. Other incentives remained and new ones arose. The "radical movement" was an established phenomenon. Many of its members had developed cynical dispositions towards government, authority and orthodox political party life generally. Some had cultivated a powerful sense of reformist conscience, still others were absorbed by the romance of dissent. The new Whitlam government, by professing the need for independent postures and reformed policies abroad, itself helped to encourage a climate in which challenge and criticism flourished. Ironically, the Labor government's own reformism became the target of radical criticism and inspiration for continuing rather than standing down the radical effort. Labor was variously seen as unfaithful to its own standards or as simply being a captive of forces within the "system" and of unregenerate electoral expediency. It was seen as quite incapable of accomplishing anything of *fundamental* importance. Labor was thereby felt to deserve derision, while the radical movement continued to hold leading responsibility for provoking public debate and applying pressure for basic change.

To say that Australian radicalism developed many countenances is not saying very much. There were persons within the spectrum of dissidents who thought of themselves less as "radicals" than as activist reformers. Many, moreover, abjured any notions of attacking the system outright. For some, for example, inspiration for protest sprung from religious convictions. Action for World Development addressed itself to such causes as more severe Australian government sanctions against South Africa and Rhodesia. The group subscribed to Christian principles and took support from the Australian Council of Churches and the Roman Catholic Church's Justice and Peace Commission. In 1973, a number of Catholics associated with Action for World

Development affiliated with Pax Christi. The group's aim was to "promote among Christians and throughout the community a greater social consciousness on the key issues of peace and justice as they relate to Australia's involvements and responsibilities. Pax Christi believes that non-violent Struggle offers the only real alternative to war and injustice." Pax Christi chose as its foremost concern the presence of "foreign military bases".[31]

In our effort to prototypify the radical movement, we probably should look outside the Christian groups as such, even though overlap of membership and sympathy existed. The two major radical "roof" organizations were the Association for International Co-operation and Disarmament (AIDC) in Sydney and the Congress for International Co-operation and Disarmament (CIDC) in Melbourne. Very important, especially in its intellectual thrust, was a circle of academics, many of them associated with the journal *Arena*. Also important was the publicity given to radical themes by the leadership of the Australian Union of Students (AUS) and the student press, which became a kind of "underground" alternative-culture vehicle.[32]

An important if not overarching assumption of the radical movement was that imperialism, largely but not exclusively practised by the United States, had become an ugly, pervasive force:

> The US sought to maintain control of the world's resources by strengthening the dependence and internal domination of the Third World countries through a series of militarily powerful, reactionary client régimes, tied to US military and economic aid; while on the other hand, attempting to resolve the global economic contraditions of the capitalist system by the economic integration of the socialist countries through a process of *détente*.[33]

Through a series of manipulations, which included the machinations of multi-national corporations, the effect was "to leave the developing countries in a state of under-industrialization, exhaustion of agricultural and mineral resources, and perpetual under-employment and poverty".[34]

For Australia, this reasoning continued, the great lesson was to acquire solidarity with the exploited peoples and definitionally to avoid complicity with, and to resist, imperialist designs. Yet, the radicals objected, Australia had done no such thing. Labor professed independence, but "contrary to the new nationalist viewpoint Australia is both a junior partner and competitor of US, British and Japanese business interests."[35] Labor's "reforms" in external policy were condemned as tokenism at best, and more accurately as a smokescreen behind which to hide. Maintenance of the US alliance, failure to oppose reactionary régimes, timidity in dealing with racist nations and the export of Australian goods and capital in exploitative roles were among the symptoms of a party inherently incapable of performing a genuine transformation. Bruce McFarlane, one of the leading critics in this area, wrote that

> What is involved is a neo-colonial policy, streamlined, brisk, efficient and ruthless. It is Technocratic Labor's attitude to its own working class and to multinational corporations projected externally. It is a carefully thought-out nexus of power/investment/trade relations; it is Technocratic Labor's own creation, its own model.[36]

What policy guidelines did the radical movement recommend? It would have undertaken an uncompromising assault on all remaining racialist states and remnants of colonialism. It would stringently have opposed what it regarded as élitist- led, imperialist-infected régimes, especially in South-East Asia. It would have embraced "peoples" and "liberation" movements, such as the Provisional Revolutionary Government in South Vietnam, before that group actually took power. It would have accelerated efforts at disarmament, purged American defence facilities from Australia and preferably dismantled Australia's connections with security alliances. It would have severely restricted the foreign economic presence in Australia and stopped the export of what it considered to be Australia's own economic subjugation of Third World peoples.[37] Australia would, unequivocally, have moved towards non-alignment and would have become an honoured champion of "progressive" forces.

As far as could be adduced from the wealth of radical movement pronouncements, the "how to achieve it" question carried no single answer. There would, of course, have been publicity about the wrong-headedness of prevailing policies, efforts at mobilizing sympathetic Labor parliamentarians and party members generally, as well as open attacks on forces and ideas held blameworthy. While we are not concentrating here on tactics and systemic and policy effects, one particular chord should be emphasized. The radical movement acknowledged that imperialism had no single national origin, but it identified the United States as by far the most powerful and culpable imperialist nation. While the United States was a target for radical movements in many countries, circumstances gave the anti-American campaign in Australia special embellishment. The American idiom in Australia had become widespread, through US investment, US corporate establishments, reliance by Australia on the US market, the ANZUS and SEATO connections, American defence installations, increasing numbers of American secondary and tertiary education staff members, the untold number of everyday reminders, from Coca-Cola to Kentucky Fried Chicken to *Time* and *Newsweek* to Ford, Chrysler and General Motors (-Holden's) cars, and so on. The recollection that Liberal governments had tied Australia's policies to the American kite, with what were regarded as disastrous results, also accentuated the anti-American feeling, though much more in corporate than in interpersonal terms. So, less directly, did the sense of disdain for a Labor government that was accused of having done nothing fundamental to dissolve the Australian–American linkage.

All this gave rise to a literature on the adverse nature of the American presence. Conspiratorial theories were widely offered in radical circles, such as alleged CIA involvement in Australian politics to the sinister role in "war research" of American educational foundations and academics. There were demonstrations at US consular facilities, at the North-West Cape signal-station, at affiliates of American companies involved in defence production, and even against an art exhibit in Adelaide, sent to Australia under the auspices of the New York Museum of Modern Art. Critics of the radical movement would have said that, as a fashion, anti-Americanism became the anti-communism of the left.

There may also have been some connection between anti-American feeling and outlooks expressed in the radical movement (but outside radical circles as well) on other matters. There was a certain affinity for China and its socialist experiment, but little affinity for the Soviet Union. In Australia, this had several causes, among them the feeling that the Soviets had become more like the Americans and less genuinely revolutionary. The Chinese, long the objects of American (and Australian) containment, were, by contrast, idealized for their sense of principle, social experimentation and their positive attention towards liberation causes, especially in Asia. The tendency in a number of radical quarters to move towards the Arab/Palestinian cause in the Middle Eastern dispute was in part affected by portrayal of Israel as an American client state, resistant to the rights of disposed people.

The radical movement did not, of course, simply address itself to opposing or promoting particular causes. Many in its ranks, though with considerably varying degrees of commitment, would have wished to remake Australian society. Only then could a sensitive approach to external affairs have been vouchsaved. Ordinary party politics or lobbying efforts were not enough. A "mass involvement" by a public all too deeply tranquilized by self-serving élites and the establishmentarian media somehow had to be brought about. Some in the movement would have subscribed to the injunction of the international research officer of the AUS. He recommended that Australia follow Ho Chi Minh's directive that "'the best way to help the Viet-.namese revolution was to make revolution in your own country'".[38]

We now turn to the Liberal and Country Parties, which in December 1972 became Australia's alternative government. There are some difficulties in providing a confident assessment of the L–CP's undergirding foreign policy assumptions and guidelines. Almost anywhere, an opposition is liable to be more free-wheeling in expressing itself than are authoritative government spokesmen. Because the L–CP was exercising a prominent *criticism* role, there is some problem of disentangling political rhetoric from basic foreign policy convictions. Necessarily, a fair amount of our analysis will reflect what the L–CP objected to as opposed to what it favoured. While Labor as a government had its share of dissident party voices on various policy questions, the opposition was literally two parties, each with its own leader and party orientations and loyalties. It was not until after the May 1974 election that a joint L–CP opposition shadow cabinet was formed. Finding itself in the unfamiliar role of opposition, the L–CP faced a multitude of tasks and concerns that prolonged or otherwise interfered with the systematic regroupment of external policy approaches. The public seemed only marginally interested in foreign and defence policy issues, while becoming preoccupied with domestic economic conditions. The opposition's attention was thereby deflected from external affairs. There was a new Liberal leader who had to establish his credentials within his party, within the combined L–CP opposition and *vis-à-vis* the country. There were issues of intra-party reorganization, of inter-coalition party relations and of rebuilding political stock. New opposition spokesmen on external subjects came forward.

The opposition's spokesmen on external topics represented some subject-matter continuity with the L–CP when it had occupied office. The previous Foreign Minister, Nigel Bowen, at first continued as Liberal spokesman in that area, but resigned from Parliament later in 1973. His replacement, Andrew Peacock, had served as Minister for the Army and as Minister for External Territories, but had never been an L–CP "inner Cabinet" man. Dr A. J. Forbes, who became defence spokesman, had held both the Army and the Immigration portfolios. B. M. Snedden, the new Liberal leader, had a considerable ministerial background, but not really central to external affairs—Immigration, National Service and Treasury. In his depth of interest, schooling and overseas contacts, he was distinctly less well-prepared than was Whitlam when the latter had served in opposition. Unlike Labor, moreover, the Liberal and Country Parties were not parties with an authoritative body of party guidelines, such as a fixed party platform from which animating principles of foreign policy could readily be drawn.

The Liberals eventually did set in motion an ordering of their foreign policy thinking. Statements on foreign policy and defence and on international economics and foreign investment were (with CP concurrence) pulled together for the 1974 election. The foreign policy/defence statement was one of the few in the Liberal package that had been given prior systematic attention, though the effort was not begun until after Peacock had replaced Bowen as Foreign Policy spokesman.[39] Later in 1974, a new federal platform was approved.[40] By September of 1974, Peacock and Forbes had begun consultations with academics, to sharpen and make more sound party policy in foreign and defence policy and to find ways to make such policies more graphic and presentable to the public. Snedden himself set out to improve his grasp of foreign policy. As leader, he began to speak more frequently in this area than when his party had been in government and he undertook occasional fact-finding trips abroad. As we will notice later, forceful external policy spokesmanship came quite easily to Malcolm Fraser, who replaced Snedden as Liberal leader in March 1975. In October 1975, shortly before the election that ousted Labor from office, the coalition parties published updated and refined versions of their external policies.[41]

In any event, once in opposition, the L–CP had both more opportunity and more incentive to reconsider its foreign policy outlooks than when it had governed. As one Liberal document admitted, while the L–CP was still is power, "Precedent proved to be to some extent a barrier to change. However, once in opposition, this was less an obstacle than it had been in government."[42] Snedden, while denying that the electoral defeat of December 1972 required an "abnegation of the past", averred that it did stimulate a healthy scrutiny of party foreign policy, to test it for currency and amenability to necessary innovation. As the world was fluid, static assumptions in foreign policy were inappropriate: "We may have been hindered at times by such assumptions in the past—I intend that we should avoid them in future."[43]

Together with opportunity, the opposition also had motive to recast its position on external affairs. Especially after Peacock had become shadow Foreign Minister, it helped to have new men in key spokesmanship roles. There was an electoral incentive to produce, or at least to appear to have produced, a more up-to-date and creative foreign policy, to shed the "men of the past" image that Labor had pinned on the L–CP. The DLP lost almost all of its previous influence over Liberal external policy. In 1972, its electoral presence had failed to insure the government's survival. In the 1974 combined House and Senate election, the DLP was in disarray and lost all five of its previous Senate seats. The opposition also had to live with what the Labor government had done; decisions that, in varying degrees, the

Liberals often regarded as desirable, or difficult or impossible to reverse, or electorally popular.

To be sure, there were some constraints on the ability of the Liberals to generate a "new image" in foreign policy. Various implications of these constraints will be examined in other contexts. Here we might quickly mention two such constraints. On the Liberal side, Snedden had been elected leader largely for his consensus qualities. His management of the party reflected this, both because of his temperament and because he appreciated the Liberals' recent history of internecine conflict. He therefore was unprepared to push too hard or too fast on foreign policy renovation. A harsh, domineering style would have been resented, and more conservative party members would have taken particular umbrage. This was exemplified by his strategy in 1973. At intervals rather than in omnibus fashion, he broached "new versions" of Liberal policy, such as acceptance of the recognition of Peking and the advisability of reshaping SEATO. By the 1974 election, some of this process had been completed and incorporated into the party's platform, though a platform not authoritative and binding on party members in the same sense that Labor's was. However, as will be indicated later, by late 1974, the pendulum of Liberal Party foreign policy "renovation" had started to swing back and became even more apparent when Fraser took over.

A second constraint on Liberal foreign policy reform was the Country Party. Not only was it a separate party, but its outlook tended, as a whole, to be more traditional. Thus a few months after moving into opposition, Anthony remarked on his party's similarity to the DLP: "They are very anti-communist, they believe in the security of the country and basically they tend to be a conservative group, such as the Country Party."[44] A year later, he was still emphasizing the anti-communist features of his party's outlook.[45]

Among Liberals in particular, as we are about to see, "communism" as an assumed portentious force and threat to Australia lost some of its earlier dogma, but by no means receded into obscurity as a factor in the party's international relations calculations. Liberal spokesmen did not, as Whitlam had, dismiss communism's effects on South-East Asian nations as "so much garbage". In his 1973 study of parliamentarians' attitudes towards foreign aid, Mendelsohn found that "Fear or at least apprehension about 'Communism' is still strong among Opposition parties, but there is no longer a belief that Australian interests will necessarily be served by open or cold warfare against communist movements or régimes."[46] What the new Liberal leadership did stress was its brand of "realism". Part of this was criticism of Labor's foreign policy approach, which was characterized as all too frequently proceeding from ideological symbolism instead of objective assessments. Part of it was a portrayal of the opposition itself as sensible and unblinkered. As Peacock wrote,

> The realities of international politics, which turn largely on the fact that relations are largely power relations and interests mainly national interests, are not particularly pleasant ones and any civilised man would wish them to be different. But they arise from the fundamental conditions of international life and they will not easily or quickly be changed.[47]

We recall that Labor made the corner-stone assumption that the international climate, primarily because of great-power *détente* and multi-polarization, had become less eruptive, more tractable. It then concluded that military responses were less relevant than before and that more room for independent manoeuvre for countries such as Australia had been opened.

The opposition reacted sceptically. It did not pointedly deny that there had been shifts away from great-power confrontational postures, and from US and Soviet domination of the international order, and overall it welcomed such movement. But it was not convinced that *détente* had progressed far, or that there no longer were many apparent or concealed sources of conflict—whether between the great powers or otherwise—that could easily overturn optimistic calculations. Despite some mutually accepted nuclear arms restraints, Washington and Moscow continued to build sophisticated weapons systems that could distort the "nuclear balance" foundation of *détente*. Active great-power rivalry was evident in many locations, perhaps most conspicuously in the Middle East. The Sino–Soviet dispute could itself spin off into a widely ramified conflict—this being one of Fraser's particular concerns. The scramble for resources was ominous for the cause of peace. Multi-polarity itself, by diffusing the *loci* of power, "may introduce new elements of instability, resulting in crisis situations in which smaller powers might eventually find themselves diplomatically helpless and militarily insecure," Peacock maintained. "To assume that modest progress in the reconciliation between states of opposite political persuasions will thereby ensure fifteen years of peace is wishful thinking: to rest one's security on an assumption of continued equilibrium between the great powers is folly."[48] Contrary to Labor's assessment, the L–CP concluded that the fall of South Vietnam and Cambodia raised, not lowered, dangers to regional security.

From this outlook followed the L–CP's approach to the role of security/military measures in the international context. The opposition saw much evidence of instability, of ongoing or potential conflicts and of a continuing brandishing of arms as a fact of life. Perhaps some of the openings created by *détente* and the American retraction from Asia did recommend more manoeuvrable and possibly less explicitly military reflexes in the external policies of many nations. But, as Forbes remarked, "Nations like individuals, need general insurance policies for an uncertain future."[49] The corollary, according to Snedden, was that "You don't need military power to have a foreign policy, but you certainly do need military self-defence capacity in order to have credible diplomacy and alliances."[50]

Phenomena such as multi-polarity and global resource competition, the L–CP believed, had created a greater, not lesser, interdependence: an interdependence measured by interests and by practical need for collaborative international effort. Moving on an interdependent course in external policy did not imply servility towards others, or seeking their approval before decisions were made. A healthy nationalism, an independence of mind, were commendable, but not Labor's so-called "new nationalism". This was "not new nationalism but old-style aggressive nationalism, a petulant self-assertiveness"[51] and a dangerous illusion about the realities of interdependence. Nations could neither afford to be brashly independent in security nor in economic terms, whether the latter touched on foreign investment or resource policy. When the Labor government vilified "outside" or "foreign" economic interests, it was flaunting its simplistic symbols, parading a distasteful xenophobia, not talking sense. On its part, of course, the L–CP's response was governed both by its assessment of what the realities of the world economic picture dictated, and by its traditionally more conservative and permissive temper in these matters. It came easily for Anthony to remark that

> I have no phobias about defending the mining companies. I've got no complex about sticking up for the multi-national corporations, provided they act in accordance with our laws. They are way ahead of most politicians in their understanding of the internationalisation of the world that has been going on in the last 50 years—and generations ahead of the Labor Party.[52]

The opposition did not, as such, dispute the government's contention that foreseeable threats to Australia were not impending. It did, however, take serious exception to three aspects of what it associated with Labor's formulation of the threat question. Unfortunately, the debate between the two sides became obscured by turgid rhetoric, semantic acrobatics and imputations of outright dishonesty.

The opposition complained that the government had, to suit its own purposes, almost certainly misrepresented the actual variables required for a sensible threat assessment. Barnard quoted the 1973 strategic basis document to the effect that "Australia's basic strategic concern is the security of our territory from attack and threat of attack and from political or economic duress."[53] That would seem to have covered a wide spectrum of contingencies. But the L–CP argued that the government had conveniently emphasized "threat" in the sense of Australia being drawn into a general war, or facing invasion or other fairly direct pressures. Instead, "In an interdependent world, it may be that indirect threats from conflicts elsewhere should weigh more heavily on the scales, with less concentration on possible direct threats to Australia."[54] There were occasional intimations from opposition quarters that the strategic basis study had been written to please the government's known proclivities, and therefore the "inconvenient", indirect facets of threat had been subordinated by the report's draftsmen. More forcefully, the opposition insinuated that while there may well have been adequate attention devoted to "indirect" threats in the official assessment, the government may have chosen to keep those portions classified. One senior opposition spokesman bluntly told the present author that Barnard had "lied". It was obvious to this L–CP spokesman, as revealed in the 1971 and 1973 strategic assessments, that Australia was not in danger of direct threat. But this was quite different from features of both reports that were far more cautious about turmoil in Asia, which could adversely affect Australia's interest and security. Imputations of this sort were heatedly denied by government spokesmen, who in turn castigated the opposition for its own disingenuousness and lingering cold-war mentality.

There is no way to resolve the dispute over what exactly was said in the 1973 strategic assessment without its full declassification, a most unlikely step. As indicated earlier, however, there is reliable internal evidence that a degree of unease was expressed in the assessment about some possibly negative security implications for Australia impinging from Indonesia or Japan, features of the report never publicly disclosed by the government. Reluctance to disclose them could, of course, have been dictated by an understandable wish not to embarrass relations with Jakarta and Tokyo, and/or by the simple fact that the report could have spoken about Indonesia and Japan in terms so remote and contingent that their mention did not constitute a genuine exception to the stated general rule of threat unlikelihood.

The question of what *constituted* a threat, or *from where* or in what *form* it might arise, was joined by a second point in controversy. Basically, it concerned the *degree* of threat expectation. Invoking the strategic assessment, the government had argued that while no one could speak categorically, it was sensible, and necessary for policy preparation, to prognosticate about likelihoods of foreseeabilities. In exuberant moments, opposition spokesmen complained about a naive Labor prophesy of the *absence* of any possible threat developing— which definitely was not the government's position. In more considered contexts, the opposition drew a distinction between "likelihood" of threat and "possibility" of threat. The international situation was not stable and all manners of breakdowns could, logically, impinge on Australia's safety and well-being. In this sense, "to argue that there is no discernible threat for a given period, is not to say that there will *therefore* be no threat during that period",[55] and that is what worried the L–CP. The coalition parties were reluctant in the extreme to subscribe to a threat assessment that not only could have been unrealistic in substantive emphasis but also in its potential for inducing complacency.

A related third area in dispute was over the *period* covered by the officially supported threat assessment. The strategic basis report and the government's own remarks made it plain that, as one progressed further into the ten-to fifteen-year projection period, the less confident could anyone be. It was also stressed that the strategic situation would remain under constant review and the estimates of threat likelihood would be adjusted if international conditions themselves changed. The opposition could not quarrel with an ongoing review programme, but in focused on the fifteen-year outside period for which low likelihood threat was being anticipated. It objected that fifteen years was in and of itself unrealistically deep into the future for meaningful, even tentative forecasting. It also objected because it felt that, like other features of Labor's threat evaluation, it could easily induce a cozy but misplaced "She'll be right" confidence. We noticed earlier that the "up to fifteen years" time frame used by the Defence Committee in the strategic basis was a quirk. Had a· more conventional ten-year period been used, the debate over Australia's safety could have been spared some mystification and the Labor government some politically trying moments.

In substance, the mainstream opposition thinking was relatively less preoccupied with a communist threat than in earlier years. More varied types of international tensions that could affect Australia's security were now assigned special salience. The evaluation of potential dangers to Australia was notably less sanguine than in Labor government quarters.

The opposition's foreign policy guidelines reflected a trend to move away from the positions of the 1960s, but to fall short of, and in some instances to disavow, Labor's policy guidelines. The L–CP was prepared to take Australia along a more independent path than before. It agreed with Labor that this had become more possible as well as desirable in the context of international developments and was possibly politically expedient as well. What it refused to countenance was a foreign policy that, contrasted with what it chose to impute to Labor, was "independent" for its own sake and brazenly executed. The opposition's version of a modified yet clearly continuing interdependence of nations in all spheres—security, diplomacy, economics—dictated what it felt was a more co-ordinate approach than Labor's.

We previously noted the opposition's contention that a viable foreign policy, and especially one that hoped to exhibit a measure of independent behaviour, required a credible defence complement. This outlook, added to its perspectives on interdependence, flavoured L–CP preferences in the security area. It meant, for one, an un-apologetic commitment to security alliances. Whereas Labor thought of ANZUS as important but wished to deflate its previous status as the centrepiece of Australia's external relations, the Liberals were not averse to claiming that Australia's association with the United States and New Zealand, as embodied in ANZUS, was of fundamental importance. The Labor government declared that Australia was an "aligned" nation, but it wished to engage the country more closely with Third World nations. The opposition was definitely less disposed to place a foot in each camp. It preferred to have a foot in one, only a toe in the other. While Snedden said that he would be on friendly terms with Third World nations, especially in trade and aid, Whitlam was said to have weakened Australia's defence system by "moving more into the Third World". The "reality is that the Third World is not really an option for us. We are part of the Western defence system and we should remain part of it."[56]

The opposition's clear endorsement of the alliance system carried certain corollaries. It meant maintaining the American defence facilities in Australia. It meant behaving as genuine partners with the United States. For Peacock, for instance, there were two sides to this coin. One was that while the Liberals welcomed something like a "special relationship" with America, they saw no reason why Washington could not respect a more independent Australian foreign policy, one that flowed from what Australia itself perceived as best for its interests. America's own foreign relations were "prosecuted along these lines in a very business-like way".[57] However, "Change and forthrightness in a relationship does not call for the abuse of a quite personal kind which has been levelled at the United States Government by the Labor Party."[58] In the post-Vietnam international setting, Fraser remarked, America's credibility was bound to be questioned. Therefore, "the United States needs to know how her friends view her situation in the world and I believe that she would understand plain and friendly talk from Australia on these matters."[59] In this sense, an "independent" Australian voice would call for American resolve.

Partly to supplement some wider allied military effort in its region, to sustain its ANZUS obligations and in self-protection against low level threats, Australia had to develop a reasonably self-reliant military capacity. Moreover, in outward contradiction to Labor's position, the opposition did not preclude the garrisoning of Australian troops overseas in situations short of all-out war; "while the defence of continental Australia, and a realistic capacity to defend continental Australia, is the first and basic aim, our forces must also be capable, should the eventuality arise, of being deployed outside Australia for so long as they continue to serve purposes common to those other countries involved and Australia's own national interests."[60]

Formulations such as these seemingly placed the L–CP very close to what it had espoused when in government. But some important caveats need to be drawn. For instance, though there was some ambivalence on this count, there was a noticeable disposition to think that arms counted for less than before. And, as Peacock expressed it, it was doubtful whether a concentration on defence would help Australia to evolve better regional relationships, "to endear us to our Asian neighbors who could scarcely do likewise without harmful effects on their vitally important development programmes".[61] Secondly, as will be explained later, opposition spokesmen admitted that under an L–CP government no major enlargement of defence capability could be expected in the short to middle run. Finally, despite in principle being prepared to post troops overseas, opposition figures did not envisage a return to a standard forward defence posture and conceded that the foreseeable circumstances for sending troops away for garrison or combat duty were remote, and that the political risks of such a step would probably be steep.

The non-security features of opposition external policy guidelines also showed both continuity and change from older outlooks. There was a restlessness over the alleged impetuosity of Labor's preferred approach to communist and Third World nations. By this, for instance, the L–CP meant Labor's haste (but not inherent error) in recognizing Peking and Hanoi. There was restlessness over Labor's alleged tendency to be severe in chastizing old friends and downplaying differences with Afro–Asian and communist states. There was displeasure over flirtations with the Third World at the expense of tried and valued friends. There also was feeling that, by ostensibly downgrading alliances and other security commitments, the Labor government was sowing confusion in Asia, thereby lowering rather than enhancing Australia's own credibility. What all this added up to was a predictably more cautious, less experimental L–CP policy style than Labor was prepared to follow.

The L–CP was prepared to practice greater initiatives in Asia than it had when in government. Some of these were of a diplomatic nature, but the stress was to be on economic dimensions of policy.

Hence it saw Australia's role in fostering South-East Asian, or Asian, co-operative efforts less in political than in aid–trade co-operation terms. Even before it had vacated office, the L–CP was sponsoring a substantial external aid programme. Now it wished to move further, both in the generosity of Australia's assistance and in action towards harmonizing the efforts of donor and recipient states. The particulars of the opposition's programme can best be examined in later context. So can its attitude towards resource policy. What we wish to say here is that the L–CP became far more cognizant of the need to evolve a resource policy than it had before December 1972. Working from its assumptions about international economic interdependence, it visualized Australia's natural wealth as a great asset. In the exploita-tion of the nation's resources, the Liberal Party had at least moved to a more "nationalist" outlook than the McMahon government had held. Hence the party's 1974 platform on overseas investment in-dicated that Liberals sought "maximum Australian control and ownership of our national resources and industries". While foreign investment was welcomed, "there are certain costs which may be as-sociated with such investment. The national interest ... is best served where the benefits of such investment are maximised and its costs minimised."[62] In theory, at least, this resembled Labor's own guidelines, though it lacked the impulses of ideology that buttressed the ALP's approach. It was on the disposition of resources that the L–CP's policy guidelines came to reflect its brand of international in-terdependence. Once again, it censured what it portrayed as Labor's proclivity for nationalist expression and for over-organizing in wrong directions. "It may appear that Australia has a choice," Snedden told an American audience in late 1974. "On the one hand, greater co-operation and shared prosperity; on the other, hoarding, pressure and eventual disruption. In reality, I believe there is no real choice. The selfish alternative could be maintained only in the short term and only at ultimate risk."[63]

The "conservative" persuasion in foreign policy criticism was not limited to Liberal and Country Party spokesmen. Some of it, matching or exceeding the force of L–CP challenges to the Labor government's assumptions and guidelines, emanated from party political or right-radical circles. Some of it came from academics. Also some ranking military officers, serving or resigned, publicly questioned the govern-ment's basic outlook on the firmness of *détente* and on the security risks foreseeably faced by Australia. The impact of these opinions on the broad external policy debate lay in the putatively non-partisan vantage-point from which they spoke: as professionals, with many years of career experience. Few officers actually chose to expose such thoughts. Some senior officers volunteered general agreement with the government's conceptions. But the critics were accorded special publicity by opposition spokesmen and by the Australian right generally. They were held up as patriotic experts, realistic about the troubled state of the world and unafraid to call a spade a spade where Australia's need to keep good friends and fix its defences was concerned.[64]

The party and lobby *political* "right" in Australia was even more amorphous than the political "left". Its composition emphasized the right wing of the Liberal and Country Parties, the DLP and its supporting bodies, patriotic organizations and a radical right fringe. As a phenomenon, however, it was less well internally co-ordinated than the left and probably enjoyed less outward publicity for its causes—unless, as some critics of the left argued, the media represented a built-in right-wing empire in Australian society. The Australian right's values leaned towards "conserving" or "restoring" rather than towards "radically innovating". Hence it generally was temperamentally offended as much by swift change and experimentation as by the substance of those governmental assumptions and policy guidelines that it found obnoxious. It also suffered from certain situational handicaps and from some ambivalence. Many of the left felt that they were moving with a tide such as the corrosion of capitalist and imperialist power, and with the tide of anti-colonialism, anti-racialism, "peoples'" resistance to establishmentarian oppression, etc. The right was worried that the public had become too preoccupied with narrow hip-pocket concerns to appreciate the downward slide of tried and tested values and of rising challenges from an unharnessed left, and to shake off pernicious illusions about the domestication of communism and the safety of Australia. The right worried about what an irresponsible and allegedly left-infected Labor government was doing, about what a "new style" L–CP opposition was trying or might try to do, namely to become more electorally attractive by displaying "trendy", wrong-headed and even principle-subverting tendencies. Power realities, unreconstructed communist or other alien designs and Australia's tested connections could not be dismissed as echoes from the past, or be shunted aside in the interest of political cosmetology.

Some ranking members of the Liberal Party itself found the experimentation of their colleagues uncongenial. Fraser, even before he became Liberal leader, was one person who held some doubts. For him, changing international power relationships had created a more dangerous situation than before, a view not unshared by his L–CP associates, but perhaps more keenly felt by him than by most others. The Labor government had drawn wholly false conclusions from what was happening and had propagated a line about the nation's security that deceived and bemused.[65] Menzies, the grand old man of the Liberal Party, wrote of how "horrified" he was with a leading opposition spokesman's comments that, apart from a few details, the spokesman had no quarrel with the government's foreign policy: "Heaven help us! The foreign policy of the present Government is the very antithesis of the foreign policy of the Liberal Party in my time;" defence through strength and close ties with powerful friends, not flirtations with communist and Third World nations did and should continue to matter.[66] In 1974, Liberal Senator George Hannan broke away from his party and stood separately for the Senate in Victoria as a "National Liberal Party" candidate. Among other things, he had become disillusioned with his old party's trendy and, as he saw it, myopic approach to international questions. By the opening of 1975, the National Liberals mated with elements from the much older, ultra-conservative League of Rights, to form a National Australian Association. Later that year, 4000 people marched in Melbourne under the auspices of the "People Against Communism Committee", in protest against communism's many-faceted evils.[67] Writing on what he called "Whitlam's Foreign Policy Myth", Hannan minced no words: "The Whitlam foreign policy, such as it is, is so oleaginously servile to Communist powers and ingratiating to third world powers that it is not an Australian foreign policy at all—it is a fraud."[68]

Hard-to-right outlooks on foreign policy and defence were not the dominant strain among the federal opposition parties, but had important pockets of strength elsewhere. Hence it is understood that the foreign policy document drawn up by Peacock's study group prior to the 1974 election enjoyed a generally positive or at least uncomplaining reaction among federal Liberal parliamentarians. But the "backwoodsmen" (as they were described to the author) in some of the party's state branches were far from captivated by the proposed "modernized" policy guidelines. Queensland, with its strong anticentralist bias and the steadfastly anti-communist National (formerly Country) Party Premier Johannes Bjelke-Petersen at its helm, evinced a notably right-wing flavour in its politics. Political material that in good part would have been inappropriate to non-Labor parties in the southern states was freely disseminated. Not unrepresentative was a newspaper advertisement placed by the President of the Captive Nations Council of Queensland, opposing the constitutional referenda the Labor government was sponsoring concurrent with the 1974 federal election. The advertisement enjoined people to reject the referenda as invasions of Australian freedom, "founded on the Christian ideal—not suppressed under harsh regimentation as in the Soviet Union (SOCIALIST REPUBLICS)".[69] Brisbane was the headquarters of the National Association of the Australian Citizens for Freedom. Its organ, *National Message*, carried the captions "Freedom, Justice and Democracy under God" and "God Save the Queen". In the December 1974 Queensland state election, a Bjelke-Petersen campaign leitmotiv was admonitory about the spectre of communism in Canberra. There had been sell-outs to communists at home and abroad, the doing of despicable deals with those who would ruin and enslave Australia, among them the Russians, the Chinese and the North Vietnamese.[70]

The DLP had for many years been a paramount publicist for a right-wing approach to external policy. In the 1974 election, though more forcefully in Victoria than in New South Wales, it continued to warn against dangers in Asia and urged vigilance and preparedness in defence. In that election, it lost all of its federal parliamentary representation. The loss of its Senate forum considerably weakened its ability to project its views on the country or to continue to leave whatever very little imprint it still could on the L–CP. The DLP's 1974 setback was very disheartening to B. A. Santamaria and his National Civic Council. Santamaria complained of "the Liberals having adopted the essence of the policies fastened on Labor by Dr Cairns and the Left".[71] Santamaria felt that, if anything because of the removal of the DLP from the federal parliamentary scene, it was imperative for those who understood and who cared to keep the external policy failings of the "identikit" Labor and Liberal Parties before the public. In time, the somnolent Australian people would rue the day they lost perspective on communism, on an unbalanced world order, on their frail security shield and ultimately on their own safety. Some of Santamaria's formulations, such as finding a linkage between a red aligning Jim Cairns and a badly duped Bill Snedden or Andrew Peacock, were most notable for their shock value, or their appeal to true believers. But Santamaria remained among the most informed and trenchant publicists of a distinctive, right-oriented alternative to Labor's outlook on foreign policy.[72]

NOTES

1. E.G. Whitlam, "Australian's Foreign Policy: New Directions, New Definitions", 24th Roy Milne Memorial Lecture, Brisbane, 30 November 1973, (Melbourne: AIIA, 1973), p. 3.
2. *Commonwealth[Australian] Parliamentary Debates (APD)*, House of Representatives (HR) (22 April 1971), p. 1925.
3. *Australia and South-East Asia*, (Canberra: Department of Foreign Affairs, 1974), p. 35.
4. D. Willesee (untitled paper, AIIA conference, Adelaide, June 1974), pp. 6–7.
5. Whitlam, address of 3 December 1973; and Department of Foreign Affairs, *Circular Memorandum*, no. 109/73 (5 December 1973).
6. Department of Foreign Affairs, *Circular Memorandum*, no. 109/73 (5 December 1973).
7. *Canberra Times*, 3 May 1974.
8. *Australian Foreign Affairs Record (AFAR)* 44 (August 1973): 530.

9. J.L. Richardson, "Australian Foreign Policy under the Labor Government", *Co-operation and Conflict*, 9, no. 1 (1974): 17.
10. *APD*, HR (7 March 1974), p. 203. Some of the clearest expositions of Australian perceptions of changes in the international order have been offered by officials. For instance, see remarks by R.A. Woolcott, "Australia and Asia in the Seventies", *AFAR* 45 (May 1974): 314–23. Also see *Submission by the Department of Foreign Affairs of the Royal Commission on Australian Government Administration (Canberra: October .1974), esp. pp. 2–6.*
11. E.G. Whitlam, address in Washington of 8 May 1975, in *Department of Foreign Affairs, News Release* no. M30 (20 May 1975), p. 5.
12. For instance, see the Barnard–Schlesinger Washington communiqué of 9 January 1974 regarding the North-West Cape signal-station renegotiations, transcript; Barnard's address in Washington, 5 January 1974, in *Defence Release*, no. 200/74 (undated) p. 8; and Barnard, *APD*, HR (9 April 1974), p. 1233.
13. A. Renouf, "The Future of Australia's Foreign Service". address of 21 November 1974, transcript, p. 9.
14. *APD*, HR (8 April 1975), p. 1261.
15. O. Mendelsohn, *Australia's Foreign Aid: The Perceptions of Parliamentarians*, (Canberra: Parliament of Australia. Parliamentary Library, 1973), p. 15.
16. *Canberra Times*, 14 August 1973.
17. See especially Barnard's speech (and quotations from the strategic assessment) to the National RSL Congress, 29 October 1973, transcript, esp. pp. 2–5. Also see Barnard, *APD*, HR (22 August 1973), pp. 238–39.
18. For instance, see the assessment by R. Skelton, Melbourne *Age*, 2 October 1975.
19. B. Dale and J. Stackhouse, *Australian Financial Review*, 13 February 1974.
20. National Press Club address, *Sydney Morning Herald*, 16 March 1973.
21. Whitlam, "Australia's Foreign Policy", p. 6.
22. Willesee, "New Directions in Australia's Development Assistance" (AIIA conference paper, Melbourne, May 1975), p. 17.
23. Willesee, "Australia's Foreign Policy (II)", statement of 19 January 1973 (Washington: Embassy of Australia, Press and Information Service) *Release* no. M23, p. 1.
24. *AFAR* 44 (February 1973): 96. Emphasis added.
25. *AFAR* 44 (January 1973): 32–33.
26. Whitlam, "Australia's Foreign Policy", p. 5. Emphasis added.
27. Melbourne *Age*, 1 January 1974.
28. Whitlam, remarks to ALP Federal Conference, *Australian*, 24 July 1973.
29. Whitlam, "Australia's Foreign Policy", p. 5.
30. On the radical movement, see R. Gordon, ed., *The Australian Left: Critical Essays and Strategy* (Melbourne: Heinemann, 1970). With special emphasis on anti-Vietnam and anti-conscription protest, see H. S. Albinski, *Politics and Foreign Policy in Australia: The impact of Vietnam and Conscription* (Durham, N.C.: Duke University Press, 1970), pp. 101–62.
31. See description in *Catholic Worker*, November 1973. For representative Christian radical opinion, see the *Newsletter* and *Political Concern* produced by the Australian Student Christian Movement.
32. On the student press, see G. Henderson, F. Timmerman, and S. Grove, contributions to "The Student Press" *Current Affairs Bulletin* 51 (November 1974): 24–27, 28–30 and 30–31, respectively.
33. *The Global Emergency* (Sydney: AICD, 1974), p. 5.
34. M. Frydman, *Australian Policies in Asia* (Melbourne: CICD, 1974), p. 2.
35. *National U* (AUS organ), 8 July 1974.
36. B. McFarlane, "A Neo-Colonial Policy for the Pacific Rim", *Arena* nos. 32–33 (1973), p. 34. For the broad argument, see R. Catley and B. McFarlane, *From Tweedledum to Tweedledee: The New Labor Government in Australia* (Sydney: ANZ Book Company, 1974). For an early but generally relevant critique of Labor's foreign policy, see J. Camilleri, "In Search of a Foreign Policy", *Arena* nos. 32–33 (1973), pp. 65–79.
37. For a summary, see "Strategic Orientation and Priorities for the Peace Movement" (Sydney: AICD, 1973).
38. P. Galvin, *Report to August Council* [of AUS] (?Carlton, Vic: AUS, 1974), p. 3.

39. Liberal Party of Australia, *The Way Ahead with a Liberal Country Party Government* (Canberra: 1974); foreign affairs on pp. 11–17, defence on pp. 18–22, minerals and energy on pp. 88–91, overseas trade on p. 92, international economic relations on pp. 94–95.
40. Liberal Party of Australia, *Federal Platform* (approved by Federal Council, October 1974) (Canberra: 1974). foreign affairs on p. 13, defence on p. 14, international economic relations on p. 15, overseas investment on pp. 61–62, mineral and energy resources on pp. 65–67.
41. See Liberal and National Country Parties, *Foreign Policy* and *Defence Policy* (Canberra: Liberal Party Federal Secretariat, 1975).
42. Derived from non-attributable source.
43. Snedden, address to AIIA, Victorian branch, 7 March 1974, transcript, pp. 2 and 5.
44. *Australian*, 16 March 1973.
45. *Sydney Morning Herald*, 26 April 1974.
46. Mendelsohn, *Australia's Foreign Aid*, p. 16.
47. Melbourne *Age*, 14 October 1974.
48. A. Peacock, "Opposition Foreign Policy: Alternatives or Bipartisanship" (AIIA conference paper, Adelaide, June 1974), p. 4. For other broad expositions of opposition policy, see Peacock, "An Alternative Foreign Policy for Australia", *World Review* 13 (July 1974): 3–11; and his "Australia and South-East Asia—An Alternative View" (AIIA conference paper, Melbourne, May 1975), *passim*; and A. J. Forbes, "A Forward Thinking, Integrated Defence Policy for Australia", address to National RSL Congress, Melbourne, 29 October 1974, transcript, *passim*; Fraser, address in Townsville of 12 April 1975, transcript, *passim*.
49. A.J. Forbes, "Reply to Statement on Defence by Defence Minister", n.d., transcript, p. 6.
50. Melbourne *Age*, 13 August 1973.
51. Peacock, *APD*, HR (20 November 1973) p. 3497.
52. J.D. Anthony, "In Defence of Mining", *New Accent*, 31 May 1974, p. 17.
53. Address at Royal Military College, Duntroon, 12 August 1974, transcript, p. 19.
54. A.J. Forbes, "National Security and Defence", in *Looking at the Liberals*, ed. R. Aitchison (Melbourne: Cheshire, 1974), p. 126.
55. Peacock, "An Alternative Foreign Policy for Australia", p. 5. Emphasis in original.
56. Interview in *Newsweek*, 13 January 1975.
57. Melbourne *Age*, 11 May 1973.
58. Peacock, "Opposition Foreign Policy", p. 2.
59. Address in Townsville of 12 April 1975, transcript, p. 18.
60. Forbes, "National Security and Defence", p. 127. Also see Forbes' remarks, Sydney *Daily Telegraph*, 25 April 1974; and J.D. Killen's remarks, *Canberra Times*, 5 April 1975.
61. Melbourne *Age*, 10 May 1973.
62. *Federal Platform* p. 61.
63. Address to Council on Foreign Relations, New York, 9 December 1974, in *Media Release*, no. 74/185, (n.d.) p. 2.
64. For instance, see the remarks of Vice-Admiral Sir Richard Peek, *Canberra Times*, 6 March 1974; of Brigadier J.G. Hooton, *Australian*, 25 June 1974; and of Admiral Sir Victor Smith, *Australian*, 18 March 1975. For representative academic criticism, see R. O'Neill, "Foreign Policy and Defence" (AIIA conference paper, Adelaide, June 1974), *passim*; and T. B. Millar, Melbourne *Herald*, 9 April 1975.
65. For instance, Fraser's remarks before the Defend Australia Committee, in Melbourne *Age*, 19 November 1973; and his speech to Jewish graduates in Melbourne, 5 May 1974, *Press Statement* of 3 May 1974.
66. *Sydney Morning Herald*, 16 December 1974.
67. Melbourne *Age*, 9 May 1975.
68. G. Hannan, "Whitlam's Foreign Policy Myth", in L. Shaw, ed., *The Shape of the Labor Régime* (Canberra: Harp Books, 1974), p. 35.
69. Brisbane *Courier-Mail*, 17 May 1974.
70. See a summary of the anti-communist campaign in Queensland by H. Lunn, *Australian*, 6 December 1974.
71. B.A. Santamaria, "Point of View" commentary, *News Weekly*, 15 May 1974.
72. See his remarks to the Victorian branch of the AIIA, *News Weekly*, 1 January 1975.

4 External Policy: Diplomatic Dimensions: I

In the preceding chapter, we examined the dominant dispositions of the Labor government, the opposition and other groups. We now begin to look at how, in diplomatic, economic and military/security terms, policy was operationalized under the Labor government. We will be interested in policy process, stylistic and political climate considerations, as well as in policy outputs as such. As far as possible, our treatment will identify and link major subject-matter themes. Here and in the following chapter we concentrate on diplomatic features of external policy.

We open with an analysis of Labor's efforts to promote a wide association of Asian and Pacific states. The choice is in part dictated by the fact that, directly or indirectly, a good deal of the government's diplomatic activity can be related to this theme. It is also a theme that connects especially well with a number of the ALP's previously outlined perceptions and assumptions.

From the beginning of its term of office, the government espoused the cause of a regional Asian–Pacific grouping.[1] It was reluctant to spell out a detailed blueprint of what it hoped for. The guidelines foreseen by Whitlam were of "an organization genuinely representative of the region, without ideological overtones."[2] Whitlam suggested the analogy of the Commonwealth of Nations. He conceived of something relatively unstructured, "not a body where decisions are made and then [made] binding, but where it is possible for heads of government regularly to exchange views which are of mutual interest."[3]

What nations would be included? Again, hard and fast specifics were not proffered, but definitely the ASEAN countries (Indonesia, Thailand, Malaysia, Singapore and the Philippines), and in all likelihood other South-East Asian nations such as the Indo-Chinese states and Burma, but the membership of South Asian states was less clear. Australia and New Zealand would of course belong. So would China and Japan, but probably not the two super-powers, the Soviet Union and the United States.[4]

How would the construction of such a new forum proceed? Slowly, without any timetable. Australia was an interested party, but the impulses mainly had to come from Asians themselves.[5]

Why was the government interested in promoting such a venture? The various reasons, stated and otherwise, were consistent with Labor's sentiments, ideological dispositions and understandings of world forces. Government spokesmen emphasized that a wider regional community could help to break down long-standing preoccupation with ideological conflicts and with defence oriented answers to fostering stability. Attachment to "containment" postures and to alliance systems had in the past served to feed, not mitigate, conflict. Great-power rivalries had destructively spilled into Asia. Now that the great-power writ was less obtrusive, new clusters of power were emerging and there seemed to be a de-emphasis on military instruments of conflict management, it was opportune to proceed with insulating the region against ideological interference from the great powers.[6] These theses not only squared with Labor's theoretical assumptions about international life but also captured some of the spirit of the party's inherent idealism. War and strife in world politics could be attacked through reasoned interchanges. If the world was not "perfectable", at least it was improvable. A new reconciliation *could* be expected among nations as different in background and politics as China, Japan, Australia and the range of South-East Asian states.

For Australia itself, encouragement of such a project could be seen as valuable beyond the large objective of working towards a less conflict-infected neighbourhood. The government's investment of time and energy in sponsoring the idea was a demonstration that Australia under Labor was capable of initiatives, of exercising an "independent" foreign policy. This was good for the soul of the party. It presumably won the applause of Asians. It helped to advance Australia's future credibility and influence in the region. Lacking direct institutionalized access to some important Asian councils such as ASEAN, Australia was well-advised to promote political machinery of which it would be a full and charter member. It would also, as Peter King remarked, serve to end Australia's traditional "obsession" with South-East Asia, to extend the nation's constituency of interests.[7] Moreover, should such a grouping of states be realized, Australia could expect to further some of its more specific favourite interests. For example, a functioning Asian—Pacific forum could become the springboard for declaring a zone of "peace, freedom and neutrality" in the region. It could not only facilitate economic co-operation and joint endeavours among the various members, but supply a base on which both resource producer and consumer nations could harmonize their activities, consistent with Labor's notions about "interdependence" and the appropriate wielding of resource policy.

As it publicized its ideas about a broad Asian–Pacific community, the Labor government took notice of the smaller groupings already present in the region. Some it chose to downgrade, others to praise and support. This variable approach was dictated by the criteria by which Labor measured the inherent value of various groupings and by its perceptions of how, if at all, they might dovetail with the envisioned broader association.

Two regional groups were downgraded by Labor. One was SEATO. It was a security pact of anti-communist origins, had very limited Asian membership, included non-Asian members and was considered to have become decrepit when Labor assumed office. As we will see later, Australia promoted a restructuring of SEATO on essentially non-military lines. But even when that was achieved in late 1973, the organization was regarded as unsuitable as a springboard for an extended Asian–Pacific association.

The Asian and Pacific Council (ASPAC) was viewed in slightly different perspective. Unlike SEATO, it included no members from outside the Asian–Pacific region and was not a security alliance but a cultural and economic association. But its membership was characteristically anti-communist. It included not only South Korea, and South Vietnam while it was still under anti-communist rule, but Taiwan, the large thorn in China's side. Some attempts had been made to turn ASPAC into an anti-communist vehicle. Moreover, by 1973, three of ASPAC's members—Australia, New Zealand and Japan—had recognized Peking, even though Taiwan remained a member. A fourth, Malaysia, withdrew from ASPAC entirely. Hence the Labor government downgraded ASPAC. It did not consider it amenable to being remodeled. It did not follow Malaysia out of the organization and continued most of its financial contributions. In mid-1975, however, it withdrew from ASPAC's Registry of Scientific and Technical Services, and increasingly watched ASPAC's apparent eclipse as a meaningful body.

On the other end of Labor's enthusiasm scale stood ASEAN. Of all the past or present groupings in Asia, Whitlam noted, "ASEAN is the only one which has a proper regional relevance, the only one which has a thriving future."[8] ASEAN contained no nations from outside the geographical area, no Taiwan and, despite the slowness with which ASEAN's members were individually willing to normalize relations with Peking, no strident or "tainted" anti-communist nations such as Thieu's South Vietnam or South Korea. Unlike ASPAC, ASEAN included Indonesia, South-East Asia's single most important nation and with whom both L–CP and Labor governments attempted to evolve an especially close relationship.[9] ASEAN was believed to be giving gradual but positive evidence of the workability of regional co-operation. Within its own ranks, it was evolving closer economic links and was helping to dampen potentially dangerous frictions, such as the Philippines' claim on Sabah, in Malaysian Borneo. It pointed the way towards an ALP ideal by subscribing to a˙zone of peace, freedom and neutrality in the area. It was beginning to fashion a common approach towards outsiders, as for instance the European Economic Community (EEC). It was investigating conditions under which other South-East Asian states could join it.[10] In other words, ASEAN was inherently good value, a springboard, or example, for launching a larger association.

The Labor government went out of its way to indicate that its own objective of an Asian–Pacific forum did not imply that ASEAN would thereby be absorbed, or even that it would be the structure that would be augmented to include many more and diverse nations.[11] Australia undertook to back up its convictions with positive gestures. For instance, in 1974, it became the first nation to support collective all-ASEAN economic development projects, in addition to continuing economic and technical assistance to ASEAN's members on a bilateral basis or through international aid consortia. Later that year, Canberra was the site of the first ASEAN Secretaries-General Conference held outside of ASEAN capitals.

The Labor government also encouraged links with other regional bodies in the area. Again the government had a dual rationale. Such bodies seemed to be performing constructive, socio-economic work and their activity held some promise for raising incentives for a wider association of Asian–Pacific nations. For instance, Australia took a keen interest in *Pacific* regional groupings. In 1973, Australia launched an initiative that later brought about a *de facto* merger of the "Commission" and the "Conference" facets of the South Pacific Commission. These were, respectively, the Western metropolitan members, plus three independent island governments on the one hand, and these governments plus dependent Pacific territories on the other. The Australian motive was to make the South Pacific Commission (then Conference) at large more viable and to remove invidious distinctions between dependencies and others.[12] Beginning under the L–CP and then continuing under Labor, support was given to the South Pacific Forum, a group of independent or self-governing states dealing with problems that could not successfully be tackled by the Commission. Among the virtues attributed to the Forum by the Labor government was that in its councils Australia was able, with

New Zealand's support, to launch a successful initiative for a resolution condemning French nuclear testing in the Pacific. Australia mentioned this Forum action in conjunction with its legal presentation against French testing before the International Court of Justice (ICJ) in The Hague. Virtue was found in Australia's ability to provide technical assistance to Forum members. Then, too, the Labor government saw a possible precedent towards building a broad regional association. There were intimations from within ASEAN's ranks that useful links between ASEAN and the Forum could be forged. [13] Placing regional co-operation in even wider perspective, Indonesian Foreign Minister Malik suggested in early 1974 that Australia's willingness to deal with ASEAN as a group was an important prelude to any more ambitious plans for regional co-operation in the South Pacific. [14]

There were other means by which Australia strived to demonstrate initiative, to anchor itself more firmly in regional programmes and groupings, and to generate a climate conducive to building a broadly gauged Asian–Pacific community. For instance, the government was especially eager to promote China's membership in ECAFE, the Economic Commission for Asia and the Far East: "The assumption of its rightful place in ECAFE by the largest country in the region should *help to accelerate the movement towards better understanding among all regional countries* and to give greater authority to the deliberations of ECAFE." [15] Under Labor, Australia (and New Zealand) acquired membership in the Ministerial Conference for Economic Development of South-East Asia, theretofore a purely non-European organization. Canberra saw this as a building-block for an even more comprehensive regional association, since the group now included most South-East Asian nations, Japan, and Australia and New Zealand. It also recognized the special role that Australia could discharge in regional affairs. The ASEAN states supported Australian and New Zealand participation because they saw their presence as something of a counterweight to Japanese influence, as well as an inherently important source of finance and expertise for their development plans. [16]

So far, we have stressed the policy features of Labor's efforts to promote a wide Asian–Pacific forum. The style in which it proceeded is equally important for us, both insofar as it helped or retarded the government's objectives and in more general process terms. In January of 1973, Whitlam met in Wellington with New Zealand's Labour Prime Minister, Norman Kirk. The idea of a broad regional association was mutually agreed upon. Whitlam raised the idea in a public address later that month. In February, he travelled to Indonesia. The proposal was put—and received very cooly. The merits of the proposal aside, Australia's approach was launched too precipitously, with inadequate testing in South-East Asian capitals. Copies of Whitlam's January statement "were produced for foreign missions, but there was little in the way of supporting material. The flurry of activity was counter-productive given the lack of detail available. ASEAN ministers in mid- February informally discussed the proposal, and rejected it as it stood."[17] New Zealand informants indicated that the genesis of the regional scheme was more Kirk's idea than Whitlam's. New Zealand was not so much angered over not receiving due credit, as it was sorrowed because Whitlam's enthusiasm in launching the proposal may have set it back. Then, too, for a time afterwards, the government found some resistance to a European Australia acting as catalyst for Asian co-operation. It found some obstacles in persuading South-East Asians of its credibility. Rightly or not, the new Australian government was suspected of being more interested in emphasizing the best possible relations with the major Asian states, China and Japan, than in promoting a higher level of confidence in South-East Asia. It is understood on good authority that, shortly before leaving office, the L–CP government was cautioned by all ASEAN governments about recognizing Peking, but this was one of earliest and most enthusiastic diplomatic steps taken by the new Labor government. Labor's promise to withdraw troops from Singapore was not only generally unwelcome among ASEAN states but was announced after only sketchy consultations with them.[18]

The Labor government continued to foster its regional objective among various Asian nations, but developed more subdued, refined and reassuring methods. The zeal for change, the personal assertiveness of Whitlam, were brought under restraint. Assurances were repeated that Australia had no intention of superseding or otherwise tampering with ASEAN, and that it could not, or would not, act as spokesman or intermediary for China *vis-à-vis* South-East Asian states. Australia would only try to give its own impressions of China and its role when treating with its South-East Asian neighbours.[19] A special section was created in the Foreign Affairs Department to concentrate on regional affairs. Australian embassies in Asia were instructed to bring their efforts to bear. Prior to his early 1974 visits to various South-East Asian capitals, Whitlam sent a personal aide to discuss the nuances of each nation's special perspectives with Australian diplomatic personnel. Each of Whitlam's speeches was carefully tailored and it became "one of the first occasions before a Prime Minister's overseas visit that Australian embassies have played a constructive role in the stance adopted through such close consultation."[20] How well, on its merits, was the idea of a broad Asian-Pacific association received? The brief answer is "cautiously". China was officially supportive, but without showing haste for the plan's consummation. Peking actually found the idea of extending its influence into South-East Asia quite attractive and began to employ its new Canberra embassy to stimulate interest among others.[21] The Japanese were more circumspect. They first wanted time to straighten out their own complex bilateral relations with China, and were unsure of what their membership in a regional grouping would do to their already bruised commercial reputation in South-East Asia.[22]

Reaction within ASEAN became more favourable after early 1973 and moved towards acceptance in principle. But, unequally among its members, sentiment remained guarded.[23] There was pride in ASEAN as a viable Asian self-devised organ. There therefore was apprehension that ASEAN could, willy-nilly, be eroded if a rapid move towards the larger and unknown quantity desired by Australia were taken. Some apprehensions felt within ASEAN were based on the kinds of reasons that the Labor government saw as *incentives* to build more ambitiously. The Asian security situation was still volatile and fighting was in progress in Indo-China. Most of ASEAN's members had undergone unhappy experiences with China and were not sure Peking should be allowed entrée to them before it was perfectly clear that it had foresaken all aggressive or subversive intentions. These feelings were not entirely dissipated, despite growing links between them and China, begun by Malaysia's recognition of Peking in 1974 (for which Australia felt it deserved a measure of credit) and by Thailand's and the Philippines' recognition of China in 1975. ASEAN states feared that, with China in a wider grouping, South-East Asia could become a sort of regional cockpit for the Sino–Soviet rivalry. They had misgivings about Japan, with its appetite for resources and for investment outlets, and an already very heavy development aid stake in the region. A cohesive group of South-East Asian states might be overshadowed and exploited by a populous and militarily potent China, an economically powerful Japan and a resource-rich Australia. Indonesia, as the single most powerful state in South-East Asia, would find its own relative influence impaired by the formal intrustion of important outside nations.

Variations on a regional theme were occasionally broached. Perhaps the most analytically interesting was raised in late 1973 by Indonesia. Together with New Zealand, it urged a quadripartite association among itself, Australia, New Zealand and Papua New Guinea. For Indonesia, this was announced as a modest step, free of great powers, towards some distant ideal of the broad Asian–Pacific association, whose time had not yet come. It was also understood to be a device for heading off problems potentially flowing from the

much more rapid development of Papua New Guinea than on Indonesia's western, Irian Jaya (West Irian) side of the island of New
Guinea.[24] The New Zealanders' interest was primarily dictated by
their disappointment at the slow pace at which the original large-
grouping idea was incubating. New Zealand had been more explicit in
admitting this than Australia and had not continued to pursue the objective as vigorously as Canberra.[25] Hence as the big idea seemed to
languish, New Zealand decided to support the stepping-stone that
could emerge from Indonesia's idea of a smaller arrangement. New
Guinea spokesmen were themselves cautious. Basically, they wanted
close regional co-operation for their country, but with more emphasis
towards the Pacific than towards South-East Asia, and in any event
did not wish to prejudge the situation before formal independence
had been acquired.[26]

Australia's reaction reflected the dilemmas involved in pursuing a
grand-scale diplomatic objective, the constraints imposed on the influence of any single international actor and the hard lessons learned
about the need for respecting South-East Asian sensibilities. The
documentary evidence indicates that Canberra did not endorse the
quadripartite idea because details were missing and because "it would
want to consider Papua New Guinean views on the proposal before
forming its own judgment on it,"[27] and Papua New Guinea was not
yet an independent state. The internal evidence suggests a somewhat
more complex picture. The above reason is acknowledged. Among
persons very close to the scene, there was some feeling but no consensus as to whether Australia stood New Zealand's position on its
head; i.e. that Canberra believed such a grouping would *distract* attention from rather than *stimulating* the wider Asian–Pacific community.
What did emerge was Australia's misgiving that China might construe such an experiment as having an anti-Chinese bent, and that
other ASEAN states might resent the central role that would probably
devolve upon Indonesia, the nation already dominant within ASEAN.

Within Australia, the Labor government's proposal of a broad
Asian–Pacific forum did not escape criticism. The critiques offered by
the L–CP opposition and by the left were instructive in that they illuminated both conceptual and normative differences with Labor.
The opposition jabbed at the government for being too brusque and
imperious in style, too little aware of Asian sensitivities, too
enamoured of its own grand designs. Part of this criticism, of course,
was aimed at scoring political points. It also reflected a somewhat different view of Asia and of Australian priorities. There was an undercurrent of displeasure that Labor's proposal was trying to draw an as-
yet untamed China into the regional home of reluctant South-East
Asians and that the scheme at large was an unwarranted departure

from Australia's more traditional definitions of security requirements.[28]

The opposition was not, however, content to be negative. It sensed
that regionalism, by whatever name or form, was a fashionable and
inherently sensible idea. The Labor government's over-ambitious plan
was weak on detail and apparently stalled. So were most other
regional proposals. The quadripartite notion was weak because it
deflected attention from building more meaningful regional structures. This, according to a Liberal document, "leaves a gap which the
Opposition has an opportunity to fill—or on which we can at least be
seen to be making a constructive and realistic effort. It ... offers an opportunity to take a significant initiative in the foreign policy area." It
would emphasize "progressive" humanitarian features, while also
making a significant contribution to regional security.[29] Snedden had
by early 1974 begun to speak of practical co-operation between
ASEAN and the South Pacific Forum, to which Australia itself
belonged, and he then moved towards the language of a more integrated developmental assistance format for various nations in the
region.[30] The new, highly co-ordinated development scheme was en-
visaged as embracing aid, trade, communications, investment and
other business ventures. It would embrace the South Pacific Forum,
ASEAN and other South-East Asian and possibly South Asian states,
and possibly even China and Japan. As an early internal Liberal formulation of the plan read, "This proposal is distinct from Labor's
'forum'—it is a strategy not an organisation; its purpose is co-
operation and development not simply consultation (though that is
part of it); it offers something practical to those who choose to participate. It would also be a step toward rationalising, in our region,
the tangled web of bilateral relationship."[31] At this time, in 1974 and
1975, the Liberal Party was undertaking efforts to establish contacts
with like-minded conservative/moderate parties in the region, for instance in New Zealand, Japan and India. After Snedden had departed
and Fraser was in charge, the Liberals' regional scheme continued to
be advertised.[32]

While the L–CP criticized the government for being too bold, and
for unguardedly and prematurely trying to introduce a communist
China into the councils of the region, left criticism insisted that
Labor's plan was a pointless and deceptive exercise. The subject was,
in particular, addressed by La Trobe University political scientist
Joseph Camilleri. One part of his thesis was that even under Labor,
Australia was unfit to advance the idea of an organization designed to
insulate the region form great-power ideological influence, since
Australia remained in firm military and economic alignment with
the United States. Moreover, and more trenchantly, one could

"interpret the Whitlam proposals for regional co-operation as an attempt to evade the fundamental problem confronting Australian
foreign policy, that is, its long-term attitude to the possibility of
radical social change in Southeast Asia and the Pacific Basin." That,
Camilleri argued, was what the affairs of the region were all about.[33]

Labor's approach to the twin themes of colonialism and racism was,
like its pursuit of regional arrangements in Asia and the Pacific, a
mixture of idealism and perceived practicality. In the latter sense, it
was regarded as a general yet supportive force behind Australia's
wish to influence a new comity in its own region. It also was a way of
following practices abroad that could temper Australian public pre-
judices: the construction of a qualitatively better, more humane
Australian ethos, in the desired context of a "new nationalism". We
will first look at colonialism, noticing general orientations,
characteristic policy movements and the treatment of concerns lying
in Australia's own immediate environment.

The remnants of colonialism were obnoxious to Labor's values.
They represented an older and largely unsavoury tradition. They
smacked of racial as well as economic and political exploitation. They
meant denial to native peoples of the right to choose their own
destinies. The party also thought of remaining colonialism as carrying the potential for strife that could exacerbate relations between
races and contribute to local, and possibly regional instability. Advocacy of the principle of self-determination (and frequently of independence as such) for dependent peoples had some practical value
for Australia. It identified Australia as being a nation thinking and
acting for itself, rather than as just another white and affluent
country with its own colonial heritage in New Guinea. L–CP governments had been cautious about confronting colonialism head on.
Labor, stressing its independent foreign policy credentials, felt it had
to move boldly. In Asia, where acceptance and influence were being
sought, energetic anti-colonialism (and anti-racialism) could help
Australia establish its bona fides.

The government's anti-colonialist posture was confirmed by
various deeds and gestures. Willesee's widely ranging visit to African
nations in 1973 was one such method. Under the L–CP, Department
of Foreign Affairs recommendations for ministerial visits to Africa
had been overriden. Another method lay in the government's
laudatory remarks about solidarity with Africa's colonial peoples,
with acclaim for events such as "Namibia [South-West Africa) Day",
which marked South Africa's illegal jurisdiction over the territory,
and in participation at such assemblies as the International
Conference on Colonialism and Apartheid. Various anti-colonialist
spokesmen were welcomed to Australia.

By and large, as we will shortly see, most of the practical steps available to Australia were diplomatic, whether through the United Nations or otherwise. But, in a late 1973 television interview, Whitlam went further than most of his colleagues, including Willesee, were prepared to go. He spoke about condoning revolutionary movements and characterized the Rhodesian and South African leaders as being "as bad as Hitler".[34] Anti-colonialist sentiment could have been expressed forcefully but less starkly. It created misunderstandings as to what the government really meant and triggered a flurry of domestic controversy that may have set back rather than advanced the cause of anti-colonialist and anti-racialist sentiment in Australia. It was an illustration both of Whitlam's deeply felt convictions and of his more impulsive side.

Still, the government wished to do something more dramatic than conventional anti-colonialist diplomacy allowed. When in Australia in March 1974, Tanzanian President Julius Nyere openly called for Australia to arm liberationist forces in Africa.[35] A national conference of Australian Young Labor had shortly before made the same appeal.[36] The government was prepared to do something exceptional, but not so dramatic as becoming the armourer of liberation movements. The tack chosen, upon a submission from the Department of Foreign Affairs, was to allocate $150 000 in 1974–75 for humanitarian assistance to African national liberation movements, channelled through established organizations such as the Organization of African Unity. This was eventually narrowed to mean aid for women and children of liberation movements who had temporarily settled in Zambia.[37] In essence, this was a fairly innocuous step. With the colonial winding-down process undertaken by the new Portuguese régime, not much "colonialism" remained in Africa, apart from the special circumstances in Southern Africa. Several other Western nations had previously committed funds for humanitarian purposes to liberation movements and the Australian contribution was very modest. But the gesture was there, and perhaps well-timed in anticipation of the forthcoming UN sessions, at which a major Australian role was foreshadowed

Labor's diplomacy on major colonial questions such as the Portuguese territories and Namibia could probably be described as "tempered enthusiasm". The switch from a more cautious L–CP approach at the United Nations came as soon as Labor had entered office. In January 1973, Australia rejoined the "decolonialization" committee or "Committee of Twenty-Four", from which the L–CP had withdrawn in 1969. Labor did this "because resumption of membership ·was consistent with the Government's policy of demonstrating Australia's continuing concern for the problems of decolonialisation".[38] Australia's behaviour on the committee was not, however, over-zealous. In 1975, Australian intervention helped to avert consideration of a resolution—strongly opposed by the United States—that would have affirmed the "inalienable" right of the people of Puerto Rico to self-determination and independence. Australia undertook to join the UN's Council on Namibia and supported resolutions on behalf of self-determination in the territory. In 1973, at the United Nations, Australia abstained on a resolution that welcomed Guinea Bissau's (Portuguese Guinea's) independence, on grounds that Guinea Bissau did not fulfil proper criteria for determining sovereign status. But by the middle of the next year, it accorded *de facto* recognition to the new Guinea Bissau régime. This was in keeping with prevailing *de facto* or *de jure* recognition practice among South-East Asian states, but unlike US and Western European practice. Australian spokesmen at the United Nations voiced reservations about the use of force to achieve complete decolonialization and refused to support some of the more extremely phrased resolutions. Still the government had moved a considerable distance. Australia's UN delegation reported that

> Australia emerged at this [1973] session of the Assembly as one of the two or three western countries most sympathetically disposed toward the anti-colonial causes that are a principal attraction to the third world. Its contribution to those causes was widely recognised not only as a direct one but as having the potential capacity also to influence other western countries to modify their attitudes.[39]

Closer to home, the Labor government's anti-colonial professions were put to some hard tests. In principle, Labor came to office determined to release Papua New Guinea to independence as early as possible:

> We regard it as unacceptable that Australia, of all countries, should be one of the world's last colonial powers. ... It is not only a question of our responsibilities to the people of Papua New Guinea, it is not only a question of our clear responsibilities under the United Nations Charter, it is a question of our responsibilities to ourselves.[40]

Labor eagerly accepted its predecessor's timetable of self-government for Papua New Guinea by 1 December 1973. This was met and acclaimed at the United Nations. An independence target of December 1974 was projected and various functions were rapidly devolved upon the Papua New Guinea government. But Australia had to accept some setbacks on the road to arranging a rapid and clean break for Papua New Guinea. The independence date had to be postponed. Papua New Guinea could not itself agree on the terms of a constitution and, if anything, Australia itself was chided by some PNG figures for pushing a bit too hard for quick independence.[41] Efforts by regionally based separatists to declare their own right to national identity had to be firmly rebuffed in Canberra.[42] The Australian and PNG governments wished to delineate the boundary between the two countries. In the Torres Strait, historical accident had placed some small and sparsely settled islands, which were Australian and more specifically Queensland territory, virtually at Papua New Guinea's doorstep. One solution, at least theoretically favoured by the Whitlam government as well as by the authorities in Port Moresby, would have been a transfer of these islands to Papua New Guinea. However, the affected islanders vocally resisted a change from Australian citizenship and Whitlam acknowledged that their wishes would need to be honoured.

Moreover, the position of the Queensland state government became an obstacle, whether respecting an outright transfer of the islands, or some form of settlement with Papua New Guinea short of the transfer of sovereignty. Queensland insisted that, under the Commonwealth Constitution, a state's boundaries could not be altered without the approval of the affected state's Parliament and electors, as well as that of the Commonwealth Parliament. Negotiations continued between Canberra and Brisbane, with Bjelke-Petersen making a variety of claims on Queensland's behalf, including over resource exploration and exploitation in the territorial waters off the contentious islands.

Bjelke-Petersen's position was an expression of his attachment to maximum state domain over the sea-bed. It also was an extension of his political warfare with the Whitlam government. Papua New Guinea leaders resented this intramural Australian haggling at their expense, and the inordinate delay of a settlement. The prospect of a Papua New Guinea appeal to the International Court of Justice was not ruled out. In sum, the Labor government's decolonialization effort had been flawed, and relations with a neighbouring and otherwise friendly nation were strained.[43]

Labor's handling of the Cocos (Keeling) Islands is also instructive. While the issue confirmed the government's concern for the welfare of dependent peoples, and in a sense for self-determination, it also showed that Labor was not unmindful of practical considerations. The Cocos Islands, lying in the Indian Ocean some 2700 kilometres north-west of Perth, were ceded to Australia by Britain in 1955. In 1974, a delegation representing the Committee of Twenty-Four went to the Australian Cocos. The visiting team was told that Australia intended to honour relevant UN resolutions and that the islands' future would be determined "with full regard to the freely expressed wishes of the inhabitants".[44] So far so good; standard high-principled language, and in form consistent with an earlier Australian gesture at the United Nations. Very shortly after entering office, Labor supported a UN resolution that called for self-determination and in-dependence timetables to be established for a variety of small dependent territories, including the Cocos. However, queried about this in the House, Whitlam said, rather disarmingly, that such resolutions all contained "aspects which would be impractical or irrelevant". One had to look "at the overall effect of them". If a resolution were 90 per cent acceptable, it deserved support; "It does not mean one votes for every individual aspect of it." What he meant was that acceptable resolutions were those that stated good intentions, subscribed to by an Australian government wishing to demonstrate its anti-colonial credentials. But, regarding the Cocos Islands, no consideration had been given to independence and no one seriously believed that such a step would be appropriate.[45]

Australia's reluctance to encourage independence for these islands, or even to consider a foreseeable referendum or other formalized self-determination action, was understandable. These were a group of islands with an area of 13 square kilometres, with a population of under 1000 and an indigenous economy no more diverse than a copra plantation. For over a hundred years the inhabitants had been under the seigniorial control of a succession of heads of the Clunies-Ross family, which enjoyed special privileges on the islands. There was an exceptional sense of interdependence between the indigenous Malay stock community and the Clunies-Ross establishment. The population was incredibly insular, conservative-minded and reasonably satisfied with the political *status quo*. Forced independence for the Cocos in the early or mid-1970s would, in nearly every way, have been a travesty on common sense.

Australia had other disincentives for not pushing the Cocos Islands out of its orbit. Spurred by the UN visit, Canberra decided to proceed with a variety of social, economic and political reforms, on the islands, though gradually, and not so as to upset the intricate lacework of relationships there. If and when the islands were to "self-determine" themselves into self-government or independence, Australia would at least have been in close charge long enough to set up an infrastructure amenable to more modern outlooks and practices. In August 1975, the Special Minister of State, Senator Douglas McClelland, visited the islands. He was unable to persuade John Clunies-Ross to undertake meaningful reforms. The following month, legislation was introduced in Parliament to strip the Clunies-Ross family of some of its powers. Essentially, it was a step towards enlarging the official Australian presence, providing residents with more genuinely consultative opportunities and towards expediting social reforms.[46] The prospect of eventual self-determination did not, however, arise. The Cocos also were valued for their use as an international stock quarantine facility. The islands' demonstrated security significance in both world wars had declined somewhat, but still mattered. This was the official opinion in the Department of Defence and was variously shared by ministers. Their location in the Indian Ocean placed them in an area of increasing super-power naval rivalry. The major landing-strip was already being used by British, New Zealand and American military aircraft, as well as by Australia. The islands' Indian Ocean surveillance potential, especially after the reopening of the Suez Canal, was believed to be considerable. In and of themselves, such considerations outweighed the islands' economic liability to Australia.[47]

Far more serious strains, and dilemmas, were imposed on the Labor government's diplomacy by Portuguese Timor. There arose a measure of conflict between "principles" and even competing appraisals of expediency. The issue brings to mind the remark of one highly perceptive observer—himself by no means unfriendly towards the government—that Labor's idealism and sense of principle were less manifest the closer and more intimate for Australia was an object of diplomatic attention.

The western half of Timor was Indonesian. The eastern portion was Portuguese from the sixteenth century. In the 1960s, the ALP, and Whitlam, had generally taken a conventional anti-colonial stance on Timor. After coming to office, the Labor government did not assert its indignation over East Timor as forcefully as it did over Portugal's African territories. Timor was close to home in more than one way. It was only 580 kilometres from Darwin and had been a staging-base for the Japanese in the Second World War. Unlike the Cocos, it was not quite a micro-country, with 19 200 square kilometres and a population of 650 000. Australia had established close and profitable links with Portuguese Timor, in air communications, in commerce and in investment. Both BHP and the Melbourne-based Timor Oil were engaged in mineral exploitation activity.

The 1974 coup in Portugal changed the entire Timorese picture. The new régime in Lisbon was quite happy to promise a genuine act of self-determination. Parties and movements surfaced. They represented pro-independence, home rule and association with Indonesia options. One group even favoured association with Australia. The government in Canberra was pleased that the yoke of colonialism was being lifted and that an expression of self-determination was foreshadowed. What queered the pitch was that all available options had drawbacks. Australian thinking was constrained not only by what a particular political outcome would mean to Australia directly but to other neighbouring states as well, notably Indonesia. Too much was at stake to permit Canberra a totally detached attitude. Continued association with Portugal seemed unreliable as a long-term proposition. It could mean economic neglect and the eventual surfacing of revolutionary forces. There were distinct Australian economic interests involved, which might be sacrificed if an independent yet politically inexperienced and vulnerable East Timor were to succumb to a radical administration. A potentially unstable, economically fragile Timor, so close to Australia, could carry adverse security implications. Moreover, there was Indonesia's attitude. Indonesia insisted it had no claim to lay against East Timor, but quickly came to favour a political outcome that would make it Indonesian. Jakarta felt that a decision favouring independence could restimulate secessionist feeling on Indonesia's own scattered home islands. It was very much worried that an independent Timor could go politically radical, even communist, creating unacceptable security risks to an Indonesia that, according to its leadership, had in the mid-1960s barely escaped a communist takeover. It was uneasy about possible secessionist and security implications for Papua New Guinea, with which Indonesia shared a border. It was also suggested that association with Indonesia, more than independent status or home rule, would be more economically sensible for Timor. The Australian Labor government took these Indonesian anxieties to heart. For Australia, Indonesia was an extremely important near neighbour, the key nation in South-East Asia, and the nation which required special handling in the furtherance of such Australian projects as a broad Asian–Pacific forum.[48] When he visited Jakarta in September 1974, Whitlam acknowledged to his hosts that the best option for Portuguese Timor was connection with Indonesia, qualified only by the taking of such a step through a genuine expression of self-determination.[49] Thus the ALP's commitment to self-determination was fulfilled, or so it seemed, but not its attachment to the principle of independence or to an open non-prejudgmental position.

If anything, Australia's endorsement of a pro-Indonesian solution sparked Indonesian enthusiasm for obtaining the desired outcome. Apprehension rose in various Australian and other quarters that Indonesia would not stop with a propaganda campaign in Timor, but might try to infiltrate agents or even resort to military force, perhaps pre-emptively. Such prospects disturbed a number of Pacific nations, which did not overlook Australia's indirect hand in the matter, as well as its ostensible support for substituting Indonesian for Portuguese overlordship. Imputations of this nature were not helpful in advancing Australia's campaign for regional co-operation. Within Australia, the complexity of the Timor question was highlighted by serious and at times brusque differences of opinion rendered by public servants. Foreign Affairs had advocated a self-determination positon for Australia, with a favoured outcome being association with Indonesia. Whitlam started by agreeing on both counts, but reversed their recommended Foreign Affairs order of importance. The Defence Department was sceptical about encouraging the Indonesians in any way, but apparently at the early key stage made no formal submission on the matter. There was unease within sections of the Australian intelligence community that their warnings against a pro-Indonesian posture had not only not been accepted but had hardly geen given attention. When Indonesian declamations rose, a "we told you so" reaction was detectable.

Political fall-out in Australia was noticeable. The Australian left felt that the government's behaviour on the issue was powerful testimony of its false radical colours. The left had been fervent in its opposition to Australian meddling in other people's affairs. On this issue, a representative radical-left document made the striking demand that the Australian government "must make very clear to the Indonesian generals that any invasion [of Timor] will be resisted militarily [*sic*] by Australia".[50]

Doubts about the wisdom of the government's position were strengthened within the ALP parliamentary caucus, in part through conversations with a touring pro-independence Timorese political figure. A reasoned brief, urging caution, was circulated among parliamentarians by a research officer of the Parliamentary Library, who had once been in Foreign Affairs and had served at the Dili consulate in Timor.[51] Some Liberal parliamentarians became interested in the discussions and exchanges of documents going round Parliament House and a mixed ALP–Liberal parliamentary delegation was planned for a fact-finding trip to Timor. For various reasons the trip was postponed and eventually a delegation composed exclusively of ALP parliamentarians went. Among their findings was that independence was the strongest popular sentiment on East Timor.[52] The opposition's tactical position on the Timor question was comfortable. Not being the government, the L–CP was not required to make the hard choices. Instead, Peacock took the high ground. Without actaully condemning a pro-Indonesian settlement, he chided Labor for prejudging and constraining an act of self-determination. He used Timor as another instance of the government's "inconsistency" and "hypocrisy", of mouthing grand anti-colonialist principles but behaving otherwise. Said Peacock: "Mr Whitlam's sanctimonious self-righteousness does not bear scrutiny."[53]

The government was for some time cross-pressured by conflicting official advice. It was challenged from within its own party and within radical ranks, mocked for its inconsistency by the opposition and compelled to readjust brave principles to pragmatic considerations. The government eventually seemed to soften its position. It backed away from announced advocacy of an "Indonesian" solution and emphasized the requirement of self-determination. It involved itself in discussions with the Portuguese and Indonesian governments and, with the latter, stressed that duress should not be applied. It seemed to move toward J. A. C. Mackie's advice that "the way the issue is resolved matters to us far more than the conclusions reached".[54]

That impression, however, was put to a very severe test by early August 1975, when civil war broke out on East Timor among competing groups. The residual Portuguese administration possessed neither will not ability to intervene. The tone of the Labor government's public position was set by Whitlam late in August. Australia desired a genuine act of self-determination in the territory. It hoped that all concerned parties, including Indonesia, would come to a peaceful understanding. Australia understood Indonesia's concern that Timor should not become a source of instability. But Australia would not intervene, either in a peace-keeping or even in a mediatory role. Australia could not, Whitlam said, be compromised by acquiring a quasi-colonial role or a *de facto* responsibility for East Timor.[55]

With very little variation, the government publicly held to these precepts during its remaining time in office, as the strife continued and Indonesia began to insinuate itself more directly into the conflict. A few days before the Australian election of 11 December, when the caretaker Fraser government was in office, Indonesia moved in in strength. Fretilin (Revolutionary Front for an Independent East Timor), the group that had won out in the civil conflict and had proclaimed independence, was defeated by Indonesian forces and East Timor eventually was incorporated into Indonesia.

Two aspects of the Labor government's position are of special interest to us. One is Whitlam's aversion to involving Australia in anything that could smack of intervention, an intervention that, however benign, could suggest a quasi-colonial role. Such feelings were not only consistent with the international image Whitlam wished to mould for Australia but were personal for him as an individual. [56]

The second point of interest is the government's attitude towards Indonesia's professed interests and Jakarta's involvement in Timor. Whitlam certainly did not favour a forcible Indonesian take-over of East Timor, but he never rescinded his 1974 view that the best solution would be Timorese association with Indonesia. This view became increasingly firm within the Foreign Affairs Department. While it was generally felt in Canberra that Fretilin was not a dangerously radical movement, Whitlam and his official advisers accepted the Indonesian position that this served as no guarantee for the future.

Quintessentially, Australia wished to placate Indonesia. Despite protestations to the contrary, there was suspicion among observers that Whitlam was willing to countenance an Indonesian take-over; concern for keeping on side with Indonesia blended with Whitlam's aversion to intruding Australia on to the scene.[57] Classified materials leaked in 1976 indicated that in October 1975, the Labor government had refused to make a public disclosure of and to express its regret over information that Indonesia was militarily involved in Portuguese Timor.[58]

Strong internal evidence tends to corroborate speculations that during the civil strife on Timor, Whitlam privately communicated to the Indonesians that he would not take umbrage if Indonesia intervened. It is also believed that he asked the Indonesians not to embarrass his government by intervening in force before an anticipated Australian election.

In the Labor government's mind, a determined anti-racialist policy was the natural complement of anti-colonialism and perhaps of even greater importance. Racism was believed to be inherently contemptible. Attacks on it, at home and abroad, were needed in order to make the Australian public more tolerant and humane; again, this was part of Labor's new nationalist conception for Australia. The image of an Australia conscientiously challenging racialism helped to cultivate an image that would enhance the nation's standing and influence abroad, especially among Third World Nations. Racialism could be the cause of pernicious, dislocative international tension. This could work contrary to Australia's interests, both at large and close to home. Australia was a white nation with a conspicuous history of racism. If it did not make its anti-racialist position abundantly clear, it was conceivable that, should there be strife in the region, its racial attitude could be bluntly called into question.

With these incentives in mind, Labor undertook to attack racism domestically, as well as *vis-à-vis* other countries. Whitlam s summary was that

> By giving the Aborigines the same status before the law and the same
> political, economic and social opportunities as white Australians, by revising immigration laws and procedures to eliminate the racial criterion, and
> by demonstrating our sympathy and understanding of the aspirations of
> the black Africans, the Government is making what it feels to be the most
> helpful contribution to the lessening of international suspicion, fear and
> hostility.[59]

The government's domestic efforts were, *inter alia*, constrained by political and constitutional factors arising out of the federal distribution of jurisdiction. It therefore could not, with an executive or

legislative sweep, institute all reforms it wanted. It worked to persuade states to expunge their residual, racially discriminatory legislation. Because of both federal factors and an unconvinced Senate, it
faced considerable delay in winning needed concurrence for the
legislative implementation of the international convention relative to
the elimination of all forms of racial discrimination.[60] The Racial
Discrimination Bill was finally enacted into law in mid-1975 and took
effect shortly before Labor was evicted from government.

The government gave serious attention to Aboriginal improvement
in Australia, though the results were mixed. Here we limit ourselves
to brief mention of government attitudes and practices bearing on external policy. We find encouragement and funding for Aboriginal
delegation visits overseas and for an Aboriginal cultural festival in
black Africa. We also find a concern for traditional Aboriginal sites
and for Aboriginal claims to land rights and entitlement to proceeds
relative to mining operations, especially in the federally controlled
Northern Territory. Such considerations impinged on foreign investment policy and on mineral sales to overseas customers. For instance,
in 1974, restraints were imposed on the exploitation of rich uranium
deposits at the Northern Territory site of Nabarlek, situated on sacred
Aboriginal lands.[61]

It is in its immigration policy that the government hoped to make
an especially prominent impact. Some of its steps were largely symbolic, but still of value. As of 1975, all persons entering Australia (except from New Zealand) had to obtain visas. This was done for several
reasons, one of which was anti-racial. The step revised a long-
standing discriminatory practice under which *European* British subjects (Commonwealth citizens) and Irish citizens, but not non-
European Commonwealth citizens, could enter Australia without visa
formalities. The removal of this distinction was regarded as a move
towards a thoroughly non-discriminatory immigration policy.

More substantive were questions bearing on opportunities for non-
Europeans to migrate to Australia. As we saw, L–CP governments had
considerably liberalized non-European migration and some thousands
of non-European were entering the country before Labor was elected.
The new government's Immigration Minister, Al Grassby, became an
energetic apostle of breaking down remaining barriers. It was
emphasized that the screening of prospective immigrants was to disregard ethnic, racial and other considerations. Non-Europeans were
placed on the same footing as Europeans in their entitlement to assisted passage. Nettlesome regulations that, in particular, affected
short-term Japanese business visitors were redone. Grassby himself
toured Asia in mid-1973, to explain the government's commitment to
anti-discriminatory principles and practices. The government's ap-

proach did not go unnoticed or unpraised. Singapore's Lee Kuan-yew, on various counts a critic of Whitlam's foreign policy, acclaimed the "decisive break with the white Australia polocy" and related issues of race and colour.[62] The favourable response from the Philippines was especially gratifying. It was there that Australia's discriminatory policies had been most acutely felt.[63] Labor's intentions nevertheless had to contend with some distractions. Grassby was defeated in the 1974 election. The Immigration Department was then merged with the Department of Labour. As we will notice in more detail later, the Foreign Affairs Department expressed a wish to take on a large portion of responsibility from Immigration, notably in the handling of non-assisted migrant visas. The belief (though only one reason for the proposed change) was that Foreign Affairs' commitment to non-European migrants was more positive than Immigration's. Therefore, an unquestionably more progressive approach would result if Foreign Affairs had a prominent hand in administering migration. A compromise of a sort was worked out after considerable bureaucratic scrapping. In the end, administrative practices came to conform to policy intentions.[64] We should also notice that the government's aim was not simply to eliminate discriminatory practices against non-Europeans but to provide visible proof of good intentions in the actual numbers of non-Europeans coming to Australia. One such opportunity arose from a proposal by the Leyland Motor Corporation to import a thousand or more skilled Filipino workers for its Sydney factory. Whitlam was enthusiastic, and the Philippine government gave its support. A pilot group was to be brought in. And so it was, but not without reservations being raised by the Australian Council of Trade Unions (ACTU). Job protection for Australians was the argument, though a number of commentators thought they heard sounds of an incompletely interred White Australia outlook.[65] By the second half of 1974, the Australian economy had taken a serious downturn. Unemployment rose to disturbing proportions and there were company failures, Leyland among them. This meant the shelving of special foreign-worker projects. It also had consequences for non-European migration at large. Economic constraints forced the government to curtail the annual migration intake. Thus although non-European applications for entry into Australia rose substantially over earlier times, the available number of places for migrants, regardless of race, shrunk. The tangible "proof of good intentions" desired by the ALP government was rendered less abundant.

The Labor government also strived to assume an anti-racialist posture in its relationship with other countries, notably Rhodesia and South Africa. Willesee's 1973 African tour was partially designed to set the mood, to knock over traces of Australia's racist tag. The government also tried to set the mood of sympathy for its anti-racialist and anti-colonialist causes through such symbolic means as referring to African countries by their African rather than their more familiar Western names. Hence the use of Namibia rather than South-West Africa. When questioned on why Australia referred to Rhodesia as Zimbabwe, Whitlam answered that "the overwhelming black majority of the people of that territory have adopted the African word 'Zimbabwe' as the name for their country, and the Australian Government sees no reason why, for everyday usage, their wishes should not be respected."[66] Both in regard to Rhodesia and to South Africa, however, Labour found its policies bedeviled by political, legal and material constraints.

On Rhodesia, the government quickly moved at the United Nations to the side of Afro–Asian nations, with far less equivocation than had L–CP governments. It did not favour armed intervention, but among its actions was support for efforts to broaden sanctions against Rhodesia, condemnation of the presence of South African security forces in Rhodesia and support for sanctions against Portugal for breaking the international embargo against Rhodesia. It endorsed resolutions calling for the rupture of all communications with Rhodesia and for the denial of landing rights to national air-carriers of countries that themselves allowed landing rights to Rhodesia. At the 1973 Commonwealth Prime Ministers Conference, Australia backed Canada's idea to send a Commonwealth police force to Rhodesia to supervise an eventual independence agreement.[67] At the 1975 Commonwealth Conference, Australia agreed with all other participants to assist newly independent Mozambique to blockade Rhodesian exports.[68]

Australia's implementation of such sentiments was generally but not invariably strict.[69] The government swiftly banned further sales of wheat to Rhodesia. The L–CP's previously stated humanitarian exceptions were no longer said to apply,[70] and trade sanctions were otherwise honoured. Strict implementation of other anti-Rhodesian measures encountered some difficulties and at times created embarrassment for the government. Almost immediately after achieving office, Labor painted itself into a predicament over a group of Rhodesian Girls' Brigade (church and missionary work) youngsters who wished to spend several days in Sydney on their way to an international congress in New Zealand. The government invoked a *discretionary* 1968 UN resolution that had urged that Rhodesian passports not be honoured. But the girls were travelling on British and South African, not Rhodesian passports, and at all events could hardly be regarded as missionaries of racialism. In the end, the government allowed them to remain overnight in Sydney.[71] The government also had some awkward moments with the Sydney-based Rhodesian Information Centre, which in some respects was acting as a *de facto* Rhodesian mission. Critics of the office, centred on the "Alternative Rhodesian Information Centre", wanted it shut down, or at least immobilized. The federal government tried to cut off postal and telephone services to the Centre, but the High Court ruled that this was improper, since the Centre had broken no existing legislation. In mid-1974, in the New South Wales state courts, the Centre lost its privilege to register its title as a business name. The action was welcomed by Willesee, who saw it as a step towards fulfilment of Australia's UN obligations and a blow at the Centre and its *de facto* Rhodesian government sponsors.[72] However, later efforts to delete the Centre's entry from Sydney telephone directories again ran foul of the High Court.

The government's approach to contact between private Australians and Rhodesia added further complications. Only very rarely were visas granted to Rhodesians and in 1975, a Rhodesian delegation was barred from attending an international air safety conference in Melbourne. But in 1974, it had been disclosed that former Australian military officers were being recruited for service with Rhodesian forces. This not only violated UN injunctions but Australian law as well. Access had apparently been gained to confidential Australian army personnel files. The recruiting was believed to be carried out occasionally by mail from Rhodesia (not all of which was being blocked by the government), through the weakened but not liquidated (Rhodesian) Information Centre and through South African contacts in Australia.[73] The government was obviously concerned and launched an investigation, but continued Rhodesian access to Australia had facilitated the recruiting efforts in the first instance. The government also took steps to block the publication of advertisements designed to encourage travel or emigration to Rhodesia, or the sale of tickets thereto. This practice had been begun under the L–CP, consistent with prevailing UN resolutions, but observance by airlines and travel agencies was found to be incomplete. The Labor government applied considerable but not legally enforceable suasion to accomplish this purpose. The Department of Foreign Affairs co-operated in its enforcement and groups such as Action for World Development exerted their own influence towards discouraging contravention.[74]

The government's overall efforts towards Rhodesia reflected the various difficulties inherent in the situation. At times it seemed zealous, at other times constrained by lack of legal power, or by hesitation to bring forward appropriate legislation, or by the ingenuity of the Rhodesians and their supporters. It wished to honour

UN obligations, but ran foul of criticism that, as a party, Labor had a professed commitment to "open government", but was willing to restrict the ventilation of certain "unpopular" ideas, or the right of Australians to travel where and how they chose. It found itself attacked by some groups, both radical and otherwise, as being pusillanimous, and by others, such as the conservative Australian–Rhodesia Association, for proceeding too harshly, or indeed for proceeding at all.

Labor's approach towards South Africa and its racial policies had both stringent and mild features. Some would have suggested that the approach bordered on the cynical, others that it remained principled throughout, and that what seemed to be exceptions were more properly classifiable as common sense than as waffling or expediency.

One area where the government took a reasonably hard line was in sport. Its position was made clear almost immediately after taking office and sharply diverged from earlier L–CP policy. Individual sportsmen (such as the golfer Gary Player) were not barred from competing in Australia, nor individual Australians from competing in South Africa. However, racially selected sporting teams were excluded from Australia and their transit through Australia to other destinations was precluded.[75] While the principal target of the ban was South Africa, it was at least in theory made generally applicable, for instance to Uganda.[76] Legally, of course, the government's right to deny visas was irreproachable. In early 1974, as the result of official pressure, the Lawn Tennis Association of Australia withdrew its intention to send players to South Africa. Some months later, the government clashed with the Australian Cricket Board over sending a team to South Africa and the Board relented. The government could in theory have denied passports, but this particular legal recourse was distasteful to it. The L–CP opposition, never reconciled to a policy of excluding South African sporting visitors, was likewise displeased with efforts to dissuade Australian teams from playing in South Africa.[77] At all events, the government's position on sport was more than a gesture of resentment against apartheid. It was felt to be part of an international effort to force changes in South Africa's approach to race in sport and to obviate the possibility that African, Asian and Caribbean nations might impose a boycott on playing against Australian teams should Australia turn a blind eye towards South African practices.

Moreover, the government was prepared to grant asylum to South Africans who claimed persecution in their own country. Neville Curtis, a radical white South African student leader, was allowed asylum in 1974. He then very quickly became associated with the Campaign Against Racial Exploitation and proceeded to write and speak on the need for Australia to pursue a tenacious anti-apartheid South African policy.[78]

Also reasonably stringent was Australia's diplomatic posture towards South Africa. Bilateral diplomatic relations were not severed, as indeed no UN resolution required this. But, in 1974, in accordance with a UN resolution that enjoined members to sever all military and defence links with South Africa, South Africa was told that it could not replace its retiring military attaché in Canberra. It was at the United Nations itself that Australia moved against South Africa, first firmly, then dramatically. Beginning in 1973, Australia co-sponsored a number of anti-South African apartheid resolutions. Only in one instance did it fail to endorse an anti-apartheid resolution, and then it abstained rather than voting against. It objected to features of a resolution declaring that only the liberation movements recognized by the Organization of African Unity were authentic representatives of the South African people and to features intended to justify the use of force in South Africa and South Africa's total international isolation. A year later, at the twenty-ninth regular UN session, Australia took the leap. While it voted against suspending the South African delegation's credentials as long as South Africa remained in the United Nations, on the Security Council it voted for a resolution calling for South Africa's expulsion from the world body.

It was a most controversial step, which the government took pains to explain. South Africa had been following repugnant and illegal practices for an inordinately long time. No amount of pleading and scolding seemed to work. This, it was said, undermined the argument that South Africa could be made more responsive to international opinion if it were in rather than outside the United Nations. Also, while Australia endorsed the principle of universality of membership in the United Nations, this "had to be weighed against the effects of the standing and efficacy of the Organization of continued membership by a nation which had clearly violated the Charter and showed no intention of reversing its policies."[79]

Was Australia's vote as simple and straightforward as that? It apparently was primarily a Whitlam decision, taken in the face of some misgivings on Willesee's part. The original Foreign Affairs submission on the matter offered no recommendations. Whitlam determined that Australia would not allow itself to be compromised, and would not abstain. Was the step taken to gain the best of both worlds, to demonstrate vividly Australia's anti-racialist credentials before Third World nations, while knowing that South Africa would not, in the event, be expelled, since a veto would be cast by one or more permanent members of the Security Council? Although Britain, France and the United States all in fact cast vetoes, the answer to the question is

almost surely not. It is understood that Foreign Affairs calculations
pointed to at most one and possibly no outright negative votes among
the permanent members of the Security Council. There was nothing
approaching a foregone conclusion that the motion to expel would be
lost. But did Australia have a special purpose in courting the Third
World by voting to expel South Africa? One possible explanation was
an alleged wish to gather support for Willesee's election to the
Presidency of the UN General Assembly at the following year's session. This was a most unlikely motive. Firstly, Australia would have
stood as the nominee of the "West Europe and Others" group, whose
turn it was to hold the Presidency. On precedent, other groupings at
the United Nations went along with the nominee of the group eligible
in rotation. Secondly, Australia's vote in the Security Council ran
counter to the wishes of France and Britain, nations that belonged to
the "WEO" group and whose possible pique at Australia could have
caused them to resist Willesee's candidacy. On its part, the United
States unsuccessfully tried to limit Australia to an abstention on the
expulsion motion.[80] Was Australia working another angle, such as
getting appropriately exercised about South Africa at the United Nations and therefore ingratiating itself with Afro-Asians, while comfor-
tably retaining economic links with South Africa, plus representation
in both countries that helped to keep such profitable relations alive
and well? Australian–South African economic links are a large subject in itself, and we pass to it now.

The government's position on trade with South Africa was quite
clear. Cairns, when Minister for Overseas Trade, said that one could
not stop trading with countries simply because of disapproval for
their politics. "If we did that, we would stop trading with just about
every country except Sweden and Switzerland."[81] Whitlam and
others added that Australia would impose a trade embargo if it were
sanctioned by the United Nations, and if South Africa's major trading
partners did so.[82] Much the same attitude was expressed by the
ACTU. Australia's trade with South Africa in 1973–74 amounted to
$91 million in exports and $36 million in imports. Australia had
become a significant exporter of cars, car parts, machinery and other
products of the sort for which it especially wished to find overseas
outlets. It imported a number of important minerals from South
Africa, including a considerable part of its industrial diamond and
asbestos requirements.[83] Moreover, as J. D. B. Miller pointed out, the
International Wool Secretariat, with headquarters in London and
financed by Australia, New Zealand and South Africa, was largely run
by Australia. It was the one international organization "in which
Australia could strike an effective blow at vital South African interests; but since these interests [research, publicity and marketing on

behalf of wool] are largely identical with Australia's, any blow at South Africa would create opposition within Australia itself, and would weaken the combined front of wool exporters struggling against the advance of synthetic fibres."[84]

The Overseas Trade Department's journal *Overseas Trading* carried promotional material on trade with South Africa and Australia's two trade commission offices in South Africa conducted considerable promotional activity. In 1974, the government declared that in future the trade commissions would act simply as facilitating bodies. In 1975, the government went one small step further. While retaining its facility in Johannesburg, it withdrew the trade commissioner from Cape Town. Impatience with what was described as half-measures was expressed among the government's critics. In 1975, the Campaign Against Racial Exploitation launched a programme to discourage public buying of selected South African imports.[85]

The Australian Labor government also perceived considerable national economic interest in not disturbing Australian investment operating in South Africa, especially since Australian overseas investment had become a prominent objective of the government and South African investments were generally highly profitable. This was challenged not only from conventional radical quarters but from among a large section of Australian church opinion. The argument was that such investment strengthened the grip of the South African régime, while at the same time tolerating procedures that exploited the native South African workforce. The government in Canberra took two slight remedial measures. It "ceased to encourage to subsidise investment by Australian companies in South Africa."[86] Moreover, Willesee wrote to Australian companies with subsidiaries or associated companies in South Africa, asking them to improve pay and working standards for their black employees.[87] The appeal was purely hortatory; no sanctions were to be applied in the event on non-compliance.

The government also assumed an essentially *laissez-faire* attitude towards South African Airways (SAA) flights to and from Australia. The principal argument for a hard line was that this link contributed to the South African tourist trade and in turn to South Africa's efforts to place a benign facade on its apartheid policies. The government fell back on a familiar argument: There were no UN prohibitions on international air arrangements with South Africa or its international flag-carrier and many lines flew to and from South Africa. Until such time as this position changed, Australia was not prepared to undertake a unilateral shift.[88] There also were practical considerations. If SAA were denied rights in Australia, Qantas rights in South Africa would undoubtedly be shut off. This would injure a profitable route and force a diversion that would require giving reciprocal landing-rights in Australia to East African Airways, thus creating competition for Qantas on the Australia–Britain run. When SAA's Australian rights licence renewal came up in 1974, it was granted. The following year, Cabinet deferred any decision on changes in airline policy.[89]

We asked earlier whether Australia's 1974 UN vote on South African expulsion might have had some bearing on Australia's economic ties with South Africa. The above narrative suggests that, in every major instance of economic and commercial liaison with South Africa, the ALP government refused to damage the relationship. Economically, its reasons were sound. Departmentally, Overseas Trade was disposed to stick to established links, and on available evidence so was Cairns personally. Once he took over the portfolio in late 1974, Frank Crean was more disposed to considering a stronger position. Foreign Affairs did not recommend breaking economic ties, but was not rigid on the subject. Furthermore, the government's position was honest, insofar as there were no UN instructions requiring a different course of action. The letter to Australian subsidiaries in South Africa, and the curtailment of trade commission functions in South Africa, were announced virtually on the eve of the UN session at which Australia voted to expel South Africa. This could be interpreted as a clever strategy· Win friends among Afro-Asian nations at the United Nations, tinker a bit to soften official acquiescence in Australian economic ties with South Africa and thereby insulate Australia from criticism, at home or abroad, that the government was not "doing enough" or living up to its avowed anti-racialist principles. Although plausible, this interpretation is not satisfactory and no corroboration could be taken for it from internal evidence. The minor screw-tightening announced in September 1974 came after many months of protest and lobbying by opposed interests and the company letter·had been in preparation for some time before it was revealed. Moreover, the decision to vote against South Africa at the United Nations was almost certainly still unsettled when the economic decisions were announced. Indeed, it would have been somewhat out of character for the Labor government to have planned and stage-managed such an elaborate strategy. The simple explanation of the government's behaviour is probably the closest to the truth. Labor was pained by apartheid, did something to express its feelings, in principle sympathized with those who wanted more drastic, punitive action, but believed that the price of an economic war against South Africa was excessive. As on a number of racial and colonial issues with which it dealt, Labor observed both principle and practicality.

NOTES

1. For an overview, see J. Knight, "Australia and Proposals for Regional Consultation and Co-operation and Co-operation in the Asian and Pacific Area", *Australian Outlook* 28 (December 1974): 259–73.
2. E.G. Whitlam, "Opening Address", in G. McCarthy, ed., *Foreign Policy for Australia: Choices for the Seventies* (Sydney: Angus and Robertson, 1973, p. 6.
3. Whitlam's Kuala Lumpur press conference of 30 January 1974, in Department of Foreign Affairs memorandum.
4. See B. Juddery's discussion, *Canberra Times*, 4 April 1973.
5. See Whitlam, *Commonwealth [Australian] Parliamentary Debates (APD)*, House of Representatives (HR) (9 October 1973), p. 1812; and *APD*, HR (2 September 1975), pp. 894–95).
6. For instance, Whitlam, "Opening Address", in *Foreign Policy for Australia*, ed. McCarthy, p. 6; Whitlam, "Australia's Foreign Policy: New Directions, New Definitions", 24th Roy Milne Memorial Lecture, Brisbane, 30 November 1973 (Melbourne: AIIA, 1973) pp. 11–12; and D. Willesee (untitled AIIA conference paper, Adelaide: June 1974), p. 11.
7. P. King, "Whither Whitlam?" *International Affairs* 29 (Summer 1974): 434.
8. Whitlam's Manila press conference of 12 February 1974, transcript, p. 4.
9. On the Australian–Indonesian–ASEAN connection, see J.A.C. Mackie, "Australia's Relations with Indonesia: Principles and Policies. I", *Australian Outlook* 28 (April 1974): 11–13.
10. For a review of ASEAN's work, see J. Rees, *Canberra Times*, 19 April 1974, and M. Richardson, Melbourne *Age*, 10 and 16 October 1975.
11. For instance, Whitlam's Jakarta press conference of 22 February 1973, transcript, p. 3; and his speech in Manila of 11 February 1974, in *Australia and South-East Asia* (Canberra: Department of Foreign Affairs, 1974), p. 48.
12. See *Australian Foreign Affairs Record (AFAR)* 44 (September 1973): 609–11; and *AFAR* 45 (March 1974): 157; Whitlam, *APD*, HR (20 March 1974), p. 687; W.D. Forsyth, *Canberra Times*, 4 March 1975; and K. McGregor, *Australian Financial Review*, 29 September 1975.
13. See M. Richardson, Melbourne *Age*, 26 April 1973
14. *Canberra Times*, 6 February 1974.
15. D. Willesee, address to ECAFE, 12 April 1973, in Department of Foreign Affairs, *News Release*, no. M/70 (3 May 1973), pp. 2–3. Emphasis added. Also see R. Duffield, *Australian*, 13 April 1973.
16. See M. Richardson, *Australian Financial Review*, 23 July 1973.
17. L. Oakes and D. Solomon, *Grab for Power: Election '74* (Melbourne: Cheshire, 1974), p. 104.
18. See, for instance, M. Richardson, Melbourne *Age*, 27 February 1973; and C. Burns, Melbourne *Age*, 8 August 1973.
19. Whitlam's Peking press conference of 4 November 1973, in *AFAR* 44 (November 1973): 771–72. For the government's assessment of the project shortly before Whitlam was dismissed, see Whitlam, *APD*, HR (2 September 1975), p. 897.
20. P. Kelly, *Australian*, 15 February 1974.
21. For instance, P. Webster, *Australian*, 20 June 1973.
22. For instance, J. Farquharson, *Canberra Times*, 18 October 1974.
23. For a summary of South-East Asian reactions, see Knight, "Australia and Proposals for Regional Consultation ... " pp. 263–70. For ASEAN reactions to post-Vietnam Asia, see B. Wilson, Melbourne *Sun News-Pictorial*, 14 May 1975 and *New York Times*, 10 June 1975.
24. For analyses of Indonesia's proposal, see P. Hastings, *Sydney Morning Herald*, 12 November 1973 and 15 March 1974; and R. Muntu, *Australian*, 5 September 1974.
25. N. Kirk, "New Zealand and South-East Asia: A Policy for the Seventies", address to Council of Returned Services Association, Wellington, 12 June 1973, New Zealand Ministry of Foreign Affairs document, pp. 4–6; and J.A. Walding, address to Asian Studies conference, Auckland, 5 July 1974, transcript, pp. 6–8.
26. A. Somare, "The Emerging Role of Papua New Guinea in World Affairs", 25th Roy Milne Memorial Lecture, Melbourne, 14 June 1974, (Melbourne, AIIA, 1974,), p.

13; A.M. Kiki, press conference account, Melbourne *Age*, 5 August 1974. Also see comment in J. Verrier, "Priorities in Papua New Guinea's Evolving Foreign Policy: Some Legacies and Lessons of History", *Australian Outlook* 28 (December 1974): 298–303.
27. Whitlam, *APD*, HR (18 July 1974), p. 459.
28. For instance, W. McMahon's article, *Sydney Morning Herald*, 3 March 1973; and Snedden's and Fraser's press conferences, Perth *West Australian*, 23 February 1973 and Melbourne *Age*, 26 July 1973, respectively.
29. Derived from non-attributable source.
30. On his ASEAN–South Pacific Forum idea, see his press conference remarks, Melbourne *Age*, 1 February 1974. For his regional development ideas, see his address to the Victorian branch of the AIIA, 7 March 1974, transcript, pp. 14–15.
31. Derived from non-attributable source.
32. A. Peacock, "Australia and South-East Asia—an Alternative View" (AIIA conference paper, Melbourne, May 1975), p. 8.
33. J. Camilleri, "A New Australian Foreign Policy?", *Arena* no. 31 (1973), p. 14. Also see his "In Search of a Foreign Policy", *Arena*, nos. 32–33 (1973), pp. 75–76.
34. Interview with Lord Chalfont, broadcast in London on 11 December 1973, recorded in Sydney on 16 September 1973; in Department of Foreign Affairs memorandum.
35. *Sydney Morning Herald*, 22 March 1974.
36. Melbourne *Age*, 28 January 1974.
37. See Whitlam, *APD*, HR (22 October 1974), p. 2622; and Willesee's remarks in Department of Foreign Affairs, *News Release* no. M/160 (22 December 1974).
38. Whitlam, *APD*, HR (10 October 1974), p. 1723.
39. Twenty-Eighth Regular Session of the General Assembly of the United Nations, New York, 18 September to 18 December 1973, *Report of the Australian Delegation* (Canberra: 1974), p. 15. On colonial and racial questions at the United Nations, see C. Clark, "Labor's Policy at the United Nations", *Australia's Neighbours*, 4th series, no. 89 (February–March 1974), pp. 5–6. For a review of Australia's uses of the United Nations, see former UN Ambassador Sir Laurence McIntyre's article, *Canberra Times*, 16 May 1975.
40. Whitlam's remarks in Jakarta, 22 February 1973, *AFAR* 44 (February 1973): 99.
41. For a résumé of these problems, see A. Aston, *Australian Financial Review*, 28 August 1974 and 3 June 1975.
42. *Sydney Morning Herald*, 20 January 1975; *Australian Financial Review*, 12 August 1975.
43. For illustrative comment, see D.J. Murphy, "Problems in Australian Foreign Policy, January to June 1973", *Australian Journal of Politics and History* 19 (December 1973): 336–37; B. Toohey, *Australian Financial Review*, 12 December 1974; F. Cranston, *Canberra Times*, 13 August 1975; and R. Skelton, Melbourne *Age*, 11 November 1975. For the federal government's exposition, see Whitlam, *APD*, HR (9 October 1975), pp. 1991–98.
44. Whitlam, *APD*, HR (23 August 1974), p. 1205.
45. Whitlam, *APD*, HR (17 May 1973), p. 2255.
46. Australia's reform programme is contained in its report of 12 November 1974 to the Committee of Twenty-four. See "Report of the U.N. Visiting Mission to Cocos: Australian Statement", Department of Foreign Affairs *New Release*, no. D/26, (13 November 1974). For the government's position in late 1975, see D. McClelland, *APD*, Senate (10 September 1975), pp. 721–24.
47. For general treatments, see F. Cranston, *Canberra Times*, 14 February 1974; P. Hastings, *Sydney Morning Herald*, 8 August 1974; A. Clark, *National Times*, 2 September 1974; and R. Duffield, *Australian*, 4 September 1975. On Defence Department advice, see *Canberra Times*, 21 March 1975.
48. For overviews, see M. Richardson, Melbourne *Age*, 5 September and 28 October 1974; A. Clark, *National Times*, 10 June 1974; P. Hastings, *Sydney Morning Herald*, 25 January and 21 February 1975; P. Hastings, "The Timor Problem—I", *Australian Outlook* 29 (April 1975): 18–33; and H. Hill, "Australia and Portuguese Timor—Between Principles and Pragmatism" (Australasian Political Studies Association conference paper, Canberra, July 1975).
49. D. Wilkie, Adelaide *Advertiser*, 10 September 1974; M. Richardson, Melbourne *Age*, 10 September 1974; H. Armfield, Melbourne *Age*, 13 September 1974; and P. Hastings, *Sydney Morning Herald*, 16 September 1974.

50. "East ('Portuguese') Timor Faces Invasion Threat from Indonesia—a Background Report", (Sydney: 9 November 1974), p. 16. 'Prepared by a member of the Committee of the Southern Africa Liberation Centre, Sydney, presaging formation of a committee to support East Timor independence and oppose intervention.'

51. J.S. Dunn, *Portuguese Timor Before and After the Coup—Options for the Future* Parliamentary Library, Legislative Research Service, 27 August 1974) esp. p. 23–24.

52. On the ALP mission, see *Australian*, 18 March 1975; *Sydney Morning Herald*, 24 March 1975; and P. Hastings, *Sydney Morning Herald*, 12 June 1975.

53. Melbourne *Age*, 2 October 1974. Also see Peacock's *Press Release*, 9 September 1974 and his remarks in *APD*, HR (25 February 1975) pp. 641–42.

54. J.A.C. Mackie, "Foreign Policy Options for Australia. The External Dimension: Regional Problems and Policy Decisions" (AIIA conference paper, Melbourne, May 1975), p. 17. For some commentaries reflecting the government's perplexities even before civil war broke out in East Timor, see A. Clark, *National Times*, 11 November 1974; F. Cranston, *Canberra Times*, 25 February 1975; R. Schneider, *Australian*, 26 February 1975; M. MacCallum, *Nation-Review*, 28 February 1975; and Hill, "Australia and Portuguese Timor".

55. Whitlam, *APD*, HR (26 August 1975), pp. 491–3. For a later exposition, see Willesee, *APD*, Senate (30 October 1975), pp. 1609–10.

56. On this point, see R. Skelton, Melbourne *Age*, 5 September 1975.

57. See especially articles by H. McDonald and J. Edwards, *National Times*, 31 May 1976.

58. See B. Juddery, *Canberra Times*, 31 May 1976.

59. Whitlam, "Australia's Foreign Policy", p. 13.

60. See statement of Attorney-General L. Murphy of 4 September 1974, Attorney-General's Department, *Circular*, no. 68/74 (n.d.); H. Mishael, *The Times* (London), 21 May 1974; and A. Clark, *National Times*, 5 May 1975.

61. *Australian*, 30 March 1974; R. Hall, Sydney *Sun-Herald*, 31 March 1974; and A. Clark, *National Times*, 15 July 1974.

62. D. Solomon, *Canberra Times*, 8 February 1974.

63. P. Webster, *Australian*, 23 June 1973; and M. Walsh, *Australian Financial Review*, 12 February 1974.

64. See *Australian Financial Review*, 3 July 1974; S. Simson, *Australian Financial Review*, 20 June and 20 August 1974; A. Clark, *National Times*, 24 June 1974; and J. Edwards, *National Times*, 24 February 1975.

65. For instance, Melbourne *Age*, 12 and 18 March 1974; *Sydney Morning Herald*, 14 March 1974; and Adelaide *Advertiser*, 18 March 1974. For an overview of the programme, see M. Richardson, *Australian Financial Review*, 5 July 1974.

66. *APD*, HR (11 December 1973), p. 4579.

67. For the Commonwealth discussions on Rhodesia, see *Australian*, 11 August 1973.

68. See the communiqué in Department of Foreign Affairs, *News Release*, no. M/28, (9 May 1975), p. 5; and P. Bowers, *Sydney Morning Herald*, 8 May 1975.

69. For an early assessment, especially on Rhodesia and South Africa, see D. Goldsworthy,"Australia and Africa: New Relationships?", *Australian Quarterly* 45 (December 1973): 58–72. For Goldsworthy's later assessment, see his "The Whitlam Government's African Policy", *Dyason House Papers*, 1 (January 1975): 1–5. Also see R.A. Higgott, "Australia's Changing African Relations?—Australian/African Relations under the Labor Government" (APSA conference paper, Canberra, July 1975).

70. Whitlam, statement of 14 December 1972, in Department of Foreign Affairs, *News Release*, no. M/7 (14 December 1972).

71. For an account, see Melbourne *Age*, 29 December 1972.

72. Willesee, statement of 31 July 1974, in *AFAR* 45 (August 1974): 549–50.

73. J. Phillips, Sydney *Sunday Mirror*, 25 August 1974; F. Cranston, *Canberra Times*, 25 September 1974; and M. Wilkinson, Melbourne *Sun News-Pictorial*, 1 October 1974.

74. For a summary, see Whitlam, *APD*, HR (30 August 1973). Also see *Sydney Morning Herald*, 12 August 1974.

75. Whitlam, statement of 8 December 1972, in *AFAR* 44 (January 1973): 34. Also see the assessment in *National Times*, 17 February 1975; and M. Ross, *National Times*, 8 September 1975. For a compilation of various Australian actions taken against South Africa, see Department of Foreign Affairs, *Australia: Relations with South Africa* (Canberra: 1975).

76. *Australian*, 30 June 1973.
77. See Senator I. Greenwood's remarks in Liberal Party of Australia, Federal Secretariat, *Press Release*, 19 January 1975. Also see Peacock, *Sydney Morning Herald*, 20 February 1975.
78. *Sydney Morning Herald*, 24 September 1974; and R. Howells, *Nation-Review*, 6 December 1974.
79. Willesee, remarks of 30 October 1974, in Department of Foreign Affairs, *News Release*, no. M139/74 (30 October 1974), p. 4.
80. For a good analysis of Australia's vote at various stages of UN consideration, see D. Goldsworthy, "The Whitlam Government's African Policy", pp. 4–5.
81. *Australian*, 27 July 1973.
82. Whitlam, press conference of 18 September 1973, transcript, pp. 4–5; and Crean, *APD*, HR (25 February 1975), p. 698.
83. For general commentary on Australia's economic links with South Africa, see B. Noone, *Australian Economic Ties with South Africa* (Carlton, Vic: AUS, May 1973). Also see R. Witton, "Australia and Apartheid: The Ties that Bind", *Australian Quarterly* 45 (June 1973), 18–31; and Higgott, "Australia's Changing African Relations?", esp. pp. 16–20.
84. J.D.B. Miller, "Australian Foreign Policy: Constraints and Opportunities—II", *International Affairs*, 50 (July 1974): 433–34.
85. See H. Hill, *Nation-Review*, 30 May 1975.
86. Whitlam, Melbourne interview of 30 April 1974, transcript, p. 7.
87. See Department of Foreign Affairs, *News Release*, no. M/125 (20 September 1974). Also see M. MacCallum's commentary, *Nation-Review*, 27 September 1974.
88. Whitlam, Melbourne interview of 30 April 1974, transcript, p. 7.
89. See especially *Sydney Morning Herald*, 1 August 1974; and Melbourne *Age*, 22 April 1975.

5 External Policy: Diplomatic Dimensions: II

The preceding chapter examined some of the Labor government's broader concerns, such as regional co-operation in Asia and the Pacific, and colonialism and racialism. Our analysis of Australian diplomacy continues under a somewhat different format. Firstly, we will consider a few representative issue areas, both for their intrinsic interest and for their wider policy process and outcome implications. We will then bring into perspective Australia's approaches to and relations with communist nations, with the Asian region and such world bodies as the United Nations, and finally with the United States.

Issues relating to the Indo-Chinese region were a highlight of Labor's foreign policy and of domestic party politics. We suggested earlier how, before December 1972, Vietnam had become a point of acerbic partisan differences. When it came to office, Labor was persuaded that its own formulations had been proved right. Emotional as well as rational considerations affected the party. Involvement in the conflict had been a major miscalculation. Military reactions to complex socio-economic problems were seen as having exacerbated rather than solved. The conflict in the region had been wasteful in blood and treasure. Western-supported régimes had shown themselves to be corrupt and lacking in popular base. These reactions stimulated a feeling that an ALP government could not be indifferent to developments in the region. Also evident were feelings that, on Indo-China as on other issues, it was desirable to demonstrate quickly, and firmly, the new government's independent turn of mind. Moreover, wider considerations were taken into account. Continuing warfare in the region meant unsettled conditions in Asia generally. There were dangers of renewed great-power friction and threats to the evolution of *détente*. Also Labor's objectives for Asia, such as an inclusive Asian–Pacific forum, would be hindered as long as the absence of a genuine peace settlement seemed to keep various South-East Asian states at a distance from China.

When Labor entered government, it almost immediately terminated the residual Australian military presence in Vietnam, by withdrawing advisers. That, literally, took Australia "out of the war". It had been a predictable step. Also predictable was Whitlam's undisguised pleasure in late January 1973 over the announcement of a Vietnamese cease-fire agreement. His praise of Nixon for having established himself "in the foremost ranks of modern statesmanship" was indeed exceptional.[1] Also, rapidly and predictably, Labor extended diplomatic recognition to the Democratic Republic of Vietnam (North Vietnam). There was some opposition carping about undue haste, and there was distress in Saigon, but Washington registered no complaints. The recognition of Hanoi left unaffected Australia's recognition of South Vietnam.

While these government actions were very popular within the ALP and excited relatively little domestic or external complaint, much of the rest of the government's reaction to Indo-Chinese events generated prominent controversy. At the heart of the matter lay the question of how the government, or certain members of it, felt about the Vietnam conflict, who was responsible for prolonging it and what needed to be done.

In late 1972, Vietnam peace negotiations broke down and almost immediately after Labor assumed office the United States resumed bombing of North Vietnam and undertook harbour-mining operations. The reactions of the new government and within the labour movement more generally detonated a fierce debate, the effects of which lingered for a very long time. Whitlam transmitted a letter of complaint to Nixon. He publicly acknowledged that a letter had been sent, but declined to disclose its content. Three newly appointed senior ministers—Cairns (Overseas Trade and Secondary Industry), Cameron (Labour) and Uren (Urban and Regional Development)—volunteered public and extremely derogatory remarks about the US President and his administration: Cameron—"maniacs"; Uren—"mass-murders"; Cairns—"corrupt" US régime. Cairns proceeded to call for public rallies to oppose the bombing.[2] Additionally, protesting dockside workers imposed a boycott on American shipping and there were threats of more widespread sanctions against American goods and services.

The implications of these reactions for US–Australian relations generally will be assessed later. Here we should say that the US administration was shocked and angered over what had happened in Australia. There were representations, intense conversations and, on the part of American unions, a retaliatory boycott against Australian shipping. Whitlam himself was not personally blameworthy for over-reacting, but impressions of him among critics in Australia, and in the United States, were unflattering. His letter to Nixon was not insulting in tone. But there was a feature of Whitlam's approach that in-furiated some persons in Washington—a promise to draw the Indone-sians and Japanese into common cause with Australia to protest against American interdiction of North Vietnam. This had not been Whitlam's idea, but rather the recommendation of a senior public ser-vant. The idea was not only offensive to Washington but proved un-workable. Whitlam dissociated himself from the more vigorous, anti-American criticisms of his ministers, but was unable to enforce their silence. Cairns, on his part, then and thereafter, said he spoke only for himself on Vietnam, not for the government or for Whitlam, and would continue to do so as his beliefs dictated,[3] principles of Cabinet responsibility notwithstanding. Whitlam .opposed the shipping boycott, but this was trade-union not government action. It lacked formal ACTU backing and brought on mediating efforts by R. J. Hawke, ALP as well as ACTU President. In other words, Whitlam, and his new government, were portrayed by critics as wrong, inept and basically not in control of their own ministers and followers. The L.-CP, still recovering from the shock of having being pushed into op-position, attacked in full force. Labor was proving the historical L-CP prediction of being irresponsible and dangerous as a party of govern-ment. Barely in office, it had severely damaged relations with the United States, abdicated its responsibilities as a cohesive government to wild men and shown its helplessness in the face of radical trade-union pressure.[4]

In the hubbub, much of the substance of the debate over ap-propriate Australian policy towards Vietnam was drowned out and a heavy coat of emotionalism was superimposed over subsequent dialogue about Vietnamese issues. Cairns in particular, though careful to represent his views as his own, on future occasions, speaking at home and overseas, was bitter against what he portrayed as a record of American aggression in Vietnam, the puppet status of the Thieu régime and deliberate efforts by Washington and Saigon to subvert the peace accords reached in early 1973, and he acclaimed the need for a "peoples'" victory in Vietnam.[5] Opposition spokesmen slapped at Cairns. His views were substantially wrong and turned a blind eye towards the behaviour of North Vietnam and the Vietcong; they con-tinued to poison relations with America; they exposed the weakness of the proposition that there was a single government with a single authoritative Prime Minister.[6]

What was the *government's* interpretation of conditions in a con-

tinually strife-torn Vietnam? Whitlam himself was noticeably uncomfortable with the régime in the South and with the background of
US interdiction of Indo-China from Thai bases—"militarily ineffective
and morally monstrous".[7] Overall, however, the official attitude,
firmly endorsed by Willesee and his department, became that blame
for the mischievous conflict in Vietnam rested with both sides. If
anything, breaches of the Paris accords by Saigon "are fully, and in
some cases more than fully, matched by breaches by the DRV and
PRG". The Paris accords were a reasonable framework within which
to work out national conciliation in Vietnam. It would be presump-
tious for outsiders to weigh the sincerity and national feeling on
either side. But this was not sufficiently explicit criticism of North
Vietnam to suit many opposition members, especially as by early 1975
they detected a more hostile Labor government tone against the
Saigon régime.[8]

What of Australia's diplomatic relations with the North and South
Vietnamese régimes? Relations with Hanoi were satisfactory and correct, though not effusive. One accomplishment, announced in 1974,
was that Australia's mission in Hanoi was to serve as a source of information and as modest conduit between North Vietnam and
Thailand, which then lacked relations with Hanoi.[9] Official and other
North Vietnamese visitors to Australia were accorded sympathetic
receptions. The government's treatment of South Vietnam was also
correct, though perhaps inclining towards coolness. The Foreign Affairs Department was certainly not disposed to impose any ostracism
on Saigon's diplomatic personnel. Departmental officials resented
what they regarded as attempts to incriminate South Vietnam, and
the department, by those who alleged that Foreign Affairs had,
despite representations from Cairns, in effect countenanced the
deportation of a number of Chinese Vietnamese from Hong Kong to
incarceration in South Vietnam.[10] The department, and indeed a
number of Labor people as well, felt embarrassed by occasional
episodes, such as at La Trobe University in 1973, when South Vietnamese spokesmen were denied public forums or otherwise harassed
by radical critics.[11] The Labor government expressed its concern to
Saigon over allegations of mistreatment of political prisoners, though
ranking Labor ministers made similar representations in other Asian
capitals, notably Jakarta and Manila. Moreover, as will be shown
more fully later, the ALP government largely resisted pressures from
some party sources and radical lobbyists to emasculate its civil
economic assistance to South Vietnam.

While it was being pilloried by the opposition for its behaviour on
Indo-China, the Whitlam government also found rising dissent
on the left, both in and outside the ALP. Some of these critics felt that,

de facto, Australia's handling of Vietnamese issues was tantamount to culpable negligence. By doing little if anything, by risking few initiatives, the government was countenancing the warfare, the preservation of a discredited régime in South Vietnam and the postponement of a political settlement under more progressive leadership, such as the Provisional Revolutionary Government (PRG). It was asserted that the Paris peace accords had recognized not only the Saigon government but also the PRG as an established administrative and political force in the region. Hence as an important start towards reconstructing its Vietnamese diplomacy, Canberra should extend diplomatic recognition to the PRG.[12]

The Whitlam government rejected these propositions. Publicly, it argued that the Paris peace accords in no way implied that the PRG was, by reason of its status, necessarily entitled to diplomatic recognition. It said that the PRG, while definitely an entity, was in no sense of the accepted word a government. Canberra already was able to maintain informal contacts with the PRG, but recognition would mean severance of relations with Saigon. The South Vietnamese régime was a government, entitled to value-free recognition, and a régime whose conduct Australia could better influence in a movement towards free elections and an overall Vietnamese settlement if formal links were maintained.[13] There were other disincentives for the government to recognize the PRG. The advice of the Foreign Affairs Department was decidedly against. South-East Asian (ASEAN) states very firmly urged Australia not to change diplomatic course. These were governments with which close ties were highly valued by Australia. The American outlook, also opposed to PRG recognition, in and of itself probably counted for less in the government's calculus. The Labor government, in some ways rather attached to legal niceties and fond of its even-handedness in its recognition policies towards the two Koreas and the two Germanies, was thus further disinclined to recognize a legally "questionable" government and to forfeit recognition of an unquestionably "legal" government. There also is an intimation that, especially on a policy choice that would have meant adhering to what was an international recognition policy limited to communist and some Third World states, Canberra felt uneasy about the solidity of precedents for a recognition of the PRG on its own part. Even Hanoi had not accorded formal "recognition" to the PRG. Finally, though not decisively, the government kept in mind the L–CP's resolute opposition to PRG recognition and its happy willingness to pin nasty labels on Labor in the course of electoral politics.

Furthermore, in the party political sense, the ALP government found itself in something of a dilemma. If it acceded to rising demands for PRG recognition and otherwise remodelled its posture on

Vietnam, it would be severely scored by the L–CP for having suc-
cumbed to left-wing and radical pressures. If it held its basic policy
ground, it would be hit harder and harder by PRG proponents. This
could lead to a formal Labor Party demand for PRG recognition
and/or to serious, electorally damaging, intra-party frictions.

Pressure on the government to recognize the PRG came from
diverse sources. The PRG itself made known its wish, both to
Australians visiting Vietnam and in Australia through touring PRG
spokesmen, for the now more independently minded Australian
government to soften its position. Cairns, though continuing to represent himself in a private capacity, urged PRG recognition. The radical
movement launched a heavy campaign. An Australia–Indo-China
Society was formed. Committees for the Recognition of the PRG were
formed and co-ordinating groups arose. Bodies such as these, plus
AICD in Sydney and CICD in Melbourne more generally, began a
systematic campaign of lobbying ALP parliamentarians. According to
spokesmen for the pro-PRG lobby, the effort among parliamentarians
was one of the radical/peace movement's most conspicuous successes.
Literature, films and visiting speakers were made available. By late
1974, nearly half of the ALP parliamentary caucus members, including several ministers, had subscribed to a manifesto on Vietnam
that, among other things, called for PRG recognition. More Labor
parliamentarians later subscribed to a call for the observance of the
Paris peace accords and a negotiated settlement, though not necessarily to literal advocacy of PRG recognition as such.

The government had never been inflexible towards the PRG and
gradually proceeded to loosen its position. At the 1973 ALP Federal
Conference, motions calling for recognition of the PRG were comfor-
tably, though not overwhelmingly, defeated. Whitlam was very firm
in opposing such instruction. His margin of victory on the resolutions
may have been increased by his promise to endorse another resolution that called for Australian representations to Saigon over political
prisoners.[14] Through indirect means, the government continued to
channel funds for humanitarian projects in Vietcong-controlled areas
of Vietnam. In 1974, it shifted its approach towards PRG representation at humanitarian-oriented international conferences to favouring
observer/forensic status for PRG delegates.[15]

The ALP met in federal conference at Terrigal, New South Wales,
in February 1975. The party's Foreign Affairs and Defence Committee, chaired by Whitlam, recommended that resolutions proposing
PRG recognition be discharged. The mood of the conference was not
so accommodating. Whitlam made a spirited defence of his government's foreign policy, including reasons not to recognize the PRG.
Then came a series of tangled events. A motion by Cairns favouring

recognition was put and passed by a single vote. Then, admidst much procedural confusion and bad-tempered remarks, Hawke, as presiding officer, ruled in order an amendment stipulating that the PRG would be allowed to establish an information office in Australia. Whitlam himself endorsed it. It passed, 31 to 0. Somehow, Cairns' motion, which had passed, slipped out of sight.[16] Whitlam, Willesee and other moderate Labor ministers had found that first caucus and then conference had taken issue with them on Vietnam, and more particularly the PRG question. The outcome at Terrigal was, on paper, a compromise. The compromise amendment worked, but its passage was fortuitous, a procedural accident. Some delegates had not realized that, at least according to the chair's ruling, support for the compromise motion negated the already approved Cairns motion. The episode was a commentary on struggles among factions or bodies within the party and varied "lobbies" that strived to effect outcomes. It was a not very edifying commentary on how Labor formulated major policy. It also was commentary on perspectives on how, and in what way, an ALP government sought to deal with a foreign policy issue both emotional and substantively complex. We will return to Vietnam shortly, after reviewing government policy towards Cambodia.

Cambodia was a less emotionally tainted subject that Vietnam and produced relatively little concerted party or outside lobbying. The government's approach was, however, affected by many of the same considerations and constraints that had shaped its Vietnam policy. As with the South Vietnamese régime, the Whitlam government had little personal sympathy for the Lon Nol régime in Cambodia. Australia was vigorously displeased by American interdiction of North Vietnam at the turn of 1972–73. Less sternly, it took the view that heavy US support for Cambodia was misguided and probably contributed to prolongation of Indo-Chinese fighting at large. The Whitlam government did not, however, find that it realistically could play a real mediatory role in the conflict. In 1973, against American advice, it withdrew from an international economic stabilization fund for Cambodia. But the programme had had an uneven reception in the United States itself, and when the LCP government joined the scheme in 1971, it did so only after heavy lobbying from Washington.[17]

Australia's diplomatic relations with Cambodia also resembled its diplomatic attitude towards South Vietnam. Recognition of the Lon Nol régime was maintained, nominally on the mechanical grounds that it effectively controlled the capital and held the Cambodian seat at the United Nations. Prince Sihanouk's government in exile in China did not meet these tests, nor did the insurgent forces operating in Cambodia. All the same, as in regard to the Vietcong/PRG in Vietnam, the Whitlam government was willing to maintain informal contacts with Sihanouk. By the end of 1973, Sihanouk had held talks with Ambassador FitzGerald in Peking, with several Australian ministers and eventually with Whitlam personally—though against Department of Foreign Affairs advice.[18]

Foreign Affairs lost its case on the Whitlam contact with Sihanouk, but otherwise its own position on Cambodia was upheld by the government. The Department counselled against a change in formal recognition policy and opposed Australian actions to install a pro-Sihanouk delegation in Cambodia's UN seat. Other influences affected the government's position. Once again we see a trace of a rather formal, legalistic approach. Moreover, Cambodia was not South Africa. Unlike South Africa, the Cambodian régime had not egregiously flaunted UN principles and directives. As on the Vietnam/PRG issue, considerable lobbying was exerted on Canberra by foreign governments not to turn Australia's back on Lon Nol. This came from Washington, from ASEAN countries and, most energetically at the 1974 UN session, from Indonesia and Japan. The argument, as with Vietnam, was that the abandonment of the Pnom Penh government would assist the cause of insurgent movements in the region and foreclose what little prospect remained for a negotiated Cambodian settlement. Hence the Australian delegation at the United Nations opposed efforts to displace the Lon Nol régime. Australia did impose one qualification. Distressed by the way the Chinese recognition issue had been handled for many years, holding to the proposition that the United Nations should be an open forum rather than a stage for procedurally delaying and obstructing tactics, the government refused to associate itself with such procedures, even though their sponsor's—America's—intent was also Australia's objective, namely salvaging the seat for the Lon Nol régime.[19]

In March 1975, following on the ALP resolution passed at Terrigal, the PRG approached Australia to establish an information office. Almost immediately, the matter became moot. Within two months, Australia had formally recognized the PRG as the government in Saigon, as well as the Royal Government of National Union of Cambodia (GRUNC) as the effecitve government in Pnom Penh. The anti-communist régimes in South Vietnam and Cambodia had collapsed. The period March–May 1975 generated fierce public controversy in Australia and requires more specific attention.

We might begin by asking whether the government and the opposition saw the outcome of communist takeovers in Indo-Chinese states as desirable or not. The question has two parts. The first is whether incumbent régimes were favoured over a communist alternative, or vice versa. The second relates to post-Vietnam forecasts for the region and for Australia's interests.

On neither side of the House was there particular sympathy for the Thieu and Lon Nol régimes, though Labor's views were more demonstrably critical. Whitlam, Willesee and others resented the venality of the Thieu régime in particular, and felt it had resisted steps towards reaching a peaceful accommodation. They were not inherently well-disposed towards communist régimes in South Vietnam and Cambodia, but reconciled themselves to them, in part because at least and at last the killing would stop when established régimes in the capitals collapsed. The opposition, though not enamoured of the Thieu and Lon Nol régimes, nevertheless felt that more should be done to sustain them, at least so as to avert a full-scale communist takeover. Remarks such as by Cairns that it would be a good thing if Thieu fell and the inevitable takeover by the other side occur were denounced. After the dénouement in Indo-China, Peacock remarked that the Liberals were unhappy not because they had unquestioningly wished to defend those who had lost, but basically because "we fear that the Government which has replaced .. [them] may have greater faults based on dogmatic ideology".[20]

More far-ranging in importance was the question of what the two party groups saw as the consequences of the end of conflict in Indo-China. Their differences were considerable and a reflection of their separate perceptions of the international order. To the government, the end of conflict was a healthy thing. It was desirable because it meant the end of carnage. It also was highly welcome because it brought to an end myths about the alleged importance to Australia of who governed in Indo-China. Australia could now concentrate on its vital interests and sources of security interest. The close of the conflict meant that great-power competition in the region was reduced and regional stability enhanced. *Détente* would be helped and international priorities otherwise set right. American resources and energies would no longer be squandered. Adventitiously, the setback in Indo-China could serve to make future American policy in Asia wiser and more constructive.[21] The opposition saw the Indo-Chinese outcome otherwise, as a destablizing event. The outcome raised the power and credit of communism generally, weakened American and anti-communist nation credit and had the potential for spreading undermining effects across South-East Asia and elsewhere in the manner of an oil slick.[22] A number of commentators interpreted the L–CP's posture as a combination of efforts to revive a sharp foreign policy debate and a return to domino-theory thinking.[23]

Another aspect of the March–May 1975 debate over Indo-China related to Australia's diplomatic role in the conflict. The exchanges were often bitter, personal and politically supercharged, and tended to obfuscate the merits of the cases argued. Essentially, the opposition maintained that Labor, and Whitlam specifically, had disguised their true feelings and had misled Parliament. The government was said not to be even-handed, but favoured the North and the PRG over South Vietnam. Labor denied the charge and said it was addressing itself to the realities of the situation. In the Senate, where Labor lacked a majority, a motion was passed condemning the government for duplicity in its dealings with the two Vietnams.

The gravamen of the L–CP's charge was that the content of leaked cables sent to Australia's missions in Hanoi and Saigon for communication to those governments had placed more blame on the South than on the North for protracting the struggle and were more gentle and accommodating towards Hanoi. Not only was this said to be wrong, but it gave the lie to Whitlam's earlier professions that Canberra was steering a middle course and that its communications would bear this out.[24] Overall, the press agreed[25] and US official opinion felt that the government had "tilted". The government tabled the contentious cables, as well as earlier letters to the two Vietnams. Taken together, the government argued, these documents proved that Australia's objective throughout had been for both sides to stop shooting and to stop their evasion of the Paris accords, so that a reasoned settlement could be reached. Its efforts had been expended consistently, in all manners of diplomatic settings. It also publicized a letter from the Hanoi authorities that chided Australia for its lack of appreciation of the situation in the South.[26] During these exchanges, the government was accused of being dishonest with Parliament, obsequious towards Hanoi and essentially hoping for a communist takeover. The L–CP was accused of having protracted a senseless and bloody war while in office, and in opposition of having contributed no reasoned proposals for its resolution. Actually, an April 1975 opposition fact-finding mission to Indo-China filed (the government would have added, very belatedly) not a recommendation for more American arms to bolster régimes there but essentially a recommendation for mutual disengagement and observance of Paris accord procedures.[27]

It is not practical to undertake an exegetic analysis of the various contentious documents over which the parties argued. Messages to the two Vietnams were not identical. They did leave an impression of partiality towards the North, or at least that Australia was placing its bets on what it was persuaded would be the winning side. Some earlier Whitlam remarks had shown particular frustration with Thieu's unwillingness to bend. But it is also possible to view the matter in perspective, in the context of Australia addressing a tottering Saigon régime while momentum and the sight of victory were clearly on the other side. Laurie Oakes' interpretation cannot be dismissed as simple apologia. In his view, cables to Saigon hoped to change Thieu's mind about subscribing to a national reconciliation council. If this were done, Whitlam's communications to Hanoi were intended to persuade North Vietnam and the PRG that they should call off their military offensive. The specific formulations of language were designed as sweeteners and incentives to Hanoi, again in recognition of the relative imbalance of strength then enjoyed by the two sides.[28]

Another facet of government policy that aroused controversy was its handling of refugees. During March–May, the government committed more funds towards international relief efforts in Vietnam and urged public donations. It allowed Cambodian and South Vietnamese students in Australia to remain. It also extended temporary residence permits to South Vietnamese and Cambodian diplomatic personnel and their families who were in Australia at the time of communist takeovers, but without guarantee of permanent residence. It participated in bringing orphans out of South Vietnam for relocation with Australian families. Its approach to accepting South Vietnamese refugees was the major bone of contention. Whitlam delayed making a judgement on this issue, in the face of Willesee's efforts for a prompt prime ministerial decision. Some Vietnamese were brought out when the Australian embassy closed, but over two hundred who had been associated with Australia and Australians in Vietnam, and who would have wished to come out, were left behind. Immigration Minister Cameron apparently concurred in a set of refugee admission criteria drawn up by the Department of Foreign Affairs, but Whitlam had the criteria tightened. Even those who met the criteria were to be treated on a case-by-case basis. Out of thousands of refugees who applied for entry into Australia, only a few hundred met the screening criteria and were otherwise deemed suitable for admission. Whitlam eventually called upon the United Nations High Commissioner for Refugees to sponsor a world effort on behalf of Vietnamese refugees scattered at various temporary reception centres, a scheme under which Australia promised to take its fair share. But the Australian offer was contingent on a multilateral effort rather than being unconditionally made. Then, in August 1975, an additional three hundred refugees were brought in. By the time Labor had left office, slightly over a thousand Vietnamese refugees had been accepted, nearly three hundred of them orphans scheduled for adoption in Australia.

The opposition complained about the government's modest and stop-and-go refugee response, and so did most of the press. Although Labor accepted more refugees for permanent settlement than any country other than the United States, Labor was castigated for being a party committed to humanitarian principles but unwilling to serve humanitarianism in an appropriately generous way. Australia had over the years been a refuge for Balts, Hungarians, Czechs and finally Chileans who wished to avoid political persecution. It had a capacity to absorb foreign, even Asian peoples. Was not the government also proud of its colour-blind migration policy? Why not South Vietnamese?[29]

Several factors seemed to have constrained the government, and Whitlam particularly. There were some technical obstacles to moving people out of South Vietnam when the old régime was disintegrating, but they were not insurmountable. When the government originally brought orphans out, Hanoi expressed concern that Australia was improperly involving itself in Vietnamese affairs. Some Cabinet members were very much concerned about the plight of refugees on humanitarian grounds, but there also was feeling that a major Australian intake of refugees could be further interpreted in Hanoi as an unfriendly gesture. Since Australia wished to have good access to Hanoi, and to a successor government in Saigon, perhaps cuation was in order. The government's principal efforts at assisting refugees came to be carried out in circumstances that could be interpreted as least likely to offend Hanoi or the incoming régime in the South. It was to be done under neutral international auspices; it was mostly to be done from refugee centres outside Vietnam, rather than directly out of Vietnam; it was mostly done after the excitement of the April–May period had subsided. One more interpretation is possible. Whitlam could remember how in 1974 the Baltic community in Australia had resented Australian recognition of Soviet sovereignty over their homelands and how much they had fuelled a partisan debate over this action. The Prime Minister may have felt that the introduction of thousands of overwhelmingly anti-communist Vietnamese could in time have created a potent lobby on behalf of hard-line Australian diplomacy and have exacerbated politics in a nation he, Whitlam, was striving to move towards a more balanced and relaxed outlook on Asia and towards communism.[30] Later in this chapter, we will more broadly examine the implications of government reactions to issues of political asylum.

As an issue area in Australian diplomacy, the Middle East outwardly lacked the sharpness and salience of Indo-China, and especially Vietnam. The Middle East was half-way round the globe rather than in the Asian neighbourhood, Australia's centre of security and diplomatic concern. Moreover, it lacked the emotive content that for years had pervaded debate over Australia's stakes and proper role in Vietnam. Nevertheless, Middle Eastern questions, most of which somehow touched on the Arab—Israeli conflict, became significant for Australia and in turn attracted considerable and heated political controversy. For Labor, the Middle East as an object of Australian diplomacy acquired importance because the conflict there was seen as destabilizing progress towards great-power *détente* and because it raised significant problems touching on such Labor Party concerns as self-determination, humanitarianism, the rights of states to exist free of intimidation and the peaceful rather than forceful settlement of disputes. Particularly after the Yom Kippur war of 1973, economic issues such as trade with the Middle East, petroleum supplies and potential investment funds for Australia required special and delicate treatment.

The basic guidelines for the Whitlam government's Middle East policies were spelled out in the party's 1973 Surfers Paradise Federal Conference resolution, passed unanimously:

> The situation in the Middle East remains the greatest threat to the peace of the world. There can be no peace until the Arab States respect and recognise Israel's sovereignty and right to exist. Equally, there can be no peace until Israeli forces have been withdrawn from occupied territories to secure and recognised boundaries and a just settlement of the refugee problem is achieved.[31]

Two important embellishments were imposed on this position by government spokesmen. The call for a "just settlement of the refugee problem" came to mean that "if the Palestinians want to create a state of their own alongside Israel, we will accept this. ... It accords with the Australian Government's attachment to the principle of the right of self-determination.[32] The other embellishment was less a matter of policy than of style or approach. Particularly for Whitlam personally, it was morally wrong and probably diplomatically counter-productive to ascribe "blame" in the Middle East conflict. For instance, though addressing a Jewish audience, he spoke of the Arabs "who [in 1973] it would seem [sic] invaded Israel". Provocative attacks by one side and retaliatory strikes by the other, for example Israel's reprisal sorties into Lebanon, were equally contemptible: "The bullying of Lebanon by Israel gets no public support. Israeli civilian women and children, Lebanese women and children, are all sacred alike. I condemn the terrorist attacks which have brought shame on both."[33] Such pronouncements, combined with Australia's actual behaviour at the United Nations and elsewhere, were publicized by the government as scrupulously even-handed, but pommelled by critics as biased and unworthy.

Unlike Vietnam and Cambodia, the Middle East did not pose problems of diplomatic recognition, but very prominently posed voting choices at the United Nations and related international agencies. At the United Nations, Australian Labor supported injunctions to the parties principal in the Middle East to reach accommodation. In

July 1973, Australia supported a Security Council resolution (though it was described by UN Ambassador McIntrye as "lacking in balance") that, *inter alia*, strongly deplored Israel's continuing occupation of territories taken in the 1967 war and its lack of co-operation with the United Nations in this matter. The resolution, sponsored by non-aligned states, was vetoed by the United States. In October 1973, following new hostilities in the Middle East, Australia joined the massive vote in favour of a resolution appealing for a cease-fire and implementation of a 1967 UN resolution that had urged a return to earlier territorial boundaries, a proper settlement of the refugee problem and the inviolability of states in the region. In November 1974, Australia abstained on a General Assembly resolution that reaffirmed the rights of the Palestinian people, because it lacked reference to Israel's right to exist as an independent state. During his visits to Yugoslavia and the Soviet Union at the turn of 1974–75, Whitlam emphasized the need for Israel's continued survival and in the USSR, supported the right of migration to Israel of Soviet Jews. All the same, there had been a report, unconfirmed, that during the Yom Kippur war Australia had spoken with US officials in criticism of the American arms airlift to Israel.[34] In 1974, following a guerrilla raid into Israel and an Israeli counterstroke against guerrilla sites in Lebanon, Australia voted for a Security Council resolution that condemned Israel's violation of Lebanon's territory and all acts of violence generally. It also supported an unsuccessful amendment that would specifically have condemned the original guerrilla raid into Israel. In 1975, Australia rejected any idea that Israel should be expelled from the United Nations or denied the right to participate in its work, and refused to support moves to equate Zionism with racism.

Australia's position on the Palestine Liberation Organization's (PLO) involvement in UN affairs was guarded. In October 1974, the General Assembly passed a resolution inviting the PLO to participate in the Assembly's plenary deliberations on the question of Palestine. The success of this resolution was a major triumph for the Arab nations and a setback for Israel. The resolution passed 105 to 4, with twenty abstentions, among them Australia and a number of other Western nations. Australia saw value in allowing spokesmanship for the PLO, but had misgivings about the procedural correctness inherent in the resolution and about its capacity to assist the delicate negotiations required for a lasting settlement in the Middle East. The following month, Australia abstained in the General Assembly, this time on a resolution granting the PLO permanent observer status at the United Nations—on procedural grounds, but without prejudice to Australia's willingness to take into account an Arab summit (Rabat) decision that the PLO should speak for all Palestinians.

Also Australia often chose to abstain or otherwise to assume a non-categorical position on matters affecting relations with UN-related agencies. For instance, in mid-1974, it supported observer status for the PLO at the World Health Organization, but later in the year it abstained on admitting the PLO to the deliberations of the International Civil Aviation Organization. It also abstained in committee when Israel sought membership in the European regional group of the United Nations Educational, Scientific and Cultural Organization (UNESCO), though in UNESCO's plenary session it voted against anti-Israeli sanctions that that body might impose. Australia also abstained on a resolution calling on UNESCO to provide aid to various liberation movements and that expressed hope that Palestine would join the community of nations under the aegis of such international bodies as UNESCO. As an official Australian publication explained, "The effect of the motion barring Israel, supported mainly by Arab and Communist countries [but on which Australia had abstained], was to maintain Israel's exclusion from participation, as of right, in the regional activities of UNESCO."[35]

In early 1975, by a very narrow margin, the ALP Cabinet decided against a PLO visit to Australia. Whitlam had previously been favourable. His explanation of the Cabinet refusal was that a visit at that time would have worsened divisions within the Australian community.[36] He later indicated a wish that such a visit could be arranged in the foreseeable future.[37] Shortly thereafter, on the invitation of the Australian Union of Students, a delegation representing the General Union of Palestinian Students, affiliated with the PLO, was allowed to enter. In June 1975, a ranking member of the PLO was allowed to tour Australia. Outwardly, he came under the sponsorship of the Arab League, not the PLO, but he was received by Whitlam and the matter of a PLO information office in Australia was broached.[38]

Given its emotional as well as diplomatic and economic dimensions, the Middle East was bound to stir internal controversy. The government insisted that it was following the best policy for Australia and for the general cause of international morality and order, a policy that scrupulously aimed at even-handedness, namely fairness to the claims of both Arabs and Israelis. A number of critics examined the government's actual behaviour and branded it as not at all even-handed, but as tilted against Israel. They maintained that this bias was itself morally wrong and diplomatically unsound. They claimed that, as with the July 1973 Security Council resolution, Labor had supported a position that inordinately threw blame on Israel for the lack of a lasting settlement. They saw Australia's lack of opposition for the right of the PLO to present its position before the UN General Assembly as *de facto* anti-Israeli and unfortunately bereft of any

Australian efforts to wring prior concessions for Israel's future security from PLO petitioners. They felt that at least part of Australia's vote on Israel and UNESCO was shameful and indefensible. At large, they bitterly complained that trying to steer even-handedly by laying as much opprobrium on Israel's reprisals as on Arab terrorist provocations mischievously confused aggressor and victim.

The chorus of criticism sprang from diverse quarters, ranging from the L–CP opposition to the inner circles of the Labor Party itself. The L–CP did not declare itself openly pro-Israeli and acknowledged the rights of Palestinians. But, conviction apart, the opposition felt it had something to gain electorally by exposing Labor's alleged hypocrisy and inconsistency—promises of high principle accompanied by deplorable favouritism and disregard for the Israeli underdog. Implicitly, there also was a tendency to look favourably upon Israel's interests because Israel was, in a sense, an American client, while the Arabs were supported by the Soviets, and the L–CP was prone to take seriously world events that brought deterioration to American influence. L–CP interest in the Middle East was reflected in the amount of internal research attention paid to the subject. Early in 1975, the first well-documented paper in the Liberals' foreign policy review process was devoted to the Middle East.[39] Yet the Liberals' sense of unease about how the Middle East conflict could adversely affect Australia was itself highlighted. It is understood that, in late 1973 and early 1974, party spokesmen deliberately refrained from remarking on the issue, in fear of exciting possible Arab retaliatory measures against Australia, such as skyjackings of aircraft or terrorism.

Another source of criticism was Australia's Jewish community. The bulk of the Jewish community of some 75000 though normally strongly Labor in voting preference, found the government's Middle East policy distasteful and entirely unsatisfactory. We will deal with some of the policy process and electoral spin-off implications of this theme later. What needs to be said here is that the Jewish community mobilized itself to question and if possible to correct Labor's policies. Its spokesmen held private as well as more open dialogues with Whitlam. Their distress over government policy helped to give birth to a pro-Israeli *Mid-East Review*, published in Melbourne. They were eager to organize a broadly based Australian Council of Concern and supported efforts by Jewish and non-Jewish ALP parliamentarians in the Friends of Israel group within caucus. In 1975, the Australian Union of Jewish Students launched a signature campaign aimed at keeping the PLO out of Australia.

This brings us to the ALP itself. The Arab-Israeli conflict touched Labor's heart-strings, and in so doing severely divided the party. A

pro-Israeli sentiment was easily understandable within important
sections of an idealistic and humanitarian party. There were
memories of the Jews as a persecuted people, victims of the
Holocaust, and then besieged and fighting for their state's and their
own survival against huge Arab odds. It was the Arabs who were the
prime villains, not Israel. It was they, despite some valid claims of
their own, who wished to dismember someone else's homeland and
who as a result had periodically incited international crises. Feelings
of sympathy for a deserving underdog were strengthened in the ALP
by the party's inclination to favour democratic and socially progressive régimes. An essentially labour/social democratic Israel fitted this
description, but the Arab states did not. Close ties between the
Australian and Israeli trade-union movements further strengthened
sympathy for Israel's cause.

This persuasion within the ALP could live with the language of the
party's 1973 conference declaration on the Middle East, but not with
many of the government's utterances and policy movements. To one
degree or another, the government's position was questioned by conference delegates, members of the Federal Executive, caucus and even
ministers. The Friends of Israel group in caucus, though not particularly effective as a lobby, was at least one evidence of intra-party
interest and concern. More evidence was found in the barbed questions on the Middle East sometimes put to Whitlam in Parliament by
members of his own party. The most dramatic evidence was Hawke
himself, the party's Federal President. Hawke was a steadfast friend
of Israel. He openly referred to the government's policy as not "even-
handed" but as "abhorrent".[40] In November 1973, Hawke, himself not
a parliamentarian, undertook to influence the Labor caucus to assume
a more aggressively stated, pro-Israeli position.[41] After a January
1974 speech on the Middle East question, Hawke told Whitlam's
senior personal adviser, Peter Wilenski, that he considered the issue
"almost as vital as the survival of the Labor government. He said he
was seriously considering resigning from the party presidency. And
he warned that if he did so he would not help in any future campaign
to get the government re-elected."[42] In February 1974, he nearly succeeded in having his charges of the government's non-even-handed
policy brought before the Federal Executive. He openly condemned
the 1975 decision to allow a known PLO member to visit Australia
and complained that had the matter gone before full Cabinet, permission would have been refused.[43]

There was another dimension to the Labor Party's thinking about
the Middle East. Again some characteristic Labor orientations were
noticeable. This view was not strictly speaking anti-Israeli. What it
emphasized was that, after the 1967 war, Israel took and tenaciously

held territories that did not belong to it. In this sense, Israel's conquest by *force majeure* could not be condoned. Nor could Israel's treatment of the Palestinian refugees, whose plight had become an international scandal. Nor was its unreasonable refusal to treat with the PLO, the most authoritative spokesman for the Palestinians. Less crystallized were some feelings that Israel, an essentially Western state, was resisting the claims of what basically were Third World nations. Also present were occasional overtones that Israel had become a pawn of America's designs in the region.

Generally, though not universally, those who took an especially sympathetic view of the Arab state and Palestinian position stood on the left of the party. One such figure was W. H. Hartley, a member of the Federal Executive. He and Hawke were the most vocal protagonists of the two competing strands within the party. Hartley opened another dimension of the intra-party and national debate in mid-1974. Returning from the Middle East as part of an unofficial ALP and trade-union delegation, he said that the PLO was receptive to opening an information office in Australia and to sending a group of its people on tour of Australia in early 1975. Such steps, Hartley and the PLO believed, were necessary to counter disproportionate Zionist propaganda in Australia.[44] Reaction from other ALP quarters, Jewish sources and the opposition was sharply critical. The PLO not only should be unwelcome in Australia because it was pledged to dismember Israel, but because it was, among other things, a terrorist organization. In the months following, not much was heard of the information office idea, but by the opening of the new year a group of PLO members was preparing for an unofficial visit to Australia. The Foreign Affairs Department undertook an intensive security check of those proposing to come. All the same, the debate exploded. Hawke and other members of the Labor Party, including ministers and South Australia's Premier Don Dunstan, members of the Jewish community and the L–CP opposition condemned the idea.[45]

There was acute embarrassment for the ALP as a party of government. The party was gravely split on the issue. Its electoral fortunes at that time were depressed and there was a possibility of another early election being forced by the opposition. Moreover, the ALP was about to meet in federal conference, where it was eagerly hoping to promote the theme of party unity. In addition to standard anti-PLO arguments, Peacock was alleging that a visit would be another and deplorable government concession to Third World agitation and inconsistent with a policy of denying visas to peaceful South African sportsmen.[46] Willesee, Immigration Minister Cameron, Whitlam and the Department of Foreign Affairs, though they would have preferred that the issue had not surfaced as it did, supported the visit. This was not done on ideological but on "fair go" grounds for the ventilation of a particular point of view and because they felt that an internationally "isolated" PLO (as China had once been) would only persist in its intransigence. Federal Cabinet met on the eve of the Federal Conference and proceeded to make the first genuinely "collective" foreign policy decision since Labor's election in December 1972. After much impassioned debate, on a very close vote, the decision was to bar the PLO visit. Whitlam's official explanation of the action was that such a visit would have worsened division within the Australian community. The explanation was superficial. More exactly, a favourable decision would have inflamed anti-PLO feeling within the party and enhanced opposition electoral fortunes. Whitlam was angry that two leading party associates, Hawke and Hartley, had in their separate ways unnecessarily envenomed debate over the Middle East.[47] Whitlam was especially vexed with Harley. Hartley's critical interventions in government foreign policy had been numerous. On this occasion, he was felt to have improperly taken over sponsorship of the PLO visit and to have precluded the consideration of visas for PLO visitors through normal diplomatic channels. The controversy did not die there. Whitlam indicated he would at some future point like to have a PLO delegation pay an unofficial call. Other exponents of a visit continued to champion their cause. Some felt a particular urgency to bringing in a PLO delegation, with whom a PLO information office could be discussed. An early election was still possible, and so was a change of government. It was therefore important to set up an office before an unsympathetic L–CP might come to office.[48] As we have seen, visits by PLO-related persons were in fact allowed by the government. Among the consequences of the visits were physical clashes between pro- and anti-PLO demonstrators. We recall Whitlam's explanation of only a few months earlier that Cabinet had rejected a PLO visit because it would likely further divide the Australian community.

Our present context is Australia's diplomacy towards the Middle East, not trade. But some comment on the diplomacy/economics nexus adds perspective to our subject. The Whitlam government's official position was that its Middle East diplomacy was quite distinct from Australia's economic interests in the region. The point is hypothetical, but we can surmise that had Australia not had a distinct economic interest in the Middle East, its diplomacy would *not* have been much different. But if its economic interests had been substantially tied to Israel and only incidentally to the Arab states and Iran, then there might have been a somewhat different diplomatic posture. Australia was dependent on Persian Gulf states for about 30 per cent of its crude oil and enjoyed a meaningful primary product export trade with the region. Prior to the outbreak of the Yom Kippur war, Canberra had dispatched a seasoned emissary to the region to deal with Australia's continuing petroleum requirements and other matters. When the war broke out, the government had already been subscribing to what it portrayed as an even-handed diplomatic policy. Although its Middle East oil bill jumped, Australia never faced an oil embargo of the sort that Middle Eastern oil-producing states imposed on ostensibly pro-Israeli nations. Plainly, Australia was interested in further insulating itself from oil and other trade difficulties.

During the 1973 Middle Eastern hostilities, a wheat sale to Egypt was in the pipeline. The Wheat Board reversed its earlier decision and now wanted Egypt to pay cash, or to have the Australian government itself bear the risks if credit were extended. The government agreed to accept 75 per cent of the risk involved in the sale. Its decision was justifiable on strictly commercial grounds. But it also told the Wheat Board that it was eager to demonstrate an even-handed, not preferential, outlook towards the conflict. Australian negativism on the wheat deal could have lent itself to an opposite, pro-Israeli interpretation.[49] Later, with strong diplomatically based arguments from Foreign Affairs, the government agreed to expedite deliveries of the wheat. After the 1975 Cabinet decision to bar a PLO delegation visit, there were indications of Arab state displeasure and intimations that Australian trade would be adversely affected.[50] Careful Foreign Affairs Department monitoring of Arab capital reaction did not, however, indicate that explicit commercial retaliation against Australia was forthcoming. Indeed, the Labor government proceeded with an enormously ambitious search for petrodollar loans, an effort that, as we will discuss later, precipitated a major political crisis in Australia.

Nuclear testing was another issue area that highlighted the confluence of values, party and interest group politics and diplomatic manoeuvre. Labor's basic view was emphatic: "We would like to see all atomic testing—by all nations—cease."[51] Within the party, the anti-nuclear view was both genuine and widespread. It was inspired by a mixture of idealism and perceived Australian and international benefit. Nuclear testing was a bad thing because it endangered human health and otherwise damaged the natural environment. Hence Australia was especially concerned about above-surface nuclear testing. Secondly, the government believed that nuclear testing was bad for the state of the world, bad for confining the ambit of conflict or for reducing its destructive consequences. Nuclear testing even by established nuclear powers could serve as an incentive for nuclear weapon proliferation among other nations and it increased chances of conventional conflict escalating to nuclear levels. Hence the ALP government very rapidly ratified the NPT and unconditionally renounced acquisition of nuclear weaponry for itself. It was interested in strengthening international nuclear information and materials exchanges for peaceful purposes. It was pained by the 1974 Indian nuclear test, despite the test's ostensible peaceful applications, and also by the British underground test in Nevada in the same year, since it occurred "at a time when other recent [i.e. Indian test] developments have justifiably increased apprehension in the international community about the nuclear arms race".[52] A final subsidiary reason for Labor's campaign against nuclear testing was that such activity by Australia provided a convenient opportunity for demonstrating the government's sense of diplomatic initiative on a virtually global stage and for demonstrating its humanitarian credentials among Third World nations.

Labor's attention was focused on the two established nuclear powers that refused to subscribe to the NPT and that continued to test in the atmosphere—France and China. Particular umbrage was taken with France, which carried out its testing in French Polynesia, in the South Pacific, meaning in Australia's general geographic neighbourhood. Moreover, France was a party to an interwar treaty that provided for peaceful settlement of international disputes, but which in this instance France claimed inoperative due to a defence exigency exception clause. Australia discounted the French exception and believed Paris was acting in direct defiance of international law. Official Australian initiatives against French testing were numerous and varied. There were diplomatic conversations, diplomatic protests when tests occurred and intimations of withdrawing the Australian ambassador from Paris. Prior to France's mid-1973 test, New Zealand dispatched a frigate and Australia a support ship to the test area around (but not within) the test/fall-out zone, to publicize displeasure. Together with New Zealand, though with a somewhat different brief, Australia went to the International Court of Justice in the Hague, to force a legal restraint on France. In an interim decision, the ICJ issued a temporary restraining injunction asking both France and Australia to refrain from aggravating the dispute, including by not proceeding with testing, until the Court could explicitly establish its own competence in the matter and render a full and binding judgement. Paris did not honour the Court's injunction. But, while Canberra continued to protest against French testing, it eventually felt that earlier official and unofficial Australian and other exertions had probably hastened France's decision to conduct tests underground. This was a safer procedure, and one against which Australian displeasure was less intensely expressed.[53]

It must be noted that the Labor government's efforts to block French testing, or to censure France for testing, or at large to condemn nuclear testing, especially in the atmosphere, were not confined to unilateral Australian or bilateral Australian–New Zealand initiatives. Especially in 1973 and in early 1974, senior Australian ministers used the United Nations and every other available international forum to press appropriate resolutions or other expressions of sentiment. These settings included the South Pacific Forum, Apia, April 1973 (Whitlam); June–July 1973 African ministerial visit (Willesee); Mexico City, July 1973 (Whitlam); Commonwealth Prime Ministers Conference, Ottawa, August 1973 (Whitlam); South Pacific Conference, Guam, September 1973 (Willesee); South Pacific Forum, Rorotonga, March 1974 (Willesee). Largely though not uniformly, Australia was able to evoke sympathetic responses in such forums. The Labor government was also able, at an early stage of its tenure in office, to display its credentials of interest, humanity and initiatory style. Several persons intimately associated with the Australian foreign policy scene remarked to the author that Australia probably gained considerable diplomatic credit through its anti-French testing diplomacy, especially among Pacific Island nations.

Action against the French nuclear-testing programme was by no means limited to official, diplomatic initiatives. On the government's part, there were some intimations that French obduracy could lead to trade reprisals, including Australia's defence procurements.[54] But the government elected not to play that game, and in fact discouraged trade-union action against France. In May 1973, Whitlam met with Hawke and requested that no industrial action against France be taken. More particularly, Whitlam urged unions to avoid a postal and telecommunications ban. Such action would not only contravene Australian obligations under international conventions on diplomatic and consular postal exchanges but could also possibly prejudice Australia's case before the ICJ.[55]

But, with the open support of several ministers, Hawke and the ACTU took their own counsel. For several months, a black ban was imposed on French shipping and air services to Australia, on the handling of French goods, on mail and telecommunications services, even on French artistic performers. The ban was not entirely successful. Inconvenience was caused to France and French interests, but equally or more so to Australia, which enjoyed a profitable and favourably balanced trade with France. There were particularly inconvenient spin-off effects upon South Pacific countries. In time, the ban petered out, with only sporadic and incidental revival afterwards.[56]

Moreover, the union boycott opened a party political controversy in Australia. Earlier L–CP governments had been very firm in con-

demning French atmospheric testing. When in opposition, the L–CP
continued this position and endorsed Labor's submission to the ICJ.
But it thought the Australian and New Zealand venture to be a case of
grandstanding, and the union boycott as counter-productive and a
sign of government helplessness in the face of outside pressures.[57]
Most of the opposition's criticism of the government was, however,
aimed at Labor's handling of Chinese nuclear testing. The L–CP's basic
charge, as for instance expressed in a motion of importance moved in
the Senate, was that the government was adhering to a double standard in its attitude towards French and Chinese nuclear testing, and
that it had exerted itself less often and less intensely in denouncing
Peking's nuclear programme; a "matter of national disgrace", Sinclair
called it.[58]

What were the facts? The government filed protests over Chinese
as well as French tests. Conversations were held with ranking
Chinese officials in Peking by top Labor figures, including Whitlam
and Cairns, and Cairns noted Chou En-lai's annoyance over the
Australian criticisms.[59] In its public pronouncements, the government
made it plain that it condemned all atmospheric tests, Chinese and
French alike. Australia brought French but not Chinese tests before
the ICJ. This was fully understandable, since China had never
covenanted to the ICJ's jurisdiction. On the other hand, the fact remains that on some occasions, in international forum or bilateral
communiqué settings, Australia pressed for a condemnation of
French tests, but wished to avoid similarly explicit chastisement of
Peking. It is also true that while there had been ministerial intimations of officially sponsored commercial pressures against France, no
comparable remarks appear to have been made about China. While
Australiá at one time toyed with recalling its ambassador from Paris,
nothing comparable was contemplated opposite China. The tone of
Australia's relations with France in 1973 over the testing issue was
more angered than it was towards China. Furthermore, at a non-
governmental level, Australian unions effectively did nothing to impose bans against Chinese goods, services or transport.

Why did there seem to be a less-severe attitude towards China?
One apparent reason was the ICJ situation. The Whitlam government
was especially piqued with France for its refusal to acknowledge the
jurisdiction of the Court in the testing matter, since France was a
party to the ICJ convention. We notice again a certain legalistic
streak in the Labor government's outlook, as well as a preoccupation
with regularized, international means of conflict settlement. The
French flaunted both principles; the Chinese, technically, neither. The
Whitlam government also was known to make a distinction between
French and Chinese testing in that France had the effrontery to set off

nuclear explosions in someone else's backyard, while China at least operated on its own soil. This view was present despite the fact that the French nuclear devices seemed "cleaner" than the Chinese and their fall-out probably potentially touched no more people than China's.

That leaves only one further explanation. For reasons of sentiment or diplomatic calculation, the Labor government did not wish to be as stern with China as with France. The present author supports Hedley Bull's conclusion: "whereas a political campaign against France on the issue suits the general line of our foreign policy, a comparable campaign against China would move so much counter to the main drift of our diplomacy as to be unthinkable."[60] This interpretation was privately accepted, with various degrees of emphasis, in circles close to the Australian foreign policy process. Labor's view had something to do with its pleasure at having helped to discard open containment practices against China, and perhaps with a fear that overreaction against Chinese nuclear tests could lead to re-estrangement between China and other countries. Labor's approach also related to its wish to be firm but not brusque with good, though admittedly ideologically distant, diplomatic colleagues. It also had something to do with the fact that China was felt to be a key factor in Labor's vision of a low-conflict Asian community, while France was not, and with Labor's wish to maintain standing and some influence with the Chinese leadership. In a nutshell, for Labor, China counted for far more than France and therefore deserved somewhat special handling, even after the original honeymoon of Chinese–ALP government relations.

We have, in several issue area contexts, mentioned Australia's reaction to various communist states. A more explicit rendering of Australian–communist state relations is helpful in unravelling the motives, diplomatic style and political constraints that operated on and within the Labor government. We will look first at Australian diplomatic initiatives towards smaller communist nations and then turn to relations with China and the Soviet Union.

Part of Labor's approach to communist nations was dictated by the conviction that realities needed to be recognized. Diplomatic connections implied nothing about political or ideological approval. Indeed, diplomatically "contained" nations were less likely, in Labor's view, to become respectably behaving members of the international community. Movement towards international *détente* had already set the tone for abandoning anachronistic postures. Sustaining Labor's feelings was the memory of the prolonged and, the ALP felt, conspicuous-.ly counter-productive isolation of China.

Labor quickly recognized East Germany (German Democratic Republic). The explanation was in part straightforward: It was to facilitate commercial as well as political relations. In part, it reflected a more particular Labor intention, namely to diversify Australia's contacts and interests beyond the traditional South-East Asian concentration.[61] It was an unconditional step. The McMahon government had itself been moving towards recognition and no political recrimination arose when Labor recognized.

Within Asia, the recognition of North Vietnam was, for reasons previously alluded to, a natural step for Labor. It was more controversial than the German step, but really more for its alleged "haste" than for its lack of justification. Relations with Saigon, we recall, were unaffected until the Thieu régime collapsed. When in 1975 there was a change of régimes in Saigon and Pnom Penh, Australia quickly recognized the new governments. Again, what criticism there was from the opposition, and from the United States, was essentially for haste, not for the wrongness of the decisions.

The recognition of North Korea (Democratic People's Republic of Korea) was a more complex enterprise. In addition to conventional political and commercial recognition considerations, the government was animated by the belief that Australian, and more generally international, recognition would place both Koreas on notice that they were two *de facto* entities, neither of which was entitled to encroach on the other, and that peaceful reunification as such might be hastened. It was a reason that carried both pragmatic and idealistic connotations. Moreover, even though recognition of North Korea had no bearing on Canberra's continuing recognition of South Korea (Republiç of Korea), there was considerable resistance expressed by Japan, the United States, and most emphatically by the South Koreans; "premature" recognition of Pyongyang would weaken Seoul's position and possibly delay a reasonable unification settlement.[62]

The process by which Australia moved towards recognition of North Korea was nearly a model of preparation and sensitivity. Early in Labor's tenure, it was decided to avoid any hostile tone of voice towards North Korea and to promote various informal exchanges. An Australian trade mission to North Korea broke some ice in 1973. The South Korean and other governments were kept apprised of what became Australia's intention to recognize North Korea. The South Koreans requested that, at minimum, Canberra ask various communist nations to consider recognizing Seoul. This was done, including with China, despite obvious Australian reservations about prospects for success. Australian–North Korean negotiations were conducted slowly, and Australian patience was apparently sorely tried. The North Koreans were ."bloody obstinate" to deal with, one well-placed observer remarked. Australia did not "give anything away" in its recognition agreement with North Korea. Nor did it hasten to establish an embassy in Pyongyang, but decided to accredit a non-residential ambassador.[63] An embassy, headed by a chargé, was not opened until April 1975. Nor was the government innocent about the Australian political scene. Once the double dissolution of Parliament had been announced in April 1974, the author was assured that nothing would be done to consummate recognition before polling-day. When, shortly before the election, South Korean objections became loud, Willesee turned the tables by taking the high road: Australians would resent any action by another country that might be interpreted as an intrusion into an Australian electoral campaign,[64] When he visited North Korea in June 1975, Willesee cautioned his hosts about bombastic and unrealistic behaviour on the subject of Korean unification.[65] Recognition had, he felt, made it easier for Australia to speak plainly.

The Labor government's meticulous efforts at sensible relations with North Korea were laid waste just before Whitlam lost office. At the end of October, the North Koreans peremptorily withdrew their personnel from Canberra and a week later ordered the Australians out of Pyongyang. A flurry of charges about "intolerably" provocative acts, sabotage of the North Korean people and harassment by Australia appeared. The Australian government was stunned, dismayed and embarrassed. The day that the government was ended by the Governor-General, Willesee was describing North Korea's allegations as "so transparently false that they do the People's Republic of Korea no credit and raise serious questions about its willingness or capacity to act in the normally accepted way."[66]

North Korea's diplomatic insult followed immediately upon a vote in the Political Committee of the United Nations, where Australia had just cast an abstention on a North Korean-favoured resolution that, *inter alia*, called for eventual Korean unification talks between North Korea and the United States only. Investigation suggests that Australia's United Nations vote was not the only and quite possibly not the major factor behind the North Korean move. Apparently, it simply was the last straw for a North Korean government already very unhappy with Australia. The North Koreans had never adapted to dealing with a Western government, and to their position in Canberra in particular. They had not appreciated admonitions (equally placed before the South Koreans) not to engage in blatant propaganda within Australia against the other Korea, nor Australia's insistence on dealing with the two Koreas as equally sovereign in their respective areas. Indeed, when Australia first made publicly known its intention to oppose the contentious United Nations resolution, and the North Koreans expressed their resentment, a decision was made to change the vote to an abstention. It was a decision taken impetuously, apparently by Whitlam personally, and satisfied no one. It failed to placate the North Koreans. It angered the Americans, to whom a negative vote had been explicitly promised. Canadians, Japanese and others also expressed their disappointment. While the resolution was expected to succeed whatever Australia's vote, it was believed that the final tally in the Political Committee was exaggerated due to the influence of Australia's early alphabetical vote.[67] In the end, the Labor government earned recrimination from both sides, ironically on an issue where its United Nations vote seemed to be more symptom than cause of the diplomatic breach with North Korea. At all events, the caretaker Fraser government returned Australia's vote to negative once the resolution came before the plenary session.

For different reasons, Cuba also proved a complex diplomatic enterprise. When Labor entered office, Australia and Cuba already recognized one another, but there was no representation on either side. For the first half year of its tenure, the Whitlam government turned aside Cuban inquiries about setting up a consulate and trade mission in Sydney. The principal public explanation as of June 1973 was that the volume of bilateral trade did not justify such a move and that Australia lacked the resources to reciprocate with a mission in Havana. Whitlam did indicate, however, that American feeling may have played a part.[68] By July 1973, while in Mexico, Whitlam explored Latin American feelings towards Cuba in relation to a possible Australian move. By January 1974, a decision was taken to accept a Cuban consulate, temporarily with no Australian post in Cuba. Australia did, in fact, have something to gain from a consulate in Sydney, given the healthy and rising sales to Cuba. Representation by one party alone suddenly proved no obstacle to accepting a consulate.

It is instructive what really did constrain Australia for a time. Canberra believed that the United States would have been furious with Australia, perhaps to the point of applying trade sanctions, had Australia made a friendly representational gesture towards Cuba in the first half of 1973. In the immediate background seemed to lie Washington's known hostility towards the Castro régime, and the climate of Canberra–Washington relations was at that time very chilly, given Whitlam's Vietnam letter to Nixon and other factors. So, to avoid further aggravation, Australia did nothing about Cuba. The truth is that these Australia concerns were decidedly exaggerated. They were based on plausible but overdrawn inferences passed from the embassy in Washington, not on actual American threats or pressures. By the second half of 1973, Australia began to realize that Washington had itself become less strident about Cuba, and Whitlam as Prime Minister had at long last paid a visit to America and in a fashion made peace with the Nixon administration. The episode showed that the new independently minded Labor government was not callous about its relations with the United States, though admittedly the issue of a Cuban consulate was peripheral to Australia's basic foreign policy concerns. The fact that Whitlam took pains to discover Latin American feelings about Cuba also illuminated a broader principle, namely his orientation towards regionalism as an international phenomenon. His interest in Latin American opinion was much more than a gesture of courtesy: it fitted his conceptions.[69]

Labor's recognition of Peking was in a political class by itself. It held topmost priority for the new government. There never was any question of continuing diplomatic links with Taiwan; it could not and would not be. The nomenclature of the Sino–Australian recognition agreement was accepted by Canberra without resistance, even though Australia "acknowledged" China's position that Taiwan was one of its provinces, rather than holding out for a softer, Canadian formula of "noting" China's claim.[70] Affirming a natural diplomatic relationship with China was then, and remained, a source of considerable pride and pleasure for the ALP government, and for Whitlam personally, who had gambled but benefited handsomely from his 1971 visit to China. Normalization of relations with China was symbolically prominent as an exercise in party vindication. The nasty past lay behind, a good and sensible future ahead. At last, things had been set right. Whitlam's October–November 1973 visit to China, now as Prime Minister, was a sentimental as well as diplomatic journey. As we have seen, Labor was convinced that, for many reasons, effective relations with China were central to building a structure of stability and regional co-operation, though the government realized that Australia had to guard against making relations with China the pivot of its foreign policy. The government underwrote its commitment to close and effective ties with China. It appointed as ambassador Dr Stephen FitzGerald, a Sinologist, expert in the language, personally known to the Chinese from his 1971 visit with the ALP delegation, and a person close to Whitlam himself. The embassy was staffed with competent Chinese-speaking personnel. The Australian commission in Hong Kong was retained, in part, to provide a supplementary source of "China-watching" data and advice to the government.

For some time, Australia had to suffer some tiresome, even meddlesome Chinese behaviour. The Chinese press celebrated the pro-Peking Communist Party of Australia (Marxist–Leninist) and played up industrial disorders and economic weaknesses in Australia. The

Chinese complained to Canberra about misinterpretations by Australian journalists of the "anti-Confucian" ideological campaign being waged in China. The Foreign Affairs Department pointed out that the Australian press was free, not controlled as in China. The department was prepared to correct errors of fact, but regarded interpretations as the right of individual journalists.[71] The Chinese asked the Australian government to prevent the screening in Australia of a film on China regarded by Peking as libelous. The government refused to intercede with Australian Broadcasting Commission decisions on screenings, or with private screenings in theatres. There had been intimations of reprisals against the ABC correspondent in Peking should the ABC run the film.[72] The government's polite but firm reactions apparently paid off. There eventually were fewer maligning articles in the Chinese press and no repetitions à la the anti-Confucian campaign and film screening complaints. Informed parties suggested two explanations for the earlier Chinese intrusions. Firstly, that they had been inspired by China's Canberra embassy, perhaps by persons inexpreienced in the ways of Australian society and politics. Secondly, that there may have been an attempt to "test" Australia, as to how far Labor as a government was prepared to concede to China in its bid to preserve favourable working relations with Peking.

More generally, how did Sino–Australian relations fare? According to the government, early and enthusiastic recognition, plus other gestures and the style of Australia's approach to China, helped to improve trading relationships.[73] We will look at this latter claim further on. The point here is that the government had seen some concrete commercial gain from a friendly diplomatic posture towards China, and then believed this had been brought about. In 1974, China's agreement to a cultural exchange package with Australia was the first of its kind negotiated since the Chinese Cultural Revolution. The Chinese invited a senior Australian diplomat to assist them in exploring certain law-of-the-sea problems and took Australian specialist advice on the development of undersea oil deposits. The Labor government welcomed such contacts. For the sake of diplomatic benefits, it seemed to treat China tenderly. Hence it walked a careful line on Chinese nuclear testing. It was hesitant to denounce Peking on such occasions as when China forcefully took over the Paracel Islands in the South China Sea from South Vietnam. It acceded to Chinese representations that Taiwanese visitors bearing official connections not be granted Australian visas, though Australia managed to protect its own position in the Pacific Area Travel Association by admitting Taiwanese delegates to the association's Sydney conference through some very delicate footwork.[74]

Whitlam, in particular, reiterated that Australia was not trying to cast itself in the role of China's advocate in the region. All the same, better understanding in the neighbourhood could be advanced by Australia: "I don't suggest that we should pose for ourselves any grandiose, pompous role as a 'bridge'. But it may well be that on certain issues and on some occasions and at all times in a general way, we can be one honest broker among others."[75] As we saw earlier, a salient feature of this conception was the wish to make China more acceptable to South-East Asian states. The quality of Australia's own relations with Peking would in turn serve as evidence of how a professedly Western and aligned nation could get on with a communist China. The ultimate purpose, or vision, was a more stabilized regional environment and broadly cast linkages in an Asian–Pacific associational context. Though the regional impact was slight, as early as May 1973, Chou En-lai urged Cairns to use his contacts among Asian leaders to stress that China would not attempt to expand its influence among overseas Chinese communities.[76] As seen, Australia's role may have affected Malaysia's recognition of China in 1974. By early 1975, there were signs that China was prepared to enter into initially confidential conversations with Australia about broad issues of disarmament. This was due in part to Australia's known interest in the subject and to its good relations with a variety of aligned and non-aligned governments. Still, as a number of people sensed, there was a danger of overstating and romanticizing Australia's Chinese connections. A serious turn for the worse between Canberra and Peking could create a major public and political let-down, and possibly cause precipitate overreaction and otherwise unnecessary disillusionment.

For the Labor government, relations with the Soviets were less critical and entailed less emotional involvement than did relations with China. All the same, Soviet–Australian relations were important. There were considerations of trade. There was the overall requirement of reasonable access to a super-power with considerable and world-wide interests. There was interest in the Soviet role in Australia's western seaboard exposure, the Indian Ocean. The Soviets themselves took an increasingly keen interest in Australia. Australia was assuming a particularly active role with various Asian states and was evolving a form of brokerage relationship among them, while reducing its earlier, heavily American-oriented dependence. Moreover, Moscow's competition with Peking seemed to recommend a strong diplomatic presence in Australia, which could help to monitor and if needed countervail possible pro-Chinese, and therefore Soviet-resented, inclinations. The Soviets upgraded their diplomatic and consular staffs in Australia and, apparently, the KGB component. Whitlam's visit to the Soviet Union in January 1975 was a testament of both sides' heightened interest in one another. On that occasion, the Soviet "interest" was extended to the electronic bugging and other forms of surveillance over the Australian visitors. At the diplomatic level, the visit produced agreement for sponsorship of a world-disarmament conference, as well as enhanced top-level bilateral contacts.[77]

The ALP government had some skirmishes with the Soviet Union that, though in and of themselves of no major substantive importance, were felt in many quarters to have been indicative of Labor's diplomatic style in relation to communist states. As a party of government, Labor prided itself on its commitment to the rights of individuals and peoples. Willesee issued a statement in which he denounced the expulsion from the USSR of writer Alexander Solzhenitsyn as "contrary to all internationally accepted forms of judicial process and respect for human rights.[78] When in the Soviet Union, Whitlam raised with Premier Kosygin issues such as Jewish migration from the Soviet Union and the treatment of political prisoners, only to be told that these were matters of domestic Soviet concern.[79] At the United Nations, Australia promoted standards of generous political asylum.

At home, however, the L–CP and considerable sections of the press concluded that the government was behaving contrary to such sentiments, presumably to curry Soviet favour. The opposition revealed an otherwise unpublicized case of an East European diplomat who, for his family and himself, had inquired about asylum in Australia through an Australian mission in a third country. Pressed, Immigration Minister Cameron conceded that the head of the Australian mission in the third country had recommended that entry be given, but that he, Cameron, had refused the request. The government declined to elaborate, leaving an impression that it had something to hide.[80] Much more dramatized was the case of Georgi Ermolenko, a young Soviet violinist. In August 1974, in Perth, at the conclusion of a concert tour of Australia, Ermolenko announced that he wished to remain in Australia. For several days there was confusion and public demonstration in Perth, and hectic activity in Perth and in Canberra. The upshot was that Ermolenko was said by Australian spokesmen to have changed his mind of his own free will, after conversations with Soviet officials. He was then spirited out of Australia on his way to the Soviet Union in an RAAF aircraft, to avoid restraining action by groups in Perth convinced Ermolenko was being intimidated into leaving. There was a widespread impression that, while Australia had a very nettlesome problem on its hands, it had bent over backwards to accommodate the Soviets, and perhaps had even colluded with the Soviets to get Ermolenko out. This was presented as a violation of

Labor's human rights professions as well as a cynical gesture to be pleasant to the Soviets, perhaps in anticipated exchange for some diplomatic or commercial favour, or more broadly, simply to be tolerant of communist practices.[81] In 1975, Ermolenko and his musician parents left the Soviet Union with exit visas for Israel, whereupon they announced they were migrating to Australia. The Labor government portrayed this as vindication of its earlier procedures. Had Ermolenko not previously been permitted to leave Australia, he could not have brought his parents out of Russia.[82] Simultaneously, Cameron announced that two Czech seamen who had jumped ship in Australia, and who for months faced the prospect of deportation, would be granted permanent residence.[83]

Another point in controversy was Labor's decision to recognize *de jure* Soviet sovereignty over the Baltic states of Latvia, Lithuania and Estonia. These states had, under duress, been incorporated into the Soviet Union at the start of the Second World War. By mid-1974, when Australia took its step, most Western and in particular NATO states had not accorded *de jure* recognition. How and why did Australia take its step? On the basis of extensive inquiries, the author feels that a close approximation of an accurate answer can be made. The public record reads that Willesee personally ordered a Foreign Affairs Department review of the matter. He may have had a hand in it, but the inspiration apparently came from Whitlam himself. He had become aware of and was disturbed by the anomalous presence of an honorary Latvian consul in Melbourne, who purported to represent a "free Latvian" government. Whitlam shot a note to Foreign Affairs to examine the matter. Then, from New Zealand, came another incentive for the government to delve into the issue. A New Zealand parliamentary delegation wished to visit the Baltic states, but the New Zealand government discovered this would be difficult, since Wellington had never granted *de jure* recognition of Soviet sovereignty over these states. In search of guidance, New Zealand contacted the Australian government. In Canberra, Foreign Affairs made a recommendation that Australia recognize *de jure* Soviet sovereignty over the Baltic states. The submission went to Willesee, as Foreign Minister. Willesee was out of the country. His office asked that the submission be held over until his return. But the submission was then placed before Whitlam, in his capacity as acting Foreign Minister. Whitlam endorsed the department's favourable recommendation, without consultation with Willesee or other Cabinet colleagues. No public announcement was issued. The decision came to light quite accidentally, when press reports picked up the fact that the Australian Ambassador to the Soviet Union had paid a call in the Baltic region.

Why was the decision taken? The British, US and other governments were consulted and raised no objections. The department's brief was decidedly positive. Foreign Affairs largely construed the step as part of the government's "cleaning-up" effort to remove remaining diplomatic anomalies. However, it is understood that the department's preparation of the submission was handled less diligently than it might have been and that some potential offshoot problems were simply overlooked; for instance, the effect on Japan, which for years had challenged Soviet occupation of its northern islands. The government's explanation of the decision was that it was a logical extension of recognizing realities. It was foolhardy and inimical to sensible East–West relations to encourage people to think that the Baltic states could somehow be recovered from the Soviet Union. Australia's gesture would also facilitate various consular relations relative to the Baltic states.[84]

These explanations, in the author's best judgement, were real, not specious, and they did generally complement Labor's overall thinking about recognition practices and about working with realities and towards useful relations with communist nations, rather than holding to nostalgic and divisive notions about what communist nations perpetrated years before. Other motives, turning on its ostensible wish to please the Soviets, were imputed to the government. Labor was charged with trying to demonstrate to the USSR that Australia was not "over-tilting" towards China; with wishing to improve its voice in Moscow over the Soviet naval build-up in the Indian Ocean; with wanting Soviet backing for Australia's UN General Assembly presidential candidacy; with looking for a cordial reception for Whitlam on his scheduled visit to the Soviet Union; with aiming to influence Soviet–Australian negotiations on the sale of beef from the depressed Australian industry. Most of these interpretations were plausible, but none, apparently, contributed to the decision.

If indeed the government was not searching for any diplomatic or commercial pay-offs from its decision, then it can be argued that its generalized motives were not worth the clamour that the decision precipitated. Australia gained next to nothing from a decision on a matter very marginal to its diplomatic concerns. Willesee said that he concurred in the decision, but there is some highly reliable internal evidence suggesting otherwise. He certainly felt that the step was precipitous and ill-timed politically, lacking the sort of gradual public conditioning that had preceded the recognition of North Korea. A number of people in the party, including ministers, were upset. Not only was it a poor decision, but it had been taken by Whitlam alone. The bypassing of caucus and Cabinet on foreign policy decisions had been routine procedure. In this case, however, it strengthened feeling that Labor parliamentarians were at large being improperly disregarded by the Prime Minister. The Baltic incident probably heightened caucus activity on the Timorese and PRG issues.

There was, moreover, a great hue and cry raised by the opposition, in much of the press and within the Baltic *émigré* community in Australia. The criticisms, taken together with attacks over Ermolenko and the East European diplomat who had sought asylum, caused the government acute political embarrassment. Critics generally believed that the government had impunged its own declarations about rights and self-determination for all peoples. Baltic people in the country felt betrayed. The opposition hammered the theme that the Whitlam government now stood exposed. The government talked a smooth line about even-handedness, but was said to be patently uneven in its practices by fawning over Third World and communist states. It attacked injustice in Rhodesia and South Africa. It gave aid to liberation movements. But it failed to distinguish between aggressor and victim in the Middle East, and now on the Baltic issue, Ermolenko, etc. This showed that the government was preoccupied with ingratiating itself with the Soviets. In broader terms, the Baltic decision was sketched out as evidence of an Australian drift into non-alignment.[85]

On the *known* evidence, the Ermolenko, East European diplomat and Baltic episodes did not justify a reasoned judgement that Labor was bending over backwards to be gracious towards the Soviets or communist nations generally. The government did not handle the Ermolenko case as efficiently and clearly as it might have. Indeed, it may have erred in thinking that Ermolenko had had a fair chance to weigh his options before he was flown out of Perth. But the government had to contend with an extraordinarily confused and sensationalized problem, most of which was played out in Perth, where the government lacked adequate personnel. The author can personally testify that, when the Ermolenko affair crested, there was a frantic atmosphere in the Department of Foreign Affairs and in the Foreign Minister's office, a clutching of heads prompted by not quite knowing what was going on and how to react next. There is no information as to why Canberra overrode its own overseas Australian mission advice and refused to grant asylum to the inquiring East European diplomat. One can surmise that Cameron did not wish to let an apparent anti-communist in or to create an untoward situation with a communist nation. But it can also be speculated that the reasons were quite different, with no bearing on ideology or politics. We simply do not know. We have suggested that the stated reasons for the Baltic states decision were probably true and the only ones. These reasons squared with Labor's overall international perceptions and had little if anything to do with tilting towards the Soviets. It was impression that led people to think otherwise. The step was quite unnecessary and, like the asylum seeker's case, was, at least originally, kept under wraps, thereby arousing suspicions of some kind of perfidy. It was stylistically mismanaged, and above all showed a noticeable lapse of political foresight. It was in these respects that the Labor government could be most tellingly faulted.

We have discussed the pattern of Australia's relations with communist states. Shortly we will appraise relations with the United States. In between, it is worthwhile to reassemble and extend a number of earlier points about Labor's general substantive and stylistic approach to international diplomacy, with emphasis on Asia.

We have noticed the Whitlam government's professions of internationalism, a "new nationalist" temper and a wish to discharge an independently concerned, constructive role in world councils. Labor saw separate yet interlocking reasons to spread Australia's diplomatic involvement widely—towards great powers, towards Third World states, towards states whose "middle power" status seemed to resemble Australia's and towards the surrounding Asian–Pacific region in particular. Establishing a far-flung network of diplomatic ties was one method of going about this. The dispatch of very senior ministers overseas, especially to areas previously understressed by L–CP governments, was another. A third method was accepting observer status at a variety of regional bodies, in Latin America, Africa and elsewhere. The ALP as a party was bestirred. For instance, in 1974, for the first time it voted money for a fraternal socialist party, in this instance Portuguese socialists, and initiated steps for an Australian meeting site for the Bureau of the Socialist International.[86] Whitlam, we recall, saw the period of Labor's advent to power as most timely for an activist Australian role abroad, to make the most of opportunities previously lost over Indo-China, China, and so on.

Relations with Japan were one sign of what the government set out to do. It saw Japan not only as a major trading partner but as a vital cog in the region, a contributor to regional economic development, and as a potential and major member in a broad Asian–Pacific forum. Moreover, Whitlam was preoccupied with the need to "break the nexus", which he associated historically with great industrial powers, a nexus between economic strength and military strength and its use. Australia could not do this alone, but it could help. It could afford Japan access to raw materials and an overseas market. In addition to economic provisions, it could also make gestures of major symbolic and possibly diplomatic importance. A 1974 proposal from Ambassador Shann in Tokyo for a large-scale Japanese–Australian foundation was rejected in Canberra as premature and too grandiose, and was not supported by the Japanese themselves.[87] Instead, a straightforward yet important cultural agreement was signed and in 1975, a modified form of the Australian–Japan foundation idea was announced by the government.

Under the L–CP, Japan's wish for a treaty of friendship, commerce and navigation had been rebuffed. Under Labor, the Interdepartmental Committee on Japan again advised against. There were various economic objections, and objections dealing with suspicious reactions that might be aroused elsewhere in Asia. Whitlam turned down the advice and had the matter reassessed. A modified umbrella concept was adumbrated; in effect, a treaty of friendship and co-operation. Such a compact would spell out various economic relationships. It would be geared to meeting the promise of Australian materials and markets for Japan. It would also, in a unique step for both sides, formalize the Canberra–Tokyo relationship and hopefully serve as reassurance for Japan and neighbouring states. China, for one, was consulted by Australia and raised no objections.[88] However, negotiations on the treaty proved long and difficult, as we will see when discussing Australia's international economic policies.

Labor's reaction to a proposal for a more formalized New Zealand–Australian relationship illuminated some of the government's diplomatic priorities and conceptions. Early in 1973, Kirk put to Whitlam the idea of a new institutionalized arrangement. Despite palpably close New Zealand–Australian ties and *rapport* between the two Labor Prime Ministers, Australia said no. In part, it was felt that existing mechanisms for consultations and exchanges were sufficient. More explicitly, Canberra wished to avoid requirements of what it regarded as constant pre-consultation, feeling this would constrain its freedom of manoeuvre, especially in a period when the new Whitlam government was undertaking so many foreign policy initiatives.[89]

Here and in other contexts we have noticed the wide span of ALP government activity. Some of this was conducted circumspectly, some of it with an air of drama and some in a plain-spoken Whitlam style. For instance, Whitlam's original Asian–Pacific scheme proposal was probably overrushed, but his visits to China and Japan in the latter part of 1973 were models of careful preparation and execution. Whitlam's early remarks about Thailand becoming a second Vietnam because of the American military presence there, and about the need to urge Thailand into closer ties with China, were at the time taken in Bangkok more as rudeness than as candour.

At the 1973 Commonwealth Prime Ministers Conference in Ottawa, Whitlam and Singapore's Lee Kuan-yew had very sharp exchanges, publicly as well as privatley, on a variety of topics. Whitlam claimed that Lee had started it all, but Whitlam was not averse to giving as much as he took. Whitlam referred to Lee as a "philosophical hawk" and a man who was "very free with his advice, but Singapore has pursued a thoroughly selfish attitude in our region". Lee had become "too authoritarian" and "more and more like Cromwell."[90]

The government's handling of political and civil violations in various nations was, as a rule, composed. The major exceptions to the rule were the South African and Rhodesian régimes. This was substantially accounted for by a personal sense of revulsion against racialism. One less-glowing explanation, to which we alluded before, was that idealism and principle faded as distance to Australia shortened. What was meant was that South Africa, Rhodesia, and perhaps the Greek and Chilean military régimes, were easy targets. Little was lost and perhaps something gained, especially among Third World nations, by roundly condemning such régimes. But towards Asian countries, with whom Australia felt it needed friendly relations and where the thrust of its diplomacy was directed, criticism was more muted.

The author feels that there is something to be said for this principle versus pragmatism interpretation, but that it should not be overstretched. Whitlam made some quite unflattering remarks about the Chilean military junta and quite pointedly said that there was much less freedom in Chile than in China.[91] But, despite vocal radical pressures and much unease among ALP parliamentarians, the government had chosen to recognize the new Chilean régime. It dealt with it, and in so doing was able, by early 1975, to arrange the passage of a number of Chilean political "non-desirables" to Australia, in itself a concrete humanitarian gesture.[92] The government issued public condemnations of the treatment of noted Soviet authors and scientists, and Whitlam raised civil liberty questions with Kosygin, though there was no particular rancour in Australia's tone on such occasions.

Political prisoner issues in Asia created the most controversy in Australia. There was a view that Australia should not countenance political oppression simply to maintain working relations with offending régimes. Régimes changed and, in any event, some argued that Australia should try to associate itself with the more, not less, progressive tendencies within the Third World. The "pro-criticism" outlook, though concentrated on the left, drew cross-party support. For example, a multi-party "amnesty" group in Parliament, though only about fifteen strong in consistent working numbers, collected some eighty parliamentary signatures on a petition handed to Whitlam prior to his 1974 and 1975 Indonesian and Soviet visits, requesting that he raise political oppression issues with leaders in the two host nations. Indonesia came in for special attack by critics, since the government seemed so intent to stay on side with the leadership there. A different view was offered by Richard Woolcott, then Deputy

Secretary of the Department of Foreign Affairs. He cautioned against imposing Australian political values on others. The government should not fall into the trap of overreacting to the point of counter-productivity. Sensitive régimes might become more repressive if over-pressed and Australia could lose needed standing among them.[93] Ministers of Whitlam's and Willesee's stature did in fact raise political repression with governments as diverse as South Vietnam (Thieu régime), Singapore, South Korea, the Philippines and Indonesia. But they generally followed Woolcott's advice. They expressed concern, but without fanfare. When Whitlam refused the parliamentary petitions pressed on him by the amnesty group, his explanation was not that the petitions were substantively improper, but that he alone, in an official capacity, would broach these matters.

The government's approach to international groupings, and especially the United Nations, requires special mention. Attachment to the United Nations fitted Labor's temperament and objectives well. The United Nations was a near-universal membership body, as heterogeneous as could be, and a genuine gathering of the family of man. It stood for noble objectives such as peace and international goodwill, and was seen as devoted more to the avoidance than to the suppression of conflict. It provided a forum where smaller powers such as Australia could more easily be noticed, and possibly exert influence, than in ordinary bilateral situations. For Labor, idealism and perceived national interest merged. In its lexicon, the United Nations was a decidedly good thing.

As a result, Labor used the United Nations energetically. It was opposed (for instance, on Cambodia) to procedural manoeuvres designed by others to block substantive deliberations. It undertook special issue area initiatives, as on diplomatic asylum and on the peaceful settlement of disputes. It proclaimed that "there was no area of actual or potential conflict anywhere in the world where loyalties, ideology or interest, should make Australian involvement ... in peace-keeping unacceptable or unwelcome.[94] Australia expressed interest in supplying troops in this capacity for service in Cyprus and in the Middle East, and actually undertook training of units in peace-keeping roles with Canadian forces.

Late in 1975, the government's position on peace-keeping became the basis of some misunderstanding: Roy Macartney, an Australian correspondent based in the United States, reported that the Labor government had demurred in the face of a United Nations query about Australian logistical troops being sent in support of the peace-keeping force in the Sinai.[95] The government acknowledged that as of late 1973, Australia had made known that it would give sympathetic consideration to a United Nations request for peace-keeping personnel and that a list of potentially available resources had been periodically revised and made available to United Nations authorities. It denied, however, that any sort of United Nations inquiry had been made in this particular case. Nor had Australia discouraged the United Nations from entering such a request.[96]

The author's inquiries indicate that the government's explanations were accurate. The Macartney stories were apparently inspired when Australia made some fairly routine queries to the United Nations about costing its ongoing contributions of an air transport in Kashmir and policemen in Cyprus. However, *once* the allegations about a purported United Nations request for troops had appeared, it seems that, internally, Australia began to question the feasibility of a troop contribution to the Middle East *if* it should be asked for one. The economics of such an effort were one consideration. Domestic politics in Australia were very likely another; there would have been reluctance to re-ignite volatile opinion on the government's Middle East policy. Another suggested constraint—intruging, originating with a reputable source but unfortunately unconfirmed—was said to have been the need to husband Australian forces for contingency use in Portuguese Timor. At any rate, it is speculation as to how an actual United Nations request would have been received in Canberra in the closing months of Labor's tenure in office.

Australia announced Willesee's candidacy for the presidency of the UN General Assembly's 30th (1975) session. The idea sprang up in the Department of Foreign Affairs. Whitlam was more enthusiastic than was Willesee. No particularly conspicuous lobbying was carried out within the "West European and Other" group, to which Australia belonged and whose turn it would have been to provide an Assembly President. Still, it was an endearing thought in some Labor quarters that Australia would be the first nation ever to have been elected to the post twice, the first time having been in the 1940s, when Evatt presided. Willesee's candidacy was withdrawn in mid-1975, mostly because an equally senior person from a nation without previous presidency experience became available.[97] Australia was pleased to find its way on to various UN committees and was active in related agencies. It strengthened its representation at the International Labour Organization headquarters in Geneva. In early 1975, it withdrew the country's previous substantive reservations to acceptance of compulsory jurisdiction of the ICJ. This was an indication of support for the Court's principles and objectives and was done because Labor felt it to be "in the interest of all States to act in accordance with international law and to accept the resolution [of disputes] by peaceful means.[98] This was a clear example of Labor's propensities: idealism, faith in peaceful and collective means of settling differences and a tinge of legalism.

Apart from the United Nations and related bodies, there was the Commonwealth of Nations. Menzies had embraced it for its intimacy and its British qualities, but felt saddened as the Commonwealth became more diverse and multi-racial. What saddened Menzies gladened Whitlam. Under the ALP, the Commonwealth once again became a championed institution.

Among other international venues, admission under observer status was sought to summit meetings of non-aligned nations. It started with a bid to attend a non-aligned nation conference in Algiers. Some precedent for such a step was seen in the Bandung conference of 1954. In the event, Australia withdrew its bid, because it was not then, nor professed a wish to become, non-aligned. However, Whitlam continued to hope that observer status in non-aligned nation settings would be possible, if only to share economic ideas.[99] In August 1975, Labor got its wish, becoming a guest at the foreign ministers conference of non-aligned countries in Lima. The only other Western nations attending in this capacity were nations that belonged to no international security alliances, and Portugal, which although a member of NATO was at the time governed by a strongly radical régime.

While not professing non-alignment, Whitlam did, for instance in Yugoslavia in 1975, say that his government supported many of the non-aligned world's causes.[100] The visit of President Julius Nyere of Tanzania in 1974 conveyed an impression that Australia under Labor had somehow been "accepted" by non-aligned states. Then there had been Whitlam's remark in New Delhi in 1973 that Australia's attitude towards UN issues would no longer be influenced mainly by consultations with America and Britain:

> On matters concerning our region—the Pacific, Asia and the Indian Ocean—We will want to consult more closely than Australia has in the past with our neighbours.

Indeed,

> Never again are we going to be put in the position of finding ourselves siding with Britain, France, Portugal [pre-coup], South Africa and the U.S. while all our neighbours are on the other side.[101]

Opposition spokesmen and other critics thought they saw a pattern in Labor's diplomatic actions and pronouncements. The essence of their position can be distilled from Peacock's rejoinders. Labor's style was depicted as confusing motion with progress; a great deal of ministerial rushing about, a posturing at times tainted by intrusiveness and rudeness. Labor's *métier* was to grab for slogans, gimmicks and formulas—Asian forums, zones of peace, aid to African revolutionaries, or whatever. "This is an advertising man's approach to foreign policy—and only someone regarding Australia's destiny as an account to be handled could proceed in this way."[102] Labor's allegedly tasteless style was depicted as a counterpart of its inability to discriminate between the lasting and the important, and the fleeting and the marginal. In its pursuit of ideological goals, Labor dissipated the nation's diplomatic resources; "With an ineptness bordering on genius it has managed to achieve the worst of both worlds, to be naive without idealism and opportunistic to no advantage."[103] Labor's thinking was not only dissheveled but dangerously airborne. Liberals, said Peacock, "do not accept the vague internationalism and the spirit of international brotherhood of socialists as espoused by this Government."[104] It was in the context of such depreciations of ALP diplomacy that critics found special fault in the government's over-involvement with the Third World and with non-aligned causes, with a markedly concessionary approach to communist states and movements and with a depressing cavalierism towards the United States.

Challenge to the government's diplomatic approach to the United States rested on two related grounds. Firstly, it was claimed that Labor was pulling Australia away from its trusted and immensely important friend and ally, while making very questionable substitutions."Mr Whitlam is seeking to take Australia away from old and trusted friends, away from Britain and America," Fraser insisted, "and in exchange he takes Australia to the third world, to China and Russia. I doubt if the average Australian will regard that as a fair exchange."[105] There also was sharp reaction to Labor's diplomatic style, but with the caveat that the L–CP would not itself accept a subservient relationship with Washington. Labor treated America rudely. This was unnecessary and gratuitous. It harmed Australia's reputation and standing: "The Liberal and Country Parties see the United States and Australia as equal partners. Forthrightness on Australia's part does not in our view require Australia to be personally abusive."[106]

The government took pains to explain its relationship with America in a quite different light. Australia's "aligned" status was often alluded to, as was the value of the US connection, through ANZUS and otherwise. Wider, more active and more constructive relationships with other nations were explained as having been gained without expense to traditional American ties, and these newer connections could actually assist Australia's chief ally in the realization of global and regional objectives. Australia's diplomacy under the L–CP had been subservient and contrary not only to Canberra's but to Washington's best interests. Australia now sought a wider range of advice and consultation than in the past. The new tone of relationship "will now rest on firmer foundations than it did in the past," Whitlam averred. "I believe that America respects and welcomes the less compliant and more independent though equally friendly, approach ... "[107] Australia and the United States were claimed not to disagree on basic matters. When disagreement arose, Australia made its views known, politely but candidly, and if possible privately. The end of the Indo-Chinese conflict was seen as opening even better opportunity for a sensible, relaxed relationship with Washington.[108]

What follows in our narrative is an attempt to explain the actual temper of Australian–American relations, especially in the context of bilateral diplomatic interchanges. Much of the analysis is based on interview material. It draws on discussions conducted in both countries with numerous Australian and American respondents.

Relations between the incoming Labor government and the United States almost immediately got off to a poor beginning. Cumulative events produced a shocked, angry reaction from Washington. Washington was *not* surprised that Labor had won the December 1972 election: But disorientation resulted because an old and faithful ally, though admittedly previously led politically by parties other than Labor, should now scold the United States in its time of travail, to "conspire" to organize international protest against American policy in Vietnam. There was resentment over personalized ministerial denunciations of the US President and administration, though American officials apparently failed to take into account the mechanics and dynamics of ALP ministerial election and the relative impunity with which caucus-elected ministers could speak their convictions. There also was distress over the union boycott of American shipping and some under-appreciation of what the Australian government could realistically do about it. These shocks were felt in the White House, in Henry Kissinger's National Secutiry Council and in the State Department. Numerous diplomatic discussions were held in Washington and Canberra. A year later, much of this classified material was obtained and published by an Australian journalist.[109] These disclosures showed considerable credit reflecting on the poise and restraint with which Australian officials conducted themselves under very difficult conditions.

For the first half of 1973 there was a torturous guessing-game as to when and if Whitlam would be able to visit Nixon. Whitlam was eager to pay a call. He was, however, also eager to avoid leaving an impression that he would beg his way into the White House, and he otherwise wished to avoid the sychophantic style he attributed to his L–CP predecessors.

There were obstacles to an early, easily arranged visit. The professionals in the State Department strongly encouraged a meeting, but the President held a serious grudge about the events of December–January. At all events, it was Kissinger's National Security Council, not the State Department, that at the time carried influence in the White House. There also was the matter of Whitlam's demeanour. We have seen that he on several occasions heaped praise on Nixon's international statesmanship. He also, however, made some distinctly unflattering and *de facto* undiplomatic allusions. In Parliament, in May, he referred to the "parlous position" of the American presidency.[110] At a private but widely attended reception at the Prime Ministerial Lodge in April, he had described Nixon as a "barbarian" and as a man who had "monstered" Vietnam.[111] The explanation for this seemingly contradictory behaviour is that Whitlam believed that Nixon *had* made a vital international contribution, but nonetheless suffered from other defects. The critical remarks further hampered a White House invitation. About Whitlam the man, they revealed a lapse of diplomatic finesse, but a sense of honesty as well.

Various factors eventually combined to produce an invitation for an informal Whitlam visit. Certain policy moves had a mollifying effect on Washington, for instance an Australian pledge to retain US defence installations. Visits to America by various Australian ministers went off smoothly. Officials on both sides struggled to make a visit possible. The two top people in the embassy in Washington, Sir James Plimsoll and Roy Fernandez, were well-known, well-liked and highly effective spokesmen for their country. Whitlam's principal personal aide, Peter Wilenski, paid a hurried call on Kissinger in May. Kissinger was mollified. In writing, he extended a personal promise to Wilenski that Whitlam could come. Various Australian opposition members, including Peacock during a trip to America, urged US officials and politicians to work for a Whitlam visit, since the stand-off increasingly appeared to be endangering long-term US–Australian relations. The new US Ambassador to Canberra, Marshall Green, exerted himself to bring about a visit. His representations were probably decisive, though the other factors also counted.

Whitlam eventually showed up in Washington in late July. Measured against the strained background of the previous months, the visit was a success. Contact with Nixon came off without incident. Whitlam saw a wide range of official and Congressional figures. He avoided captious remarks, and generally, in his speeches, interviews and the like, left a very favourable impression. But Whitlam apparently did not lose his distaste for facets of Nixon the man. Shortly after leaving Washington, he remarked that Watergate had "purified and strengthened" America.[112] It is believed that, as the Watergate scandal's proportions grew, Whitlam would not have bothered to visit Nixon again, even if opportunity had arisen. Nixon himself thought better of snubbing Whitlam. When Labor was returned to office in May 1974, Nixon promptly sent warm congratulations. Whitlam and the new American President, Gerald Ford, struck an easy relationship. When in the United States in late 1974, Whitlam was accorded praise as well as courtesy. The US Ambassador to the United Nations, John Scali, called Whitlam's UN address "magnificent". The irony was remarked upon: "it was Nixon's departure in disgrace that made it possible for Mr Whitlam to have his nice week in the U.S. and to put Australian–American relations—at least on a personal basis—back to a moderately comfortable square one."[113]

A few basic points should be stressed before we continue our assessment of Australian–American relations. One is that the connection was between two states that *shared* an intimate interest in many international concerns. The Labor government's diplomacy emphasized initiative and innovation. The United States remained a super-power. Therefore, their contacts were bound to be numerous. A second point was the extensive and intricate bilateral relationship in economic, diplomatic, defence and other areas. A third point to remember is that the two governments, by the admission and preference of both parties, sought to thrash out rather than blithely overlook their differences of opinion. In other words, it would have been difficult to imagine that the relationship could have proceeded casually and wholly undisturbed.

At various times, each side expressed concern over what the other was or might be doing. Australia did not like the American interdiction of North Vietnam and took exception to US naval and air facility upgrading in the Indian Ocean and to aspects of Washington's role in the 1973 Middle East hostilities. The United States for example, wanted a stronger Australian UN stand on Cambodia, resented Australia's sudden shift on the Korean resolution at the United Nations in 1975, resisted Australian plans to vote South Africa out of the United Nations, disapproved of the prospect of a joint Soviet–Australian space-science installation in Australia (which Australia itself refused) and was unhappy about a possible PRG information office in Australia before the incumbent Saigon régime collapsed. On the other hand, often unnoticed, were areas of Australian policy not congruent with prevailing American policy where the United States expressed no opposition, or even assumed a benign posture. Included in this category were Australia's recognition of Peking and of Hanoi, recognition of *de jure* Soviet sovereignty over the Baltic states, the eventual decision to invite a Cuban consulate into Sydney and Australia's wish to reconstitute SEATO.

When senior Australian ministers such as Cairns, or even Whitlam himself, offered public remarks that went beyond standing Australian policy or were openly derisive of US motives or policies, the Americans sought explanations. Such US reactions were, according to one very highly placed Australian official, not really "protests" but "mildly couched" representations. Indeed, it is understood that the Americans came to believe that, by calling attention, such representations eventually proved useful in reducing the number and force of ministerial "out of school" comments, thereby enhancing the overall climate of bilateral relations. The point is interesting, but most difficult to verify.

American reaction to Australia was at times unmistakably firm, as on the controversy over US bombing in Vietnam, or the South African UN membership vote, on which the United States tried hard to limit Australia to an abstention. At other times it was restrained, but misconstrued as being otherwise. It seems useful to reconstruct one such episode, namely the 1975 ALP conference decision to allow a PRG information office in Australia. Wide currency was given in the Australian press to what were described as strong American representations.[114] The impression given was of American heavy-handedness, especially to be resented in Australia because this had been only a party not an official decision. As it was, US officials had scheduled a meeting with Ambassador Shaw on other matters. The PRG issue was simply tacked on later to the agenda and represented a statement of US thinking, nothing more. The ambassador had not been "summoned" to receive anything approaching a "protest". The conversation would probably not even have been made public had an Australian correspondent in Washington not guessed that the PRG issue would be raised. When asked directly, US sources acknowledged that it had been. The US embassy in Canberra, with Ambassador Green being away at the time, "confirmed" that the matter had been broached in Washington. Inexplicably, however, since it did so on an educated guess basis, not yet having been formally appraised of what, if anything, and in what form, had happened in Washington. This US embassy "admission" of some sort of American objection to a PRG office heightened an impression of American anger with Australia. A further irony was that the decision in Washington to approach Shaw was taken on a more senior level than the State Department's own ANZ desk or the US embassy in Canberra. It was more a response to worried inputs from "key" (read South-East Asian) US embassies. What emerged was more a conjunction of happenstance, misinformation and bureaucratic jumble than an advanced case of American heavy-handedness.

The United States did take seriously Australian security lapses. At the opening of its term in office, probably out of some sense of "open government" practice, Whitlam's personal staff was not required to undergo security clearances. The United States took a dim view, since this could have compromised the normal intelligence flow and further weakened what already were frayed US–Australian relations. The Labor government acceded.[115] The United States is known to have expressed reservations about the advisability of releasing highly sensitive information to Cairns, particularly after he had become Deputy Prime Minister and, at times, acting Prime Minister. But Cairns himself apparently never asked to be briefed on such matters as the role of the top-secret US facilities at Pine Gap and Nurrungar, and Whitlam did not see fit to encourage him to find out. What also worried the United States was a succession of major security breaches. The 1972–73 Vietnam issue transcripts of conversations and of cables were revealed a year after the fact. Shortly thereafter, details of conversations with Shaw regarding Whitlam's indiscreet remarks on the use of Thai bases for bombing North Vietnam were disclosed. So were details of Soviet approaches for a joint space-science station in Australia and the ensuing American objections. Both Washington and Canberra were deeply concerned, and Canberra was especially embarrassed. Security was tightened and investigations launched, but nothing definite came to light. The dominant *speculation* among Australians and Americans who were asked was that the leaks were not attributable to a single source. They did not represent a concerted effort to compromise US–Australian relations. They may have originated among ministerial staff members who passed information to journalists. Just prior to the sacking of Whitlam by the Governor-General, a report appeared that the CIA had apparently undertaken, through ASIO, to inquire into security breaches by the Prime Minister himself.[116]

Both sides seemed to share the blame for a breakdown in communications when, during the Yom Kippur war, Nixon declared a US armed forces alert. Being world-wide, the alert affected the North-West Cape and other US facilities in Australia. US personnel were placed on the alert *before* the Australian government was notified. The incident brought a sharp rebuke from Whitlam, both for the lack of consulative propriety and because he felt the alert had been a Nixon gesture designed for American domestic consumption. Green advised the Australian government of the alert "moments" after the fact, as soon as he personally knew of it. The United States tried to explain the oversight as best as it could. It took exceptionally serious umbrage at what it thought to be unfair and overreactive remarks from Whitlam at a time when, the author was reminded, America was in difficulties with its European allies over transit rights for US aircraft carrying arms to Israel. As the United States saw it, the European injury was compounded by the Australian insult.[117]

An inference to be drawn is that it was on those occasions when the United States felt itself most internationally beleaguered—Vietnam in 1972–73, the Middle East later in 1973—that it was the most unsparing in its retorts to adverse Australian criticism. Another precipitant was Indo-China at large, a consuming American interest that bred hypersensitivity, some of which spilled over on to Australia's Labor government.

The historically close Australian–American relationship withstood the kinds of jostles we have noted. As will be shown in another context, defence-related co-operation if anything improved under Labor. Intelligence data continued to move in both directions and senior and experienced Australian officials noticed no serious omissions or "cooking" of data from the United States. America continued to maintain CIA and other intelligence personnel in Australia, known to the Australian government and who worked closely with JIO and other sectors of the Australian intelligence community. Relations between US and Australian officials continued at a very close and usually cordial level in both capitals. The felt sense of kinship was, if anything, more evident among Australian than American officials. Late in 1974, Foreign Affairs Secretary Renouf explained that Australia's relations with a host of foreign nations were "useful but not intimate", in contrast with Americans, Britons and Canadians. With these three national groups, and presumably with New Zealanders as well, "we can get policy-makers and policy people together and have a really intimate exchange of views".[118]

After Labor came to office, the ANZ desk at the State Department was expanded, though arguably still shorthanded. All the same, the embassy in Canberra was enlarged to provide for the care of more and more specialized functions and US reporting from state-based consulates was upgraded. By appointing Sir Patrick Shaw, the Labor government continued the practice of sending a very senior ambassador to Washington. After years of sending to Canberra political appointees whose talents and style ranged from average to embarrassing the United States sent Marshall Green, a seasoned professional. It was a sign that the United States was taking Australia less for granted than in the past. From the point of Green's departure in mid-1975 to the end of Labor's period in office, the US ambassadorship remained vacant. Part of this delay was due to skirmishing in Washington over whether another career appointment should be made, a view favoured by the State Department. The lack of urgency to appoint a replacement also reflected the American opinion that relations with Australia had improved noticeably since 1973. In the end, the appointment went to a non-career man, James Hargrove. To minimize any impressions of American partisanship, his name was submitted for *agrément* on the eve of the 13 December election, rather than after the election outcome was known.

To some critics, the American presence in Australia, highlighted by the Green appointment, was ominous. In mid-1974, Victorian ALP Senator W. C. Brown made a number of remarks that condemned Green and his purpose in Australia. Green was alleged to have spent years as a diplomatic "hatchetman" and was said to have been a hirer of killers. His posting to Australia was within this tradition. He had been sent to protect at all costs American imperialist interests in the form of investments and defence facilities. He was aiming to subvert the Labor government and was working in tandem with such groups as the L–CP opposition, the Australian–American Educational Foundation, the Ford Foundation, the US Chamber of Commerce and the CIA.[119] About this time, too, but not necessarily connected with Brown's allegations, charges appeared that the CIA was operating in Australia on a large scale, in part without Australia's knowledge and with imputed nefarious designs on Australia.[120]

Brown never furnished hard evidence for his accusations. Several of the charges he levelled against Americans or Australians ostensibly implicated in enterprises inimical to Australian interests were confused and demonstrably inaccurate. His motives for having launched the anti-Green campaign were obscure. The dominant interpretations among Australians of various political persuasions, and among American officials, was that Brown was being used by a left-wing faction within his home Victorian Labor Party branch. The effects of his remarks seemed counter-productive. There were some anti-American demonstrations in capital cities on the Fourth of July, the peak of Brown's campaign, but such manifestations would probably have occurred without the catalyst of the Senator's remarks. A number of known radical figures appeared embarrassed by Brown, since his charges carried so little substantiation that the radical cause suffered some loss of credibility. With very few exceptions, Labor Party people turned against Brown, condemning him for rudeness as well as for fatuousness. Hawke, Barnard and Whitlam himself (without prompting from American officials) repudiated Brown. Whitlam referred to Brown's attack as unfounded in fact and "a miserable, in fact a cowardly thing."[121] The US embassy and American consulates were blanketed with calls, wires and letters fom ordinary persons, many of them self-identified ALP members, who felt it necessary to dissociate themselves, and Australians generally, from Brown.

The CIA charge is more difficult to assess since, by definition, covert enterprises of this sort go unmentioned or are denied. CIA agents did and do operate in Australia, often in conjunction with JIO and other Australian intelligence and security bodies. By long-standing agreement, Australia is to be informed of the identity of US intelligence operatives and of their activities. Revelations such as the CIA's role in helping to "destabilize" the Allende régime in Chile cast some doubts in Australia as to whether the United States was fully honouring its agreement with Canberra and possibly lent some credence to allegations that some agents, possibly under deep cover, were in the country to reverse "leftist" or otherwise anti-American interest tendencies. This is not impossible, but highly implausible. Cairns, for instance, a frequent critic of US policy and with good connections in the radical movement, said he knew nothing of improper CIA behaviour in Australia.[122] Victor Marchetti, a former CIA agent who exposed numerous other agency activities, denied that the CIA operated in this manner in Australia: "the relationship is too good, too important. They just don't screw around with another guy's internal affairs."[123] That would seem to have been the nub of the matter. The United States already had considerable access to Australian data and officials. It worked in an open not a closed society. Subversive or highly partisan behaviour would, if uncovered, have enormously handicapped the American economic and defence stake in Australia. We will have more to say about alleged CIA interventions in Australian politics in a later context. In any event, the ALP as a party of government could not be indicted for concerted anti-Americanism and therefore was not a natural target for American conspiracies.

It became the public as well as private posture of the US government that the ALP was not running an anti-American government. According to this view, Australia and the United States had consistently agreed on the large issues. The difficulties in 1973 were not a welcome episode, but probably had a salutary effect. Relations became more mature. Differences were handled in a businesslike way, though in an atmosphere of genuine *rapport*. Green *publicly* criticized the earlier L–CP tendency towards wholehearted embrace of the United States and called it an embarrassment to Australia at that time and to subsequent Australian governments. For Green, "Too rigid relations can snap in the winds of controversy: if it's flexible, it bends with the wind. I think that this is a more resilient, healthy, enduring relationship that we have today."[124] Furthermore, "Now all the parties—Labor, Liberal, Country Party—are in favor of a nationalistic policy in Australia. We understand that and agree with it."[125] All internal evidence points to this having been Green's actual, rather than a diplomatically sugar-coated, sentiment.

Expressions such as these were remarkably harmonious with the Labor government's own conceptions of what was appropriate in the Canberra–Washington relationship. In practice, on both sides, there was backsliding from the high intent. When the style or substance of one side's policies aggravated the other, untoward incidents did occur. But, as we argued before, these were predictable facets of a relationship between two separate nations with numerous and complex concerns in common.

NOTES

1. E. G. Whitlam, statement of 24 January 1973, in *Australian Foreign Affairs Review (AFAR)* 44 (January 1973): 57.
2. For instance, see Melbourne *Age*, 21 December 1972; and P. Hastings, *Sydney Morning Herald*, 1 January 1973.
3. *Sydney Morning Herald*, 11 January 1973.
4. See Snedden, cited in *Australian*, 6, 9 and 11 January 1973; Sinclair, cited in *Australian*, 10 January 1973; and Anthony, cited in *Australian*, 12 January 1973.
5. Melbourne *Age*, 11 and 12 December 1973; and Department of Foreign Affairs transcript of 15 December 1973 Bangkok press conference; remarks reprinted in "-Vietnam: It's Still America's War" (Melbourne: CICD, October 1974).
6. For example, Snedden and Peacock, Melbourne *Age*, 22 December 1973; and *Media Releases* of Liberal MHR Don Cameron, 8 and 16 January 1975.
7. *Australian*, 4 March 1974.
8. D. Willesee, *Commonwealth [Australian] Parliamentary Debates (APD)* Senate, (16 August 1974), p. 1067. Also see Whitlam, *APD*, House of Representatives (HR) (5 March 1975), p. 1037. For an example of opposition criticism, see Anthony's *Media Release*, 18 March 1975. For an overview, see P. Samuel, *Bulletin*, 8 March 1975.
9. M. Richardson, *Sydney Morning Herald*, 4 June 1974.
10. For the anti-Foreign Affairs version of the incident, see C. Beck *Nation-Review*, 26 July 1974. Also see *Canberra Times*, 22 July 1974.
11. For instance, *Sunday Independent*, 7 September 1973.
12. For a good summary of this thesis, see "Breaking Faith in Vietnam" (AICD Occasional Paper no. 6, Sydney: July 1974).
13. For a full exposition, see D. Willesee, *APD*, Senate (16 August 1974), esp. p. 1066.
14. See *Direct Action*, 19 July 1973.
15. See K.D. Suter, "Foreign Policy: Australia's 'New Image' Sags" (AICD Information Paper, Sydney: June 1974); Whitlam, *APD*, HR (2 August 1974), p. 1114; Willesee, *APD*, Senate (16 August 1974), p. 1066; and *Australian Financial Review*, 2 August 1974.
16. See accounts in *Sydney Morning Herald*, 7 February 1975 and *Australian*, 8 February 1975. For the various resolutions introduced prior to and during the conference, see Foreign Affairs and Defence Committee, *Report* [with addenda], Thirty-first ALP Federal Conference, Terrigal, February 1975.
17. See M. Richardson, Melbourne *Age*, 16 November 1973.
18. *Canberra Times*, 3 November 1973; *Australian*, 3 November 1973; and B. Johns, *Sydney Morning Herald*, 5 November 1973.
19. Whitlam, *APD*, HR (2 August 1974), pp. 1107-8; M. Walsh, *Australian Financial Review*, 21 December 1973; and M. Richardson, Melbourne *Age*, 28 October and 1 November 1974.
20. A. Peacock, "Australia and South-East Asia—An Alternative View" (AIIA conference paper, Melbourne, May 1975), p. 1. For Cairns' remarks, and Peacock's and Fraser's retorts, see Melbourne *Age*, 1 April 1975. Also see Anthony's *Media Release*, 2 April 1975.
21. For instance, Whitlam's remarks, cited in *Australian*, 14 April 1975; Whitlam's address in Washington of 8 May 1975, in *AFAR* 46 (May 1975): 265-68; and Willesee's interview in *Newsweek*, 28 April 1975.
22. For instance, Peacock, "Australia and South-East Asia", pp. 1-2; Fraser, *Media Release*, no. 116/75 (1 April 1975), p. 3; and Anthony, *Media Release*, 30 April 1975.
23. M. Grattan and C. Burns, Melbourne *Age*, 5 April 1975; and M. MacCallum, *Nation-Review*, 4 April 1975.

24. For the opposition argument, see Fraser, *APD*, HR (8 April 1975), pp. 1260–66 and *APD*, HR (13 May 1975), pp. 2112–17; and Fraser, *Press Releases*, 1 and 2 May 1975.
25. For representative opinion, see Melbourne *Age*, 29 April 1975 and *Australian* and *Sydney Morning Herald*, 30 April 1975.
26. See especially Whitlam, *APD*, HR (8 April 1975), pp. 1256–60 and *APD*, HR (13 May 1975), pp. 2117–22 (these pages include tabled documents); and Morrison, Department of Foreign Affairs, *News Release*, no. M24 (29 April 1975).
27. Liberal Party of Australia, *News Release*, no. 189/75 (21 April 1975).
28. L. Oakes, Melbourne *Sun News-Pictorial*, 30 April 1975.
29. For representative opinion, see P. Samuel, *Bulletin*, 12 April 1975; *Sydney Morning Herald*, 30 April 1975; C. Forell, Melbourne *Age*, 1 May 1975; B. Juddery, *Canberra Times*, 2 May 1975; *Canberra Times*, 8 May 1975; and D. Warner, Melbourne *Herald*, 21 May 1975.
30. For some of the fuller speculations on government motives, see H. Steketee, *Australian*, 29 April 1975; and R. Haupt, *Australian Financial Review*, 22 August 1975. For examples of the government's own explanations of policy, see Morrison, Department of Foreign Affairs, *News Release*, no. M23 (29 April 1975); and Whitlam, *APD*, HR (15 May 1975), pp. 2306–8 and *APD*, HR (21 August 1975), p. 380.
31. Thirtieth ALP Federal Conference, Surfers Paradise, July 1973, transcript of proceedings, p. 40.
32. Remarks by Sir Laurence McIntyre, Australian Ambassador to the United Nations, UN General Assembly, 21 November 1974, in Department of Foreign Affairs *News Release*, no. D27 (22 November 1974), p. 3; also see Whitlam *APD*, HR (5 March 1975), pp. 1039–40.
33. Derived from non-attributable source.
34. P. Samuel, *Bulletin*, 3 November 1973.
35. *AFAR* 45 (November 1974): 808. For the government's explanation of its position on the PLO's status in international bodies, see Willesee, *APD*, Senate (7 October 1975), pp. 955–6.
36. *Australian*, 30 January 1975.
37. *Australian*, 5 March 1975.
38. For instance, *Sydney Morning Herald*, 9 and 11 June 1975.
39. A. Peacock, "Foreign Policy Position Paper: Middle East Situation" (working document: March 1975).
40. *Sydney Morning Herald*, 4 July 1974.
41. V. Matthews, Melbourne *Herald*, 1 December 1973.
42. L. Oakes and D. Solomon, *Grab for Power: Election '74* (Melbourne: Cheshire, 1974), p. 162.
43. Melbourne *Age*, 26 May 1975.
44. J. Hurst, *Australian*, 2 July 1974; and F. Cranston, *Canberra Times*, 4 July 1974.
45. For instance, see *Australian*, 27 and 28 January 1974.
46. Peacock, Liberal Party, *Media Release*, 27 January 1975; his remarks cited in Melbourne *Age*, 3 March 1975.
47. *Australian*, 30 January 1975; and M. MacCallum, *Nation-Review*, 31 January 1975.
48. *Australian*, 5 and 6 March 1975; and P. Samuel, *Bulletin*, 8 March 1975.
49. Senator K. Wriedt, Minister for Agriculture, *Press Release*, 30 October 1973. Also see M. Walsh, *Australian Financial Review*, 22 November 1973.
50. *Sydney Morning Herald*, 31 January 1975; and *Canberra Times*, 19 February 1975. For earlier intimations of tying of Arab trade to Australia's foreign policy, see *Australian*, 10 August 1975; and *Canberra Times*, 12 November 1974.
51. Willesee, *Australian*, 20 June 1974.
52. Whitlam, *Sydney Morning Herald*, 26 June 1974.
53. For a review of Australian government approaches to nuclear testing, both before and during Labor, see "Australia Presents Its Case Against Nuclear Testing", *AFAR*, 44 (May 1973): 322–27. For the ICJ ruling, see *AFAR* 44 (June 1973): 409–10.
54. L. Murphy, *Australian*, 19 April 1973.
55. See Whitlam, *APD*, HR (16 May 1973), pp. 2165–66; and *Direct Action*, 24 May 1973.
56. For discussions of the ban and its effects, see H. Frizell, *Sydney Morning Herald*, 2 July 1973; and *Bulletin*, 1 September 1973. For some French reactions to the Australian position generally, see remarks of French Ambassador Gabriel VAn Laethem, 1 August 1973, in Department of Foreign Affairs memorandum; and C. Dyer, "French

Attitudes to Nuclear Experiments in the South Pacific, 1971–1973", *Australian Outlook* 27 (August 1973):172–78.
57. Snedden's remarks, Melbourne *Age*, 8 and 10 May 1973; and Peacock's article, Melbourne *Age*, 16 December 1974.
58. *Media Release*, 25 March 1974.
59. *Australian*, 19 May 1973 and Melbourne *Age*, 1 June 1973.
60. H. Bull, "Australian Perceptions of Our Role in the World" (AIIA conference paper, Adelaide, June 1974), p. 7.
61. Whitlam, statement of 22 December 1972, in *Current Notes on International Affairs* 43 (December 1972): 529–30.
62. *Australian*, 10 May 1974; and G. Clark, *Australian*, 6 June and 2 August 1974.
63. See Willesee, Department of Foreign Affairs, *News Release* no. M/106, (31 July 1974); Whitlam, *APD*, HR (15 October 1974), p. 2392 and *APD*, HR (22 October 1974), p. 2714; F. Cranston, *Canberra Times*, 5 June 1974; and H. Armfield, Melbourne *Age*, 1 August 1974.
64. Willesee, Department of Foreign Affairs, *News Release*, no M/71 (9 May 1974).
65. See B. Toohey, Melbourne *Age*, 16 June 1975; and R. Duffield, *Australian*, 26 June 1975.
66. Willesee, *APD*, Senate (11 November 1975), p. 1874.
67. On foreign and especially American reactions, see F. Cranston, *Canberra Times*, 13 and 18 November 1975. ·
68. Press conference 12 of June 1973, transcript, pp. 9–11 and press conference of 19 June 1973, transcript, p. 1.
69. See D. Solomon's comments on the Latin American factor, *Canberra Times*, 15 June and 30 July 1973.
70. See the joint Sino–Australian communiqué of 21 December 1972 in *Current Notes on International Affairs* 43 (December 1972): 632–33.
71. See the account in *Australian*, 7 March 1974.
72. For instance, *Australian*, 24 May and 1 June 1974; and M. Jones, *Sydney Morning Herald*, 13 June 1974.
73. See Rex Patterson's press statement of 31 May 1973, in *AFAR* 44 (May 1973): 362; Cairns' address of 15 March 1974, transcript, p. 5; and Whitlam, Perth radio interview of 2 May 1974, transcript, p. 16.
74. See especially J. Stackhouse, *Australian Financial Review*, 9 September 1974; and F. Cranston, *Canberra Times*, 20 February 1975. On earlier Taiwan visitor problems, see Whitlam, *APD*, HR (15 May 1973), pp. 2055–56.
75. Whitlam address of 8 November 1973, transcript, p. 8. Also see the observations of A. Barnes, Melbourne *Age*, 5 November 1973.
76. G. Clark, *Australian*, 18 May 1973.
77. See R. Schneider, *Australian*, 18 January 1975. On increased Soviet interest in Australia, see M. Richardson, *Australian Financial Review*, 3 April 1974; D. Mukarka, *Bulletin*, 25 May 1974; D. Warner, *Sydney Morning Herald*, 7 March 1975; and *Soviet News* (London), 22 October 1974.
78. *Sydney Morning Herald*, 15 February 1974.
79. *Sydney Morning Herald*, 17 January 1974.
80. *APD*, HR (16 October 1974), p. 2407. Also see P. Hastings, *Sydney Morning Herald*, 3 October 1974; also opposition criticisms, *Canberra Times*, 23 October 1974.
81. For two of the sharpest criticisms, see *Focus* (DLP journal), August 1974; and P. O'Brien, *Bulletin*, 24 August 1974.
82. Cameron, Melbourne *Age*, 5 March 1975.
83. *Australian*, 6 March 1975.
84. See Willesee, *APD*, Senate (13 August 1974), pp. 781–82; and Whitlam, press conference of 10 October 1974, in *AFAR* 45 (October 1974): 664–65. ·
85. See, for instance, Snedden's address to the Baltic Council of Australia, 8 September 1974, transcript, and the attached exchange of telegrams between Snedden and Willesee; also Peacock, Melbourne *Age*, 2 October 1974 and *APD*, HR (30 October 1974), pp. 3043–44. For a book-length condemnation of the government's behaviour, see E. Dunsdorfs, *The Baltic Dilemma: The Case of the De Jure Recognition by Australia of the Incorporation of the Baltic States into the Soviet Union* (New York: Robert Speller, 1975).

86. See, for instance, the remarks of K. Sibraa in *Tne Radical* (NSW ALP branch journal), December 1974; and Federal ALP Secretary David Combe's comments in the same issue.
87. B. Toohey, *Australian Financial Review*, 30 May 1974; and A. Clark, *National Times*, 29 July 1974.
88. For accounts of early stages of the idea, see F. Brenchley, *National Times*, 21 May 1973 and 11 March 1974; and G. Clark, *Australian*, 26 October 1973. For versions of Australian–Japanese relations at large, see *Japan: Report from the Senate Standing Committee on Foreign Affairs and Defence* (Canberra: 1973); and "Australia and Japan—Expanding Co-operation", *AFAR* 45 (March 1974): 136–41.
89. For a review of Australian–New Zealand relations, see Seminar on New Zealand–Australia Co-operation, *Proceedings and Papers*, August–September 1973, (Wellington: Published under the auspices of the Department of University Extension, Victoria University of Wellington, 1974).
90. See D. Solomon, *Canberra Times*, 14 August 1973; and Whitlam's television interview with David Frost, 18 August 1973, transcript, p. 6. For commentaries on the exchanges, see R. Haupt, *Australian Financial Review*, 9 August 1973; and D. Bloodworth, *Bulletin*, 25 August 1973.
91. Whitlam's television interview with David Frost, 11 May 1974, transcript, pp. 13–14.
92. Sydney *Sun*, 8 March 1975.
93. R.A. Woolcott, "Australia and Asia in the Seventies", *AFAR* 45 (May 1974): 321. For supportive argument with regard to Indonesia, see J.A.C. Mackie, "Australia's Relations with Indonesia", *Australian Outlook* 28 (August 1974): esp. 175–78. One of the best-framed "pro-criticism" arguments was by A. Pickering, *National U*, 22 July 1974.
94. Whitlam, UN General Assembly address, 30 September 1974, in Department of Foreign Affairs, *News Release*, no. M/128 (1 October 1974).
95. R. Macartney, Melbourne *Age*, 17, 18 and 25 September 1975.
96. On the government's position, see Willesee, *APD*, Senate (30 September 1975), p. 768; and Whitlam, *APD*, HR (4 November 1975), p. 2774.
97. See the analysis of Australia's candidacy by R. Duffield, *Australian*, 20 February 1975; and the announcement of the withdrawal, *Canberra Times*, 27 June 1975.
98. Whitlam, Department of Foreign Affairs, *News Release*, no. M/12 (14 March 1975).
99. Whitlam, Lima press conference of 25 April 1975, in Department of Foreign Affairs, *News Release*, no. D30 (28 April 1975), p. 3; and Kingston press conference of 5 May 1975, in *Canberra Times*, 6 May 1975. For Willesee's assessment, see his remarks in *AFAR*, 46 (November 1975): 619–20. Also see the note "Australia and the Non-Aligned Movement," *AFAR*, 46 (August 1975): 446.
100. *The Times* (London), 11 January 1975.
101. Melbourne *Age*, 7 June 1973.
102. Peacock, article in Melbourne *Age*, 14 October 1974.
103. Peacock, article in Melbourne *Age*, 16 December 1974.
104. *APD*, HR (14 March 1974), p. 455.
105. Address to Jewish graduates, Melbourne, 5 May 1974, transcript digest, p. 4.
106. Peacock, *Media Release, 9 May 1974*.
107. *APD*, HR (22 August 1973), p. 200. Also, in particular, see his Washington address of 30 July 1973, in *AFAR* 44 (August 1973): esp. 528–29; and his address in Sydney to the Australian–American Association, 4 July 1975, transcript, *passim*.
108. See R. Duffield, *Australian*, 13 May 1975.
109. M. MacCallum, *Nation-Review*, 11 January 1974.
110. *APD*, HR (30 May 1973), p. 2385.
111. See D. Warner, *Sydney Morning Herald*, 18 January 1974.
112. See *Australian*, 10 August 1973.
113. P. Costigan, Melbourne *Herald*, 5 October 1974.
114. For instance, R. Macartney, *Sydney Morning Herald*, 10 February 1975 and *Australian Financial Review*, 11 February 1975.
115. For the government's formal position, see Whitlam, *APD*, HR (28 February 1973), pp. 33 and 39; and *APD*, HR (1 March 1973), p. 196.
116. See B. Toohey, *Australian Financial Review*, 20 February 1976.

117. For summaries, see *Sydney Morning Herald*, 22 November 1973; and C. Burns, Melbourne *Age*, 24 November 1973.
118. Cited in *New Accent*, 25 October 1974.
119. For instance, see Brown's remarks in *Australian*, 3 July 1974, *Sydney Morning Herald*, 5 and 6 July 1974; and his interview in *Rabelais* (La Trobe University newspaper), 17 July 1974. For supportive comment, see W. Richards, "Is Australia's Political and Economic Future at Stake?—The Senator Brown and Marshall Green Affair", mimeograph (n.d.).
120. For instance, see J. Halpin, *Digger*, 16 February 1974.
121. *Canberra Times*, 3 July 1974.
122. Melbourne *Age*, 30 October 1974.
123. See *National Times*, 8 July 1974.
124. Interview with K. Randall, *National Times*, 1 February 1975.
125. *Australian*, 13 March 1975. Also, at large, see his interview comments to R. Duffield, *National Times*, 28 July 1975.

6 External Policy: Economic Dimensions

The present chapter concentrates on the economic dimensions of Australia's external relations. We will especially wish to appraise the relationship between economic policy formulation and outputs and broader foreign policy considerations. We will concentrate on external assistance, foreign investment, resource policy and trade.

The principle of Australian development aid has for many years enjoyed bipartisan approval. The rationale behind such programmes has entailed a mixture of considerations. As we saw earlier, Labor as a party was more emotionally attracted to foreign aid than the L–CP. It was more disposed to interpret international events, and especially competition, as being guided by economic forces. It placed greater trust in non-military techniques of conflict avoidance. It was more reflexively inspired by a humanitarian wish to devise strategies to provide better, more decent lives for ordinary people. On its part, the L–CP tended to devote more attention to the instrumental values of foreign aid, i.e. the tangible benefits for Australia's own perceived diplomatic or economic interests. After Labor came to office, these inter-party inflections seemed to narrow and the debate was more over particulars, such as who should be getting how much aid and in what form. It was generally recognized on both sides, for instance, that as a wealthy nation involved in the affairs of the region, Australia needed to make a meaningful contribution. This became especially true as the United States retracted its own presence and scope of assistance.

One rough index of Labor's performance in external development assistance was the amount and rate of change of spending. In the 1975–6 budget, $378 million in official development aid was allocated. This represented a 14.7 per cent increase on funds spent the previous financial year. However, between 1972–3 and 1973–4 the allocation had increased by 21 per cent and between 1973–4 and

1974–5 by a substantial 31 per cent. Moreover, applying other indices, overseas aid spending under Labor was not uniformly impressive. Labor was on record as wishing to reach the UN target of "advanced" nation aid donations of 0.7 per cent per annum of GNP as soon as possible, but no later than the close of the 1970s. In 1972–3, largely based on the L–CP's last budget, the Australian figure was 0.53 per cent. In 1973–4, based on Labor's first budget, it was 0.52 per cent. For 1974–5, it moved up to 0.55 per cent, but on the basis of the 1975–6 budget projections, fell back to 0.53 per cent. Inflation reduced the value of aid dollars spent, as did the September 1974 devaluation of the Australian dollar. Domestic economic conditions inspired overall spending constraint in the 1975–6 budget. International comparisons of aid as per cent of GNP showed Australia slipping somewhat from the very high position it occupied just before Labor entered office. Aid figure assessment in such terms is subject to various conceptual and statistical difficulties. All the same, in its early years in government, even though decidedly more dollars were spent, Labor failed to open a major gap between its own contribution level and that of its predecessors, as the L–CP did not hesitate to point out.[1] In partial mitigation, it should be remembered that, especially after 1973, in a period of severe inflation, heavy demands were being imposed on budgets by a variety of ALP spending programmes.

Who were the beneficiaries of Labor's aid programmes? Understandably, and as under L–CP governments, Australia's overwhelming concentration was on the Asia–Pacific region. Also, again in keeping with established practice, most of the assistance was devoted to Papua New Guinea. Of the $378 million projected for 1975–6, $210 million was earmarked for Papua New Guinea; in 1974, the government pledged itself to some $500 million over a three-year period to a prospectively independent Papua New Guinea. With so much flowing to Papua New Guinea, funds remaining for other countries were, of course, relatively modest. Of the $49 million overall aid increase planned for 1975–6, about $40 million of that figure was accounted for by money pledged to Papua New Guinea; even so, a fair proportion of the money for Papua New Guinea was actually payable to Australians serving there or otherwise not directly available for PNG development.[2]

Apart from Papua New Guinea, the most heavily endowed recipient of Labor's aid programmes, compatible with previous practice, was Indonesia, which took about a tenth of Australia's official aid. We noticed in a number of earlier contexts why Australia assigned special importance to its large near-neighbour. The Indonesian aid emphasis was generally approved in Australia, but with some reservations. Left opinion was particularly disturbed by Indonesia's closed politics, the presence of political prisoners and diplomatic postures such as Indonesia's interest in associating East Timor with itself. In economic terms, this criticism was augmented by allegations of misspent and misdirected aid funds, especially as benefit was alleged to have accrued more to the Indonesian élite than to the broad public.[3]

Aid to Indonesia elicited only marginal political controversy, but the Labor government found itself sharply attacked from its left flank for its aid programmes towards South Vietnam and Cambodia before their rightist régimes fell in 1975. Labor's professed guideline was that "we would give generous aid to post-war [i.e. post-January 1973] reconstruction of the whole of Indo-China without regard to governments or their ideologies".[4] Some Australian aid projects were not in dispute, among them contributions to all of Indo-China (and including Vietcong-held areas) through such agencies as UNICEF, the International Red Cross and the Office of the UN High Commissioner for Refugees. The last of these programmes was given special official attention during the mass flight of South Vietnamese refugees in the Australian autumn of 1975 and the public was encouraged to make donations. In the 1975–6 budget, reconstruction aid for Indo-China was given special mention. In October 1975, the first shipment of direct, bilateral commodity aid to Communist-held South Vietnam, valued at $2.4 million, was announced.

What was controversial was Australia's aid to the two Vietnams *per se*. Strong critics of the Thieu régime in South Vietnam were in principle uncomfortable about aiding it, since even non-military aid could be construed as helping to prop up that government. More specifically, the argument was that Australia's aid programme had *de facto* favoured South Vietnam over North Vietnam. In 1973–4, South Vietnam received $3.5 million in aid, North Vietnam only $600000, and the large disparity persisted into 1974–5. In 1974, particular warning was levelled in radical circles and among some Labor people against Australian involvement in international aid projects for South Vietnam under the World Bank and the Asian Development Bank. The claim was that such projects would constitute blatant bias in favour of South Vietnam and a propping up of its unwholesome régime.[5] The disparities in Australian aid to the two parts of Vietnam were in part due to the fact that, when Labor came to power, there already were ongoing aid programmes for the South, but not for the North. A more important reason related to North Vietnam itself. Australia was for some time unsure of what, exactly, Hanoi wanted in the form of aid. Funds earmarked for the North went unspent and considerable Australian effort was needed to clear the pipeline. By November 1974, it finally was possible to announce a $2 million commodity gift to North Vietnam. Another problem was Hanoi's resistance to most forms of multilateral assistance. The Australian government regretted Hanoi's attitude. But, outwardly in keeping with its own professions of even-handedness, with clamour from critics rising, it decided that it would be

> inappropriate to join in a consultative group for South Vietnam so long as North Vietnam holds to ... [its] attitude ... To do so would be to join in preferential treatment for the South, with Australia coming under pressure to increase its contributions when, as an act of policy, we are trying to establish some balance in aid allocations between North and South.[6]

A year earlier, as we have seen, the government had withdrawn from an economic stabilization consortium that was funnelling hard currency to Cambodia. With the collapse of the Thieu régime in 1975, the problem of how much and what sort of aid to extend to Saigon disappeared.

The form and execution of Australia's foreign aid programmes also caused some difficulties. By the time Labor was elected to office, Australia was already underwriting a large and diverse aid programme. Reporting in early 1973 the Parliamentary Joint Committee on Foreign Affairs, which examined Australia's overseas aid, noted various difficulties, such as inadequate aid project evaluation and a tangle of bureaucratic responsibilities.[7] An interdepartmental task force was set up to work on the whole issue of foreign aid administration. What emerged, first on a provisional and then on a permanent basis, was the Australian Development Assistance Agency (ADAA). Labor as a party had previously advocated an independent aid agency. ADAA became a full-fledged body with a permanent staff and head equivalent to a departmental secretary. It acquired a number of former Foreign Affairs officers and reported directly to the Minister for Foreign Affairs. In the short run, at least, ADAA failed to satisfy the high aspirations that some had held for it. There were differences between former External Territories and Foreign Affairs members of ADAA as to how best to deal with Papua New Guinea, the single largest target of Australia's external aid. The Foreign Affairs Department was uneasy about the evolving policy orientation of ADAA. It forcefully argued that ADAA would create, and to an extent already was creating, a nightmare of crossed and blurred responsibilities between itself and the department, thereby handicapping rather than facilitating planning and execution in overseas aid.[8]

Some identified Foreign Affairs' complaints as another symptom of the department's "aggrandizing" designs to control all key levers of Australia's external relations. At all events, under Labor, Australia's overseas aid programme assumed more and more complex characteristics, placing a premium on an efficient system of foreign aid administration. The range of aid programmes was very wide. There were project and equipment programmes, technical personnel projects, training programmes, food aid programmes, trade incentive schemes, and so on. Labor extended or initiated special forms of assistance. For example, together with New Zealand, Australia made efforts to sustain the work of a new South Pacific Bureau for Economic Co-operation. It joined the Ministerial Conference for Economic Development of South-East Asia. It began to make grants to ASEAN corporatively. It made payments to improve international air navigation in several Asian countries, without publicity, in part so as not to offend recipient nations' sensibilities about their ability to operate their own airways systems. Labor shifted some of the foreign aid programme's emphasis. More attention was to be given to social aspects of aid, an important aspect of which was to be the strengthening of rural sectors of developing economies.[9] Government and opposition at times seemed to vie for innovative approaches to aid. The government somewhat stepped up official assistance to voluntary aid groups, administered in conjunction with the Australian Council for Overseas Aid. In the 1974 electoral campaign, the L–CP produced a plan for an Australian Aid Corps, a domestic programme modelled on the overseas related Community Aid Abroad scheme. The Whitlam government floated its wide-ranging Asian–Pacific proposal. The opposition countered with its own "regional development strategy".

Several other structural changes began to appear in Australia's aid programme and thereby partially alleviated some long-standing criticisms. The proportionately large increase in multilaterally framed aid for 1975–6 (by either 14 or 33 per cent, depending on the reading of the data) was not a sign that the traditional dominance of bilateral aid was about to disappear. But it reflected a greater flexibility and a recognition of the value of many consortially organized aid efforts. There was an extension of "programme" as opposed to the more familiar "project" bilateral aid approach, which facilitated "forward" development planning. As of 1975, bilateral aid generally remained "tied", i.e. aid funds needed to be spent in Australia or on Australian products, but the objective, especially in consultation with other donors, was to move towards untying. An untying of the multilateral portions of Australian assistance had largely been completed. In 1975, for instance, Australia announced the untying of its contribution to the Asian Development Bank's multi-purpose special aid fund and of the local currency part of Australia's subscription to the bank's technical assistance special fund.[10] Aid tying had long been defended as an instance of enlightened self-interest, defined as assisting development in needy nations while stimulating Australia's domestic economy. Several other forms of official commitment to the economic enhancement of developing states were also, implicitly or explicitly, believed to serve Australia's own economic interests. We will examine them under the wider rubrics of foreign investment, resource policy and trade.

The prominent overseas investment stake in Australia became contentious. Sometimes overlooked, however, was Australia's own private investment activity abroad. Because of anxiety over balance of payments, investment abroad had been discouraged during many of the L–CP years. By 1970–1, *new* private Australian investment within developing countries was only about $40 million, most of it in Papua New Guinea. Between 1972–3 and 1973–4, the proportion of Australian investment in South-East Asia relative to total overseas investment actually dropped, from 64 per cent to 40 per cent. All the same, Australia's accumulated investments in the South Pacific already exceeded those of any other Western nation. The Labor government made a firm commitment to encourage investment in developing countries. Its guidelines were not unlike those it framed for overseas investment in Australia—the host government's right to regulate investment, where investment would be welcome and useful, under conditions consistent with advanced labour relations and environmental policies, and if possible with considerable local equity included. Private overseas investment was visualized as meeting several desirable objectives. It would serve as a complement to official developmental aid efforts, with assumed economic and humanitarian benefits. It would serve a wider foreign policy objective in embellishing the image of a caring Australian presence among developing and especially Asian–Pacific states. It would stimulate local Australian business. Some radical critics saw it somewhat differently. Australian investment testified to Labor's implication in a "Pacific Rim" strategy, an Australian partnership with American and other international capitalist interests, the net effect of which would be the social dislocation and economic domination imposed upon developing states.[11]

Official encouragement for private overseas investment in developing states was accelerated. For instance, investment survey missions were organized. Pre-investment feasibility funds were made available to potential investors. Trade commissioner services were upgraded. Overseas investment coverage opportunities under the Export Finance Insurance Corporation (formerly Export Payments Insurance Corporation) were expanded. A bilateral agreement with Indonesia guaranteeing the security of private Australian funds was negotiated.

There was marked response among both Australian-owned as well as Australian-based but largely foreign-owned companies. Some investing companies were small, others among the largest in Australia, for instance Broken Hill Proprietary and Conzinc Riotino of Australia. BHP undertook negotiations for a steel mill in Saudi Arabia and in minerals and oil exploration in the Philippines, CRA in energy projects in Indonesia.

Not all went smoothly, however. Criticism simmered over the inordinately high Australian investment stake in Fiji, three-quarters of whose business was in Australian hands and from which returns taken by Australian companies were exceptionally high. By 1974, CSR (formerly Colonial Sugar Refining) had its sugar-marketing concession withdrawn by the Fijian government, and there were other rumblings in Suva about the Australian presence.[12] In Papua New Guinea, where Australian investment was especially prominent, the Somare government undertook a stiff line with foreign investors and wrung a massively revised tax agreement from Bougainville Copper, a group controlled by Conzinc Riotinto. In this instance, the Australian government, despite appeals from the company, refused to be drawn in to support Bougainville/Conzinc Riotinto's negotiating position with the PNG authorities.[13]

The Australian government itself increasingly had to cope with some difficult foreign policy spin-offs of its foreign investment encouragment posture. There were difficulties relative to Australian investment in South Africa, as we saw earlier. There was a territorial jurisdiction dispute with Portugal, both before and after the 1974 coup in Lisbon, over oil exploration in the Timor Sea, between Timor and Australia. Ironically, Woodside-Burmah, which was conducting explorations off Australia's North-West Shelf, had also been granted Timorese exploration concessions by Portugal. In 1974, BHP and Conzinc Riotinto of Australia were granted off-shore exploration leases by South Vietnam, a step that did not escape criticism from elements in the ALP. On its part, the PRG claimed that when it took control. oil-exploration leases let by its predecessors in Saigon would be nullified. Moreover, China and Indonesia, two nations with which Canberra earnestly desired amicable relations, claimed jurisdiction over portions of the seas in which the leases had been let.[14] By the close of Labor's time in government, however, North Vietnamese authorities, acting as spokesmen for the PRG, were indicating South Vietnam's interest in reviving exploration activities.[15] At the UN law-of-the-sea conferences, Australia's own interests dictated a position that provided for an exclusive sea-bed resources area extending to a maximum of 322 kilometres off-shore, or to the edge of the continental margin, whichever was farther, except where a boundary could be negotiated bilaterally, as it was with Indonesia.[16]

Once Labor came to office, one factor that induced Australian-owned or -based companies to search for overseas investment opportunities was their concern about the viability of the investment climate within Australia. We now turn specifically to foreign investment in Australia, a subject that excited considerable political as well as. economic interest.

Australia had for some years been identified as an excellent target for overseas investors. It had a growing population, a high standard of living and an increasingly diversified and sophisticated economy. Its political system was orderly. Its currency was strong and under-valued. Overseas investment was extended official encouragement under the L–CP and broadly welcomed by the public. Australia also possessed unusual natural riches and eventually ranked among the world's five main producers of bauxite, iron-ore, tin, nickel, silver, lead, zinc, manganese and uranium. In 1974, the world's largest high-grade deposit of uranium oxide was discovered in the Northern Territory. The peak of overseas investment inflow during the L–CP period was in 1970–1 ($1.5 billion) and dropped only slightly, to $1.4 billion, in 1971–2. British investment had for long dominated, but by 1974 the United States had caught up, with each country supplying about 45 per cent of Australia's total foreign investment. By 1973, American-owned companies in Australia were exporting well over $300 million in goods to Third World countries and Australia had become regional headquarters for 170 American firms. Several key sectors of the Australian economy, among them motor vehicles and industrial chemicals, fell under principal foreign ownership. A number of minerals were dominated by foreigners. Overall, in 1972–3, the mining industry, exclusive of processing, was just under 50 per cent foreign-owned and 57 per cent foreign-controlled; both figures represented a slight rise over 1971–2.[17]

L–CP governments had been persuaded that foreign investment was a most important contribution to the nation's economic growth. As a result, their foreign investment policies were extremely permissive. Only in a very limited number of enterprises, such as Australian banks, broadcasting media, civil aviation and life insurance, was foreign ownership penetration restricted. Handsome tax concessions were extended to the mining industry, in which foreign investment was considerable. Official efforts to increase local equity were essentially hortatory. In 1971, the Australian Industry Development Corporation (AIDC) came into operation. One of its missions was to maximize local ownership and control in enterprises for which it provided finance, but its capital resources were limited. The principal measure of the L–CP period was not brought forward until September 1972, when the McMahon government introduced machinery to forestall takeovers by foreign interests under specified circumstances.[18] In spirit, at least, it had been Gorton more than McMahon who had questioned an open-door investment policy.

Labor entered government against this background. We will first assess its approach, disposition and intentions towards foreign investment generally and then its actual programmes.

The ALP's view of foreign investment was a complex mixture of visceral reaction, ideological predisposition, politics and economic calculation. Moreover, the party's general principles were not consistently presented and within its ranks there were decided differences of emphasis. R.F.X. (Rex) Connor, the Minister for Minerals and Energy during virtually the entire Labor period, took a nearly consistent hard line, and so did Clyde Cameron. Whitlam and some ministers with economically related portfolios, such as Cairns, Hayden and Crean were relatively "softer" on foreign investment.

There was a noticeable emotive-ideological component in Labor's thinking. While a mixed economy rather than a straightforward socialist party, the ALP nevertheless harboured suspicions of big, powerful and wealthy business. Its suspicions were accentuated when that business was foreign-dominated. Foreign big business, especially in key sectors such as automobiles and minerals, implied foreign-based decisions often made for parent company benefit and possibly were beyond Australia's ability to counter. Also foreign big business offended sensibilities about national Australian pride and independence as goals or symbols in and of themselves. Giant multinational companies were on both counts deserving of scrutiny, and reaction to them sharpened with reports of their alleged misdoings elsewhere; for instance, ITT's unsavoury role in attempting to unseat the Allende régime in Chile and disclosures of pay-offs to influential foreigners by various American companies.

It was not uncommon for Labor ministers to take point-blank shots at foreign investors. Connor took pride that, under Labor, overseas "racketeers" in the extractive industry could no longer write their own tickets.[19] Cameron denounced the "greed" of multi-nationals and forecast that their international activities would in time bring most Western economies to their knees.[20] When the 1974 electoral campaign opened, Whitlam felt he had an emotional as well as winning issue to stress: multi-nationals. Connor was very plain about this just before the double dissolution: "The major problem facing Australia, both in the forthcoming Federal Election, and also in its economic policy, is Who Owns Australia? How do we stem the tide? How do we turn it back?"[21] There were various occasions on which Labor resentment spilled over and perhaps was seen in part as the good oil of politics. There was a pained outcry when an American was appointed the new managing director of General Motors-Holden's. When in late 1974, General Motors-Holden's threatened to stand down several thousand employees because of severely depressed car sales, the company's announcement was denounced as a case of anti-Australian dictation from Detroit: "The monstrous and intolerable situation in Australia is that General Motors' subsidiary there has attempted to stand over the Australian Government," Whitlam charged: "I never thought even General Motors would have the gall to be so overt about it. These ugly American companies."[22] There were more imputations that multi-nationals as such bore heavy personal responsibility for Australia's high rate of inflation. Threats to combat multi-nationals by local or international action were also, at various times, expressed by trade-union spokesmen.

In Labor's view, there was a specific economic case to be made against aspects of foreign investment. L–CP governments were claimed to have created an unconscionably free climate for investors, who in turn exploited their opportunities to the hilt. For example, relying on the *Fitzgerald Report* on the mineral industry,[23] the government pointed to the way in which tax concessions, paltry royalty arrangements and other factors had resulted in more money being awarded in assistance to mining companies by the government than they paid in taxes, while earning, and repatriating, great sums of income. Another argument was that, in 1971 and 1972, the large amount of inflowing capital had not been translated into additional resources for consumption and investment within Australia but rather into massive overseas reserves, thereby inducing excessive domestic liquidity. Another argument, familiar to Connor, was that the Australian economy had already been given the necessary boosts for economic growth. At all events, Australia generated an impressive 80 per cent plus of its own capital requirements and was claimed by Connor to be able to generate all or most of the remainder, if necessary.[24]

Altogether, however, what were Labor's guiding principles towards foreign investment? Experience in office, worsening economic conditions in Australia, decline in the political mileage that could be earned from strictness towards foreign investment and other factors had by the second half of 1974 brought mellowing; not consistently, but enough so as to be identifiable. In an illuminating November 1974 speech, Treasurer Frank Crean said that the stage had been set for a resumption of net capital inflow at moderate and digestible levels: "there has necessarily been some evolution in our policy towards overseas capital and this has been emphasized by the need to meet changing economic cirsumstances."[25] Australian remarks and submissions to the United Nations respecting the development of a multi-national company code by that body were guarded and balanced, though admittedly the inputs were primarily from Foreign Affairs and Treasury, not from Minerals and Energy.[26] Within a few months of its exit from office, Labor's outlook took an even more abruptly adaptive and permissive turn. Treasurer Hayden offered high praise for foreign investment, about which it was "silly and, in some cases, extreme irresponsibility, to argue that we can do without."[27]

Approaches to the vital mineral sector also were modified, but nearly throughout Labor's tenure in office it was unclear which version of the precepts expressed was authoritative or what could be expected next. The very broad outlines for the resource/extractive industry were stated early and remained as guide-posts: (i) satisfaction of the nation's own future energy and industrial requirements; (ii) an enlargement of the domestic Australian stake; (iii) more mineral processing within Australia; (iv) fair prices for resources on world markets; (v) consideration of the effects of mineral exploitation on Aboriginal land rights; and (vi) regard for environmental and conservation considerations.[28] It is unnecessary to reconstruct all the permutations of Labor's position, but some illustration is needed. In 1973, in Japan, Whitlam indicated that Australia wished to achieve the highest possible level of local ownership of its resources and industries, meaning "the highest Australian equity which can be achieved in negotiations, project by project, consistent with justice to all parties ... and ... consistent with Australia's limited capacity to provide capital for development".[29] *Energy* projects were originally made an exception to the rule that allowed an overseas investment content, but this exception was lifted in late 1974. Moreover, about that time, lingering confusion as to whether the government was primarily interested in checking majority foreign *ownership* as opposed to foreign *control* were ostensibly resolved, with control emerging as the key concern.[30]

But the big issues remained unsettled, as evidenced by the party's Terrigal conference and by ministerial remarks made in the months following. At Terrigal, Connor made a characteristically hard-line speech, claiming that "To talk of control without having ownership is crazy", and moved that "Labor will achieve and maintain full ownership and control of coal, oil, natural gas, uranium and all other fuel and energy resources." Cairns, then Treasurer, defended foreign investment as essential to an Australian growth rate required by both workers and consumers. He asked that in areas such as oil, gas and coal, foreign investment be kept to a *minimum*, i.e. short of *absent*. The Connor position was unanimously endorsed.[31] After Terrigal, Whitlam announced oil exploration guidelines that *de facto* retreated from the Terrigal declaration. Foreign companies undertaking oil exploration no longer necessarily needed to seek local participation at the initial or grass-roots level.[32] In the meantime, Connor conveyed the impression that his talk of 100 per cent ownership gave him "sufficiently wide an umbrella within which to get the highest degree of local ownership consistent with a profitable deal for each project as it comes up".[33] But, in August 1975, when asked which was his first priority, Australian ownership or development of Australian resources regardless of ownership, he did not hesitate to reply "Australian ownership comes first. It must."[34]

Labor's policy responses to foreign investment broadly coincided with the party's economic and ideological dispositions. The policies reflected some of the tensions between more, and less, restrictionist views within the party. Overall, they tended to be tougher for the first eighteen months or so of the Labor government than thereafter.[35]

Even without new legislation, the government enjoyed effective command over investment flow through such means as its control over monetary policy and its ability to impose export controls. An example was the variable deposit requirement (VDR). The government imposed a 25 per cent interest-free deposit requirement upon long-term foreign borrowings and then raised the amount of the VDR to $33\frac{1}{3}$ per cent. The net effect was to make investments more expensive and therefore less attractive. The VDR was mainly a liquidity control measure, but had the effect of discouraging overseas investment as such. In 1974, when the Australian economy entered a tight liquidity stage, there was a softening on foreign investment. The VDR ratio was gradually lowered and then abolished. Moreover, an early government embargo on short-term foreign borrowings was eventually eased.

Labor inherited from the McMahon government legislation on foreign takeovers. This provided for a review mechanism of proposed takeovers of Australian businesses should such proposed takeovers be found to violate various national interest criteria, economic and otherwise. Labor proceeded to strengthen its purview over takeovers, for instance by extending blocking authority beyond share to asset acquisitions. In practice, takeovers were not treated with anything approaching unfailing severity. As of mid-1974, some 16 per cent of takeover notifications had been formally prohibited or withdrawn after detailed investigation, though some takeover bids were deterred by the very existence of the review procedures. In the thirteen-month period ending 31 July 1975, over 90 per cent of takeover notifications went unprohibited. Gradually, takeover bids were acted upon more on merit than on blanket opposition to takeover intrusion into certain sensitive areas. Financial institutions had been targeted as one such area, but in early 1975, permission was given for acquisition of a major finance company by American interests. On the other hand, in the same year, Labor introduced legislation to create a Government Insurance Corporation, in part to counter the heavy foreign stake in this lucrative field; the legislation was rejected in the Senate. Meanwhile, takeovers in the mineral industry remained among those most severely scrutinized. By mid-1974, a second interdepartmental committee had been established to screen, and upon which to send advice to the political level, foreign investments of a non-takeover character. Eventually, plans were laid to combine the two into a Foreign Investment Advisory Committee.

Labor in other ways reconstructed previous policies towards foreign investment. Under certain circumstances, Australian firms were to be extended preference in purchases made by the federal government. Income tax concessions on mining shares were done away with, as were subsidies paid to companies searching for oil. Ironically, the main adverse impact was not on large overseas companies but on smaller Australian firms, for which special buffering was then promised. Indeed, even the highly conservative Queensland state government intruded itself to acquire higher royalties from mining companies. By September 1975, however, as part of its overall reconsideration of minerals policy, the government introduced a two-tier pricing arrangement for crude oil, providing special incentives for new exploration.

One of the large issues faced by the government was the extent to which local equity would need to be offered by foreign interests. Here again the record is mixed. We saw that, by 1975, the government was saying that oil interests would not necessarily need to seek local participation at early stages of exploration. In early 1974, the government scotched the major foreign-dominated Alwest alumina project in Western Australia. One objection dealt with Australian equity. The consortium involved eventually agreed to substantial local equity arrangements and the project was approved in Canberra. But the episode also dispelled suspicions that key sectors of the extractive industry might need to be wholly domestically owned. In 1974, Labor-controlled South Australia became the first Australian state to set a future limit on foreign equity in mining operations—49 per cent. In his major foreign investment policy statement of 24 September 1975, Whitlam announced a major concession on minerals other than uranium. Henceforth, foreign investment proposals would be presumed prima facie acceptable if foreign content did not exceed 50 per cent, unless special circumstances warranted otherwise.[36]

The foremost exception to government leniency was in uranium. In part, this was because of the vast return that Australia expected for itself from uranium sales, in light of the size of deposits and anticipated world-market demands. In part, the government believed that it already possessed most formal entitlements over uranium. The great majority of Australian uranium was in the Northern Territory and was owned by the federal government. Pre-Whitlam government legislation had entitled the federal government to extract, process and even (apart from the Northern Territory deposits) to market uranium. Early in the Labor government's life, attempts by prospecting companies to sell to foreign interests part of the uranium deposits they had successfully explored were blocked. The government desired uranium processing within Australia. It invited foreign nations to consider supplying capital and technology for uranium enrichment, but insisted that no foreign equity would be entertained. Indeed, payback would occur in the form of inexpensive enriched uranium supplies. By late 1974, official policy had evolved to read that while private companies would be permitted to continue uranium exploration under standing exploration licences, all new exploration within the Northern Territory would be undertaken by the Australian Atomic Energy Commission.[37] Just before Labor left office, permission in principle was granted for an overseas uranium sale. This was a breach of standing practice, but came too late for a sale to be consummated during the Labor government, or for conclusions to be drawn as to how far, with Connor no longer as minister, Labor would have proceeded in amending earlier uranium policy.

Direct government involvement in ventures designed to limit or redirect foreign investment was most prominently to be placed in the care of two government instrumentalities, AIDC and the Petroleum and Minerals Authority (PMA). As we saw, AIDC had been started under the L–CP. One of its objectives was to supply finance to make possible greater Australian ownership and control in various manufacturing and mining development projects. Joint ventures in which foreign ownership predominated were not excluded. Under Labor, underwriting of AIDC was increased and its functions and scope of financial operations broadened. Nationalization of non-Australian enterprises, directly or "by stealth", was emphatically denied as an objective of AIDC. AIDC was to be a catalyst to investment, not an alternative to it. At best, AIDC's "buying back of Australia" role could be expected to be modest. One feature of AIDC's work was that the interdepartmental committee on foreign takeovers referred all important cases to the corporation, giving it first opportunity at local shares being offered to foreign investors. Another aspect of AIDC's work was its eagerness to develop government-to-government investment arrangements, with particular emphasis as of 1974 on petrodollar-rich Middle Eastern states. AIDC's "public" role was expressed by offers to ordinary citizens to purchase its stock. Paid advertisements stressed benefits of high return, safe investment and finally helping Australia—"Congratulations, you're doing something for yourself and your country."[38]

The PMA was designed along more specialized lines than was AIDC. We will assess its evolution mostly from the vantage-point of petroleum, an energy resource the importance of which was acutely felt in the aftermath of the Yom Kippur war. There also was the central consideration that Australia's own oil resources, themselves never completely adequate, were, on forecasts made in the mid-1970s, scheduled to be exhausted in ten to fifteen years.

The government undertook to disallow farm-in proposals by petroleum consortia. Takeover regulations were applied to the petroleum industry. The government promised critical re-examination of off-shore oil exploration leases that were scheduled to expire. Some would be renewed, some not. The government itself would for the first time insert itself into an active oil exploration role.[39]

Such steps foreshadowed the government's Petroleum and Minerals Authority. In Connor's words, the PMA would function "by partnership and farm-out in the case of off-shore oil and gas exploration ... by a partnership between the national government providing natural resources and experienced explorers providing the risk capital, technology and expertise". Moreover, small Australian-based companies that otherwise required large-scale infusion of capital to start projects would be assisted by the PMA.[40] Labor's rationale for the PMA was to safeguard and fully exploit a precious resource asset, to insure appropriate guidelines for the character, intensity and "responsibility" of exploration and to include a more comprehensive local Australian stake. The PMA's first major action, in early 1975, was to sign an agreement to buy into the multimillion-dollar Cooper Basin oil and natural gas reserves from an American concern, to insure aggregate Australian ownership in excess of 50 per cent.

To Labor's distress, the PMA experienced considerable difficulty in getting established and then in maintaining itself. Owing to Senate opposition, its enabling legislation was delayed by over a year. Then came challenge from the states, several of which went to the High Court to contest the constitutionality not only of the PMA but of the 1973 Seas and Submerged Lands Act's provisions of federal jurisdiction over territorial (5 kilometres from shore) waters, the sea-bed and air space. The court challenge brought into sharp relief the multitude of factors that can affect policy outputs. At stake were among the more important of the Whitlam government's resource and foreign investment policies. The states, including Labor-governed South

Australia, were reluctant to undermine their own economic interests. Whitlam insisted that the policies were not only right, but that their legislative underpinnings were constitutionally proper, under federal power to regulate overseas and interstate trade and as derived from general powers for the defence of Australia.[41] More on the political and legal implications of these High Court challenges when we deal with the policy process features of external affairs. We need to mention here that in 1975, the High Court overturned the PMA on a technicality, namely a flaw in the legislative procedures by which it had been handled in 1974. Its substantive validity remained juridically undetermined and the government moved to reintroduce it in Parliament.[42] The Seas and Submerged Lands Act was upheld, but not until after Labor had been ousted from power.

The state legal challenge was only one aspect of a widespread and diversified attack against the government's foreign investment policies. Some of the criticisms emanated from radical circles, where the *inadequacy* of official policies was deplored, mostly as a sell-out to the cause of capitalism. There even were imputations that an ultra-radical group, the Worker–Student Alliance, had fomented industrial sabotage within foreign-owned plants, notably in South Australia.[43] Far more prominent were criticisms from quite different quarters. We will wish to examine the tenor of those criticisms, their source and whatever counter-measures against government policies may have been launched by the critics themselves.

When Labor was first elected, there was some trepidation among foreign investment interests, but the feeling was by no means universal. There is some internal evidence suggesting that among US interests there probably was more sentiment acceptive of the ALP than among Australian businessmen, who as a group were more conservative. But the climate changed. It became clear that Labor's philosophy towards overseas investment was not shared by the bulk of investors, or indeed by the L–CP opposition. Specific policies aside, it became a dialogue between a highly nationalist-minded, state-interventionist government and those more devoted to the private sector. Anthony's summation was that "The Liberal and Country parties do not share Labor's xenophobia over overseas capital."[44] In early 1974, an American business magazine asked rhetorically whether Australia was a good place in which to invest. It wrote that "Power has gone to the government's head and prosperity to the trade unions'. The answer to the investing question, therefore, must be: Not at the moment."[45]

It was argued that overseas investment, especially in resource exploration, required the vast amounts of high-risk capital and expertise lacked by Australia. Connor's boast that Australia already supplied well over 80 per cent of its own capital requirements and could easily improve on this figure was dismissed as idle. The "missing" percentage was for types of ventures in which Australians would not or could not afford to invest. Hence in the low investment year of 1973–74, mineral exploration, exclusive of petroleum, was still more than 90 per cent foreign-financed. As of 1975, it was estimated by the chairman of AIDC itself that Australia's mining and industrial needs would likely require $15 billion in foreign capital over the following decade.[46] It was further estimated that, from 1975 to 1996, $8 billion would have to be spent on exploration and development to give Australia any chance of approaching self-sufficiency in oil, assuming the deposits were there, to avert huge oil bills and the chance of being embargoed by foreign suppliers.[47] In the light of this, critics pointed to the scarcity of new major mining projects under Labor, to a steep decline in oil exploration activity and to slowdown and even withdrawal of existing overseas ventures. Within a year of Labor's appearance in office, a survey by the American Chamber of Commerce in Australia (AMCHAM) showed a nearly across-the-board investment retraction by US firms in Australia and a sense of noticeable caution about the future.[48]

Business and the opposition attributed some of the decline in overseas investment to broader economic movements, such as removal of some protective tariffs from industry at large, currency realignment and industrial unrest. Some of it was attributed to the effects of specific policies, such as the originally high VDR on foreign borrowings, local equity requirements, prohibitions on farm-outs and blockages imposed against proposed takeovers of mining companies. Another depressant was a deterioration in the climate of business confidence generally. Foreign investors were either uncertain as to where the next government policy steps were going to lead, or were confused by frequent shifts or contradictions in government guidelines, or were simply disheartened by what they construed as rather threatening gestures by Connor particularly. They were never quite certain when and how to separate government rhetoric from actual intent. They could not be sure whether the government was really as much concerned about ownership as about control, nor were they entirely clear as to the strictness that would be applied towards a foreign equity stake in energy resources. They knew that AIDC was in some degree going to be more active under Labor than it had been under the L–CP, and that the PMA's future was clouded. As long as the particular terms on which such agencies would operate remained unsettled, there was a reaction to hold back, to wait and see.

In part, delays in clarifying what the government would do were not of its own doing. For instance, opposition party obstruction in the Senate held up the PMA's legislative authorization for many months and state challenges before the High Court further obfuscated the government's known authority to implement its off-shore exploration policies. At all events, there was a feeling in some quarters that foreign investors had overreacted, perhaps for effect, to the ostensibly dark investment picture. Indeed, American officials concerned with the subject took a less-pessimistic view than did American investors as a whole, and some informed opinion argued that decline in US investment activity in Australia was as much due to the opening of attractive investment prospects elsewhere as to hostile Australian government policies.

Those who denigrated Labor's approach to foreign investment found it advisable to offer something in return. The opposition's basic philosophical temperament was offended by what Labor said and did. The L–CP often, and tartly, ridiculed the government's policies as needless or counter-productive. But its actual counter-proposals were not radically different from Labor's. The opposition did come to appreciate the need for controls and supervision, both on the merits and as an acknowledgement of a broad public mood. For instance, a late-1973 opinion survey found 33 per cent of respondents feeling that the government was doing about enough to control foreign ownership, 44 per cent felt it was not doing enough and only 11 per cent believed it was doing too much. The proportion of "not doing enough" respondents was *greater* among L–CP than among Labor voters.[49]

Despite some variations between the Liberal and the Country Parties, a discernible pattern in opposition thinking evolved. Included were proposals for mandatory requirements for majority Australian ownership in key economic areas, sponsorship of joint ventures between foreign and Australian interests, oversight of mandatory guidelines for all overseas companies respecting information disclosure and their use of Australian senior management, and the obligation to control the flow of "hot" overseas investments. By October 1975, as part of their overall policy review, the coalition parties produced a foreign investment document that, in most substantive respects, did not diverge from the guidelines announced by the Labor government the preceding month. There was no real quarrel with AIDC. To be sure, the PMA was opposed. But a number of opposition members privately felt that they could live with the PMA, and the heart of the argument against it was that other less "statist" mechanisms could achieve sovereignty over the off-shore exploration industry and regulate its behaviour.[50] Basically, the L–CP was saying that it was better fitted than Labor to restore clarity and foreign investment confidence. It would deal with foreign investment more on its "merits", but it was not prepared to be casually permissive.

Foreign investors also replied. Apart from questioning policy features they found especially obnoxious, or deploring the policy inconsistencies and the climate of investment uncertainty, they worked to build the best possible image for foreign investment in Australia. This effort was especially conspicuous within AMCHAM. A year after Labor's election, an AMCHAM survey among its own membership concluded that "although reaction to multinationals is not generally considered serious at this stage, many respondents indicated that they felt such reaction was growing and could become a problem." Some companies had noticed adverse reaction among employees, a few among customers and several discerned prejudice at middle levels of the public service.[51] There is some internal evidence that younger, or more recently arrived, US investors were less agitated than their older colleagues, who had lived for years in a highly permissive foreign investment climate under the L–CP.

Foreign investment's technological research and development, foreign reserve, job-generating national economic expansion and other contributions were publicized. It was stressed that, especially, US firms had cultivated a burgeoning export trade, thereby complementing the economic and foreign policy objectives that the government itself felt should be sought through active commerce. Similarly, data were offered to show that those multi-nationals in Australia that were not given a free hand by parent companies to export were few and declining in number. Publicity was directed at demonstrating that foreign firms were rapidly increasing the ratio of local purchases to imports. The gates to Australian senior management and executive board directorates were said to have swung noticeably more open. Incomes of foreign- and Australian-owned firms were said to be more or less comparable. Local equity was generally easily accepted by overseas investors.[52] By 1974, the previously low-profile Australia-British Trade Association had joined AMCHAM in trying to counter adverse publicity respecting foreign investment. By 1975, the Australian Mining Industry Council was reported to be launching a publicity effort, possibly worth $100000, to win favourable public sentiment.[53]

Just how eager were foreign investment interests to rectify what they construed as wrong-headed Labor policies? As seen, there were intensified efforts within the resident overseas investment community to accentuate the positive. On a few occasions, however, concerned remarks by such groups as AMCHAM or by visiting business people were badly received in Australia. There even was a feeling among some American officials in Australia that the publication of AMCHAM's survey of its members was ill-timed and possible grist for the mill of anti-investment and anti-American sentiment. Foreign investors maintained liaison with Australian ministers and public servants. Their reactions were that while Connor was seldom approachable, other ministers, particularly Cairns, as well as most public servants, were both accessible and constructive in their attitude. Senator Ken Wriedt, who in October 1975 replaced Connor in the Minerals and Energy portfolio, gave definite signs in his brief tenure that he would be far more accessible than his predecessor had been.

Various charges were laid against foreign investment interests for undertakings characterized as sinister or otherwise improper. For example, Senator Brown and others deplored the Australian foreign investment survey conducted by the Centre for Strategic and International Studies at Georgetown University, in Washington. The centre was portrayed as a highly conservative, big-business supported American "think-tank". It was said to have tapped the opinions of American and Australian respondents, "comprador academics" and others, in order to provide US foreign investors with data and advice on how to subvert Australia's legitimate economic nationalism interests, and perhaps to undermine the perceived investment-hostile Labor government as well. It is true that parts of the survey questionnaire were awkwardly or overpointedly drawn and invited criticism of what the survey was all about. However,the project was initiated before Labor came to office, and even before the McMahon government had introduced its takeover legislation. Contributions to the survey were sought from persons representing a wide political spectrum. The survey was not couched in secrecy. Its preparation was known to Australian governments, L–CP and then Labor, and they raised no critical comment. At point of writing, the survey findings had not been published. But it is known that, at various stages of collation and disucssion, the opinions of participants reflected considerable understanding and even sympathy for Labor's keen interest in directing foreign investment and in aspects of the "new nationalism" temper.[54]

Another criticism of foreign-investment interests was that they helped to underwrite the L–CP and in so doing worked to undermine Labor. Labor government spokesmen themselves indulged in such imputations. The charge was literally correct, but perspective is needed to make sense of what happened. Prior to and then during the 1972, 1974 and 1975 elections, federal legislation governing political contributions and their uses was virtually non-existent. There was nothing illegal about even the largest business contributions to parties, nor about their non-disclosure. Most business contributions, including in 1972, 1974 and 1975, understandably went to the more conservative side of Australia's party system, the L–CP. Most political contributions by business were, moreover, *solicited* by parties rather than being independently volunteered. Strongly inferential evidence suggests that the bulk of business donations to the L–CP was from Australian rather than foreign-owned enterprises. Both major party groups had rules about accepting political donations from overseas. When multi-nationals contributed, they did so from their Australian branches rather than from parent companies. There is reason to believe that, even though they had grown restive under Labor between December 1972 and May 1974, foreign investors were reluctant to contribute lavishly to the L–CP, if only to avoid the obvious charge and possible backlash effects of political interference. In 1972, Labor was able to attract a measure of business financial support, but less so in 1974. Like the L–CP, Labor preferred not to publicize the business donation sources, or those firms, locally or foreign-owned, whom it solicited. In late 1974, Federal ALP Secretary David Combe visited the United States. While there he asked American firms with Australian subsidiaries if they would contribute towards the building of Labor's new Canberra headquarters, Curtin House. He was advised to ask the subsidiaries themselves, advice which the ALP eventually followed. The episode underscored the "business and politics" or, if one prefers, the "international business and politics" connection in Australia, from which neither major party group was exempt.[55] We might also mention, however, that in a 1975 series of investigative articles in the *Australian Financial Review*, based on both Australian and US sources of information, foreign and especially American arms and equipment companies were acquitted not only of having made donations to political parties but of having engaged in corrupt pay-off practices to individuals.[56] Well into 1976, there were no known documented instances of malpractices of this character.

Another accusation was that foreign-investment interests, especially American, worked hand-in-hand with their national governments to exert pressure on the Labor government. This is a theme the author pursued closely with Australian officials, American officials and with spokesmen of the US business community in Australia. AMCHAM established liaison with Ambassador Green and other persons in the US official establishment in Australia. There is no question that US officials knew of the businessmen's cares and worries. All the same, close checking in Australia and the United States suggested that US officialdom almost consistently was less troubled about foreign investment impediments under Labor than were corporate US investment interests themselves. It is plain that, at least throughout the first two years or so of Labor's rule, the United States never made any official "representations" on behalf of the business community or on the

US government's own behalf. Conversations did occur, but they were largely a search for policy clarification by US participants. Apparently at no time was Australia threatened with American commercial or other reprisals if Canberra failed to correct its foreign investment policies. An unusually well-placed Australian source illustrated the relative mildness of the American official position by recalling that the US Treasury Department had regarded Labor's VDR impositions as a "sensible" step. By the close of 1974, US investors continued to be apprehensive. But Green personally arranged an American visit for Cairns so that the then Deputy Prime Minister could discuss Australia's investment opportunities with interested private and official parties. By that time, Green and the US administration had come to the conclusion that the Australian foreign investment climate had brightened.[57] It is a fair surmise that the US government's low-profile stance on foreign investment may have hastened the repair of Canberra–Washington relations generally, after the troubled months of early 1973.

As an example of government-to-government relations in the foreign investment sphere, the United States and Australia were better off than were Japan and Australia. The value of Japan's investments in Australia was very low, about $260 million in 1973, compared to the many billions in US and British hands. The Japanese were not eager to compete in the US–UK class, but they did have a great stake in their continuing access to Australia's mineral resources. These they did not wish to control, but generally preferred minority equity in the minerals and their processing, as protection for themselves. As we will see, the exceptional nature of Japanese–Australian economic links led to special complications in the playing out of Canberra's resource and trading policies. But it had spin-off effects upon the question of Japanese investments as well, especially in the key and closely guarded mineral resources area.

There were protracted negotiations, moments of real distress in both capitals, some well-publicized turns of Japanese capital to other resource markets and delicate problems in writing mutually acceptable language for the long-awaited treaty of friendship and cooperation, the treaty of NARA.[58] The treaty was under negotiation since late 1973. By early 1975, most terms had been approved by both sides. The remaining clauses were dismissed for the record by Australian spokesmen as minor and technical. Some press reports were less sanguine, indicating that one major sticking-point was Japan's insistence that its foreign investment stake under any future Australian government not be treated any less leniently than the investment stakes of any other nations.[59] The author understands that Australia received this Japanese demand with utmost concern. One intimately placed Australian described it as a Japanese demand for preferential treatment, "more preferred" than available to others, and comparable to the freedom enjoyed by US investors in the halcyon years of the 1950s and 1960s. This was not only resisted by Australia, but resented.

Having reviewed the role of overseas investment in Australia's economy and in the policy debate, we pass to the rationales and policies that guided the distribution of the nation's economic resources. We will deal first with resource policy and then with overseas trade.

The notion of resource policy, or "diplomacy", emphasizes not only a presumably integrated approach to the management of resource distribution but its international politics dimensions as well. Labor ascended to power in an era associated with international developments, such as the energy crisis, that placed a premium on the development of a coherent national approach to resources. There were additional stimuli, peculiar to the ALP. As we have pointed out, Labor as a party was especially struck by the salience of the economic dimensions of interstate relations. Whitlam personally took a very broadly conceived view of Australia's international role. A specially designed *Australian*-oriented resource policy/diplomacy was consistent with new nationalism professions. The idea of a highly co-ordinated resource programme complemented Labor's preference for palnning and state direction. Finally, Australia's very considerable natural wealth, and the already established requirements of resource-short nations for this wealth, made it more natural to proceed on an increasingly co-ordinated basis.

Whitlam argued that patterns of global resource consumption introduced new complexity into Australia's strategic thinking and into various bilateral connections. As Australia became the object of others' resource strategies, it needed to respond. The national Australian interest would be taken into account; for instance, in relation to the country's own resource requirements, and appropriate Australian ownership of them, and equitable price returns. But he abjured-the idea of resource transactions between producers and consumers as a test of strength, of Australia's "possession of natural wealth as some sort of economic, political or diplomatic weapon or that we should sit selfishly on that wealth or that we should gang up with the producers against the users."[60]

Our analysis of Australia's resource policy will first consider bilateral relations, particularly with Japan. Japan was Australia's best customer. In 1974, it took about 55 per cent of Australia's mineral exports, including 46 per cent of all the iron-ore and black coal required by Japan's steel industry. Officially, on a number of occasions, Australia spokesmen reassured Japan that its mineral supplies would be maintained. Australia did not wish to tempt Japan to rearm, should it become desperate for resources. It wanted to draw Japan into closer and more economically productive links with the rest of Asia. Australia's own international reputation, in Japan and at large, could depend on the trustworthiness and reliability it displayed.[61]

The federal Labor government reacted with outrage when someone else tried to squeeze the Japanese. At the turn of 1974–75, Queensland government authorities declared that they would consider denying coal-mining leases in their state unless Japan made purchases from Queensland's depressed beef industry. Not only the Whitlam government but the federal opposition and the press reacted unsympathetically. Federal government spokesmen claimed that Queensland's action could wreck the entire carefully fitted structure of trade relations between Australia and Japan. It could lead to Japanese retaliation against a recently signed sugar contract and at minimum, generate confusion and uncertainty in Tokyo.[62]

What was federal Labor's own record? It was lauded by some, denounced by others. Imputations were raised of hard bargaining in resources bordering on blackmail. Resentment appeared in the Department of Foreign Affairs against Connor and his Department of Minerals and Energy for what was interpreted as narrowness and ir-responsibility. The Japanese themselves were in fact often confused and annoyed.

One important step taken by Connor was to compel a series of renegotiations of standing iron-ore and coal contracts with Japan, with the Australian side operating on a joint government/industry rather than industry alone or individual company bargaining basis. In effect, Connor told the Japanese to put up or shut up; no price adjustments, no minerals. He knew that the Japanese were gradually diversifying their iron-ore purchases by buying in Brazil, but was persuaded that their Australian dependency would remain intact for the foreseeable future. Japan's industry faced soaring oil costs and a shortage of coal supplies, so the Australian market was needed. Significant upward price renegotiations were obtained. Australian producers were pleased, especially since mining contracts, written in US dollars, had meant losses for them when Labor originally upvalued the Australian dollar. In 1975, Connor's intervention made possible the signing of an enormous coal contract with Japan, worth about $7 billion over five years, with assurance of Japanese purchases built in.[63]

In Australia, questions were raised as to where the fine line between astute resource policy and blackmail lay. If the Japanese construed it as blackmail, warned the *Australian Financial Review*, "this could have ramifications for the Australian economy far wider than the price interests of iron-ore products."[64] The Japanese on most occasions only grudgingly gave in to the mineral price revisions. They interpreted much of what was happening as one-sided, to Australia's advantage. They pictured themselves as very substantial and long-term buyers and therefore deserving of some price consideration. Unhappy experiences with forced price revisions of mineral contracts also helped to delay complicated NARA treaty negotiations. Based on their experiences with Connor, the Japanese wanted mineral price stipulations predicated on free competition, rather than on Canberra's preference for allowing official intervention. Not for several months into 1975 did the Japanese agree to abandon a supply and demand price position.[65]

The Japanese were also perplexed by what exactly Australia's position was on resource criteria other than prices. They found Australian ministers saying first one thing and then another about levels of Australian equity required for energy resources. They could not be sure just how strict Canberra was prepared to be about requiring the co-operation of consumer nations in creating domestic processing facilities for Australian resources. Not until late 1974 did Japan receive reasonable assurances of continuing Australian coal and uranium supplies, but upon Japan's promise to provide funds for a coal hydrogenation project and a uranium enrichment plant.

Before we return to Japan, and to uranium, something should be said of the ALP government's resource policy *vis-à-vis* the Middle East. High-level exchanges took place between Australian and Arab nation and Iranian officials in 1974 and 1975. In 1974, the Shah of Iran paid a state visit to Australia. Some aspects of the negotiations were unremarkable. What was somewhat special was Australia's wish to create two-way economic arrangements and to link trade and investment programmes. Australia was not really fearful that it could become a special target of a Middle Eastern oil embargo, but all the same there was no harm in cultivating close and interdependent economic relations with oil-producing states. Moreover, Australia was interested in getting its share of petrodollar investments or loans. Some Canberra circles seemed to perceive that the Shah saw Australia as a fellow Indian Ocean region country, somewhat in a mediating role and endowed with abundant but not fully developed economic potential. When a mission led by Cairns visited Bahrain, Kuwait and Iran in 1975, no demands were placed on Australia regarding its Middle Eastern diplomatic policy. Plans were laid for upgrading Australian exports to the Middle East. The commodities would be varied, for instance to include meat and grain, as well as technology and minerals. Here was to be resource diplomacy in action. In exchange for minerals, the recipient states were to invest in Australia, especially in the mineral resource field. It was to be done in assorted combinations, but with stress on the role of a public Australian presence, especially through AIDC.[66]

In mid-1975, however, Australian politics were rocked by revelations that the government, through Connor's and Cairns' efforts, had sought enormous multibillion sums in Arab petrodollar loans. More on this later. What matters here is that the government's intention was to raise these funds to finance a number of energy projects, in keeping with development policy and with strengthening local Australian control. The opposition and much of the press condemned the loan-raising efforts as alternatively unnecessary, overly expensive to finance and as having been undertaken with deplorable secretiveness and fragile authority. Connor was unrepentant. In the House, opening a defence of his actions, he exclaimed that

> The same international forces and their Opposition puppets which frustrated the early birth of the Industry Development Corporation and which destroyed Prime Minister Gorton now turn their malice, their spleen and their venom on an Australian Government which stands in their path as they seek to enlarge further their grip on Australia's resources of minerals and energy.[67]

One of the minerals broached for possible sale to Iran was uranium, and herein lies an interesting facet of Labor's resource policy. When Labor came to office, Connor allowed existing uranium contract arrangements to continue, but banned new ones. One reason for this temporizing policy was to allow the price of uranium to appreciate before further contracts were let. The same rationale influenced disposition towards eventually selling not crude uranium oxide (yellowcake) but enriched uranium, i.e. uranium with a considerably higher price- tag. Connor's zest for capturing price advantages was expressed in another way. There were intimations to the Japanese that uranium contracts let during the closing months of the McMahon government might not be allowed to proceed until Australia's desired price in iron-ore renegotiations was met. By the close of 1974, with general assurances of supplies extended to the Japanese, the Australian position seemed reasonably clear. Uranium would involve a combination of Japanese capital, Australian ownership and suitable third-party—probably European—technology relative to uranium enrichment.[68] Whitlam's December 1974–January 1975 visit to Europe was partially a testing of interest in getting technological investment in return for enriched uranium for European nations.[69] As 1975 went on, the Japanese chose to keep their options open and were cautious about committing themselves to a major uranium deal with Australia.

On the Australian government's part, however, uranium policy remained unclear in some significant respects. Depending on whose language was most current, Whitlam's or Connor's, it was unclear whether in a triangular uranium project Australia would require "maximum" or "100 per cent" ownership, or indeed·whether there was an understanding between the two ministers on the control–ownership distinction. Another unclear point was whether uranium sales would be tied to some kind of further *quid pro quo*. In December 1974, in prepared remarks in Brussels, Whitlam intimated that the availability of Australia's energy resources could not be divorced from the larger picture of entry opportunities for other Australian commodities.[70]

Another unclarity related to broader foreign policy considerations. One argument favouring uranium processing in Australia was that enrichment could be held below levels suitable for nuclear weapon development. In keeping with its condemnation of nuclear testing and proliferation, Labor refused in principle to consider sales of uranium to France and other non-NPT signatories. The selling of uranium to Iran was not, even notionally, easily received in Labor circles. Iran was an NPT signatory, but was undertaking a massive conventional military build-up and was suspected of wishing to keep its nuclear options open.[71] At a Paris press conference in January 1975, Whitlam persistently darted around questions that asked how uranium deals with France might be affected by France's continued non-adherance to the NPT or by its decision to move its nuclear tests from the atmosphere to underground.[72] In 1975, Germany provided Brazil with extensive nuclear technology in return for access to uranium supplies. The deal was frowned upon in various capitals, including Canberra and Washington, because of conceivable potential by Brazil, a non-NPT signatory, to apply the German nuclear technology towards military purposes. There were intimations from German sources that Bonn's decision to enter the deal was, ironically, contributed to by Australia's reluctance to part with the uranium in its own ground.[3]

Australia's approach to the multilateral management of resources was less haphazard than it was in bilateral relations. Australia became affiliated with international bodies representing producers of minerals in whose production Australia itself was prominent, for instance bauxite and iron-ore. The government's first foray into the area of producer-nation commodity policy was both tentative and short-lived. Whitlam visited Mexico in July 1973. There he broached the idea that Australia and other producers might co-ordinate their mineral selling and pricing policies. The idea was general and exploratory. It found little favourable reception in Mexico City and brought critical reaction at home. Whitlam made efforts to soften the impression that he had been urging a sellers' cartel.[74] One uncharitable interpretation of the Mexico City "initiative" was "Whitlamesque impulsiveness stimulated by lack of substantial matters to discuss with the President of Mexico, apart from the state of the local ruins".[75]

Thereafter, Australian policy toward producers' organizations was cautious. To be sure, at the Ottawa Commonwealth Prime Ministers Conference, shortly following his Mexican visit, Whitlam was a strong advocate of international producers' groups. Subsequently, Labor ministers expressed hope for a fair and orderly production and trade, and for a reasonable price return for producers, but emphatically rejected any notion of cartels and of efforts to manipulate supplies and to exploit mineral consumers through the drastic raising of mineral prices. When Australia joined the new Association of Iron Ore Exporting Countries, it was dissappointed that its proposal for including iron consumers had been overriden. When it joined the International Bauxite Association, one of its rationales was that it, as the world's single largest bauxite producer, could more effectively exert a tempering influence as a full member than as an observer or as a nonmember.

There were a number of reasons behind Australia's cautious approach. One was the realization that producers' organizations could not comprehensively impose their writ. Not all major producers necessarily belonged to such bodies, Canada's reluctance to participate in producer-exclusive groups being a strong example. Within the groups, there was no necessary identity of interests or long-term ability to hang together. Secondly, it was recognized that producers were also consumers, no nation being self-sufficient. A form of resource warfare inspired by producers' blocs could easily unhinge the world economy and profit few, if any, nations. As we saw earlier, Labor also appreciated that highly resource-dependent nations such as Japan could, if inordinately squeezed, attempt to secure their economic objectives by non-pacific means. The Arab oil boycott and the subsequent radically upward push of petroleum prices by members of the Organization of Petroleum Exporting Countries (OPEC) had a sobering effect on Canberra. The event seemed to show how resource power could be abused and that a super-power such as the United States could, however remotely, consider military intervention if threatened with strangulation. International producers' bodies could be very useful to the poorer, less-developed states. Aiming at reasonable resource returns could accelerate their growth potential. At all events, Labor's foreign policy theme of active collaboration with such nations would be advanced through multilateral

producers' venues. But the ALP government was unwilling to subscribe to a tough-minded producers' cartel proposal, even when it was
being importuned by some less-developed nations, as at the 1975
Commonwealth Prime Ministers Conference in Kingston, Jamaica.[76]

The internal politics of multilateral resource policy also affected the
government's attitude. Among protagonists of the cautious position
were such key ministers as Whitlam, Willesee and Cairns. Despite
holding the Minerals and Energy portfolio, Connor took relatively little interest in this aspect of resource policy, preferring to concentrate
on the bilateral side of the terms on which Australian resources could
be exploited and sold. Connor's general detachment from the multilateral side helped to minimize the back-and-forth, often conflicting
tendencies that characterized other features of Australia's resource
policy. Moreover, with ministers such as Whitlam, Willesee and, for a
time, Cairns carrying much of the responsibility for multilateral
aspects of resource policy, it was more natural that a noticeable
foreign policy, rather than a more narrowly nationalist-economic,
content should have animated multilateral approaches.

Indeed, the Labor government was admonished on all sides not to
translate resource policy into exploitation of consumer nations. The
United States took pains to explain, at both political and official
levels, its concerns for consumer nations and its apprehensions about
hard-lining, price-lifting, producers' cartels. But it did not oppose
Australian membership in multilateral producers' bodies. If anything,
it encouraged Australia, on the belief that Australia would exert a
restraining influence.

Within Australia, the Foreign Affairs Department strongly supported the government's temperate position on producers' commodity bodies. Both the public literature and internal evidence
demonstrated the department's concern over international political
and economic reverberations that could be occasioned by a hard-line
posture. This concern was itself a reflection of the department's disposition to think that the important international issues were increasingly economic rather than "security" based. This concern carried other consequences. As will be discussed in another context,
when we give explicit attention to the Australian external policy
process, the department became antagonized by the Connor/Minerals
and Energy Department views on resource policy and tried to increase its voice in such matters by asking for general supervisory
privileges over Australia's external relations, among them economic.

The L–CP was critical of a number of the government's country-to-
country features of resource policy. It alleged rash and/or confused
foreign investment ground rules, the bullying of overseas customers,
unrealistic delays on uranium exploitation, etc. Otherwise, much of

its rhetoric was a recognition of international economic interdependence and of Australia's role as a reliable, even generous, supplier of resources and technology. There was a clear aversion expressed towards producers' price cartels, to a point not shared by Labor; for instance, that Australia should take diplomatic initiatives to break down the more flagrantly behaving resource cartels, OPEC in particular.

Criticism was launched from the flanks. One tangent was basically political, representing an attack on Labor's credibility. Resource policy was said to expose the ALP's basic incoherence. Resource policy had

> sometimes been discussed in the rhetoric of strident nationalism, sometimes in the rhetoric of Third World havenots, sometimes in the rhetoric of responsible partnership with the industrial countries. Who, in the end, knows what our resources policy is—if indeed there is any policy beneath these layers of rhetoric?[77]

A second line of attack was more substantive. The basic message was that in its naive quest for distinctive posturing policies, Australia under Labor had done itself a disservice. Contrary to its own professions, the government had forgotten the interweave of economic, security, diplomatic and other international factors. For instance, it had overlooked that an "independently" formulated resource policy could not permit a run-down of defence forces to the point where the country was actually more dependent on others.[78] Or, as Fraser expressed it in one of his early major speeches after becoming Liberal leader, Australia and Middle Eastern countries alike had applied the resource diplomacy instrument in a way that "challenged economic stability around the world ... When nations start to export their economic ills to their trading partners, they head the world towards greater difficulty." Thereby, Labor's comfortable vision of *détente* was said to have become further degraded.[79]

We have left the foreign trade facet of Australia's international economic behaviour to the last. It is a subject that closely interfaces with such earlier themes as foreign aid, investment and resource policy. It is well to remind ourselves of the exceptional position occupied by foreign trade in Australia's economy. By 1974–75, the total value of Australia's imports and exports had reached about $16 billion, a virtual doubling since Labor took office and a figure by no means fully offset by inflationary trends. Export of goods and services in 1974–75 constituted about 16 per cent of Australia's gross domestic product, versus comparative 1973 figures of 7.3 per cent for Japan and 10.8 per cent for the United States. Moreover, by the late 1960s and early 1970s, the character of Australia's exports had become considerably diversified, with far more emphasis on minerals and manufactured goods than in the past, when primary agricultural commodities had been pre-eminent. The scope and variety of Australia's external trade strongly influenced the nation's economic development. The traditional dominant pattern of trade with Britain had under the L–CP been replaced by a concentration on Japan and other Pacific Basin nations, the region in which Australia's principal external interests rested.

There were various incentives for Labor to give attention to trade with less-developed nations. It was thought desirable to diversify trading outlets. By 1975, about 65 per cent of Australia's trade was with Japan, North America and the European Economic Community nations. Yet market opportunities in these industrialized nations were not expected to rise at the rate they once had. Their own growth rates had slowed and energy and other costs were eroding their overseas payments position. When Labor took office, Australia's exports to the developing countries had, in absolute terms, been climbing steadily, but had shown little change as a proportion (about a quarter) of total exports. Among the areas not previously well represented but targeted by Labor for heavier trade-market emphasis were South-East Asia, the Middle East and nations with centrally planned economies. There were foreseen Australian economic benefits in pressing trade in these areas. For instance, the vast oil-income wealth of Middle Eastern countries had given them incentive to buy goods and technology from the West on an expanded scale. There also were broader considerations. Whitlam asserted that "increasingly our foreign policy in South East Asia will be related to our efforts to develop mutually advantageous trade."[80] Like the L–CP, Labor visualized trade as an important base for promoting economic development among trading partners and as a dimension of external aid, i.e. as part of general foreign policy. The tying of various forms of Australian foreign aid to purchases of Australian goods, though downgraded under Labor, could still complement and enhance the trade drive. And, as a Liberal document argued, "Expansion of our manufactured exports [in the Asian region] could bring to Australia the benefits of economies of expanded scale of operations, thereby increasing domestic productivity and providing greater scope for the rationalisation of our industrial base."[81]

As a facet of external assistance, trade was intended to expand and improve Australia's visibility and influence among developing states. But, with exceptions to be noted later, the government in principle acknowledged that commerce was a two-way proposition. Australia had perennially enjoyed a substantial balance of payments advantage in its trade with developing states, including South-East Asian.

Economic sense dictated that further market opportunities ought to be opened for these nations within Australia. Superimposed were certain ALP ideals about how the world was, or ought to be, ordered: "We believe that the world needs some redress of the balance of power of the developed countries and their multinational oligopoly in relation to the much less organised economies of the developing states," Crean observed.[82]

Labor proceeded with various policies designed to promote two-way trade with developing nations. Some of this was an extension of earlier L–CP practices and some was new. The movement of Australian trade missions to far-flung places was accelerated and trade-commission posts were increased. In 1973–4, provision was made for developing countries to purchase Australian wheat on specially extended credit terms. Apart from business undertaken by the Export Payments Insurance Corporation on its own account, the government assumed large contingent liabilities on behalf of credit sales to developing nations. The corporation's own efforts in insuring overseas sales were extended. In 1974, two-thirds of the value of insured shipments were destined for developing nations, 38 per cent to South and South-East Asia. In early 1975, the Export Payments Insurance Corporation was reconstituted as the Export Finance and Insurance Corporation, with powers to operate as an export-financing institution as well as a credit and investment insurer and guarantor. The Labor government laid plans for an overseas trading corporation to supplement, but not to supplant or to take preference over, private trading efforts *vis-à-vis* centrally planned economies and with developing countries. To encourage the seeking out and cultivation of overseas markets generally, an export market development grants scheme was introduced. Labor continued the "Devisa Kredit" (formerly bonus export) scheme for Indonesia. Introduced under the L–CP, this programme was tailored to conserve Indonesia's foreign exchange reserves, to channel rupiah funds from the private sector into the country's development budget. In effect, it involved the purchase of Australian goods by Indonesia in rupiahs and the compensation of Australian sellers with Australian currency. The programme decidedly stimulated Australian sales to Indonesia, though eventually Indonesia's increased oil revenues were felt by Labor to have obviated the need for an extension of the programme beyond 1976.

Labor also undertook various measures to facilitate the sale of developing-nation goods to Australia. A special export-promotion facility within the Department of Overseas Trade was created to assist such nations in exploiting the Australian market. An earlier L–CP-initiated scheme of tariff preferences for a wide range of goods entering Australia from developing countries was enlarged and improved upon. On top of this, in 1973, the Labor government undertook an across-the-board 25 per cent reduction in tariffs on goods imported from all sources. With the approach of Papua New Guinea's independence, Canberra provisionally pledged a continuation of existing duty-free and low-tariff entry for goods entering Australia.

Such measures did have a positive effect upon developing-nation exports to Australia. In 1972–3, their share of Australia's total imports rose to 9.1 per cent, in 1973–4 to 12.4 per cent, and for the first half of 1974–5 it was running at a respectable 18 per cent rate. Nevertheless, import promotion endeavours were neither free of criticism not consistently pursued. The Devisa Kredit scheme was queried in some quarters for disproportionately siphoning development goods to Indonesia's urban sector. Sales by countries eligible under the tariff preference scheme had never equalled the value of goods under what for most of the programme's life was the available quota. The 12 per cent devaluation of the Australian dollar in the second half of 1974 reduced the value of earnings for nations selling to Australia.

Moreover, by 1974, Australia's deteriorating employment situation brought demands for relief from a variety of labour-intensive Australian industries producing goods that were entering the Australian market from developing nations. The number of Australians actually thrown out of work by such foreign competition was relatively small, but the arguments for official relief were insistent. For instance, between 1972–3 and 1973–4, the value of imported basic textiles rose by 67 per cent and the value of clothing and accessories by 97 per cent. Australian textile production declined 30 per cent between 1973–4 and 1974–5. Export licence controls were peremptorily imposed on textile goods originating in Taiwan, which did not belong to GATT, the General Agreement on Tariffs and Trade. Textile quota restraints were negotiated with China, India, Hong Kong and, very belatedly, with South Korea. Penalty tariffs on textile goods followed, and then came negotiated apparel import quotas with Hong Kong and Macao. By mid-1975, further voluntary restraint arrangements became increasingly difficult to obtain. Import quotas were therefore imposed on knitted garments from Singapore, Thailand and the Philippines, and upon textiles from China, itself not a party to GATT. Import quotas were imposed on other goods, such as footwear. The government was worried about the economy and sensitive to trade-union protests. It did not conceal the protectionist features of its policies, but Cairns found them "not incompatible with expanding world trade. The expansion of world trade requires a world of expanding domestic economies. The solution to our problems will come from a combined policy of internally induced expansion and international co-operation."[83] Some observers were not so sanguine. They acknowledged that some ministers, such as Senator James McClelland, Minister for Manufacturing Industry, held serious reservations about strong protectionism. But in the evolving practices they noticed, they deplored what they felt to be an overreactive protectionist trend, or a subversion of the government's professions about appropriate economic and foreign policy strategies towards developing countries, or both.[84]

Much of Labor's approach to trade with developing countries reflected an "enlightened self-interest" quality. It also appeared that, faced with difficult options, the government chose to come down on the side of domestic economic practicalities by heeding the appeals of vocal interests. As we continue, our interest lies in uncovering the extent and manner in which Labor may have applied a pragmatic hand to Australia's trading relationships more generally, and with what results.

We have already noticed Labor's reaction to South Africa. Despite moral revulsion among ministers and a wish to promote Australia's anti-racialist image abroad, only gradual and essentailly inconsequential barriers to a normal trading relationship were imposed. The size of Australia's economic stake in the South African economy took precedence. In the South African case, even heavy lobbying by a variety of critics failed to force a policy turnabout. Chile represented another instance of the foreign policy/trade interest group nexus. After the overthrow of the Allende régime, a ban on shipment to Chile was imposed by most Australian maritime unions. In early 1975, with wheat stocks abundant in Australia, the Wheat Board had an opportunity to make a fairly substantial sale to Chile, traditionally one of Australia's better wheat customers. The Minister for Agriculture, Senator Wriedt, advised (but did not order) the Wheat Board to withhold the sale, since obstruction was expected. The ACTU was unable to resolve the matter and the issue remained suspended for some time. The Labor government resented the post-Allende, Chilean military junta, but its "advice" to the board was largely taken to avert turmoil and to avert being placed in the position of either backing down in the face of union defiance or of sanctioning force to move the grain. It was, however, a welcome political wedge for Fraser, then shadow Minister for Labor. Wriedt, the reputed farmers' friend, Fraser charged, had betrayed the farmer to mollify sections of the trade-union movement. Who ran Australia—the government or the unions? Was this not more evidence of Labor's siding with leftists in the party and the unions to court Third World and communist nations?[85]

Labor carried out vigorous trade promotion towards communist nations and results were generally grafifying. As was expected, early in its life the Labor government lifted remaining special export controls on goods destined for communist countries. Trade treaties were signed with the Soviet Union and some East European states. Some notable sales contracts were negotiated, especially with East Germany (minerals, grain and wool) and with the Soviets. Trade diversification was an early and major commitment of the Whitlam government and the agency devised to deal with centrally controlled economies was a practical expression of this intent. The government probably was pleased, politically, with commercial success in communist capitals, seeing them as a complement to diplomatic relations. However, there is no evidence that sales terms were adjusted just to placate communist nations. Indeed, in 1974, after Canberra's recognition of Moscow's *de jure* sovereignty over the Baltic states, the Soviets refused an Australian offer of beef, at the time a considerably depressed commodity in Australia. Instead, they bought less-expensive Argentine beef. Only later did they resume buying Australian beef. What probably did help to spark trade with Berlin was that normal diplomatic relations had been established, though that step had been in the works when the L–CP left office.[86] Australia was interested in raising its trade with North Korea, but before formal diplomatic relations were established, the Labor government demurred in the creation of a North Korean trade office in Australia on Pyongyang's terms and admitted that this refusal would delay bilateral trade expansion.[87] When the diplomatic breach with North Korea occurred late in 1975, bilateral trade had made little progress. Indeed, the North Koreans were in arears on their Australian purchases.

Australian trade with North Vietnam and China should be considered separately, because of special political considerations. By the close of 1974, Australia had signed a trade agreement with Hanoi. For Cairns, then Minister for Overseas Trade, and others in the government, this step had special meaning. The agreement, together with earlier diplomatic recognition of Hanoi, symbolized Labor's policy turn-around from a time when Australian troops were engaged in Vietnam. In a way, the agreement, quite generously written by Australia, was a kind of restitution for wrongs committed. It was to be a token of new friendly relations, as well as a spur for assisting the war-damaged North Vietnamese economy.[88]

Trade with China at least as explicitly, reflected special Labor government perceptions. This is not to belittle straightforward economic considerations. China for some years under the L–CP had been an excellent customer, especially in wheat, and it was desirable to revive, enlarge and diversify sales now that Labor was in office.

Also it was believed to be in Australia's interests somewhat to lessen its dependence on its two largest export markets, Japan and the United States. However, the Labor Party felt a special need to establish close and broadly gauged relations with China. Senior ministers such as Whitlam and Cairns had personal, even emotional reasons for moving in this direction. There was disdain for the L–CP's previous antagonism towards China and recollection of the years when, because they disapproved of L–CP foreign policy, the Chinese had refused to buy Australian wheat. Whitlam had made his breakthrough and personally rewarding visit to China in 1971, and Cairns had long been sympathetic towards aspects of the Chinese social experiment. In any event, as we saw in other contexts, Labor was very eager to be on excellent terms with China, in part to bring influence to bear on a more accommodative climate in Asia.

Labor almost immediately extended diplomatic recognition to China. By May 1973, Cairns had led an impressive official and business trade mission to China. Then and thereafter, Cairns stressed that Labor's diplomatic and other friendly gestures towards China were responsible for realizing an enhanced trading relationship between the two countries. This cause and effect relationship is not easy to demonstrate, but there is inferential support for it. In July 1973, an important agreement was signed, providing the framework for much of subsequent trade between China and Australia. Its terms included encouragement for China's long-term contract purchases of various Australian commodities, specification of reciprocal, most favoured nation treatment and arrangements for extensive trade promotion activity by both sides.[89] When the preceding May trade tour was made known, 2000 Australian businessmen reportedly applied to go along. Those who did go were highly commendatory of Cairns' professional, sensitive performance. New contacts sparked the formation of an Australia–China Business Co-Operation Committee and of a joint Sino–Australian trade committee. For the first time, Australian businessmen could deal directly with Chinese corporations and their regional branches without relying on the semi-annual Canton fairs, though these continued to be useful venues. Movement between the two countries of private and official persons on commercial business became easier and more frequent. The trade value of these developments aside, Cairns saw them as a breaking down of Australian suspicions of China: "He has forced a significant cross-section of top Australian businessmen to look at China as it is and not as they are told it is. The results have been encouraging."[90]

The 1973 trade agreement was not easily achieved. The Chinese had traditionally resisted long-term commercial agreements with foreign countries, and Cairns had difficulty in persuading them to accept this one. He averred, however, that the Chinese had limited it to three years "so that, in the event of a change of government in Australia, the position could be re-examined".[91] In other words, good relations with the ALP government probably helped to gain a long-term agreement, and its time limitation indicated Chinese uncertainty as to whether an L–CP government could, or should, be dealt with in the same manner. Important long-term agreements were subsequently signed, primarily in sugar and wheat. In 1973–4, for the first time ever, two-way trade exceeded $200 million, reflecting an increase of over 100 per cent from the 1972–3 figure. By 1974–5, the value of Australian sales to China had risen to $257 million, while purchases from China were worth $81 million.

The trading relationship was not, however, free from criticism, or some nagging problems. The long-term agreements called for annual price negotiations. This somewhat weakened the Australian bargaining position and left uncertainty as to how much, exactly, to expect in income. Questions were raised as to whether Australia had quietly, for political reasons, promised low concessionary prices to China. This was publicly denied and is not definitely resolvable.[92] Nor were Australian officials and businessmen overly optimistic about the Chinese market. They recognized China's drive for self-sufficiency in various goods and its reluctance to tolerate serious long-term balance of payments deficit with trading partners. Quietly but firmly, the Australians were told of China's concern over the wide export–import gap. This concern was hardly relieved by the 1974 imposition of restraints on Chinese textile goods shipments to Australia and the imposition of import quotas on apparel in 1975.[93] In early 1975, however, China offered to sell crude oil to Australia, in part to help reduce the more than two-to-one favourable Australian trade balance.

The prospect of obtaining some Chinese oil was encouraging, if only because Australia wished to insulate itself against possible interruptions of its traditional sources of overseas supply. We suggested earlier that, during and after the October 1973 Middle East war, the Labor government was very eager to insure the shipment of goods to Middle Eastern countries, to forestall political fall-out, which imaginably could have affected oil shipments from the region. Efforts in 1974 and onwards to reach investment and trade agreements with Arab states and Iran also were attached to this consideration. The Cairns mission to the region in early 1975 returned with high hopes for new trade and investment arrangements, as well as with general assurances of continuing Australian access to oil. There was relief in Canberra when, after the refusal in January 1975 of visas to a PLO delegation, suspicions that Middle Eastern states might retaliate at the commercial level proved groundless. At all events, persons associated with the PLO were later allowed to visit Australia.

Special political considerations aside, Australia found much incentive to pursue Middle Eastern markets. States in the region had considerable funds on hand, a point underlined by 1975 disclosures of ministerial inquiries about raising billions in petrodollar loans. There were connections between investment projects and the extension of trade. Australia could make special contributions to the region's requirements—in grains, meats, sugar, dry agriculture technology and, possibly, even uranium. Impetus for dealing with the region came not only from Canberra but from Australian states. Non-Labor states such as Western Australia and New South Wales had no reservations about dealing with the politically left, radical régime in Libya. At the national level, the growing relationship was symbolized by a major long-term trade contract with Iran. A joint Iranian–Australian trading venture, "Austirian", was launched. On the Australian side, the consortium included an AIDC component as well as a considerable private stake. Overall, the commercial pay-off from Middle Eastern connections was heartening. By early 1975, an observer noted that "Middle East countries are now buying Australian products so fast that suddenly the region is reaching parity with Britain as a major export market."[94]

In various degrees, wide international economic and foreign policy considerations, not just a simple search for commercial outlets, affected Australia's trade drive in the Middle East. Wider considerations also appeared in Australia's trading relationship with more established, industrially developed partners.

While in Europe at the turn of 1974-5, Whitlam gave very positive encouragement to the EEC. But he did not hesitate to lecture the EEC countries, Japan and the United States—Australia's best trading partners—for behaving "reprehensibly" in their bans or limitations on Australian beef exports. Australia was in the process of restricting various products from Japan and other less-developed Asian countries, to protect its home industries. But Whitlam reproached affluent countries for setting a "bad example" because *they* were animated by domestic politics, while "Australia tries, even at the cost of some hardship to herself and her people, to have good trading relations. We would expect other countries, bigger ones in most cases, to be no less principled and progressive in matters of trade."[95] We noticed earlier Whitlam's intimation that the availability of Australia's energy resources could not be separated from opportunities for entry into Europe of other Australian commodities. We have also commented on Japan's dependence on Australian mineral resources, official Australian intervention to renegotiate upwards coal and iron-ore contracts with Japan and the various conditions Australia developed in connection with prospective uranium sales. Australia benefited greatly from Japan, its single best customer. In 1974–5, exports to Japan were valued at $2.4 billion, or 28 per cent of Australia's total export market, though imports from Japan were valued at only $1.4 billion. The Japanese export market was not only large but diverse. For instance, in 1975, Japan signed the biggest single contract ever negotiated for Australian sugar, and later in the year came the giant coal contract.

The Labor government insisted that it would never impose resource blackmail in order to gain trade advantages and denounced Bjelke-Petersen's threats to curtail mineral sales to Japan unless Queensland beef was bought. But the beef issue proved to be a serious point of Australian–Japanese friction. Japan imposed a ban on Australian beef in early 1974, partialĺy in response to its own domestic meat lobby. The ban came at an especially regrettable time, since EEC nations then cut off Australian beef and the United States pressed for a reduction through a voluntary beef import quota. Unquestionably, the Australian beef industry was badly bruised. Australia undertook a vigorous campaign to induce Tokyo to lift its beef ban. At one point, Japanese officials were reported to have claimed that Australia had threatened cuts in other areas of Japan's trade unelss the ban was removed.[96] The Japanese themselves had grounds for complaint. The trade balance was lop-sidedly in Australia's favour. Yet in 1974 and 1975, Australia imposed import restrictions on various Japanese goods, including textiles, motor cars, electric products and steel bearings, and Japan wished to have these curbs eased or rescinded. Eventually, in 1975, the Japanese allowed a modest quota for Australian beef. Also, with misgivings, the Japanese consented to the idea of a joint Japanese–Australian small-car manufacturing consortium in Australia (in which AIDC was then scheduled to hold a stake), though they still wished to export vehicles to Australia. In the short run at least, Australian trade bargaining with Japan had won out. The Australians had proved themselves to be hard, even obstinate negotiators, not sentimentalists. In a number of areas, they extracted demonstrable concessions, but stopped short of causing a rupture between themselves and the Japanese. Some observers were not overly impressed. They foresaw disturbing commercial strains in the bilateral relationship that official words of reassurance would not be able to assuage.[97]

Japan illustrated Australia's relationship with a large, economically powerful, yet highly raw-material dependent nation. Perhaps equally elucidating were Australia's relations with two other nations, New Zealand and the United States, both very closely joined to Australia in many ways, including commercially.

By 1974–5, the total value of trans-Tasman trade had reached over $700 million, a considerable amount for two nations whose combined populations numbered only about 16 million. New Zealand had become Australia's fourth-best export market and sixth-ranking source of imports. Each country was the other's main market for manufactured exports. The near quintupling of total trade since 1966 was considerably attributable to the institution of the New Zealand–Australian Free Trade Agreement. Overall, both nations benefited from NAFTA, which as revised, contained schedules for aspects of trade that were entirely tariff free, free in one direction or the other, or partially tariff free.

It was generally understood in both capitals that a near balance of trade was not possible, but it was hoped that NAFTA arrangements would help to stimulate some economic rationalization within both countries. Such hopes largely went unrealized. For instance, Australia refused to allow the products of its inefficient but politically influential dairy industry to come under the pact. Criticisms on both sides were to be expected, but by 1975, New Zealand opinion had become openly disconcerted. The country faced a general and massive trade deficit and slumping retail sales at home. Trade between the two countries was nearly three to one in Australia's favour, and rising. Moreover, worried about its unemployment problem and the health of some of its domestic industries, Australia was beginning to press for a voluntary reduction in some of New Zealand's manufactured imports. High-level official discussions in early 1975 failed to resolve much, apart from extending existing arrangements for a twelve-month period. Discussions later in 1975 were also disappointing to New Zealand.

There seemed to be a larger lesson in this than two nations undergoing cycles in their trading relationship, with one enjoying more advantage than the other. Much of New Zealand's foreign policy is dominated by international economic movements. For New Zealand, Australia's image has long been that of a kind of friendly giant, at times prone to patronizing and taking the New Zealanders for granted, even when the two countries are governed by parties of similar political complexion. A New Zealand observer was quite correct that "actual and imagined shared defence interests have been overused as an excuse for enforced co-operation in economic and other fields where the community of interest was much less certain".[98] When in 1975, New Zealand's trade picture with Australia became disturbing, there was ill-disguised reaction that Australia was not only being unhelpful but downright nasty. Australia might think it held most of the cards, but one New Zealand commentator was moved to suggest: "Let us have action in the form of economic retaliation until the Australians are prepared to trade on a two-way basis so that we can sell where we buy."[99] In turn, trading disputes such as this prompted Wellington to do things in foreign and defence policy areas a bit more independently of Canberra. One or two of these instances have already been noted. Others will be covered in our succeeding chapter.

Trade relations with the United States, another major Australian trading partner, were also instructive. In 1973–4, though enjoying a nearly two to one trade advantage, the United States was Australia's second-best customer. It bought $750 million worth of goods, about half of this amount in meat, of which the vast majority was beef. Australia had come to supply over half of all of America's beef imports. But the history of beef sales to the United States was checkered. Restrictions on access to the US market had been imposed between 1968 and mid-1972. The restrictions were suspended and Australia responded to Washington's call for more meat imports. Then, in 1974, under pressure from the cattlemen's lobby and some Congressional sources, the United States again moved to restrict beef imports. Washington was looking for a reduction in beef imports, not a shutdown. Australia voluntarily reduced its beef imports in 1974. A quota for 1975 was negotiated by the two parties and then slightly enlarged by the United States later that year. Through an Australian initiative, an International Meat Consulative Group was formed within the framework of GATT in early 1975. But the American move to restrict beef imports had come at a particularly inauspicious time, for Japan and the EEC countries were halting their purchases. Crean found fault in America's beef import restrictions. To him, they seemed to flaunt American wishes for freer international trade, represented a disconcerting retreat from the 1972 encouragement given to beef imports and showed lack of sensitivity to the plight of the Australian beef industry.[100]

US officials might have replied that, in a time of world beef surpluses, the American beef industry deserved tender treatment no less than its Australian counterpart, and that in 1974 and 1975, Australia, more than the United States, was backsliding on its earlier positive steps towards liberalizing the entry of goods from abroad. What seemed more interesting, however, were the background factors affecting US–Australian trade relations. Particularly after the May 1974 Australian election, Washington–Canberra relations improved. On its part, the United States approached its relations with the Labor government in a more relaxed, mature manner. It would have been regarded as counter-productive to shout down or brashly threaten Australia when trade differences, such as over beef, then arose. It would also have been counter-productive to attempt retaliation against Australia if, on a matter such as trade or the treatment of foreign investment, Australian policy ran across stated American interests. Careful checking by the author failed to uncover any instance of punitive US measures against Australia. Indeed, regarding trade differences, the United States was circumspect and tried to minimize damage to Australia. Washington seemed to understand that aspects of the most vital American stakes in Australia, such as the defence facilities, depended on large doses of mutual goodwill.

There also was evidence that, on its part, Australia could afford to be selective in its trade with America. In a late 1974 interview, Renouf drew an illuminating example. Australia would soon need to decide on a wide-body civilian aircraft. The options were between US models and the multi-nationally built European airbus. Australia should buy the airbus, Renouf said, for "good diplomatic and political reasons". Australia's relations with the United States were strong enough to withstand Australian rejection of American aircraft; "It is in our interests that we should be looking after the Europeans. In any case, this is the sort of line Foreign Affairs will be taking to the Government."[101]

The record seemed to indicate that, under Labor, overseas trade was carried out with a conspicuously pragmatic hand, and with good results. There was some evidence of combining a drive for export markets with a reluctance to reciprocate with ample opportunities for imports, but this occurred without visible counter-productive consequences. Where foreign policy considerations intruded on trade, their effect, at least in the short to middle term, appeared to range from neutral to positive. Of the three pillars of international economic policy—foreign investment, resource management and trade—it was trade that seemed to be most coherently, and successfully, pursued.

NOTES

1. For aid performance under L–CP governments, see Parliamentary Joint Committee on Foreign Affairs, *Report on Australia's Foreign Aid* (Canberra: 1973). For material that includes the Labor period, see Australian Development Assistance Agency, *Australian Aid to Developing Countries* (Canberra: 1975); *Australia's Overseas Development Assistance, 1975–76,* Budget Paper no. 10 (Canberra: 1975); and B. Juddery's assessment, *Canberra Times,* 23 August 1975. For representative opposition criticisms, see Peacock's *News Releases* of 17 April and 13 May 1974, and his remarks in *Commonwealth [Australian] Parliamentary Debates (APD),* House of Representatives (HR), (18 September 1974), pp. 1480–81.
2. For a review of Australia's Papua New Guinea aid programme and its drawbacks, see C. Ashton, *National Times,* 2 December 1974; and B. Toohey, *Australian Financial Review,* 24 July 1975. For some adverse PNG reactions to Australian aid, see B. Toohey, *Australian Financial Review,* 24 July 1975 and Melbourne *Age,* 13 August 1975.

3. For example, A. Pickering, *National U*, 25 March 1974.
4. D. Willesee, *APD*, Senate (1 August 1974), p. 695.
5. See D. McLean and K. McLeod, "Going Back on Vietnam", in AICD, *Breaking Faith in Vietnam* (Occasional Paper no. 6, Sydney, July 1974; *Digger*, 30 May 1974; *Tribune*, 6 August 1974; and the review by P. Manning, *Bulletin*, 27 July 1974.
6. Willesee, *APD*, Senate (16 August 1974), p. 1066. Also see Willesee, *APD*, Senate (1 August 1974), p. 695; and Crean, *APD*, HR (23 August 1974), pp. 1189–90.
7. *Report on Australia's Foreign Aid*, esp. pp. 30–44.
8. *Submission by the Department of Foreign Affairs to the Royal Commission on Australian Government Administration* (Canberra: October 1974), p. 17.
9. See remarks of Sir John Phillips to Asian Development Bank meeting, 26 April 1974, Department of Foreign Affairs memorandum; and Senator K. Wriedt (Minister for Agriculture), remarks in Rome at World Food Conference, 6 November 1974, Office of the Australian Minister for Agriculture *Release*.
10. For commentaries, see G. Davidson, *Canberra Times*, 22 March 1974; and C. Beck, *Nation-Review*, 12 October 1974. For an exposition of Australia's changing aid emphasis, see Willesee, "New Directions in Australia's Development Assistance" (AIIA conference paper, Melbourne, May 1975), *passim*.
11. On broad government objectives, see E.G. Whitlam, remarks in Bangkok of 1 February 1974, in *Australia and South-East Asia* (Canberra: Department of Foreign Affairs, 1974), pp. 21–22; and *APD*, HR (7 March 1974); and M. Walsh, *Australian Financial Review*, 29 January 1974. For an overall assessment, see J.B. Reid, "Australian Investment in South-East Asia" (AIIA conference paper, Melbourne, May 1975). One of the fullest official expositions is Renouf's address of 20 August 1974, "Some Foreign Policy Aspects of Private Investments in Asian and Pacific Countries", issued by the Department of Foreign Affairs. On "Pacific Rim" criticisms, see R. Catley and B. McFarlane, *From Tweedledum to Tweedledee: The New Labor Government in Australia* (Sydney: Australia and New Zealand Book Company, 1974); and B. McFarlane, "A Neo-Colonial Policy for the Pacific Rim", *Arena*, nos. 32–33 (1973), pp. 29–34.
12. On Fijian investment, see P. Hastings, *Sydney Morning Herald*, 13 January 1973; J Stewart, *Nation-Review*, 15 November 1974; and "Fiji: A Developing Australian Colony" (Fitzroy, Vic.: n.d.).
13. See B. Toohey, *Australian Financial Review*, 10 October 1974; and C. Ashton, *National Times*, 14 October 1974. For critical comment on CRA in Papua New Guinea, see J. Halfpenny, *Nation-Review*, 13 September 1974. On PNG's foreign investment approach generally, see A. Ashton, *Australian Financial Review*, 7 July 1975; and I. Parameter, *Canberra Times*, 3 September 1975.
14. For example, M. Richardson, *Canberra Times*, 31 May 1974; and B. Toohey, *Canberra Times*, 1 August and 14 November 1974.
15. See *Canberra Times*, 31 October 1975.
16. See Willesee's outline of Australia's basic position at the Law of the Sea Conference, Caracas, 2 July 1974, in Department of Foreign Affairs, *News Release*, no. M/93 (3 July 1974).
17. For data, see *Overseas Investment in Australia*, Treasury Economic Paper no. 1 (Canberra: 1972); *Overseas Investment 1972–73*, Reference no. 5.20 (Canberra: Australian Bureau of Statistics, 1974); and T.M. Fitzgerald, *The Contribution of the Mineral Industry to Australian Welfare*, Report to the Minister for Minerals and Energy (Canberra: 1974). For critical assessments, see G. McCarthy, *The Great Big Australian Takeover Book* (Sydney: Angus and Robertson, 1973); and L. Fox, *Australia Taken Over?* (Potts Point, NSW: published by the author, 1974).
18. For a general review, see R. Cranston, "Foreign Investment Restrictions: Defending Economic Sovereignty in Canada and Australia", *Harvard International Law Journal* 14 (Spring 1973): 345–67. For a summary, see Senate Select Committee on Foreign Ownership and the Control of Australian Resources, *Report No. 1*, October 1972, Parliamentary Paper no. 216 (Canberra: 1973), pp. 4–7.
19. Connor, *APD*, HR (18 September 1973), p. 1139.
20. *Australian*, 31 December 1974.
21. Address on "The Role of the Mutinationals in the Australian Mining Industry", 2 April 1974, transcript, p. 1.
22. Sydney *Sun-Herald*, 22 December 1974.

23. Fitzgerald, *Contribution of the Mineral Industry to Australian Welfare*, esp. pp. 73–77.
24. See interview with Connor by K. Davidson, Melbourne *Age*, 12 March 1975.
25. Address of 22 November 1974, in Department of the Treasury, *Press Release*, no. 97 (22 November 1974), p. 1.
26. See Willesee, remarks to the UN General Assembly of 7 October 1974, in Department of Foreign Affairs. *News Release*, no. M/129 (8 October 1974); Australian Mission to the United Nations, *Australian Statement on the Report of Eminent Persons to Study the Role of Multinational Corporations on Development and on International Relations* (March 1975), *passim*; and B. Toohey, *Australian Financial Review*, 17 April 1975.
27. See Hayden's remarks reported in Melbourne *Age*, 11 October 1975.
28. See Whitlam, remarks of 19 March 1973, in *AFAR* 44 (April 1973): 274–78.
29. See, *AFAR* 44 (November 1973): 752.
30. See Whitlam's guidelines in Office of the Prime Minister, *Press Release*, 2 November 1974: and the commentary by K. Davidson, Melbourne *Age*, 4 November 1974. For representative academic treatments of mineral policy, see S. Bambrick, *The Changing Relationship: The Australian Government and the Mining Industry* M. Series, no. 42, (Sydney: Committee for Economic Development of Australia, 1975); and the same author's "Australian Resource Development: Some Long Term Issues", *Dyason House Papers* 2 (October 1975): 4–8.
31. See transcripts of Connor's and Cairns' 4 February 1975 speeches; and commentary by R. Haupt, *Australian Financial Review*, 5 February 1975.
32. *AFAR* 46 (March 1975): 142–43; and R. Ackland, *Australian Financial Review*, 13 March 1975.
33. Interview by K. Davidson, Melbourne *Age*, 13 March 1975.
34. ABC television interview, Melbourne *Age*, 12 August 1975.
35. For an overview of foreign investment policies, see Crean's address of 2 October 1974, in *AFAR* 45 (October 1974): 676–77. For an earlier review, see G. Bruns, "Restricting Foreign Investment in Australia", *Round Table*, no. 251 (July 1973), pp. 391–401.
36. See Whitlam's statement of 24 September 1975 in *Australian Government Weekly Digest* 1 (22–28 September 1975): 835–44.
37. For official expressions, see, for example, Connor's statements of 31 October 1974 and 6 March 1975, transcripts; and his interview with K. Davidson, Melbourne *Age*, 17 March 1975.
38. For instance, see advertisement in *Australian*, 21 November 1974. For details on AIDC's operations, see its *Annual Reports*. For some public discussion of AIDC, see A. Wood, *Sydney Morning Herald*, 25 and 26 March 1974; T. Thomas, Melbourne *Age*, 17 May 1974; A. Clark, *National Times*, 3 June 1974; and *Australian Financial Review*, 17 July 1975. See Cairns' explanations in his address "The Policy and Intention of the Government for Industry in Australia", 15 March 1974, transcript, esp. pp. 6–9.
39. See a digest of Connor's attitude in Australian Information Service, *Finance and Commerce Newsletter*, 2 April 1974.
40. *APD*, Joint Sitting (7 August 1974), p. 135.
41. For commentaries, see H. Lunn, *Australian*, 28 June 1974; M. Steketee, *Australian*, 28 June and 6 July 1974; R. Ackland and B. Toohey, *Australian Financial Review*, 26 June 1974; and N. Swancott, *Australian Financial Review*, 6 November 1974.
42. For a summary see R. Ackland, *Australian Financial Review*, 25 June and 31 October 1975.
43. On the Worker–Student Alliance, see *Canberra Times*, 12 February 1975.
44. Australian Country Party National Secretariat, *Media Release*, 3 May 1974, p. 1.
45. *Forbes* magazine, 15 April 1974, p. 46.
46. Sir A. Westerman, cited in *Australian Financial Review*, 24 April 1975.
47. A.J. Knights, remarks to Australian Petroleum Exploration Association, Melbourne *Age*, 18 March 1975.
48. See *Commerce* (AMCHAM organ), January–February 1974, special supplement of US business opinion, pp. 11–14. Also see follow-up, supportive data in ACCA *News Letter*, 23 May and 25 July 1974. For an overview of investment slow-downs, see J. Byrne, *Australian Financial Review*, 18 July 1975 and *Australian*, 24 July 1975. For a general indictment of Labor's international economic policies, see R.L. Stock, "Labor's External Economic Policy—A Businessman's View", *Dyason House Papers* 1 (March 1975): 1–5. Also see the "inventory" of "losses" suffered by Australia as the result of restrictive policies, in I. Huntley, *Bulletin*, 2 August 1975.

49. *Sydney Morning Herald*, 14 November 1973 (Australian Gallup Polls).
50. For instance, see Liberal Party of Australia, *Federal Platform* (Canberra: October 1974), pp. 61–62; Snedden's remarks before the Council on Foreign Relations, New York, 9 December 1974, *Media Release*, no. 7/185 (9 December 1974), pp. 5–7; and Anthony, "A Mining Policy for Australia", address of 17 February 1975, transcript. For commentary on the evolution of L–CP foreign investment policy, see B. Toohey, *Australian Financial Review*, 3 January 1975; and Liberal and National Country Parties, *Foreign Investment Policy* (Canberra: Liberal Party Federal Secretariat, 1975).
51. *Commerce*, January–February 1974, p. 13.
52. *Commerce*, July–August 1973 and November–December 1974.
53. See A. Clark, *National Times*, 31 March 1975.
54. A verbatim text of the original Georgetown questionnaire was reprinted in Dissent, no. 29 (Summer 1972), pp. 25–27. See related articles by M. Richards, R. Witton, and C. Lang in this issue, and the commentary in *Nation-Review*, 5 July 1974.
55. For examples of L–CP indignation over charges of being in the pay of foreign interests, see remarks of R.J. Southey, Liberal Party Federal President, *Sydney Morning Herald*, 13 October 1973; Snedden, *Media Release*, no. 73/179 (17 October 1973); Sinclair, Australian Country Party National Secretariat, *Media Release*, 30 April 1974; and Fraser, *Media Release*, 9 May 1974.
56. See J. Stackhouse and B. Toohey, *Australian Financial Review*, 9 and 10 July 1975, respectively.
57. For assessments of the Cairns' visit, especially in its US–Australian relations connotations, see B. Toohey, *Australian Financial Review*, 31 October 1974; M. Adams, *Australian Financial Review*, 13 November 1974; and P. Costigan, Melbourne *Sun News-Pictorial*, 11 November 1974.
58. For treatments of the issue of Japanese investment in Australia, see G. Clark, *Australian*, 3 December 1973 and 14 June 1974; R. Haupt, *Australian Financial Review*, 1 November 1974; and K. Davidson's interview with Connor, Melbourne *Age*, 14 March 1975.
59. Most prominently, see B. Toohey, *Australian Financial Review*, 13 February 1975.
60. Whitlam, "Australia's Foreign Policy: New Directions, New Definitions", 24th Roy Milne Memorial Lecture, Brisbane, 30 November 1973 (Melbourne, AIIA, 1973), p.9. Also see Whitlam, *APD*, HR (24 May 1973), pp. 2650–51; and his New York address of 1 August 1973, in *AFAR* 44 (August 1973): 532–33. For more explicit resource guidelines, see Connor's Tokyo address of 29 October 1973, Department of Minerals and Energy transcript, *passim*. For commentaries, see H.W. Arndt, "Australian Resource Diplomacy" (AIIA conference paper, Adelaide, June 1974); and J.W.C. Cummes, "Australia and Resources Diplomacy" (Auckland conference paper, August 1974).
61. On Australia and Japan's energy needs, see R.J. McGavin, "Australian and Canadian Involvement in the Japanese and American Energy Crisis", *Australia's Neighbours*, 4th series, no. 84 (February–March 1973), pp. 1–5. For a summary of the government's position, see Whitlam's Canberra address of 8 November 1973, transcript, pp. 3–4. For a general statement of the economic relationship see J.A.A. Stockwin, "Australia's Relations with Japan: Complementarity and Strain", *Round Table*, no. 258 (April 1975), pp. 149–58; and E. Lachica's interview with Ambassador Shann, *Australian*, 19 May 1975.
62. For summaries of the controversy, see B. Toohey, *Australian Financial Review*, 15 and 20 February 1975; and C. Allen, *Australian Financial Review*, 17 February 1975. Also see the press releases of Dr Rex Patterson, Minister for Northern Development (17 February 1975) and of Crean, Minister for Overseas Trade (19 February 1975).*
63. See J. Rentsch, Melbourne *Age*, 7 July 1975.
64. 2Australian Financial Review1, 13 August 1974.
65. On Japanese disquiet, see G. Clark, *Australian*, 24 March and 26 June 1974; E. Lachica, *Australian*, 3 June 1975; J. O'Farrell, *Sydney Morning Herald*, 7 August 1974. On NARA problems, see A. Chiba, *Australian Financial Review*, 11 February 1975; and B. Toohey, *Australian Financial Review*, 13 February 1975; *Canberra Times*, 5 May 1975; B. Murray, *Australian*, 19 May 1975; and A. Clark, *National Times*, 26 May 1975.
66. For comment on the Iranian connection in particular, see G. Davidson, *Canberra Times*, 31 May 1974; M. Woolocott, *Guardian Weekly* (London), 12 October 1974; and *Australian Financial Review*, 15 August 1974. Also see the *Press Release* of the Office of

the Australian Minister for Agriculture, "Australian Ministerial Visit to Bahrain, Saudi Arabia, Iran and Kuwait—March 1975", 25 March 1975.

67. *APD*, HR (9 July 1973), p. 3610. For the major parliamentary debate contributions, see *APD*, HR (9 July 1973), pp. 3556–60.

68. On Australian–Japanese uranium negotiations, see G. Clark, *Australian*, 3 December 1973 and 30 April and 1 November 1974; T. Thomas, Melbourne *Age*, 27 September 1974; M. MacCallum, *Nation-Review*, 4 April 1975; and A. Chiba, *Australian Financial Review*, 1 August 1975.

69. See Whitlam's report to the nation following his European mission, reproduced in *Sydney Morning Herald*, 23 January 1975. Also see I. Frykberg's assessment, *Sydney Morning Herald*, 21 January 1975.

70. See his speech of 18 December 1974 in Department of Foreign Affairs, *News Release*, no. D.4 (15 January 1975), p. 4; and his press conference of the same date in *News Release*, no. D.5 (15 January 1975), p. 5. For an assessment of this interpretation, see R. Haupt, *Australian Financial Review*, 20 December 1974; J. Byrne, *Australian Financial Review*, 5 June 1975 and 7 July 1975; and R. Schneider, *Australian*, 21 January 1975.

71. See B. Toohey, *Australian Financial Review*, 3 April 1975.

72. Press conference of 7 January 1975, in Department of Foreign Affairs *News Release*, no. D.11 (17 January 1975), pp. 1–2. See commentary in *Canberra Times*, 11 January 1975.

73. B. Toohey, *Australian Financial Review*, 17 July 1975.

74. On the Whitlam idea, see A. Ramsey, *Australian*, 27 and 28 July 1973; and D. Solomon, *Canberra Times*, 30 July 1973. For typical reaction, see J. Jost, Melbourne *Age*, 1 August 1973.

75. R. O'Neill, "Australian Security and Resources Diplomacy: Alliance Problems" (ANZAAS conference paper, Canberra, January 1975), p. 3.

76. For representative ministerial expressions on producer groups, see Whitlam's address to the UN General Assembly of 30 September 1974, in Department of Foreign Affairs, *News Release*, no. M/128 (30 September 1974), pp. 7–8; Whitlam's Kingston press conference of 4 May 1975, in *News Release*, no. M/29 (9 May 1975), p. 2; Willesee's remarks at the meeting of iron-ore exporting countries, 2 April 1975, in *News Release*, no. M/16 (2 April 1975), *passim*; and his remarks before the UN General Assembly special session, 8 September 1975, transcript, pp. 3–6; Cairns' press conference statement of 10 March 1974, Department of Foreign Affairs memorandum of 11 March 1974; and his remarks as cited in *Australian Financial Review*, 4 September 1974. For elaborate commentary on Australia's position at the Kingston conference, where resource policy was widely discussed, see R. Haupt, *Australian Financial Review*, 6 May 1975.

77. Peacock, article in Melbourne *Age*, 14 October 1974. Also see the general assessment in Snedden's Council on Foreign Relations speech, *Media Release*, no. 7/185 *passim*. For analyses of opposition resource policy, see B. Toohey, *Australian Financial Review*, 24 April and 2 May 1974.

78. Peacock, *APD*, HR (11 February 1975), pp. 75–76; and Killen, cited in *Canberra Times*, 5 April 1975. For an interesting variant on this theme—a scenario in which Australia's resource diplomacy leads to depreciation of its defence capacity and American interest in sustaining ANZUS—see O'Neill, "Australian Security and Resources Diplomacy", pp. 8–9.

79. Address in Townsville of 12 April 1975, transcript, p. 8.

80. *APD*, HR (7 March 1974), p. 204. For background on trade aspects of foreign aid, see *Report on Australia's Foreign Aid*, pp. 85–92. With special reference to Indonesia, see I. Parmeter, *Canberra Times*, 16 August 1975.

81. Derived from non-attributable source.

82. Address in Perth of 21 March 1975. transcript, p. 8.

83. ALP conference address, Terrigal, 4 February 1975, p. 6. For other ministerial expressions on protection, see Whitlam, Prime Minister's *Press Statement*, no. 403 (9 December 1974); remarks of Senator J. McClelland, Minister for Manufacturing Industry, 14 February 1975, transcript; and his address of 23 May 1975, *Australian Weekly Digest* (19 May to 25 May 1975): 249–57.

84. For anti-protectionist comments, see P.P. McGuiness, *Australian Financial Review*, 22 January 1975; A. Wood, *Sydney Morning Herald*, 5 February 1975; and K. Davidson, Melbourne *Age*, 3 April 1975. A consistent critic of the government's policies' effect

on developing nations was the *Australian Financial Review's* Brian Toohey. See his articles of 26 September 1974 and of 13 March and 10 April 1975. For an analysis of competing economic interests in Australia, see D. Marr, *Bulletin*, 14 June 1975. For a general treatment of the Australian economy's capacity to sustain a major trade–aid programme in Asia, see W.P. Hogan, "Australian Economic Policy Opportunities in Asia and the Pacific", *Australian Outlook* 28 (April 1974): 15–23.

85. Fraser, *Press Statement* of 15 January 1975. For descriptive material, see *Australian*, 23 January and 15 February 1975; and *Australian Financial Review*, 24 April 1975.
86. See the commentary by G. Hawtin, *Australian Financial Review*, 16 April 1974.
87. Cairns, *APD*, HR (15 October 1973), p. 2066.
88. For instance, see Cairns' remarks, cited in *Australian Financial Review*, 17 December 1973; and in the text of the *Trade Agreement Between Australia and the Democratic Republic of Vietnam*, 26 November 1974.
89. For terms of the agreement, see *AFAR* 44 (July 1973): 472–74. For a résumé of the May 1973 trade mission, see *AFAR* 44 (May 1973): 362–65.
90. G. Clark, *Australian*, 29 May 1973.
91. *APD*, HR (15 October 1973), p. 2056.
92. On these criticisms, see P. Samuel, *Bulletin*, 17 November 1973 and 6 July 1974; and E.J. Donath, *Nation-Review*, 30 August 1974.
93. For instance, *Canberra Times*, 5 April 1974; D. Lamb, *Los Angeles Times*, 24 July 1974; B. Toohey, *Australian Financial Review*, 12 June 1975; and R. Haupt, *Australian Financial Review*, 1 July 1975.
94. P. Terry, *Australian*, 8 April 1975. For other commentaries, see D. Haselhurst, *Bulletin*, 1 February 1975; G. Negus, *Australian Financial Review*, 21 April 1975; and R. Joseph, *Canberra Times*, 5 May 1975.
95. Cited in *Sydney Morning Herald*, 9 January 1975.
96. G. Clark, *Australian*, 29 July 1974.
97. For instance, J. Penberthy, Melbourne *Herald*, 14 April 1975; M. Steketee, *Australian*, 2 May 1975; *Canberra Times*, 7 May 1975; and F. Martin, *Far Eastern Economic Review*, 16 May 1975.
98. A. Hass, *Trans Tasman Cooperation in Asia and the Pacific* (Wellington: Asia Pacific Research Unit, 1974), p. 5.
99. J.A. Young, *Dominion* (Wellington), 24 April 1975. For other opinion critical of Australia's attitude, see T. Garner, *Bulletin*, 29 March 1975; Melbourne *Age*, 29 April 1975; *Australian*, 8 July 1975; *Canberra Times*, 19 July 1975; and Ian Templeton, *Australian Financial Review*, 12 September 1975. For general analyses of the trading relationship, see various contributions in W.C. Cook, F.W. Holmes, and A.D. Robinson, eds., *New Zealand–Australia Co-operation*, (Wellington: Department of University Extension, Victoria University of Wellington, Proceedings and Papers, 1974); R. Ackland, *Australian Financial Review*, 30 September 1974; B. Juddery, *Canberra Times*, 18 July 1975; and *Canberra Times*, 19 September 1975.
100. See Crean's *Press Release*, 1 January 1975. For commentaries on beef imports to the United States, see P. Costigan's articles in Adelaide *Advertiser*, 23 October and 2 November 1974. For the 1975 quota settlement, see *Australian Financial Review*, 3 April 1975.
101. Interview remarks in *New Accent*, 25 October 1974.

7 External Policy: Defence Dimensions

We now turn to defence, our final policy area theme. We will first assess a basic instrument of the defence policy, the military establishment. Our attention will then turn to Australia's role in security alliances, and lastly to regional and Australian-based approaches to nuclear affairs, arms control and neutralization.

We begin by inquiring into the assigned role of Australia's armed forces: what they were supposed to do and why. We will then be better placed to evaluate their capabilities, measured by such criteria as numbers, organization, training and equipment, industrial and economic back-up, and the like.

Much of the perspective needed for our present subject was set out in Chapter 3, where we reviewed the external policy assumptions of the Labor government, and of the opposition and other critics. We noticed that Labor did not anticipate a serious threat to Australia in the foreseeable future. The ALP had a general aversion to military "solutions" to international problems. It repudiated the "forward" defence strategy subscribed to by its predecessors. It wished to be less reliant on traditional defence partners such as the United States. Above all, Labor was persuaded that foreign policy considerations had to dictate defence policy, not vice versa.

In principle, Labor as a party did not disavow the need for a defence capability. Article XX of the party's platform stipulated that "a strong and valid defence must be maintained. This defence intention must be so effective as to demonstrate beyond all doubt Australia's intention to defend itself and her vital interests." Once Labor had translated itself from opposition to government, and in light of international developments after December 1972, the role of Australia's armed forces had to be spelled out in considerably more detail. A perceived low-threat climate did not require massive forces. Changes in the climate were unlikely to be sudden, allowing Australia lead time to adjust its defence planning. Hence, as the 1974 *Defence Report* argued, Australia's forces needed to be maintained "to be able to cope with forseeable [i.e. mostly low-level threat] tasks; to provide backing for a more independent political posture; to sustain and practice an adequate range of military skills, and to provide an evident basis for expansion if this should be required."[1] Barnard, Morrison and other government spokesmen emphasized "continentalism". The concentration was to be on protecting Australia itself, not an outspread environment, from attack or other forms of duress.

As we saw earlier, the L–CP and others objected that the government's views on world conditions, on *détente*, and on the prospect of threats posed by tensions exclusive of great-power confrontation, were far too sanguine and dangerous. They felt that defence planning ought not to shrug off "contingencies" quite so lightly, or to impose an interdict, in principle, upon the use of armed forces in sole or supportive roles outside Australia and its immediate neighbourhood. They did not necessarily dismiss Labor's assertion that an active and constructive diplomacy could reduce the prospect of security dangers. But they often turned the argument around, claiming that an independent foreign policy lacked credibility if based on a weak or misplaced defence policy. The essence of the opposition's strategic thinking was to provide a core of forces "which can be expanded to meet a major threat in a time *less* than the likely warning time associated with the threat", as well as to develop "ready-reaction forces to meet low-level contingencies at very short notice anywhere within Australia and her territories".[2]

Into what specific roles were the armed forces placed, or projected for, under the Labor government? Some roles were not strictly military as such, or were only peripherally military. For instance, attention was given to utilizing troops during natural emergencies at home. This was done both because the services could make significant contributions and to inspire a more positive image of the military. Troops assisted during flood and other disasters in several states. In 1974, a National Disasters Organization was created, with a retired senior army officer as its first director. The NDO relied very heavily on help from all three armed services in the aftermath of the Christmas Day, 1974 cyclone that devastated Darwin. Another role, basically of a police nature, performed primarily by the RAN, was in trying to chase away or apprehend Indonesian and Taiwanese fishermen and poachers off Australian shores. Moreover, it might be recalled that in Australia's experience, troops had occasionally been called out to deal with civil disturbances. One such case was in 1949, when the Chifley Labor government brought troops to coal mines closed by industrial action. Under the Whitlam government, a spokesman indicated that while members of the army were not given riot or internal security training, "A number of training courses for officers include some lectures and instruction in the theoretical aspects of assistance by the Defence Force to the civil authorities."[3] Parenthetically, it should be said that, when industrial unrest became aggravated, a number of middle-grade officers were privately indicating their concern that more was not being done to train troops to cope with civil disorder.

What of armed forces roles outside Australia and its territorial waters? There were occasions when the services were called upon to perform essentially humanitarian duties. These included RAAF shipments of medical supplies to flood-stricken areas of Thailand, and the transport to Australia of Vietnamese orphans and refugees and of persons caught up in the strife that gripped Portuguese Timor later in 1975. We have already noticed the government's commitment in principle to contribute troops to UN-sponsored peace-keeping operations and the actual training of some Australian troops in Canada to learn from Canada's experience in this area. In 1975, an RAAF aircraft and crew were provided in support of the UN's Military Observer Group in India and Pakistan. Australian policemen had been serving in Cyprus since L–CP days. Willingness to place troops at UN disposal was a reflection of Labor's commitment to the United Nations and to the orderly settlement of international disputes. It also in part was an effort by the government to demonstrate to its own party sceptics that the armed forces had constructive "healing" functions to discharge. It also served to arrange more interesting career outlets for servicemen. From the beginning of the Second World War, Australia had stationed at least a battalion of troops abroad. With Labor's appearance in office and the withdrawal of combat troops from Singapore, the tradition was ended.

However, the shut-down of overseas troop garrisoning concerned only a combat troop presence overseas. Under Labor, numerous personnel from all services remained on foreign postings. A principal role for them was the training of military personnel from neighbouring countries. It was a reminder that the government did not disparage the value of armed forces' contributions to national self-defence or to the maintenance of civil order. Indeed, a complementary rationale was that if South-East Asian and Pacific nations had reasonably effective defence forces, this would lessen prospects of future summons from them for outside help, as for instance from Australia. Moreover, the Labor government saw a potentially important civil development role for such military establishments. It also found it valuable to enjoy overseas training sites for its own forces, for receiving Australian naval and air units and for joint military exercises profitable both to hosts and guests.

A few illustrations will underscore the extent of the Australian military's overseas roles. From late 1972 to early 1975, an RAAF advisory unit assisted Indonesians to fly and maintain Sabre fighter aircraft donated by Australia. When the unit's basic task was ended, some RAAF personnel remained behind to advise on engineering and equipment problems. Australia withdrew its combat troops and the DSD monitoring unit from Singapore by the beginning of 1974. But at least 1500 personnel of all services were still to be found in Malaysia/Singapore at any one time. About 150 men remained in Singapore to provide technical assistance and to help maintain an Australian frigate and submarine stationed in neighbouring waters. The remainder were in Malaysia, primarily in connection with the two squadrons of Australian Mirage aircraft based at Butterworth. The Mirages were to remain as a contribution to Malaysia's air defence and training until such time as the Malaysians determined that the aircraft were no longer required. Furthermore, Australia rotated an infantry company through the Butterworth base. Technically, this was not "stationing" but a "training and exercise" role. A final example comes from Papua New Guinea. A sizable Australian military presence was maintained there, primarily to train the PNG Defence Force in preparation for independence. But even after independence, training roles and service in technical fields such as logistics and signals were maintained, involving several hundred Australian servicemen.[4]

What, however, of Labor's disclaimer to sending combat troops overseas, apart from the very special case of peace-keeping under UN aegis or in response to a *direct* military threat to Australia? The question is hypothetical and may never be put to a test, though the L–CP made its point that it would not preclude an overseas intervention. There are some instructive observations that can be made respecting Papua New Guinea. Papua New Guinea's perceived security value to Australia declined considerably after the mid-1960s. The prospect that an independent Papua New Guinea would be attacked or militarily harassed by another nation was believed slight, though with Indonesia being the most likely candidate within this calculus of improbabilities. Australian and PNG authorities agreed that Australia should make no commitments to assist Papua New Guinea, either in international hostilities or if internal order broke down; for instance, through secessionist activity and should the PNG Defence Force of 3500 prove insufficient. Sir Albert Maori Kiki, Papua New Guinea's Minister for Defence and Foreign Relations, remarked that "These are things which we should be able to cope with ourselves. We do not want to be left with no alternative but to invite, or permit, foreign forces to come in and deal with the situation."[5] On its part, Australia

was hardly eager to be pulled in, especially with its own service personnel scheduled to play a key role in Papua New Guinea's defence establishment for the forseeable future.

At least hypothetically, however, that apparently was not where
the Australian government and its advisers felt that the matter
rested. Simply stated, the Labor government appeared not to preclude
the possibility of an Australian military intervention in the event of a
major security emergency in Papua New Guinea, whether externally
or domestically inspired. The combination of internal and public
evidence supporting this conclusion is reasonably impressive. The internal evidence, based on questions put to a number of key persons,
was consistently reinforcing. One interviewee remarked that
Australia had not asked for a formal defence commitment with
Papua New Guinea because it had wished to stay "on side" with Asian
countries, before which it had publicized its non-interventionalist
credentials. Another person pointed out that Labor's platform objected to the *garrisoning* of troops overseas, a prohibition that would
not preclude an *intervention* as such. At all events, whether or not these
particular *interpretations* were inherently correct, the consensus was
that intervention was not excluded as an option.

The public evidence is decidedly more inferential, but nonetheless
compatible with the conclusion. For instance, Barnard averred that,
in the absence of a formal Australian–PNG defence commitment,
"there can no longer by any thought of automatic involvement of
Australian forces in Papua New Guinea.[6] The point seemed to be
Australia's reluctance to be automatically involved rather than a flat
proscription of an interventionist role. At the ALP's 1975 party conference, Whitlam successfully argued against removal from the platform of support for treaties of non-aggression and of mutual defence
arrangements. In his remarks, on two occasions, he specifically mentioned Papua New Guinea as possibly carrying relevance for mutual
defence arrangements.[7] A final piece of substantiation, reinforced by
internal evidence, comes from the experience of the Priorities Review
Staff, a kind of far-looking "think-tank" unit created by the incoming
Labor government. In a draft that preceded its public interim report
in late 1973, the PRS criticized the government for having developed
technical/operational plans to intervene in Papua New Guinea in the
event of domestic turmoil, but for having failed to develop contingency plans for when, and in what circumstances, intervention
would be justified. The draft leaked out. Partially because the government wished to avoid indelicate material in a public document, the
PRS excluded all mention of Papua New Guinea in the foreign policy
section of its report. In any event, the government was unhappy not
only because the PRS had raised a sensitive issue, but because it saw

the PRS's criticism as unfounded; there *were* contingency plans for a military intervention of one sort or another, in addition to technical preparations.[8]

We have examined the actual and projected roles of Australia's armed forces. Now we turn to the resources Labor made available to them and their capabilities. Financial resources represented one rough index of the government's commitment to the armed forces establishment. The index is crude because it presents some difficulties in identifying the most salient data and poses problems of data comparability. Moreover, partisan discussion of defence expenditure fell victim to exchanges of political debating points and at times was depressingly unedifying. Basically, the government insisted that it was making a proper, even generous financial contribution to defence, while the L–CP disagreed.

In dollar terms, defence expenditure under Labor rose steadily. In 1973–74, it was up by $127 million over the last L–CP year. Then, in 1974–75, actual defence spending rose by $303 million. In the 1975–76 budget estimates, submitted in August 1975, defence spending was scheduled to rise by an additional $172 million, to a grand total of $1.8 billion. As a percentage of the federal budget, the projected defence allocation for 1975–76 was 8.2 per cent—down sharply from 1974–75 and roughly back to the figure for 1973–74. Opposition and other critics insisted that claims of steady improvement in defence spending, or of the adequacy of money budgeted or spent, were deceptive. For instance, both in the 1974–75 and 1975–76 budget estimates, the rise in defence expenditure represented the smallest proportional increase among any major budget items. Furthermore, it was pointed out that inflation had seriously eroded the value of the dollar, thereby invalidating government boasts of aggregate spending increases—the "less bang for the buck" argument. Hence although defence spending was scheduled to rise by nearly 11 per cent in 1975—76, it could actually be interpreted as a decline in what could be bought for the money, since it needed to be seen against a real increase of 17 per cent in the rate of inflation.

Enter the dispute over the proportionality of defence spending. In the last years of the L–CP, the annual amount spent on defence's share of national income had slipped from 4.8 per cent to 3.4 per cent and of gross domestic product from 4.3 per cent to 3.1 per cent. Under Labor, this decline continued, and then only in the most marginal terms was reversed. The national income proportions were 2.8 per cent in 1973–74 and 2.9 per cent in 1974–75; the estimate for 1975–76 was for no more than 3 per cent. Hence while the L–CP could not deny that *it* had allowed a relative "deterioration" in defence spending, it could claim that Labor had allowed even more deterioration. Defence spending as a proportion of national income was not much different than Germany's, and well above Canada's and New Zealand's—the latter two being, like Australia, Western "middle" powers. Labor had promised in the 1972 electoral campaign that it would not reduce relative spending below the level it inherited from the L–CP, so the opposition later argued that Labor had defaulted on its promise. The government of course claimed that, given its own national security calculations, and in light of other priorities, what was being spent on defence was adequate. In 1973, Barnard and Whitlam agreed that, over a five-year peiod, efforts would be made to increase defence spending by 1 to 2 per cent in real terms. An example of failure to match the promise with performance was the 1975–76 defence allocation—under 11 per cent projected rise in dollar spending, against a background of 17 per cent inflation.

From time to time, the opposition's criticism of Labor carried the strong implication that, if returned to office, the L–CP would rectify Labor's financial neglect of defence. But in the midst of the 1974 electoral campaign, the opposition stressed financial austerity as a means of combating inflation. In an interview, Anthony allowed that, because of financial constraints and the not altogether unfavourable international situation, "We just cannot spend any more money at the moment."[9] Snedden then followed by saying that, if in office to prepare the 1974–75 budget, the L–CP would increase defence expenditure by about $200 million.[10] Labor's budgeted increase for 1974–75 came to $166 million, and actual spending by the close of 1974–75 represented an increase over 1973–74 of just over $300 million. Later in 1974, the L–CP defence spokesman, Dr Forbes, said that it was "imperative" for an L–CP government "to substantially increase the resources going to defence".[11] But in early 1975, he was saying that this would only come about "in a few years".[12] In his reply to the government's 1975–76 budget statement, Fraser, himself a "strong defence" man, attacked Labor for not trimming expenditures enough to combat inflation and recommended an overall cut of a billion dollars in the government's overall planned outlays. The opposition's October 1975 statement on defence policy was equivocal. Promise was made to restore defence expenditure to "appropriate and realistic levels", but the coalition parties explicitly refused to commit themselves to any absolute or proportionate estimates of what they would spend.[13] A variety of evidence, public and internal, suggested that the L–CP was not, indeed, prepared to insure a quantum leap in defence spending certainly not in the short run. Such inconsistencies within the opposition's position made it easier for the government to justify its own defence spending effort. When Anthony made his remarks, Barnard was quick off the mark. He "welcomed" Anthony's "endorsement" of the government's current level of defence expenditure and his "acceptance" of Labor's strategic assessment.[14]

The net conclusion to be drawn seemed to be that while Labor had *de facto* decreased financial resources available for defence, the opposition was unprepared to do much more.

We now need to ask on what the money was being spent, and we start with the size of the military establishment. Labor inherited an establishment that at mid-1972 had stood at 80 900 regular forces, including conscripts serving in the army; the post-Second World War peak of about 86 000 had been reached in 1970. The new Labor government abolished National Service and allowed conscript soldiers to resign. It still, however, had to deal with the questions of what was appropriate service strength. There was no longer an Australian military presence in Vietnam, the battalion in Singapore was to be withdrawn and future overseas commitments were to be avoided. The strategic assumption was for little prospect of foreseeable threat to Australia. Labor at large was not well-disposed towards a sizable establishment, and its domestic priorities likewise imposed constraints. On the other hand, there was recognition of the need to maintain reasonable force levels to deal with contingencies and to provide a base for expansion in case of serious emergency. Under Labor, regular armed forces strength first declined quite sharply, then underwent gradual increase. Numbers stood at 69 100 as of mid-1975. They had been scheduled to rise to 73 000 in 1975, essentially through increases in army strength, but this promise was rescinded in the 1975–76 budget projections. Government spokesmen were quick to accentuate the positive. Even a 69 000-strong establishment was the same size as the number of *volunteers* serving when the L–CP left office. Under Labor, the services were much larger—by a third—than they had been in 1964, before conscription was introduced, before the services generally were expanded and before a combat commitment in Vietnam had been undertaken. The services in 1975 were only about 9000 fewer than in Canada and far above ANZUS partner New Zealand's, whose personnel numbered under 13 000, even though New Zealand continued to garrison combat troops in Singapore longer than Australia.

Among the services, RAN and RAAF strength was kept fairly consistent with levels reached in the late 1960s: about 16 100 for the RAN, 21 500 for the RAAF. It was the strength of the army that underwent the greatest fluctuations and therefore drew the heaviest criticism. Service advice under the Liberals was that a 40 000 figure was needed. When Labor came to office, this was scaled down to 38 000. Barnard, originally considered building up to a 36 000 figure, but settled for 34 000, to be reached in 1976. Some Labor ministers wanted to set the ceiling even lower, but were overriden. A move in caucus to revise to 31 000 was defeated by 18 for and 59 against.[15] However, by mid-1975, army strength had inched up to only 31 500 and, as we have seen, was not scheduled for an increase in 1975–76.

Barnard devoted considerable effort to promoting service strength, efficiency and satisfaction. Service pay and amenities were rapidly and very generously improved. The office of a services ombudsman was created. Sympathetic reaction was expressed to the idea of a servicemen's union, should servicemen themselves wish one. Results from expensive recruitment campaigns were generally acceptable. Officer resignations became worrisome for a time, but that subject we leave for another context. The *Millar Report* had pointed up deterioration in numbers and capabilities of the Citizen Military Forces. Steps were undertaken to up-grade what was to become an Army Reserve and to merge it more effectively with roles performed by the regular army. It was recognized that, since for Labor conscription was repugnant and otherwise politically impracticable in Australia, special attention had to be devoted to back-up forces.[16] Moreover, despite cutbacks from its pre-1973 strength level, the army was about to claim a favourable manpower intensive ratio of field force to support personnel. By mid-1975, there were 11 800 in the former category and 19 700 in the latter.

Where, then, lay the criticisms? There was a fair amount of bluster within the L–CP and, when it was in Parliament, among DLP senators. For instance, urgency motions were moved in the non-Labor-controlled Senate to discuss what was alleged to have been the appalling state of Australia's defence capacity and capability, in manpower terms and otherwise. One specific criticism, and on which senior service advice was overridden by the government, was over the compression of the army's structure from nine battalions to six. The government argued that this move would make battalion units more sturdy and effective. Critics rejoined that a nine-battalion structure was needed if a major overseas commitment had to be made and also to mitigate strains if army strength expansion were undertaken. It was also felt that, although the army was theoretically organized around a divisional structure, such a structure was not capable of being operationalized, regardless of battalion structure.[17] At bottom, manpower was at issue. Internal evidence indicated considerable Defence Department disquiet over the adequacy of manpower levels (and equipment) to fulfil a continental defence role properly.

In practical terms, the L–CP did not have much to offer. It made it clear that conscription would not be reintroduced, short of a real and direct threat to Australia. What of the preferred size of a volunteer army? The L–CP seemed to have scaled its sights down to about 36000, only 2000 short of Labor's original 1976 target of 34000, but 5500 higher than the 31500 figure at which the army was to be held into 1976. But internal evidence suggested that only the most marginal, if any, expansion of the forces would be launched by a L–CP government. No real political advantage was foreseen in pushing for a major expansion of the forces at a time when the public was preoccupied with bread-and-butter concerns and no threat to Australia was imminent. Paying for a larger establishment would, as we saw, upset the creed of economy in government. The L–CP's main promise seemed to be that it would restore a "sense of purpose" into the services.[18]

No proper evaluation of armed services capability is possible without reference to how the forces were armed and equipped. It is in this area that the opposition was especially contemptuous of Labor's performance. J.D. Killen, Forbes' successor as L–CP shadow Defence Minister, applied his familiar rhetorical flair to the subject. He claimed that the government had forgotten the admonition that "You cannot wage war with a map."[19] Australia's defence equipment situation was not critical, not grave; it was "plainly desperate".[20]

A continental and sea and air approach defence doctrine was adopted by the government and presumably would be reflected in equipment procurement policy. Apart from financial constraints, the government felt that equipment purchases needed to provide for a "modest military capacity for operations at short notice" and enough hardware on hand to maintain the state of the art, so as to "expand our capability more quickly than a threat, relevant to that capability, can develop". It was inadvisable to try to anticipate the changes constantly occurring in weapons technology or to place orders for equipment that, given the size and mission of the armed forces, would be indigestible.[21] Within this context the government asserted that Australia's forces were, and would continue to be, very well armed and equipped.

Criticisms of the government's equipment policy emanated from the opposition, from a number of retired, and even serving senior officers and were found in Defence Department circles. Some of the criticism followed from a rejection of a continentalist strategic doctrine as such and thereby proceeded to accuse the government of not having done enough to equip the forces for roles that, on its part, the government did not envision. But there also were criticisms that, *given* the government's own continentalist assumptions, and apart from whether Labor might have been overly sanguine in anticipating threats, the equipment picture was unsatisfactory. It was said that, if as claimed, Australia was to become more militarily self-reliant and had to anticipate, detect and, if needed, repel incursions upon itself or its immediate air and sea environment, it required exceptional rather than unexceptional equipment for the job.[22]

As of the 1975–76 budget projections, Australia had, or was intent on acquiring, some very sophisticated equipment. Acquisitions arranged by L–CP governments included twenty-four American F-111 strike aircraft. Australia had in service four conventionally powered but highly advanced British-made Oberon-class submarines and two additional boats were under construction. Also from Britain, the Labor government had ordered ten advanced-design Sea King anti-submarine helicopters. Labor also ordered eight Orion maritime patrol aircraft from the United States. During Barnard's ministry, fifty-three Leopard main-battle tanks were scheduled for acquisition from Germany and an additional thirty-four were pledged by Morrison. All the same, a number of critics saw these acquisitions as inadequate, in numbers or otherwise. Much of Australia was ideal "tank country", but even eighty-seven Leopards could do little more than literally keep the "state of the art" alive. Some felt that a meaningful number would be double what Labor had in mind. Only eight Orions were ordered, an alleged shortfall of at least 50 per cent, in the light of Australia's exceptional 19 000-kilometre coastline. The government also contracted for two American patrol (later renamed guided-missile) frigates. Not only were only two frigates deemed a small gesture, but their cruising capacity, single-screw character and armaments were claimed to be inadequate, especially in comparison with larger destroyer vessels that could have been selected. The frigates were chosen because, it was often charged, they were the cheapest.

Other equipment already in the inventory was also brought under criticism for being outdated or insufficient in quantity. As of 1975, field artillery was vintage and anti-aircraft equipment scarce, despite a pledge in the 1975–76 budget to look to artillery replacements and to acquire some Rapier surface-to-air guided missiles. Many vessels were approaching the end of their useful service and there were no plans to replace the aging carrier *Melbourne*, the RAN's flagship. There were exceptional delays in moving towards a replacement of Australia's aging Mirage fighters, though this project was given priority for 1975–76. Indeed, in the interests of economy, a Mirage squadron was stood down, leaving a single operational fighter squadron based in Australia. Under Barnard, flying time for aircraft and steaming time for vessels had been reduced. Morrison authorized more steaming time and mileage for tanks and other fighting vehicles, but not increased flying time.

Transport capabilities came under criticism. Because of Australia's vastness and absence of adequate surface-transport facilities in many regions, and a small army, which had to rely on rapid mobile transport, airlift capacity was termed sorely inadequate. When the services undertook to supply cyclone-stricken Darwin and to evacuate displaced persons, critics pointed to the lack of big cargo aircraft, such as the American Galaxy, which could have facilitated such a civilian relief task, as well as enhancing the nation's military posture. At the time of the Darwin disaster, mention was also made of the absence from the relief fleet of a combat supply ship.[23] Such a vessel was, however, promised in the 1975–76 budget. So were new transport aircraft, but not of the range or airlift capacity of the Galaxy. Western Australia's coastline was also brought up. Despite considerable great power naval activity in the Indian Ocean, and the state's enormous (and allegedly inviting) natural riches, the RAN was virtually absent from the area and construction at the Cockburn Sound naval facility had been slowed by the Labor government. In fact, Indonesian and Taiwanese poachers off the West Australian coast more often than not went undetected. The RAN's patrol vessel fleet was small and became even smaller with the gift of some vessels of this ("Attack") class to Papua New Guinea and to Indonesia.[24] Coastal surveillance was stepped up in 1975, especially during Morrison's ministry and—very belatedly and ambiguously, critics mantained—plans were set in 1975 "eventually" to replace the remaining Australian patrol-boats.

The government was correct that equipment contracts and expenditures usually were long-term and that a re-equipment programme would not necessarily be reflected in a given year's budget. Moreover, the government bargained long and well to obtain good terms for its overseas capital equipment purchases. It failed to scale down remaining payments on the exhorbitantly expensive F-111 aircraft, but won explicit protections against comparable cost overruns on the patrol frigate contract.[25] All the same, with the possible exception of the 1975–76 budget allocations, capital expenditures suffered under the ALP. In April 1974, Cabinet agreed to a long- term $330 million capital-spending programme. The project enjoyed Barnard's personal endorsement. But it is plain that the timing of the announcement, and Cabinet endorsement as such, were encouraged by the impending election. In the last three L–CP financial years, capital expenditure as a percentage of defence expenditure had averaged about 12 per cent. Under Labor, in 1973–74, it was 7.2 per cent and in 1974–75, 6.7 per cent. It was projected to reach 10 per cent in 1975–76; an improvement on earlier Labor years, but still behind what the Liberals had been doing. Only in part, however, was this the result of any overt "neglect" of equipment. Because Labor made a very substantial contribution to the pay and benefits of service personnel, less remained for capital expenditures.[26] To have done well for both personnel and their equipment would have necessitated a substantially greater outlay of funds. The proportionate increase in capital expenditures for 1975–76 was accomplished only by keeping manpower numbers constant and by introducing other economies. When in government, the L–CP had expressed its intention to raise the proportion spent on new equipment to 20 per cent by the close of a five-year rolling defence programme. By the mid-1970s, however, neither the government nor the opposition could credibly promise anything approaching that scale. Neither side was willing to reduce personnel, or to cut back on employment perquisites, *or* appreciably to raise annual defence spending.

It is also helpful to comment on the scientific/industrial back-up available to Australia's defence forces. This kind of capability can mean equipment especially suited to Australia and its allies. It can help to insulate Australia from interruptions in outside sources of supply and provide a basis for expansion in case of emergency. It can produce various benefits to civilian industry and to the national economy at large.

Under Labor, existing advisory groups such as the Defence (Industrial) Committee and the Defence Science Board were continued or embellished. This provided ongoing liasion between industry and government in matters of defence-related research, development and production, as well as forward mobilization planning. Members from industry and commerce were able to attend industry mobilization courses sponsored by the Department of Defence. In mid-1974, a variety of government research and development establishments, employing some 1000 scientists and engineers and costing about $60 million per year, were brought together under the Defence Department's wing. All the same, Labor allowed a number of research and development (R & D) activities to run down, in part because of decline of work. Among these were the Aeronautical Research Laboratories, the Woomera rocket range and missile-testing range and associated research at the Weapons Research Establishment at Salisbury, South Australia. The industrial R & D proportion of the Australian gross national product had always been low by Western nation standards and continued to be so under Labor. This was so despite the fact that 75 to 80 per cent of the value of the country's military supplies that were domestically produced were 'obtained from private industry. As of early 1975, the government was not providing any financial support for defence-related R & D programmes in the non-government area. Subcontracts to industry for scientific research and development tasks in 1974–75 were only about $1 million.[27] In the 1975–76 budget, the "defence science and technology establishments" sector of the defence budget was $84.7 million, a relative increase on the previous year's spending of only 5.1 per cent, half of the proportionate increase in the defence budget at large.

Despite various constraints before and during Labor, Australia made important defence-related contributions. Part of this was due to quality skills and to enterprise. Part of it was to the special Australian defence requirements, especially in the air and sea context of a nation continent. Part of it flowed from defence science-project sharing and information exchanges with larger nations, such as Britain and the United States. Australian research helped to develop the F-111 aircraft, which Australia purchased from the United States. Australia produced the highly successful Jendivik and Turana pilotless target aircraft, the Ikara anti-submarine weapon system, the Mulloka sonar and Jindalee over-horizon radar and the Barra sonics system, which was to be incorporated into the new Orion maritime patrol aircraft. It produced the outstanding short take-off and landing (STOL) Nomad utility aircraft.[28]

The Nomad was an example of Australian inventiveness, but also illustrated some of the shortcomings and dilemmas of the Australian defence production industry. Designed at the Government Aircraft Factories in Melbourne, the Nomad first flew in 1972. Delays and need for remodelling had been compounded by run-down in expertise at the GAF. The aircraft was redesigned. Its price rose, but cost over-runs were difficult to absorb by a small enterprise. Its domestic market was limited. Its overseas market was potentially good, but was reduced by political decisions under Labor not to sell it to certain nations that could refit it for military use; for instance, Portugal at one time and some Middle Eastern governments. By mid-1975, Nomads had been sold to or ordered by countries as diverse as Indonesia, the Philippines, Kenya and Peru. Overall firm orders, however, remained about two-thirds short of the Nomad's financial break-even point. Trade unionists insisted that the aircraft be manufactured entirely in Australia and the plane in measure became a device for employing workers who would otherwise have been threatened with redundancy.[29]

When Labor came to office, it wished to economize on defence spending. Savings were sought in what often were under-economical defence factories. No major equipment resupply projects were envisioned. In general, it was felt that quality equipment, often at lower prices than at home, could be had from abroad. But this would have endangered jobs in Australia. Hawke and other union spokesmen interceded. Union bans on servicing naval vessels were threatened or actually carried out. The government reacted in patchwork fashion, which is probably all it could have done. Some foreign purchases, or refittings, were to be reconsidered. Defence factories were encouraged to diversify their work. Special retraining for redundant workers was provided. Some measures were not altogether in step with highest standards of efficiency or economy. Ironically, because of the Labor government's sensitivity to trade-union leverage, the Australian defence industry was given a transfusion. Also there is strong inferential evidence that the very size of the Labor government's defence budgets, and thereby military capability, were improved because of trade-union pressures. Labor ministers and caucus members were understandably happier about defence expenditures if Australian worker interests were thereby being advanced.[30] A corollary was vigorous and often successful ALP government efforts to maximize production-offset opportunities when buying equipment overseas. In a 1973 agreement, the United States, for the first time with any nation, undertook to use its "best endeavours" to provide Australia with production rights to military equipment for US forces to the value of 25 per cent of any equipment purchase from American manufacturers. The patrol frigate contract, originally resisted by unionists because ships were to be bought overseas, incorporated explicit terms for Australian industry participation.[31]

We have examined the Australian armed forces capabilities in terms of financial resources committed to them, their numbers, their equipment and the scientific and industrial supports available to them. We finally need to comment on the state of satisfaction, or morale, within the officer corps. Under Labor, officer resignations rose sharply. During Labor's first two years in office, over 10 per cent of officers tendered their resignations. Among them were general-grade officers and large numbers from key middle ranks, major or lieutenant-colonel or the equivalent. One Australian close to the scene told the author that 75 per cent of the resigned officers were persons the Defence Department was not especially keen to keep anyway. Perhaps so. Moreover, a number of the early retirement resignations were prompted less by inherent dissatisfaction than by attractive retirement plans introduced by the Labor government. By 1975, the resignation rate had slowed. All the same, a number of officers, both recently retired or who were still in the service, spoke up about their concerns, which in one respect or another reflected on Labor's policies. There was some general dissatisfaction with the low-threat, allegedly over-optimistic, strategic assessments and other features of assumptions and doctrine. More particularly, the target was the state of the armed forces, and also there was resentment over reorganizational changes planned for the Department of Defence.[32]

Steps towards Defence Department reorganization began shortly after Labor entered office and were capped by the introduction of the

Defence Forces Reorganization Bill two and a half years later. The government's basic intentions were to unify the three services under explicit Defence Department control and to reconstitute and streamline the structure of advice and responsibility within the department. A number of officers found fault in these changes. There already was a disposition to feel that, under Labor, the armed services' capabilities had been allowed to deteriorate. In gist, charges now arose that, in a revamped Department of Defence, there would be insufficient uniformed services policy input or access to the Minister for Defence. There were other specific doubts about administrative efficiency under the new system. These imputations were, of course, denied by political and Defence Department spokesmen.[33] Of the various points on which the opposition took Labor's armed forces/defence capability policy to task, Defence Department reorganization was one place where the L–CP could in fact have followed a critical course, without getting stuck on the issue of expenditures. Yet the opposition was itself committed to Defence Department unification. Its protest was therefore that Labor was moving too quickly, and too radically, in reconstituting the Department. It seized on officer resignations and complaints as signs that Labor was bypassing the opinions of informed professionals, not just of the L–CP. The particulars of Defence Department reorganization were portrayed as more of the same: a shunting aside of military advice and a further demoralization of the armed forces.[34]

The Australian debate over military preparedness was over real not specious issues—men, *matériel*, morale. Its major drawback was that for ideological, electoral, economic and other reasons neither party group was in a position to depart significantly from what was in fact done. It was mainly on the doctrine of the uses of armed forces that the two sides seemed to be at variance. We now turn to how, in the context of alliance systems, security considerations were treated by Labor and its opponents.

When Labor entered office, Australia was involved in three multilateral regional security arrangements. These were the Five Power Agreement and its supportive ANZUK force, SEATO and ANZUS, and we will examine them in that order. The Five Power Agreement bound Australia, New Zealand, Britain, Singapore and Malaysia to consult in the event of actual or threatened attack on Singapore or Malaysia and to assist these two nations with training and equipment. ANZUK, comprising Britain, Australia and New Zealand, was an integrated military force stationed at Singapore, supplementing but not required by the Five Power Agreement. As Australia's contribution to ANZUK, the L–CP government had provided an infantry battalion, an artillery battery and various support troops. The Labor government withdrew the combat elements by the turn of 1973–74 and, apart from a few training and facility servicing personnel, took out the remaining personnel a year later.

Labor did not repudiate the Five Power Agreement, but its decision to end the ground presence in Singapore had been foreseen. The party was on record as opposing overseas stationing of combat troops. The Vietnam involvement was in the immediate background. Withdrawal from ANZUK would make concrete Labor's wish to portray Australia as a nation looking less to military measures than it had in the past. As preceding governments, Labor was somewhat uneasy about the possibility of its ANZUK troops becoming caught up in internal disputes. It was not much impressed by any forecasts that Malaysia or Singapore faced foreseeable externally induced security threats, and saw Malaysia and Singapore as becoming increasingly self-sufficient in providing for their own defence. In other words, Malaysia and Singapore simply were not believed to need a shielding Australian garrison any more.[35]

It is instructive to reconstruct the process followed in disengaging the troops and the reactions produced on various sides. The new government quickly (and without first seeking a submission from the Department of Defence) pledged to remove the combat garrison from Singapore, but indicated the desirability of retaining several hundred support and logistical troops. In early February 1973, an article appeared in which it was revealed that Australia had for some time been maintaining a DSD radio-monitoring and code-breaking unit in Singapore.[36] Whitlam then called a non-attributable "background" briefing for selected media people and there admitted the presence of the DSD unit. The briefing was a public relations fiasco. Whitlam had almost certainly decided to admit the unit's existence without the knowledge (and to the befuddlement) of the Defence Department, Defence Minister Barnard and his own personal aides.

The importance of the matter, however, lies in what Whitlam wished to accomplish and why. The new government had been told of the DSD unit's operations and was persuaded by Defence Department officials that the unit was performing valuable work, not only for Australia but in what could be shared with allies. Contrary to some speculation, the view that the DSD unit was operating without the Singapore government's knowledge should be discounted. Whitlam's public explanation for repatriating the unit to Australia was that "We do not believe that we should operate a defence unit in another country unless that other country shares in the management of it. This was an Australian unit." In any event, the Gorton government had itself initiated plans to transfer the operation, but the project had stalled.[37] It would not seem critical whether Whitlam's official reason was especially convincing, since the unit was not after all being liquidated, only moved.

When the government decided to retain the DSD unit long enough to arrange alternative facilities in Darwin, it decided to mask their presence in Singapore by retaining a "cover" force of several hundred men. But when the government announced that several hundred personnel would be retained in Singapore for "logistical" and other tasks, there were serious reverberations within the ALP. The council of the Victorian ALP branch roundly condemned plans to retain logistical personnel and Cairns personally endorsed the Victorian resolution.[38] Whitlam wished to avoid an open battle within the party so early in the life of the new government. He felt there were more important issues on which, if needed, he might wish to confront party critics; for instance, the American defence facilities in Australia. Since the existence of the DSD unit had eventually been leaked anyway, Whitlam's announcement of it in the background briefing was designed to ease the rationale for eventually declaring that the "masking force"—the logistical personnel—would, in addition to combat troops, be withdrawn. Party criticism against retaining support troops continued. In early July 1973, on the eve of Labor's Surfers Paradise Federal Conference, Barnard explicitly announced that, after an interval, logistical personnel would follow combat troops out of Singapore.[39]

While the evidence points to the logistical troops having been conceived of as camouflage for the DSD unit until it could be removed to Australia, there is also an intimation that the government thought of them as performing inherently useful service for the remaining British and New Zealand partners in the ANZUK force. Both before and after the DSD unit revelations, Barnard seemed to be putting this view, and indeed apparently had held it even before Labor had won the election and before he had become aware of the monitoring unit's existence.[40] It is quite true that logistical personnel were not withdrawn until some two years after Labor entered office. But to the extent that Barnard and others had believed them to serve an intrinsically useful function, other than screening the DSD unit, this seemed to suggest the weight of intra-party constraints on the government's defence policy judgement to return them to Australia.

What of the more explicit foreign and defence policy aspects of Labor's handling of the Singapore troop issue? Firstly, we consider relations with ANZUK partners Britain and New Zealand. Labor decided to pull its troops out against British and New Zealand advice. London and Wellington were somewhat concerned about the decline in ANZUK strength if Australian combat troops were withdrawn, but

were more concerned if support troops left, since Australian personnel were assigned prime logistical responsibility on behalf of the integrated ANZUK brigade. The structure that had slowly and with
some difficulty been built up would now be dismantled, or would require extensive rebuilding.[41]

In 1973, Britain continued to be under a Conservative government,
but Labour was by then governing in New Zealand. Despite all the
rhetoric about mutuality of trans-Tasman interests, Australia and
New Zealand went separate ways on stationing troops in Singapore.
Interpretations offered by New Zealanders and Australians illuminate
the nuance of approach and of one nation's perceptions of the other.
One New Zealand explanation, heard twice, was that the personable
Norman Kirk was able to get on far better with Lee Kuan-yew than
was the headstrong Gough Whitlam, who cared little for the
Singapore Prime Minister's ideas, including Lee's wish that
Australian troops remain. Another New Zealand interpretation, more
plausible than the first, was that the New Zealand Labour Party was
not as burdened by a need to repudiate the past or to honour explicit
party doctrine on overseas troop commitments as was its counterpart
in Australia. After his early 1973 swing through South-East Asia, New
Zealand Defence Minister Faulkner reported to Wellington that the
countries in the region preferred ANZUK to remain intact. This
helped to persuade New Zealand. But, according to New Zealanders,
when the Australians had this view imparted to them, they seemed to
take a "couldn't care less" attitude. Australian sources pictured the
conversations differently. The New Zealanders were said to have been
"gratuitous" in presenting their case. On the Singapore troop issue,
the New Zealanders were said to have been eager to appear "different" from Australia—a case of little brother asserting his independence, of trying to make plain his attachment to South-East
Asian problems in a way unnecessary for the more seasoned
Australians. Actually, apart from taking Asian reactions to a troop
withdrawal more to heart than Canberra, the government in Wellington was eventually not all that unhappy about fending more for
itself in Singapore. New Zealand's 1974 *Defence Report* stated that
"New Zealand thus now has a nationally identifiable force based on
Singapore. This will facilitate implementation of the Government's
policy of strengthening and extending New Zealand's bilateral
relationships in this area."[42] The author was unable to follow up on
Australian opinion that New Zealand had been told by Britain that
keeping troops in Singapore would be a sound investment in obtaining trade concessions from the EEC, which by then Britain had joined
and in whose councils it enjoyed influence.

At all events, as Faulkner testified, 1973 opinion in South-East

Asian capitals, and especially in Singapore, favoured the retention of Australian troops and of the ANZUK force generally. The ANZUK force was not really thought of as a trip-wire in case of attack. It was a less-tangible, yet meaningful expression of confidence and reassurance in what still was a fluid region. Also, to Lee at least, ANZUK filled a power vacuum in the region, which the great powers would otherwise reach to exploit.[43] These conceptions were not shared in Canberra. For Whitlam, Lee was a "theoretical" hawk in his perceptions of the security picture.

The L–CP strenuously attacked the government's Singapore troop position; for reneging on ANZUK, for flaunting South-East Asian opinion, for underestimating dangers in the region, for being hostage to left-wing elements in the ALP, and so on. On 1 March 1973, the opposition launched its first motion of censure against the new government; it was based on criticism of Singapore policy. In the Senate, non-Labor forces brought this issue forward as a motion of urgency. Snedden called Barnard's July 1973 promise of troop withdrawal an act of· "sickening irresponsibility".[44] Increasingly, however, the L–CP's options to reverse government policy shrank and then virtually disappeared. By late 1973 and well into 1974, the opposition's position was that it would be willing to send the troops back to rejoin other ANZUK forces, but of course this would take place only after consultations with concerned parties, notably Singapore.[45] By the latter part of 1974, quite compelling internal evidence indicated the L–CP felt the likelihood of Australian troops returning to Singapore would be very slight. Lee himself had reconciled himself to the withdrawal of Australian troops and did not wish the issue to become a football in Australian politics. By 1974 and then more directly into 1975, the ASEAN states were by and large searching for ways to reach a *modus vivendi* with China and to adjust to the communist victories in Indo-Chinese countries. With Australia's pull-out, at the opening of 1975 the three-nation ANZUK force in Singapore ceased to exist. Moreover, the Wilson Labour government in Britain, for reasons of economy and because of its European concentration, had just announced its intention to withdraw the great majority of its troops from Singapore. That would have left the New Zealanders as the only remaining ground force. In May 1975, New Zealand announced that its troops would undertake a phased withdrawal from Singapore, a step to which Lee had not voiced objection.[46] The ANZUK idea was gone. Time and circumstances had pushed the Liberals to a "no change" policy. Indeed, the Labor government had not only never repudiated the Five Power Agreement as such but had often spoken of its value, a value that was foreseen to continue until the South-East Asian region underwent "neutralization".[47]

When in Singapore in early 1974, Whitlam remarked that "Some components of Australian forces are going home, but Australia is not going away."[48] In part, his meaning was that his government was prepared to continue defence co-operation aid to Malaysia/ Singapore, and indeed to other nations in the region as well. This was an aspect of defence policy that enjoyed bipartisan support in Parliament. The rationale for such assistance was that it was a logical extension of Australia's own defence effort. It promoted self-reliance among recipient nations to resist external threats, consistent with Labor's perceptions of reducing reliance on great powers and their involvement in the region's affairs, and in turn strengthening regional impulses. Also defence aid was viewed as an adjunct of civilian assistance programmes.[49] For 1975–76, Australia budgeted $39.2 million for defence co-operation. The fact that this figure was less than half of what had been spent in 1974–75 was deceptive, since a very large and exceptional defence co-operation grant had been made to Papua New Guinea in 1974–75. For Indonesia (the single largest recipient apart from Papua New Guinea), Malaysia, Singapore and some other countries, the defence aid budgeted for 1975–76 was essentially the same as spent in the preceding year. The defence assistance programme was diverse. It included the training of Asian and Pacific military personnel in their own countries and in Australia. Most of this, including the RAAF's instructional defence presence at Butterworth, was conventional training. But it included instruction for Asian police security forces at the Australian Army Intelligence Centre (originally located at Woodside, South Australia), and in Melbourne under ASIO direction and Foreign Affairs funding. Criticism of such training came from persons who already were uncomfortable about the treatment of political dissidents in countries such as Indonesia. Nor did especially close defence co-operation with Indonesia escape the attention of those who saw Indonesia as a nation coveting East Timor. Arms and equipment were given under military aid programmes, including aircraft and small naval and patrol vessels. The Indonesian air force commander reported that Indonesians were receiving missile training in Australia.[50] The government eventually came to believe that the focus should fall more on training and technology than on provision of hardware.[51]

The government made much point of encouraging joint defence exercises, in and away from Australia, between Australian and Asian nations. This was in keeping with its concept of regional co-operation.[52] It did not, however, forego the familiar war-game exercises with traditional Western allies. We now more explicitly examine defence co-operation through the older security systems, SEATO and ANZUS.

The ALP's approach to SEATO exemplified its outlook on Asia, its foreign policy priorities and, as its stand on the Five Power Agreement and defence aid indicated, its general willingness to be adaptive rather than iconoclastic in matters of defence policy. Labor had for years disapproved of SEATO, and continued to do so when elected to office. The party interpreted SEATO as an anachronism at best, and at worst, repugnant. SEATO had been formed to contain China, but now China was being courted rather than confronted by SEATO members themselves. The intervention in Vietnam had been encouraged by the Chinese containment doctrine, and Vietnam had proved the error of plunging into Asian civil conflicts, which had been falsely advertised as stemming from Chinese aggressive designs.[53] At all events, the Labor government wished to prompt China into a more responsible regional role, as well as to reassure South-East Asian states that China was not an ogre. An association such as SEATO only provoked China and extended the day when Asia's regional relations could be normalized. Under the L–CP, Australia and New Zealand had been the only SEATO members to have established in their own national budgets specific SEATO aid funds. An Australian major-general served in SEATO's military planning office. There had been military planning operations and joint air and naval exercises, directly or indirectly pointed at China. For Australian Labor, such contributions to SEATO were discardable. the sooner the better.

What did Labor plan to do about Australia's membership in SEATO? When in opposition, Whitlam and other party spokesmen had continuously reproved SEATO as "moribund", while the party was on record favouring SEATO's reconstruction along socio-cultural lines. Interviewed before the 1972 election, Whitlam stated that labor would not drop out of SEATO, but would give it little notice.[54] All the same, in many minds it was an open question whether a Labor government would actually terminate SEATO membership. On the left of the party, that was the preferred course. There are various indications that, from very early in its term of office, the government was not in principle prepared to pull Australia out. However, it probably was prepared to pull out, or at least to suspend contacts with the organization, unless SEATO underwent basic reforms. This essentially meant that Australia favoured "a less militant and less ideologically-oriented posture on the part of the Organisation, and major changes in its institutions and activities, including the elimination of the elaborate, but unrealistic, military planning activity".[55] In the interim, it meant pressing against the continuation of South Vietnam's observer status at SEATO Council meetings. It also meant refusal to participate in SEATO naval exercises that, in particular, could be offensive to China. One such exercise was planned for late in

1973. Planning had reached an advanced stage and Barnard had personally approved of it. But Whitlam's personal advisers caught the matter and brought it to his notice. Whitlam promptly cancelled Australia's participation. He could not countenance such an exercise in the South China Sea and at a time when he was scheduled to visit China. Imputations that Whitlam took this step to pacify his party, which was about to meet in federal conference, are largely discountable. If the decision had that effect, if was fortuitous.[56]

Australia's willingness to remain in SEATO was reinforced by representations from its two ANZUS partners. The evidence from Wellington suggests that Kirk had originally been more inclined than Whitlam to leave SEATO. But Kirk and his government shifted their thinking. On various occasions, in definite terms, the New Zealand government expressed its wish to remain in SEATO, but wished that the organization could be revised. A number of Asian countries, both in and outside of SEATO, had urged New Zealand not to withdraw or otherwise to precipitate its collapse. SEATO was regarded as a stabilizing influence. New Zealand also may have been taken somewhat aback by the cool reception given to the Asian–Pacific forum idea Kirk and Whitlam had developed and was aware that much of South-East Asian official opinion objected to Australia's decision to pull troops out of Singapore.[57] The US argument concentrated on Thailand. Thailand was beginning to reassess its own foreign policy, including towards China. But it required some form of security guarantee and some basis for a bargaining position while its policies were in transition. Apart from the Manila Pact, Thailand only had SEATO rather than special bilateral guarantees from the United States and others. Moreover, the United States argued that the alliance systems in the region were interlocked and there could be some denigration of ANZUS, for instance, if SEATO went unceremoniously.[58]

The Australian government stayed in SEATO, which was in fact reconstituted. Military planning was scaled down. Military/naval exercises were to be strictly limited and no longer directed at China or at North Vietnam. SEATO was to acquire a predominantly economic developmental role. Had Australia been pushed into remaining in SEATO? It was presented with arguments, but that apparently was all. Reliable Australian and New Zealand sources cross-confirmed that Washington had not engaged in "arm twisting", as for instance threatening that ANZUS would be reconsidered if SEATO collapsed. The United States apparently was itself a prime instigator of a remodeled SEATO, in part to make it more palatable to Canberra and .Wellington, and it was the Thais who helped draft the organization's revised terms. The Whitlam government liked the idea of a security group realigning itself in socio-economic directions. After the poor South-East Asian reception of its Singapore troop withdrawal decision, it was more receptive to arguments that Asians themselves did not wish to have all the psychological security props knocked out. Labor did not object to the Manila treaty and its security pledge clauses as such, as distinct from SEATO's military overtones. Whitlam said it succinctly: "underpin confidence, yes, underwrite containment, no."[59] Of course, in the event of trouble in the area, Australia would impose its own judgement as to how to proceed. In mid-1975, both the Thai and the Philippine governments expressed a wish that SEATO be phased out entirely, though Thailand wished to preserve the Manila treaty. The wars in Indo-China were over and the tempo of accommodation with China was rising. Australia, New Zealand and the United States raised no objection and plans were set in motion to close SEATO down.[60]

There is parallelism between the Labor government's decisions on Singapore and on SEATO. In both instances, the more conspicuous military features were objected to and rescinded, but some military overtones remained. Additionally, the government was quite willing to maintain its approval of collective consultation and perhaps response of some order as contained in the Five Power Agreement and SEATO once it had been reconstructed, or for that matter to the Manila Pact. It did not attempt to upset the Five Power Agreement and was not the moving force behind the 1975 agreement that SEATO should be stood down completely. After SEATO was by mutual consent of its members refurbished, and then especially when its membership decided to disband the organization, L–CP opportunities to criticize Labor's approach to SEATO were lost. Australia had moved with, not against, the grain of American policy.

We now turn to ANZUS, Australia's oldest and in a way most intimate security alliance. Government spokesmen often referred to the need to place ANZUS in perspective. They objected to what they saw as an L–CP habit of invoking ANZUS as the corner-stone of a very special relationship with America. Labor claimed that ANZUS was "not the be-all and end-all" of ties with the United States and it denied that ties with the United States were the only significant factor in Australia's foreign relations.[61] Such descriptions were fully consistent with the government's wish to diversify its principal foreign policy contact points, as well as with its refusal to be overawed by the American connection. This latter sense underscored the government's efforts to project a more "independent" foreign policy line. Some of this was symbolic, some substantive. For instance, Australia's ANZUS connection did not preclude the Whitlam message to Nixon over Vietnam, or other openly stated differences of opinion with Washington.

These shadings aside, the Whitlam government not only stayed in ANZUS, but often and with scarce reserve defended it. Yet in a mid-1975 special report on Australia, *Time* magazine's Pacific edition wrote that "Whitlam feels that the ANZUS treaty is anachronistic and useful essentially only as a piece of paper to reassure some Australians about threats that no longer exist."[62] In the present author's opinion, this conclusion was unwarranted, and seriously misleading.

In one negative sense, ANZUS was approved because it was unobjectionable. It had no standing force of its own, did not call upon Australia to maintain overseas garrisons and was not actually pointed at China. It was regionally *Pacific* rather than greater Asian in its application. Its language spoke of insuring the integrity of its members and their armed forces, not of defending someone else. To a minor extent, a Labor government may have been attracted to ANZUS because its mutual defence provisions made less urgent the maintenance of powerful Australian armed forces. ANZUS's elaborate technical co-operation and exchange features continued to allow Australia's intelligence and defence science investments to be kept within acceptable bounds.

So far as ANZUS might over the years have contributed to promoting a peaceful climate in the Pacific, with favourable implications for Asia, that too was good. It was good because peace was better than conflict. It had thereby enlarged opportunities for a Labor-led Australia to enhance its room for manoeuvre and influence in the greater Asian–Pacific region. Symbolically at least, ANZUS demonstrated some movement towards "change" in a direction attractive to Labor. At the February 1974 ANZUS Council meeting, particular attention was accorded to Asian–Pacific economic problems. Economic themes were again given some attention at the April 1975 Council meeting. However, ANZUS's central concern, and its day-to-day co-ordinative work, remained tied to security/military subjects as such.[63] At the 1975 Council meeting, the New Zealanders pushed for ANZUS to co-ordinate economic programmes in South-East Asia. The Americans objected. They argued that there probably wasn't money to be had from Congress, new ANZUS administrative layers were undesirable and ANZUS should not be diverted from its principal security task. The Australians remained largely passive. They may have seen some theoretical virtue in the New Zealand position, but basically accepted the American argument and were unwilling to engage in boat-rocking.

At bottom, ANZUS's premier justification remained its security value. The organization gave access to American thinking, intelligence and defence technology. It improved Australia's ability to bring influence to bear on American defence conceptions and policies.

The key ANZUS clauses (Articles IV and V) stipulated that an armed attack on any party or its armed forces in the Pacific area would bring about action in accordance with the constitutional processes of each signatory. Especially in an era of intense resource competition, ANZUS thus provided a measure of extra reassurance in the event, however unlikely, of non-general military conflicts.[64] Also Whitlam acknowledged that "in the ultimate circumstances Australia's security is tied with America. In the case of a world war there is no question where Australia's interest would lie."[65] True, Whitlam also remarked that "ANZUS should not be debased into a general cover-all for any military project that the scientists or soldiers of any of the signatories might choose to dream up."[66] All the same, Labor believed that the world nuclear balance was a contribution to reducing great-power tensions and to *détente* as such, and that ANZUS was connected to this circumstance. This was not so much because of the expressed common resolve of the signatories, but because, as will be explained in more detail later, Australia was the site of various US defence installations, which served this end. Australia's continued acceptance of these facilities was viewed as an expression of its ANZUS bona fides. When in early 1974, there was an amicable resolution of Australia's wish for a larger share in the North-West Cape communication station from which signals were sent to nuclearly armed submarines, an instructive clause was included in the joint communiqué. Barnard and US Defence Secretary Schlesinger "noted the status of the station as a bilateral arrangement in the framework of the ANZUS Treaty. They reaffirmed their support for that Treaty and their recognition of the continuity of the important common interests that sustained the Treaty."[67] Similarly, the opening paragraphs of the 1974 and 1975 *Defence Reports* stated that, in the ANZUS context, one of the salient evidences of the Australian–US defence relationship related to the "global balance".[68]

The Labor government's allegiance to ANZUS did not go unanswered. Some persons in the party who leaned towards non-alignment and greater Australian diplomatic freedom would have been happier without ANZUS, or at least a denatured ANZUS, especially when they considered the connection between ANZUS and the American defence installations. Others, whether they agreed with this position or not, felt that the government had too readily assumed that the United States would spring to Australia's defence, by conventional or by nuclear means.[69] It is possible, but not definite, that the government's mild interest in "stretching" ANZUS's socio-economic concerns was partially inspired by a wish to make the organization somewhat more palatable to its detractors.

On its part, the United States consistently reaffirmed its attachment to ANZUS and to its commitment to defend Australia. Whitlam accepted such assurances, but noted that, in the climate of post-Vietnam American politics, congressional as well as presidential support would need to be realized.[70] As seen, the surprise American military alert in 1973 ruffled Canberra's feelings and created some unease as to whether the intimate consultations expected under ANZUS had been honoured. But reassurances of improvement in future intergovernmental communication were exchanged and apparently accepted by Labor as genuine, and the normal ANZUS relationship continued, even prospered. There were joint training exercises and exchanges of visits among senior ANZUS military officers. The intelligence-take exchanges and defence science co-operation were uninterrupted. The author's impression is that Australia remained the only country to receive regular detailed data about the movement of US surface vessels in the Indian Ocean. With the winding-down of SEATO's military functions, some military personnel sensed that ANZUS's own military co-operation/planning activities had actually been stepped up. US naval vessels continued to have access to Cockburn Sound and US aircraft to the Cocos Islands. American defence facilities in Australia remained in place.

We now focus on nuclear arms control and neutralization issues. Labor's opposition to the spread of nuclear armaments was generally clear and consistent. The government unequivocally renounced Australian development or acquisition of nuclear weapons. It quickly signed the NPT and adhered to inspection safeguard arrangements under the International Atomic Energy Agency. The L–CP opposition's view was short of categorical. A nuclear option for Australia was neither foreseen nor welcomed. But spokesmen such as Fraser and Killen left open the theoretical prospect that Australia might have to reassess its position if nuclear weapons became very widespread among other nations.[71]

We have seen that Labor opposed nuclear testing by other nations. Above-ground tests contaminated the environment. Tests in general encouraged proliferation. Among the great powers further testing meant a spiralling of deadly military preparations. This could upset the already delicate nuclear balance and further inhibit disarmament prospects. There was adverse official reaction to French and Chinese and Indian above-surface tests, and even to underground tests by established nuclear powers. Some of Australia's neighbours, such as Indonesia, were urged to refrain from considering a nuclear capability and to subscribe to the NPT. At the United Nations, Australia assumed various initiatives, including urging a comprehensive nuclear-weapon test-ban treaty and the strengthening of inspection procedures. International disarmament forums were encouraged and actively participated in.[72]

We argued earlier that while Labor disapproved of nuclear arms both on emotional and practical grounds, the Soviet–American nuclear equipoise was admitted to carry redeeming features. Movement towards *détente* was a good thing in many ways and the superpower nuclear stand-off in its way upheld *détente*: "Because of various factors, but above all the compelling restraints of the nuclear balance, the long-term prospect for global stability and avoidance of conflicts remains favourable."[73]

The ALP needed to adjust its displeasure with arms build-ups, and with nuclear arms more specifically, with what it itself conceived to be the security requirements/realities around Australia. Hence the government welcomed ASEAN's subscription to the 1971 Kuala Lumpur declaration, which had called for a South-East Asian zone of peace, freedom and neutrality, free from any manner of interference from outside powers. If fulfilled, such a concept would benefit not only the states in the region but would advance *détente*, were the great powers able to consent not to use the region as a field for destructive rivalry. But Labor understood the South-East Asian peace zone idea to be far from realization. It saw the region as containing security-conscious states and as a place which in fact remained unsettled. It therefore did not unilaterally press the United States to abandon its military facilities in the Philippines or to scale down its military presence in Thailand. In mid-1975, after the United States had used military force to recover the merchant-ship *Mayaguez*, which had been seized by Cambodia, it is understood to have explicitly urged the United States to retain a military presence in Thailand. The Labor government was assuming these positions about the time that Thailand and the Philippines were themselves recognizing Peking, reconsidering the status of American defence facilities on their soil, crystallizing their thoughts about phasing out SEATO and speaking more openly about eventual neutralization in the region.[74] While it pulled troops out of Singapore, Labor maintained a military assistance and training programme for Singapore, Malaysia, Indonesia and others, and continued to station Mirages at Butterworth. While the *concept* of a zone of peace was valid, the provision of security measures could itself stimulate conditions conducive to making neutralization a more generally acceptable proposition.[75]

In principle, Australia also endorsed the idea of nuclear-free zones. They were not construed as a substitute for comprehensive disarmament, or for an effective NPT, but nonetheless a potential contribution to reducing tensions and enhancing stability.[76] Again, however, the ALP government adjusted long-term objectives to short- and middle-range circumstances, as it saw them. In the first half of 1975, in various contexts, New Zealand suggested the idea of a nuclear-free zone in the Pacific area. The Australians were unprepared to take direct public issue with New Zealand. But they did little more than to endorse the concept's ultimate desirability. They broadly subscribed to Washington's objection that such an arrangement would deny passage and porting/landing rights to American nuclear-armed forces, which themselves were, for the time being, serving a usefully deterrent nuclear-balance function.[77] Shortly before leaving office, the government had committed itself to vote at the United Nations for a proposal, initiated by New Zealand and co-sponsored by Papua New Guinea and Fiji, endorsing the idea of a nuclear weapons-free zone in the South Pacific. In its form, this was not a dramatic proposal. It was subject to later study of its scope and content. Australia was not even a co-sponsor with countries that otherwise were its very close associates, and it continued to be ambivalent about the idea generally.

A somewhat more detailed assessment of Australia's approach to the Indian Ocean region is in order. The government was disturbed by the US and Soviet naval build-up in the Indian Ocean, which had been relatively free from the great-power competition such as had earlier intruded into the North Atlantic and the Western Pacific, and into the Mediterranean. While Australia recognized that the Indian Ocean was an international byway where anyone could sail, it did not wish it to be the scene of great-power rivalry and military and naval escalation. In short, Canberra wanted the Indian Ocean to be declared a zone of peace. Australian efforts at seeking support for this principle were widespread. They included backing for a UN resolution to make the area a zone of peace and Australian membership on the United Nation's *ad hoc* committee on the Indian Ocean. Efforts were made to solicit supportive declarations from other littoral states, such as India and Iran. The government recognized American and Soviet difficulties associated with altering their Indian Ocean deployment independent of their other global strategic commitments. Nevertheless, beginning in early 1974, Australian representations were made to the US and Soviet governments, urging them to enter into serious dialogue between themselves about mutual restraint and step-by-step force reductions.[78]

The government's objectives faced considerable obstacles. India and Iran both endorsed the zone of peace idea, but the Indian nuclear test and Iran's heavy military build-up were hardly regarded as positive contributions. The Soviets and the Americans were also, in principle, opposed to escalation, but of course blamed one another for forcing the pace of build-up and for destabilizing the military balance there. Both Moscow and Washington listened politely to what

Australia urged, but neither took much heed. The internal evidence is quite plain. By mid-1975, Australia had raised the matter of Soviet facilities in the Indian Ocean (whose presence Moscow publicly denied) in other littoral state capitals, and the Soviets apparently replied with a reminder of the presence of the US naval communication station at the North-West Cape. When asked by Australia to press the Soviet Union on naval limitations, India was told by the Soviets that they objected to the matter having being raised at all. It is evident that the Americans thought the Australian initiative to be quite superflous, since Washington had adequate access to Soviet officials and could talk about Indian Ocean issues at its convenience. Well-placed Australians on both the political and the official side remarked that the Australian "bringing together" or "intermediary" role could not be taken very seriously. It was remarked that the government felt such efforts had to be undertaken, but the description offered was of ornamentation. Phrases such as "image building" and even "posturing" were used. At least one Australian minister thought that the United States may, however, have given some credence to Australia's appeal for restraint as such. Returning from an American visit in August 1975, Morrison remarked that the United States had taken Australia's concern seriously. "I've been told America would have increased … [its] activities in the Indian Ocean if our concern had not been expressed."[79] The Indian Ocean as a "zone of peace" was, all the same, seen as resting in the distant future. The opposition saw some danger in Australia's promotional effort as such. The idea of a zone of peace was not disparaged, but "To take such worthy aspirations and concepts as immediate objectives is to run the risk of misjudgement and distortion in policy making."[80]

What of the specifics of Australia's reaction to great-power activity in the Indian Ocean? On balance, the record indicates a reluctance to offer serious resistance to an American military presence. American military aircraft continued to enjoy the use of the Cocos Islands as an occasional staging-point for air supply and surveillance in the Indian Ocean. American ships called in Western Australia from time to time, though the issue of porting privileges did not arise.

The key was Diego Garcia. Diego Garcia was a group of British-owned, virtually uninhabited islands in the middle of the Indian Ocean, where the United States already enjoyed some air and naval privileges. The US government wished to up-grade these facilities, as a reaction to the Soviet presence in the ocean, to display the flag more prominently and conceivably to gain better access to the Middle East. However, some American opinion, including within the CIA, felt that the up-grading venture would only spiral the Soviet naval presence.[81] The United States sought permission from Britain for the required improvements. The Wilson Labour government acceded to the request in May 1974, allowing "modest" refurbishing. About the same time, a special expert group appointed by the United Nation's *ad hoc* committee on the Indian Ocean filed a report on the military situation there. It claimed that up-grading plans for Diego Garcia were ambitious and could serve B-52 and other strategic weapons systems. It also claimed, similar to CIA testimony, that up-grading would evoke an equal if not stronger Soviet response. Many nations, the Soviet Union and the United States included, were patently unhappy about portions of the report. A revised version was drawn up. This version was less dramatic about the Diego Garcia proposal and drew no conclusions about a Soviet riposte.[82]

A number of the government's critics insisted that it needed to endorse the Diego Garcia project. There was objective need to counter the Soviet build-up, Australia itself had almost no naval capability in the Indian Ocean and the spirit (and desired results from) ANZUS required it.[83] The Chinese themselves, concerned about Soviet power in the area, supported up-grading at Diego Garcia as a counterweight.

The government's reaction to Diego Garcia can be reconstructed with reasonable accuracy. By the second half of 1973, the government had persuaded itself that the Diego Garcia idea was on balance wrong: it would set back plans for Indian Ocean pacification. This judgement (and its communication to the United States) was in the author's understanding almost certainly reached without a prior request for a submission from the Department of Defence, just as Defence had not been consulted before the Singapore troop withdrawal was announced. The prevailing judgement in Defence, and perhaps to only a slightly less explicit degree in Foreign Affairs, was that improvement of Diego Garcia should proceed.[84] In December 1974, Wilson personally reassured Whitlam that the build-up would be modest and essentially for resupplying rather than operational base purposes. That helped to moderate Canberra's position, as apparently did intelligence reports of growing Soviet facilities in the region, especially at Berbera, in Somalia. Prior to mid-1975, at least, the United States had not for some months received any expressions of Australian disquiet over Diego Garcia. By then, the Australians were telling the Americans that the Australian *government* was not overly perturbed about Diego Garcia, though in principle Australia remained opposed. When Whitlam visited Washington in May 1975, he apparently did not find it objectionable that development at Diego Garcia was to proceed *prior* to further Soviet–American consultations on the Indian Ocean. Morrison made his first visit to the United States as Defence Minister in August 1975. He seemed to express a somewhat more concerned view about Diego Garcia than had Barnard.[85] This may well have indicated a few degrees' turn in thinking, but could also be read as a Morrison reminder, or illustration, that Australia was unhappy about Indian Ocean escalation generally, by either party. It is also quite likely that Morrison, at the time very new to his portfolio, was exceeding his brief in the tone and vigour of his remarks about Diego Garcia.

The Diego Garcia issue was instructive in several respects. It suggested a familiar, though in this instance fairly minor, Labor government tension: between its principles and longer objectives, and its relative amenability to a variant on the strategic balance concept. It suggested a measure of tractability in government thinking, though we should grant that the issue was not in itself of overriding importance. The government's tempered criticism, at times approaching begrudging acquiescence in the project, may have been influenced by official advice. It was not surprising, however, that in its initiative-minded first year in office, the government should have reached a judgement without having called for a departmental brief. Australia was originally not averse to stepping in with criticism of Diego Garcia in part, because it knew that there were divisions within official Washington itself; that is, Diego Garcia was an open, debatable question. But US officials were rather nettled, since they regarded an Australian expression of view under such circumstances as intrusion into American politics.

A tangent of the Diego Garcia issue was whether the government could sensibly be critical of Diego Garcia while preserving the American naval communication station at North-West Cape in Western Australia. The facility, run by the US Navy, had been negotiated in 1963 for a 25-year period. Its principal objective was communication with submarines, including with nuclearly armed boats operating in the Indian Ocean. The station's messages could range from the mundane to, theoretically, a "fire" signal as part of a general war. No secret was made of the station's function, though Australia was barred from access to message content and codes, and lacked potential veto power over message transmission.

However, the Labor Party had officially declared itself "opposed to the existence of foreign-owned, -controlled or -operated bases and facilities in Australian territory, especially if such bases involve a derogation of Australian sovereignty."[86] In other words, the party opposed installations such as the North-West Cape station, but not categorically. Whitlam, Barnard and others could not overlook the party position. As will be shown later, there were important forces in the ALP whose preference was to dispense with the signal-station entirely, as well as with other US defence-related installations. Ministers indicated that an agreement such as governed the North-West Cape would not have been approved by a Labor government and that, at minimum North-West Cape would have to come under Australian control, should be joint in nature and should otherwise protect Australian interests.[87] As matters stood, while Australia was able to use the station for occasional communication with its own submarines, the "control" and "sovereignty" criteria were decidedly not being met. Moreover, Whitlam's annoyance over the October 1973 US military alert was heightened by the fact that the North-West Cape facility, without Canberra's knowledge, had been affected as well.

Australia made it quite clear early in Labor's term of office that it wished to renegotiate the terms of the North-West Cape agreement. The American view was set. Washington was quite willing to renegotiate various features of the station's use and administration. It was willing to negotiate at Australia's preferred pace. To forestall adverse Labor Party criticism, especially on the eve of the 1973 Federal Conference, it was eager that the visit of an Australian technical team should show progress. What the United States declared to be absolutely non-negotiable was the heart of the station's work. There could be no Australian access to message content and no Australain message veto rights. This was placed virtually on a "take it or leave it" basis to Canberra. What eventuated in the Barnard–Schlesinger agreement of early 1974 was that the United States protected its non-negotiable terms, but provided a number of sweeteners to Australia, such as an Australian deputy commander, more Australian personnel at the installation, an adjoining Australian signal facility and promise of improved future consultations. In 1975, some changes in administrative procedures for the running of the North-West Cape facility were arranged by Morrison, but the substance of American prerogatives remained intact. For the Labor government, honour had been redeemed and the United States not pushed against the wall. The 1974 agreement also was a symbolic statement of the more mature, pragmatic yet close relationship between the two nations. Explicitly rather than tacitly, it also was an affirmation by the Whitlam government that the North-West Cape, be it as a corollary of the ANZUS alliance or otherwise, contributed to the nuclear balance in the region, and therefore to Labor's broad objectives.[88]

The revision of the North-West Cape agreement had other results. Politically, opposition criticism of Labor's relations with Washington was to a degree disarmed. More substantively, two American nuclear monitoring stations in Australia were to be fully turned over to Australia. Also, as part of the promise of improved consultation, Australia was given even more access than in the past to America's global strategic policy orientations. At a Washington meeting later in 1974, Australian officials were fully briefed on the implications of Schlesinger's "counterforce" nuclear concept. Every indication pointed to Australia having been reassured on this matter, even though critics at home felt that the counterforce doctrine could more quickly draw Australia into a nuclear conflict.

Two other American defence installations in Australia posed tough problems for the Labor government. These were the Joint Defence Space Research Facility at Pine Gap and the Joint Defence Space Communications Station at Nurrungar. As we will shortly see, they, and the North-West Cape station as well, brought out intricate debate and manoeuvre in and around the Labor Party. For now, we concentrate on government policy and its justification.

The actual functions of Pine Gap and Nurrungar continued to be highly classified. When Labor entered government, Whitlam and some of his key colleagues were given detailed briefings and for the first time learned of the uses of the two facilities. From that point onwards, ministers who knew about the facilities defended them. Ministers often declared that the two facilities had no war-making capability, nor could they involve Australia in warlike operations. They denied that the facilities had been used for any irregular purpose, such as in connection with guiding US operations in Vietnam. They also repeated that from the outset the facilities had been jointly maintained. Australia knew what was going on there and could, if it wished, halt what was happening. After the Barnard–Schlesinger agreement on the North-West Cape, the flow of US data from the facilities to the Australian Defence Department was apparently extended.[89] In addition, apart from saying that data gathered by the facilities were useful to Australia as well as to the United States, ministers were notably silent on what positive purpose was being served. Whitlam perhaps came closest to an explanation, early in 1973: "They help to see that the great powers do not have the ignorance and suspicion of each other that leads to war."[90] His reference at the time presumably was to the nuclear test and firing monitoring/processing/early warning functions of the facilities. Educated surmise plus considerable questioning of Australian figures close to the scene suggested three government reasons, all harmonious with what we already have said about its dispositions, for supporting the facilities. One was that surveillance of communist nations and weapons systems contributed strategic arms limitation/arms control objectives. Another was that the information gathered was valuable to maintaining the nuclear balance. A final, more amorphous, but not necessarily less important reason was to provide tangible support for ANZUS and the American connection's perceived benefits generally.

Further clarification of the government's priorities could be read into the handling of the Soviet request for a joint space-science facility in Australia, raised by the Soviets less than two months before the 1974 double dissolution. The offer was rejected, for three reasons. The government did not, in principle, wish to introduce any more foreign installations that carried any sort of even remotely military connotation. What in part would have given the facility a military overtone related to the second reason why the offer was rejected. The United States objected vigorously to the proposal, on grounds that it could impair the confidentiality and effectiveness of its own defence installations in Australia and thereby prejudice the value Australia itself assigned to them. Thirdly, it is quite plain that the government needed to reject the Soviet offer before the forthcoming election, to avoid political damage from the opposition. Willesee, who personally lobbied against the Soviet installation, had said that it would need to be examined "from a scientific point of view, from a political point of view and in the context of the Indian Ocean".[91]

It is also instructive that the government emphasized the retention of the American facilities, and the protection of their classified functions, as an expression of honouring Australia's word. The "respect of pledge" theme was recurrent in Labor's external policy presentations generally: honouring of exploration and overseas sales contracts drawn up under the L–CP, honouring of the Five Power Agreement, honouring of the American installation agreements. Part of this can be interpreted as good politics, as reassurance at home that Labor was not a capricious, irresponsible government. Part of it was a signal to outsiders that Australia was a trustworthy nation. In the instance of American facilities, it had a bearing on keeping the United States persuaded that, apart from various Australian–American disagreements, as over Vietnam, Australia was quite solicitous of the ANZUS alliance and what it implied. Hence earlier Whitlam expressions about the Australian public's "right to know" about the US installations were reversed once in office. Australia did not reveal "other people's secrets" and, at any rate, Whitlam had concluded that "to state the general purpose of the satellites involved in the communications of these bases would render the operation of them quite futile".[92] Steps were taken to insure maximum security of information. Very few officials were identified as having a "right to know"; apparently only two in the entire Department of Foreign Affairs were fully briefed, as of early 1975. Five ministers had been briefed—Whitlam, Willesee, Barnard, Morrison and Bishop. Cairns was not briefed, even after he became Deputy Prime Minister in mid-1974. Cairns did not press to be informed, to the relief of his colleagues. Moreover, the United States had made known its anxiety about such classified data reaching Cairns, and the anxiety did not go unshared in Canberra.

The government had decided to protect the presence and integrity of the installations. But for how long? Pine Gap and Nurrungar had originally been transacted for ten-year periods. They were to continue beyond, unless repudiated by one of the contracting parties, with one year of notice required. For Pine Gap, the ten years was to expire in 1976; for Nurrungar, in 1979. In April 1974, responding in the House to a question without notice, Whitlam averred that "We do not favour the extension or prolongation of any of those existing [installations] ... The agreements stand but there will not be extensions or proliferations."[93] It is not clear whether at that time Whitlam meant what his words appeared to convey. Probably not, or at least he quickly regretted having spoken in this way. In the months following, a variety of Australian and American official and political persons conveyed the view that extension would be allowed. Whitlam apparently personally expressed this to Green. No specific step was, of course, needed to extend. Inaction meant continuation. Finally, at Terrigal in February 1975, Whitlam made it explicit. A non-renewal notice could be given on Pine Gap by the end of the year, but "I would give no such notice."[94]

In the Australian spring of 1975, however, the journalist Andrew Clark wrote that, because of the state of Australian politics at that time and uncertainties about the future, the United States was examining the option of removing its interior facilities from Australia.[95] The author's own inquiries suggested a variant on this theme. The intimation was that such an option was indeed broached, though in a general and quite tentative way. It was recognized that shifting the facilities would be extremely expensive and would entail some loss of capability. The incentive for raising the subject apparently was a lingering uncertainty whether the Labor government would allow the facilities to remain and some uneasiness that sooner or later some Labor government might choose to remove them. By this account, however, the Americans were largely put at ease when Whitlam conveyed unequivocal assurances in September 1975. This account therefore fails to agree with Clark's view that it was the October–November political crisis that caused re-examination in Washington.

Opposition to all or some aspects of US defence installations in Australia was expressed in various quarters. It was found among members of the academic community, among both the "old" and the "new" left, within the small but articulate Australia Party, within important (and by no means only in conventionally "left") sections of the ALP. A "Campaign Against Foreign Military Bases in Australia" was formed and in May 1974, a long protest march to the North-West Cape was staged. Cairns became President of the Melbourne-based

Congress for International Co-operation and Disarmament, whose
programme included the removal of American defence facilities from
the Asian region, as well as from Australia as such.

The facilities were criticized on diverse grounds and from various
vantage-points. It is helpful to summarize these complaints, in part to
show how opposition was able to become widespread. Intra-party
criticism was heightened by what many believed to be government
contravention of authoritative party directives. This criticism stressed
that Labor was "opposed" to the existence of foreign-owned,
-controlled or -operated bases and facilities in Australia. The Whitlam
government's attempt to circumvent this proscription was seen as unfounded and devious. So was the government's insistence, in violation
of a 1971 party conference edict, that the general purpose of the interior facilities could not be revealed. It left an impression that the
government may have been trying to camouflage some sinister uses of
the installations and that it was "covering up" no less than the L–CP
had. The promise of "open government" under Labor had lost
credibility. Suspicion of government disingenuousness was spurred by
its moderate, allegedly party platform violating, approach to leaving
service personnel in Malaysia and Singapore. Party and other critics
also believed that the continuation of the American facilities con-
flicted with certain desirable Australian foreign policy objectives,
such as de-emphasis on militarily related programmes, international
disarmament, intimacy with the Third World and, to some, a move
towards neutralism. In some quarters, the installations were distasteful because they were an obvious manifestation of American
over-influence in the country—cultural, economic, diplomatic and
military. Some of this reaction was outright anti-Americanism; a
good deal of it was more reasoned and selective.[96]

In addition, various substantive objections were raised against the
installations; against their purported function or, on the basis of
scenarios, on account of their potential danger to Australia. These
arguments were at times broached in rigorous, highly researched
terms and in themselves became a contribution to the serious
literature on strategic and nuclear questions. Only a bare synopsis can
be rendered here. In any event, no authoritative rejoinders were
available to critics' imputations of what the installations did or did
not do, and retorts to conclusions about dangers to Australia's safety
were difficult to marshal, because of the shroud of secrecy surrounding the interior facilities.

We can begin with the North-West Cape station. Technically, Hartley
was correct that, in the last resort, the amended North-West Cape
agreement was mostly decorative: "Australia still has no guarantee of
a voice in the vital decisions which could mean war or peace."[97] The

United States could order a nuclear strike order to submarines without Australia's knowledge or consent. Such orders, as well as signals allegedly transmitted in relation to the mining of North Vietnamese ports and the bombing of Cambodian targets, were said to be facilitated by the Pine Gap installation, through its control of satellite surveillance. Indeed, Pine Gap was said to have acquired a new dimension: from checking on nuclear tests and shots to directing *American* nuclear shots, information then relayable through the North-West Cape station. This meant that Australia was the site of a US offensive or retaliatory strike capability. As an integral part of the American strategic nuclear system, the facilities were·a target for hostile action, either as part of a "nuclear blackmail" scheme to force Australia's capitulation or as an actual bombardment target. Secretary Schlesinger's "counterforce" doctrine was thought to be equally disturbing. If the United States embarked on a metropolis saving, limited nuclear response, designed at most to exchange remote targets, US facilities in Australia would become attractive enemy targets. In sum, the facilities made Australia a hostage to American strategic decisions and logically susceptible to attack that might not otherwise occur if Australia did not host the installations.[98]

It was therefore no surprise that the installations caused anguish and infighting within the ALP. By early March 1973, a number of Labor parliamentarians were disturbed about the government's refusal to explain what the facilities did, and some simply wanted the facilities out, explanation or not. The government's refusal to disclose the facilities' mission was challenged in caucus. A motion to recommit the government's position to cabinet was carried by 39 to 26, ten ministers voting with the majority. Only on a technicality, i.e. the lack of an absolute majority of all caucus members (rather than of those attending), was the motion declared lost. Very likely, a majority of the then ninety-three caucus members would have been found ranged against the government. Some party moderates were as unhappy with the government's "guard the secrets" position as were those on the left side. Heavy pressure by Whitlam persuaded caucus to approve a proposed government parliamentary statement on the subject. When the statement came, it disappointed the critics, given its vague references to renegotiations and its absence of any real hint as to what Pine Gap and Nurrungar were about.[99]

The party was scheduled to convene in federal conference in July. Eager to forestall a conference defeat on the installations, Whitlam lobbied among various state branches, and even managed temporarily to conciliate the hard-line Victorians. Faced by dissent in state branches, in caucus, even among his ministers, Whitlam invoked a variety of appeals. There were the merits of the issue as he saw them.

There was a need to be faithful to other people's secrets. The L–CP should bear the onus for having imposed the installations, in their existing form, on Australia. The party platform, in Whitlam's interpretation, *was* consistent with government policy. Whitlam also wished to avert the familiar, politically damaging charge that a Labor government would be controlled by "outside" party interests and wished to assert his personal authority in the formative stage of the new administration. He even evolved a special thesis of electoral mandate. Constitutional propriety prohibited the government from undertaking major policies not promised at the previous general election. Since disbanding the facilities or revealing Pine Gap and Nurrungar secrets had not been promised, even authoritative party resolutions could not be implemented in the life of the current Parliament. Whitlam probably believed in this principle, but it also was a very considerable political convenience to him. That certainly was the opinion of persons close to the Prime Minister. The author is not aware of any context in which Whitlam publicly invoked the mandate doctrine, apart from the US defence installation issue.[100]

At the 1973 Federal Conference, Whitlam again succeeded in diverting party opposition to the installations. A resolution urging Labor to seek to end the presence of military forces in countries other than their own was moved by Whitlam himself, and passed. Whitlam did not, however, construe this as a directive to harness the government's energies to phase out the installations. Pine Gap and Nurrungar were not even "renegotiated". The North-West Cape station was. This renegotiation provided some substantive and symbolic value for Australia, but of course crucial American control was left undisturbed. The renegotiation effort was, in part, a government gesture to the party; a pacifier, as it were. A number of people in the ALP were not·impressed. Some party members openly supported the May 1974 protest march to the North-West Cape. The inspiration behind Senator Brown's series of attacks on Green, and on what Brown felt to be an excessive and nefarious American presence in Australia, included the presence of the defence facilities. At the Terrigal conference, a motion urging that foreign bases be allowed only if they were under Australian control and involved no derogation of sovereignty was defeated. Whitlam argued that control already existed and that no derogation of sovereignty was at issue, and repeated that the facilities carried no war-making potential. He also polished up the electoral mandate argument. At Surfers Paradise, in July 1973, Labor had been basking in its new status as a party of government, and Whitlam personally had made victory in 1972 possible. There was some reluctance to tear this spirit away with an angry confrontation over the installations. At Terrigal, in February 1975, Labor's electoral stock was badly depressed. There was then a chance the opposition might force another early election. The ALP was bitterly divided over a PLO visit. A premium was therefore placed on painting Terrigal in the image of a "unity" conference. For political reasons, it was sensed that a confrontation over the installations could have been seriously injurious. Things were bad enough at Terrigal with the anticipated (and eventually raucous) battle over recognizing the PRG.

The controversy surrounding American defence installations in Australia produced instructive by-product effects, not the least of which concerned Omega. Omega is a globally distributed, all-weather navigational system for vessels and aircraft, developed by the United States. It relies on a chain of eventually eight stations, located in various countries. An Australian station was to have completed the network. Relatively inexpensive receiving equipment on ships and aircraft could receive signals and considerably enhance the fixing of positions. All aspects of the Omega technology were unclassified and receivers were commercially available. Ships and aircraft of all nations could use the system. The stations themselves were completely operated by host countries and transmission could, if desired, be interrupted at any time. In 1972, negotiations to install an Omega station in Australia were at an advanced stage when the L–CP lost office and the question of what to do about the facility fell to the new Labor government. The virtues of Omega were touted in various quarters, among them local and overseas shipping companies operating in Australia, the RAN and the RAAF, the Department of Transport (under whose authority Omega would be placed) and the Transport Minister himself, Charles Jones.[101]

The propriety of establishing an Omega facility in Australia became contentious. Some of the substantive objections were not unlike those raised against the North-West Cape and the interior defence facilities—improper military applications and potentially treacherous consequences for Australia's safety. Supporters of Omega acknowledged that, like most navigational aides (such as lighthouses), it did have value for military ships and aircraft, but that this was a secondary by-product value of its essentially civilian role. While military craft could be equipped with Omega receivers, the system was insufficiently exact for nuclearly armed submarines and would not be installed on them. Critics retorted that Omega's military applications were definite all the same (for instance, as an aide to hunter killer submarines), and they even doubted whether Omega would be truly irrelevant to an American nuclear-strike capability. While all nations could benefit equally from Omega's civilian (or military) applications, some critics feared that, in a confrontational setting, the Soviets might well find the regional Omega station in

Australia disadvantageous to their interests and could thereby threaten to or actually "take it out" with a nuclear strike. Moscow and Peking had for years offered no complaints about Omega stations going up around the world, but eventually the Soviets denounced the network as a fixture in America's global strategic system. Hence, ran the argument, whether the Soviets were inherently right or wrong, what seemed to. matter was what they felt; their objection could thereby be interpreted as making Australia more vulnerable. The emplacement of Omega would add an increment of danger to that already posed by the presence of explicitly defence-related US facilities in Australia.[102]

Substantive objectives were fuelled by other situational and political factors. When in the late 1960s, the United States first expressed an interest in locating an Omega station in the South-West Pacific region, it explored both New Zealand and Australia as sites. There has been speculation that New Zealand was rejected by the United States for technical reasons. To an extent, that appeared to be true. However, in the author's judgement, the most reliable evidence is that, faced with considerable anti-Omega public antipathy, Wellington advised the United States that it would be unwise to select a site in New Zealand.[103] For us, the main importance of the matter is that many protest/left-group people in Australia themselves believed that New Zealand critics had succeeded in blocking Omega there. Inspiration was therefore added to resisting Omega in Australia. The United States first approached Canberra about a possible Australian Omega site in 1967. Five years later, there still was no final go-ahead decision. Part of the delay was due to site evaluation and terms of cost-sharing and administration negotiations. During this lengthy period, a number of comments were offered by L–CP spokesmen. Taken together, they were received by critics as evasive, contradictory and even dissembling, especially in regard to Omega's military implications.[104] L–CP government comments may well have left that impression. Ironically, there is fairly sound evidence that the inordinate delay was contributed to by the government's wish to assure itself, and thereby to defuse criticism, that an Omega facility would *not* have prominent military functions and would *not* increase Australia's susceptibility as a nuclear target.

.Opposition to Omega after Labor entered office was hardened by special considerations. A number of people in and outside the Labor Party were dumbfounded by the government's policy on the North-West Cape, Pine Gap and Nurrungar. They thought the policy wrong in substance, violative of standing Labor policy, unnecessarily secretive and enforced by overbearing tactics by Whitlam and his associates. In this sense, the Labor government's credibility was lowered. Who could then be trusted to tell the truth about Omega itself? What deals had been worked out with Washington? Could not Omega be interpreted as another mischievous factor in Australia's already massive dependence on the United States?

While Omega was broadly felt to be less inherently obnoxious than the established US defence facilities, steady challenges to it could be expected, for the simple reason that it was pending, not an established fact. It was, at any rate, clear Labor policy to oppose any *new* defence-related installations in Australia.

Once they had entered government, the Whitlam–Barnard– Willesee ministerial group became persuaded that Omega was desirable in itself, not a danger to the country, and that, probably, its rejection would be exploited by the opposition to Labor's disadvantage. The conduct of these ministers was, however, conspicuously subdued. They made no speeches in support of Omega and turned queries aside, referring them to Transport Minister Jones. Jones was a strong protagonist of Omega and he gave his views considerable publicity. He at one point is believed to have phoned his New Zealand counterpart to request a submission about Omega's navigational value for presentation to the parliamentary committee that studied the subject. But Jones was no heavyweight in Cabinet and in the party, and could not hope to exert real leverage if the Prime Minister and others stood aside. Whitlam and other ministers who favoured Omega felt that the intra-party climate was such that they had to tread cautiously. In late March 1973, Whitlam considered bringing a pro-Omega brief from Jones befor Cabinet, but reconsidered. It is doubtful that a favourable Cabinet majority could then have been mobilized. Instead Whitlam promised to assign the Omega subject to the Parliamentary Joint Committtteee on Foreign Affairs and Defence.[105] It was a stalliing manoeuvre, to stretch and in degreee neutralize the issue within the party. Also, Whitlam probably hoped for a favourable recommendation from the committee, based on Omega supporters from among opposition members of the committee and some, perhaps a majority of, Labor members.

Some difficulties intervened. Within a week, the ALP caucus elected as the committee's chairman Senator John Wheeldon, an Omega critic. Omega came up at the July Federal Conference at Surfers Paradise. With Whitlam's approval, after jockeying on various motions, a compromise of a sort was worked out and passed. The party went on record opposing Omega unless it—the Labor Party as distinct from the Labor government—were fully assured that the system could not be used for hostile acts without Australia's consent. Throughout, Whitlam claimed that it was premature for the party to judge Omega, since the parliamentary committee had the subject under advisement. Wheeldon was perfectly correct in claiming that, whatever recommendation issued from his committee, that could in no way be constured as equivalent to a *party* judgement.[106] Whitlam had never precisely said it could be, but he hoped that, somehow, pro-Omega advice from the committee would improve chances for a favourable, and not overly party-straining, government decision.

Following Surfers Paradise, anti-Omega sentiment was sporadically expressed. Some took the form of a "Stop Omega" campaign, being conducted primarily within radical circles. There also were admonitions from Hartley that if Omega were approved, unions might blackban the facility's site.[107] The issue was dropped at Terrigal, since Wheeldon's committee report was not yet available. The committee took a very long time producing its findings. By accounts from both government and opposition committee members, committee sessions were carried out in a fair and unemotional manner. Some members thought the subject rather too technical and possibly not appropriate for a "foreign affairs and defence" committee. Also, by general consensus, the quality of submissions was higher on the "pro-" than on the "anti-" Omega side. What emerged in May 1975 was a report favouring Omega's installation in Australia. The majority consisted of all opposition members, but the majority of Labor members, Wheeldon included, attached a dissenting report. Essentially, the dissenting members objected to Omaga's military applications, to possible dangers posed to Australia in the event of great-power conflict and to some of its technical value for Australia if sited within the country. The majority report had indicated that internationalization of an Omega facility in Australia would be desirable. The dissenters felt internationalization should be a prerequisite to the building of any Omega station in Australia.[108]

Whitlam and other pro-Omega ministers could not reasonably say that the test of a *party* clean bill of health for Omega had been granted. Not only was the committee a parliamentary rather than a party body, but most of its Labor members had dissented, though their reservations did not represent a recommendation of a flat rejection of Omega under any and all circumstances. Some other mechanism would need to be found to justify a conclusion that the party was in favour. The United States plainly wanted a favourable decision. But the United States was not willing to overpress its case, recognizing that the ALP would be hyper-sensitive to being leaned on heavily by Washington. If political realities dictated a choice, the United States preferred to abandon Omega in Australia in favour of not having the boat rocked on the established defence facilities. Shortly before Terrigal, Green repeated America's strong preference for an early pro-Omega decision to Willesee. After that, despite some US

Navy notions that stronger representations should be made, the United States assumed a fairly relaxed posture. All the same, official rejection of Omega would be potential ammunition for the opposition. As leader, Fraser had sharpened the L–CP's tone of foreign and defence policy criticism, including accusations against Labor of narrow-minded anti-Americanism. For the rest of its time in office, the Labor government simply kept a decision about Omega in abeyance and barely raised the subject in public settings. Omega, an ostensibly civilian navigational system, illuminated many of the complexities of defence policy conduct under the Labor government and the range of critical opinion capable of being generated.

NOTES

1. *Defence Report 1974* (Canberra: 1974), p. 5. For representative Barnard speeches, see *Commonwealth [Australian] Parliamentary Debates (APD)*, House of Representatives (HR), (9 April 1974), esp. pp. 1232–43; and his speech at Cooma, 10 May 1975, transcript, pp. 6–8. For Morrison, see his television interview remarks ("Federal File"), transcript, esp. p. 4. There are a number of sources that synthesize Labor's defence doctrines and policies. For instance, see Barnard's article in *Bulletin*, 3 May 1975; and *Australian Defence: Major Decisions Since December 1972* (Canberra: 1975), *passim*, and T.B. Millar, "Defence Under Labor", *Current Affairs Bulletin* 52 (December 1975): 4–18.

2. Forbes, address to RSL national congress, Melbourne, 29 October 1974, Liberal Party Federal Executive *Release*, p. 3. Emphasis added. Also see his "Defence Under a Liberal Government", *Pacific Defence Reporter* (October 1974): 9–11. Also see Liberal and National Country Parties, *Defence Policy* (Canberra: Liberal Party Federal Secretariat, 1975), esp. pp. 1–2. Much valuable material on strategic assumptions and the role of the armed forces is contained in *United Service* 28 (October 1974), which includes papers from the seminar on "The Defence of Australia 1974". Also see the chapter on "Strategic Considerations" in Committee of Inquiry into the Citizen Military Forces [Millar Committee] *Report* (Canberra: 1974), pp. 27–34.

3. Senator R. Bishop (representing the Minister for Defence), APD Senate (11 February 1975), p. 57.

4. Overviews of overseas military activities are found in the annual *Defence Reports*. On Australia's role in Malaysia/Singapore, see M. Richardson, *Sydney Morning Herald*, 15 July 1974. On its role in PNG, see P. Hastings, *Sydney Morning Herald*, 18 April 1974; and Barnard's statement "Transfer of Defence Power to Papua New Guinea", tabled in the House of Representatives, 4 March 1975. For an inventory of army personnel overseas, see Barnard, *APD*, HR (18 February 1975), p. 418.

5. Cited in *Sydney Morning Herald*, 25 July 1974. Also Kiki, cited in *Sydney Morning Herald*, 7 December 1974; and Barnard, *Australian Defence Estimates 1974–75* (24 October 1974), pp. 29–33. In the academic literature, see H. Smith, "Internal Conflict in an Independent Papua New Guinea: Problems of Australian Involvement", *Australian Outlook* 28 (August 1974): 160–67; and J. Camilleri's "'Internal Conflict in an Independent New Guinea': A Rejoinder", *Australian Outlook* 28 (December 1974): 308–12; H. Bull, "Australia's Involvement in Independent Papua-New Guinea", *World Review* 13 (March 1974): 1–18; and P. Mench, "After Independence ... Australian Military Involvement?" *New Guinea and Australia, the Pacific and South East Asia* 9 (January 1975): 42–54. For representative press commentaries, see P. Hastings, *Sydney Morning Herald*, 27 April 1973; I. Hicks, Melbourne *Age*, 6 July 1973 and *Sydney Morning Herald*, 30 June 1975; M. Hollingsworth, *Australian*, 9 May 1975; and F. Cranston, *Canberra Times*, 8 September 1975.

6. Barnard, address Royal Military College, Duntroon, 12 August 1974, transcript, p. 10.

7. Based on the author's personal notes.
8. For a public source on this incident, see R. Haupt, *Australian Financial Review*, 5 February 1974. On earlier training plans, see B. Toohey, *Australian Financial Review*, 15 August 1973; and P. Hastings, *Sydney Morning Herald*, 16 August 1973. The PRS's foreign policy statement is contained in Priorities Review Staff, *Goals and Strategies: Interim Report. December 1973* (Canberra: 1974), pp. 26–28.
9. Cited in *Australian*, 4 May 1974.
10. Adelaide press conference of 6 May 1974, transcript, p. 10.
11. *Press Release*, 26 November 1974.
12. Liberal Party Federal Secretariat, *Media Release*, 14 January 1975.
13. Liberal and National Country Parties, *Defence Policy*, p. 2.
14. *Press Statement*, no. 263/74 (3 May 1974). For other Barnard replies in the defence spending controversy, see *APD*, HR (30 October 1974), pp. 3029–30 and *APD*, HR (23 April 1975), p. 2022.
15. For representative Barnard comments on service strength, see *Defence Estimates 1974–75* (24 October 1974), pp. 5–7; and *APD*, HR (23 April 1975), pp. 2021–22. On competing service strength proposals, see H. Armfield, Melbourne *Age*, 10 May 1974.
16. See *Millar Report, passim*; Barnard, *APD*, HR (4 April 1974), esp. pp. 1006–7; and Barnard's address in Cairns, 10 November 1974, transcript, pp. 6–12.
17. B. Baudino and D. Armstrong, *Australian*, 19 May 1973; and *The Australian Army. Report from the Senate Standing Committee on Foreign Affairs and Defence* (Canberra: 1974), esp. pp. 29–46.
18. For instance, see Forbes, *Press Release*, 14 May 1974; and Snedden, *Press Statement*, no. 74/93 (15 May 1974).
19. *APD*, HR (23 April 1975), p. 2029.
20. "Federal File" television interview, cited in Melbourne *Age*, 7 April 1975.
21. D. McGaurr (former Barnard personal adviser), *National Times*, 24 February 1975. Also see Barnard, article in *Bulletin*, 3 May 1975; and his address in Cooma, 10 May 1975, transcript, pp. 6–8. On the implications of continental defence, see F. Cranston, *Canberra Times* 9 July 1974.
22. For instance, see Vice-Admiral Sir Alan McNicoll, "Defence of the Approaches", *United Service* 28 (October 1974): 28–32; Vice-Admiral Sir Richard Peek's remarks, cited in Melbourne *Age*, 18 March 1975; Rear-Admiral G.J. Crabb's remarks, cited in Melbourne *Sun News-Pictorial*, 20 March 1975; and (former Major) P. Young, *Sydney Morning Herald*, 8 May 1974. Various issues of the *Pacific Defence Reporter* address themselves to this issue. For reflections following the 1975–6 budget, see *Aircraft*, November 1975.
23. For examples of explicit criticisms of armed forces equipment, see W. Crouch, *Bulletin*, 6 October 1973; P. Samuel, *Bulletin*, 19 April 1975; J. Stackhouse, *Australian Financial Review*, 18 and 19 September 1973; R. O'Neill, "AM" interview transcript, 8 April 1974; and G. Harris, *Canberra Times*, 23 June 1975. On the opposition side, see Forbes, RSL national congress address, Melbourne, 29 October 1974, transcript, p. 1; and Killen, *APD*, HR (23 April 1975), pp. 2028–30. The government's presentation is found in Barnard, *APD*, HR (23 April 1975), pp. 2022–24; and Morrison, *APD*, HR (28 August 1975), pp. 712–19.
24. On Western Australian problems, see A. Thomas *Canberra Times*, 9 May and 31 August 1974; H. Schmitt, Adelaide *Sunday Mail*, 8 September 1974; F. Cranston, *Canberra Times* 26 September 1974; P. Hastings, *Sydney Morning Herald*, 12 and 13 August 1975; and J. McIlwraith, *Australian Financial Review*, 15 September 1975. For a general treatment, see J.R. Robertson, "Are Western Australians Worth Defending?", *Australian Outlook* 28 (April 1974): 57–70.
25. The patrol (guided-missile) frigate terms make very enlightening reading. See *Patrol Frigate: Memorandum of Arrangements Between the United States and Australia*. [And] *Explanatory Notes Prepared by Australian Department of Defence* (Canberra: October 1974).
26. For comparative figures on expenditure proportions devoted to major defence categories, see *Defence Report 1974*, p. 48; and *Budget Speech 1975–76*, Budget Paper no. 1, p. 24.
27. Barnard, *APD*, HR (12 Feburary 1975), p. 199. See the "Science and Defence" series by D. Warner, *Sydney Morning Herald*, 20, 21 and 22 August 1974; W.J. Henderson, *Australian*, 13 August 1973 and 8 July 1974; and B. Toohey, *Australian Financial Review*, 18 July 1974.

28. For a summary of defence inventions and government defence factory facilities, see K. Enderby (then Minister for Manufacturing Industry), *Pacific Defence Reporter*, December 1974, pp. 8–10.
29. On the Nomad, see J. Stackhouse's articles in *Australian Financial Review* 26 February, 6 and 7 March and 1 May 1975. On political issues in sales, see *Australian Financial Review*, 21 March 1974; *Australian*, 28 March 1974; S. Brogden, *Sydney Morning Herald*, 15 July 1974; P. Samuel, *Bulletin*, 23 November 1974; D. Balderstone, *Bulletin*, 24 May 1975; and S. Brogden, *Aviation News*, 1 July 1975. For a wider view of the subject, see D. Ball and R.E. Babbage, "The Australian Aircraft Industry—A Defence Point of View", *Australian Quarterly* 47 (June 1975): 62–78.
30. For good summaries of the problem, and of government reactions, see N. Swancott, *Australian Financial Review*, 16 July 1974; and Whitlam's address at Lithgow, NSW, 3 August 1974, transcript. Also see J. Smith, *Australian* 7 July 1975; and B. Toohey, *Australian Financial Review* 10 July 1975.
31. A good summary of the government's efforts in domestic defence production is found in Barnard's address at Richmond RAAF base, "The Implications of Offset Programmes for Defence Industry in Australia", 24 February 1975, transcript.
32. For representative cases, see the remarks of Brig. J.G. Hooton, *Sydney Morning Herald*, 23 April 1974; and of Air-Marshall C.H. Read, *Canberra Times*, 22 March 1975. For critical summaries, see P. Samuel, *Bulletin*, 9 February 1974; and P. Young, *Pacific Defence Reporter*, March 1975, pp. 2–3.
33. For proposals and their defence, see *Australian Defence: Report on the Reorganisation of the Defence Group of Departments*, presented to the Minister for Defence November 1973; Tange's submission to the Royal Commission on Australian Government and Administration, dated 9 October 1974, and his remarks on "Departmental Organisation and the Profession of Arms—A Civilian Perspective", in *Canberra Times*, 2 July 1975; Barnard's statement "Reorganisation of the Defence Group of Departments", 4 December 1974, transcript; and Barnard, *APD*, HR (29 May 1975), pp. 3025–26. For a summary of pro and con arguments, see B. Juddery, *Canberra Times*, 29 November 1974. For historical accounts of organizational change, see B. White, "Defence and its Environment" (APSA conference paper, Canberra, July 1975); and D. Ball, "The Politics of Defence Decision-Making in Australia—The Reorganisation of the Defence Group of Departments" (background paper, August 1975).
34. For instance, see Forbes, *News Release*, 6 May 1974 and in Liberal Party Federal Secretariat, *Media Releases*, 2 and 5 January 1975. For a concise academic criticism of reorganization, see T.B. Millar's articles in *Canberra Times*, 3 and 4 July 1975.
35. See Barnard's radio interview of 30 April 1973 and Singapore press conference of 6 May 1973, contained in Department of Foreign Affairs memoranda; and B. Toohey's review, *Australian Financial Review*, 9 May 1974.
36. F. Brenchley, *National Times*, 12 February 1973.
37. *APD*, HR (1 March 1973), p. 129. For commentaries on the unit, see Brenchley's second article, *National Times*, 19 February 1973. Also see M. Richardson and A. Barnes, Melbourne *Age*, 17 February 1973.
38. See Melbourne *Age*, 12 and 13 February 1973.
39. Statement of 4 July 1973, cited in *Australian Foreign Affairs Record (AFAR)* 44 (July 1973): 487.
40. For instance, Barnard, 5 February 1973, in *AFAR* 44 (February 1973): 138; and radio interview of 30 April 1973, in Department of Foreign Affairs memorandum.
41. See M. Richardson, Melbourne *Age*, 29 June 1973; and B. Kinsella, *Canberra Times*, 12 December 1973.
42. New Zealand, *Report of the Ministry of Defence for the Year Ended 21 March 1974* (Wellington: 1974), p. 6. Also see the comment of H. Templeton, "'New Era' for 'The Happy Isles': The First Six Months of Labour Government Foreign Policy in New Zealand", *Australian Outlook* 27 (August 1973): 164.
43. See analyses by D. Warner, *Sydney Morning Herald*, 16 February and 20 October 1973, and Brisbane *Courier-Mail* 22 October 1973; A. Barnes, Melbourne *Age*, 6 August 1973; and M. Richardson, Melbourne *Age*, 31 August 1973.
44. Cited in *Sydney Morning Herald*, 6 July 1973. Also, for example, see Snedden, *APD*, HR (1 March 1973), pp. 110–15; and McMahon's article *Sydney Morning Herald*, 3 March 1973.

45. Snedden, cited in *Australian*, 10 April 1974; and Snedden, *APD*, HR (14 March 1974), p. 446; and Peacock, Brisbane AIIA address, 22 March 1974, transcript, p. 6.
46. W.A. Fraser, New Zealand Minister for Defence, *Press Statement* 6 May 1975. On the disbandment of the ANZUK force, see *AFAR* 46 (January 1975): 44.
47. For instance, Willesee, "Australian Foreign Policy (II)", remarks of 19 January 1973, Embassy of Australia, Washington, Press and Information Office *Release*, p. 7; Barnard, Kuala Lumpur press conference of 8 May 1973, Department of Foreign Affairs memorandum; and Barnard, *APD*, HR (22 August 1973), pp. 238–39.
48. Address of 8 February 1974, in Department of Foreign Affairs, *Australia and South-East Asia* (Canberra: 1974), p. 36.
49. See *Australia's External Aid 1974–75*, Budget Paper no. 9 (1974), pp. 3–5; and Barnard, Jakarta statement of 7 April 1973, Department of Foreign Affairs memorandum.
50. Marshal Saleh Basarah, cited in *Sydney Morning Herald*, 17 June 1975.
51. See M. Richardson, *Sydney Morning Herald*, 20 December 1974.
52. On the rationale for military exercises with smaller/regional powers, see F. Brenchley, *National Times*, 11 March 1974.
53. For instance, Whitlam, Bangkok address of 31 January 1974, in DFA, *Australia and South-East Asia*, p. 22; Ottawa television interview with K. Begg of 7 August 1973, transcript, pp. 1–2; and television interview with David Frost, 18 August 1973, transcript, pp. 24–25.
54. ABC television interview of 1 October 1972, transcript.
55. *Defence Report 1973* (Canberra: 1973), p. 6.
56. A similar account of the event is given by L. Oakes and D. Solomon, *Grab for Power: Election '74* (Melbourne: Cheshire, 1974), p. 97. For an example of the party argument, see *Canberra Times*, 12 July 1973.
57. For New Zealand expressions, see Kirk, remarks of 31 March 1973, *New Zealand Foreign Affairs Review* 23 (June 1973): 8; "New Zealand and South-East Asia, a Policy for the Seventies", address of 12 June 1973, transcript, p. 7; and comment by C. Forell, Melbourne *Age*, 26 March 1973.
58. For instance, see Marshall Green's remarks, cited in *Australian Financial Review*, 15 June 1973; and of 9 August 1973, in US Department of State memorandum; and M. Richardson, *National Times*, 1 January 1973; R. Trumbell, *New York Times*, 22 January 1973; and A. Barnes, Melbourne *Age*, 4 August 1973.
59. Address in Bangkok of 1 February 1974, in DFA, *Australia and South-East Asia*, p. 22.
60. See V. Condon, Melbourne *Herald*, 28 July 1975; and F. Cranston, *Canberra Times*, 13 August 1975; Willesee, *APD*, Senate (20 August 1975), p. 66; and Whitlam's review of Australia's SEATO role, *APD* HR (4 September 1975), pp. 1100–1101.
61. Whitlam, Washington address of 30 July 1973, in *AFAR* 44 (August 1973): 528. Also see his 12 July 1973 ALP conference address, Department of Foreign Affairs memorandum.
62. *Time*, 23 June 1975.
63. See Willesee's remarks of 27 February 1974, in Department of Foreign Affairs memorandum; ANZUS Council communiqué of 25 April 1975, in *Australian Government Weekly Digest* 1 (5 May to 11 May 1975): 165–67.
64. The secruity/resource connection is elaborated on by J.W.C. Cumes, "Australia and Resources Diplomacy" (Auckland seminar paper, August 1974), esp. pp. 14–15; and by R. O'Neill, in "Australian Security and Resources Diplomacy: Alliance Problems" (ANZAAS conference paper, Canberra, January 1975).
65. American television interview, 6 October 1974, transcript, p. 4.
66. Cited in *Australian Financial Review*, 9 March 1973.
67. See [Australian] Department of Defence, Barnard–Schlesinger, *Joint Statement* (10 January 1974), clause 2, p. 1.
68. *Defence Report 1974*, p. 5; and *Defence Report 1975*, p. 6.
69. For some representative criticisms of ANZUS, see J. Camilleri, "A New Australian Foreign Policy?", *Arena*, no, 31 (1973), p. 13; J. Camilleri and M. Teichmann, *Security and Survival: The New Era in International Relations* (Melbourne: Heinemann Educational, 1973), pp. 60–61; remarks of Senator J. Wheeldon, cited in *Sydney Morning Herald*, 18 June 1973; and of W. Hartley, *Australian* 3 January 1974.
70. For US assurances, see Australian television interview remarks of Philip Habib, US

Assistant Secretary of State for East Asia and the Pacific, *Australian* 24 May 1975. On Whitlam's caveat, see remarks cited in *Canberra Times*, 6 May 1975.

71. See Fraser, interview with P. Samuel, *Bulletin*, 29 March 1975; and Killen, television interview remarks, cited in Melbourne *Age*, 7 April 1975. For digests of a feasibility study of a nuclear option for Australia, prepared by the United Service Institution of the ACT, see F. Cranston, *Canberra Times*, 18 August 1975; and D. Dale, *National Times*, 18 August 1975. For a critical view of an Australian nuclear capability, see R. Butler, *Bulletin*, 30 August 1975.

72. See Whitlam's exposition in his UN General Assmbly remarks of 30 September 1974, in Department of Foreign Affairs, *News Release*, no. M/128 (30 September 1974), pp. 3–5; and its explanation by P.C.J. Curtis (Department of Foreign Affairs), in *AFAR* 45 (November 1974): 751–52; and Willesee, address before UN General Assembly, 23 September 1975, Australian Mission to the United Nations transcript, pp. 4–6.

73. Barnard, *APD*, HR (9 April 1974), p. 1233.

74. On the Thai and Filipino reaction, see *New York Times*, 15 May, 10 June and 25 July 1975.

75. For instance, Barnard, Kuala Lumpur press conference of 8 May 1973, in Department of Foreign Affairs memorandum; Whitlam, Kuala Lumpur address of 29 January 1974, in DFA, *Australia and South-East Asia*, p. 12.

76. Whitlam, UN General Assembly address of 30 September 1974, in DFA, *News Release*, no. M/129 (30 September 1974), p. 5; and Willesee, remarks cited in Department of Foreign Affairs, *News Release*, no. M/19 (16 April 1975).

77. For press reports, see P. Costigan, Melbourne *Herald*, 29 April 1975; and J. Jost, Melbourne *Age*, 30 April 1975.

78. See Whitlam's summary of the position in *APD*, HR (22 October 1974), p. 2715.

79. Cited in *Canberra Times*, 14 August 1975.

80. Peacock, Brisbane AIIA address, 22 March 1974, transcript, p. 7.

81. For a summary of Diego Garcia's value to the US, see B. Weintraub, *New York Times*, 2 June 1974.

82. UN General Assembly, *Ad Hoc* Committee on the Indian Ocean. *Declaration of the Indian Ocean as a Zone of Peace. Report ...* , A/AC. 159/1 (3 May 1974), esp. pp. 12 and 20; and A/AC. 159/1, Rev. 1 (11 July 1974), p. 12.

83. For instance, Snedden, *Media Release*, no. 74/21 (11 February 1974); Peacock, *APD*, HR (11 February 1975), p. 70; and Vice-Admiral Sir Alan McNicoll, *Sydney Morning Herald*, 1 April 1974.

84. For summaries of early positions in the departments and in the government, see K. Randall *New Accent*, 22 March 1974, p. 6, and S.P. Seth, *New Accent*, 10 May 1974, p. 13.

85. *Australian*, 6 August 1975.

86. ALP federal platform, XXI, 5.

87. See Barnard, remarks of 22 November 1973, cited in *National Times*, 10 December 1973; and Whitlam, Colombo press conference remark of 15 December 1974, in Department of Foreign Affairs, *News Release*, no. D/2 (14 January 1975), pp. 2–3.

88. For the text of the agreement, see the Barnard–Schlesinger *Joint Statement*. Also see Barnard's Washington address of 4 January 1974, in Defence Department, *Press Release*, no. 200/74 (4 January 1974); Barnard's *Press Release*, no. 202/74 (10 January 1974); and the Whitlam–Green follow-up *Memorandum* of understandings of 21 March 1974.

89. For ministerial expressions, see Barnard, *APD*, HR (28 February 1973), pp. 67–69; Willesee, *APD*, Senate (8 March 1973), pp. 303–4; Whitlam, Washington press conference of 30 July 1973, in Department of Foreign Affairs memorandum; and Whitlam, remarks at Terrigal conference, cited in *Australian*, 7 February 1975. On the 1974 increase in data sharing, see B. Toohey, *Australian Financial Review*, 10 January 1974.

90. Cited in *Sydney Morning Herald*, 26 March 1973.

91. Interview of 1 April 1974, in Department of Foreign Affairs memorandum.

92. Cited in *Australian*, 7 March 1973. On Whitlam's view while in opposition, see his remarks in *APD*, HR (29 April 1969), pp. 1413–16.

93. *APD*, HR (3 April 1974), p. 905.

94. *Australian*, 7 February 1975.

95. A. Clark, *National Times,* 17 November 1975.
96. For representative summaries of some of these criticisms, see D. Ball, "Promise and Performance of the Labor Government Defence and Foreign Policy" (Fabian Society conference paper, Sydney, September 1974), esp. pp. 11–15; Pax Christi circular, "Foreign Military Bases in Australia" (West Footscray, Vic., March 1973); and Campaign Against Foreign Military Bases in Australia, Industrial Group, "US Bases Threaten Australia" (Brickfield Hill, NSW, February 1974).
97. Cited in *Australian,* 11 January 1974.
98. As a sample, see D.J. Ball, "United States Strategic Doctrine and Policy—With Some Implications for Australia" (ANU seminar paper, July 1974), as well as his "American Bases in Australia: The Strategic Implications", *Current Affairs Bulletin* 51 (March 1975): 4–17; and P. King, "Notes on the Bases—Pro and (Mostly) Con" (ANU seminar paper, July 1974). On implications of the Schlesinger doctrine in particular, see B. Toohey, *Australian Financial Review,* 11 July 1974; A. Clark, *National Times,* 9 September 1974; and D. Dale, *National Times,* 10 March 1975.
99. For commentaries, see M. Walsh, *Australian Financial Review,* 4 and 9 March 1973.
100. Whitlam's mandate thesis in the context of American installations is analysed in C.J. Lloyd and G.S. Reid, *Out of the Wilderness: The Return of Labor* (Melbourne: Cassell, 1974), pp. 206–8.
101. Helpful summaries of Omega's characteristics and of the background of negotiations are found in the Department of Foreign Affairs submission to the Parliamentary Joint Committee on Foreign Affairs and Defence, *Omega Navigational Installation* (Canberra: 8 June 1973); and in the Committee's own report, *Omega Navigational Installation* (Canberra: 1975).
102. For a summary of criticisms, see Stop Omega Research Group, *Omega, Poseidon, and the Arms Race: Why Omega is an Aggressive War Base* (AICD Occasional Paper no. 5, Sydney, January 1974); A. Clark, *National Times,* 9 December 1974; and *Omega Navigational Installation* report, "Dissenting Report" section, pp. 109–13.
103. For a summary of the opposition movement in New Zealand, see O. Wilkes, *Protest: Demonstrations Against the American Military Presence in New Zealand,* (Wellington: Taylor, February 1973), esp. pp. 7–16.
104. For a critical review of L–CP and Labor expressions, especially before 1973, see Stop Omega Campaign, *Ghosts from the Past: Stop Omega* (Norwood, SA: 1973).
105. See *Canberra Times,* Melbourne *Age* and *Australian,* 27 March 1973.
106. For accounts, see B. Johns, *Sydney Morning Herald,* 13 July 1973; P. Edwards, *Direct Action,* 19 July 1973; and *Nation-Review,* 20 July 1973.
107. *Australian,* 3 and 15 August 1973.
108. *Omega Navigational Installation* report, "Dissenting Report", pp. 109–13.

⑧ The External Policy Process

In the present chapter we sharpen our focus on the policy process.[1] Borrowing in part from material previously introduced, we cast our analysis in terms of the variables within the Australian political system that shaped external policy outputs and presentation. What was the jurisdictional distribution of decision-making power? What was the relative influence of various office-holders or structures? In what ways were decision-makers, and their judgements, affected by advisers, by organized interests and by Labor as a party? In the final chapter, we will consider the related theme of the interplay between electoral politics and the making and presentation of external policy.

We begin with the basic generalization that the Australian federal government is pre-eminent in external policy.[2] It achieves this dominance through constitutionally granted monopoly over such areas as defence, external affairs and overseas trade. However, there always have been some constraints on Canberra's freedom to pursue external policy objectives at will, largely but not exclusively because of Australia's federal structure. Constitutional, practical and political constraints all can be inhibiting upon federal authority. The several states are jealous of their prerogatives and often are led by powerful political figures. Political considerations can impel the states to resist federal initiatives and can dissuade governments in Canberra from relentless pursuit of their desired policies. In some respects, however, federal–state co-operation has proved indispensable. The High Court has ruled that, under Section 92 of the Constitution, Canberra may engage in interstate trade, but not so as to enjoy a monopoly over the interstate movement of goods. Hence the Wheat Board's *de facto* monopoly over overseas wheat marketing, a very important component of Australia's overseas trade, is predicated on the sufferance of periodically amended, complementary federal and state legislation.

Friction between federal Labor and the states was heightened by two considerations. The first was that for most of Labor's time in office, four of the six states, among them the largest and most important, were under non-labor administration. The second reason was that, as a particularly active, innovative, reformist and indeed centralist government, Labor generated more circumstances for conflict with the states than ordinarily might have been expected under a less-experimental L–CP government.

Some of the federal–state tensions that arose were not strictly constitutional in nature, but all the same affected the federal government's policy judgements or the effectiveness of policies taken. All state governments, including the ALP governments of South Australia and Tasmania, criticized the prospect of a PLO delegation visit to Australia. They threatened to impose an official boycott on any PLO visitors who might come and to refuse to register offices of any PLO mission.[3] This state outcry, coupled with intra-party and other criticisms, encouraged the Cabinet decision in late January 1975 to reject a PLO visit for the time being. When a PLO visitor did come later, hostility expressed by the states was hardly welcomed by a federal government wishing to attract goodwill among Arab states. In another episode, we noticed the legal and political difficulties that snarled the federal government's efforts to liquidate the Rhodesian Information Centre in Sydney and thereby frustrated federal Labor's efforts to sustain its anti-racialist objectives. In another instance, the Labor government wished to appoint Mr Justice Hope of the NSW judiciary to conduct an inquiry into Australia's security and intelligence services. NSW's Liberal Premier, Sir Robert Askin, had reservations about the inquiry and about losing still another valued state judge to a federal assignment. Askin eventually acceded. But, as one commentator noticed, "The fate of the Federal inquiry—on which entire ALP policy on and integrity of ASIO, ASIS, JIO and other security-intelligence operations stands—seems to rely on the acquiescence of the hostile NSW Government.[4]

On several occasions, state–federal conflicts threatened to, or actually did, become entangled in even more substantial policy areas. We recall that Queensland Premier Bjelke-Petersen complicated Canberra's wish to rearrange the international boundary-line between Australia and Papua New Guinea. Bjelke-Petersen also insisted that Japan resume buying Queensland beef before his government would ratify future coking-coal projects in the state. While the federal government enjoyed undoubted powers over exports, the states retained a voice in granting on-shore mining leases. The Japanese did resume buying Australian beef. But, if executed, Bjelke-Petersen's threat could have severely disrupted Australia's resource policy towards Japan, and Canberra–Tokyo relations generally.

Several states threatened to withhold ore-mining leases in instances where they felt that the new PMA would be improperly intervening.[5] Early in 1974, West Australia had a change of government, from Labor to L–CP. Both the state Labor and L–CP governments vigorously protested the federal government's reluctance to approve the multimillion-dollar Alwest Aluminium project. The state ALP even felt that its defeat at the polls had been hastened by the position of the federal Labor government. Liberal Premier Sir Charles Court personally assumed negotiations with Canberra; eventually, an appropriate formula was found for the project.[6] In late 1975, Canberra liberalized its foreign investment guidelines and Connor was replaced in the Minerals and Energy portfolio by the far more tractable Wriedt. All the same, the state mines ministers drafted a statement that argued that "the administration of foreign investment in the mineral industry would continue to involve conflict between the States and the Commonwealth in the control of the mining industry."[7]

We have seen that, through state legal intervention, the federal government faced fundamental challenges to its resource and investment programme. All six states went before the High Court to challenge the Seas and Submerged Lands Act. Much of the argument turned on whether, by extension, the federal government's control over external affairs entitled it to proceed with establishing sovereignty in territorial waters for exploration, exploitation and conservation purposes. When the High Court validated the Act, it accepted the applicability of the external affairs power, but as we have seen, its judgement postdated Labor's period in office. The Petroleum and Mineral Authority Act also ran afoul of state challenge. We recall that the PMA was designed for such purposes as government involvement in direct equity investment, loans to Australian companies and farm-outs. Its critics felt it was neither economically necessary nor desirable and urged the High Court to declare it *ultra vires* under the Constitution. In June 1975, the High Court invalidated the Petroleum and Mineral Authority Act. The judgement was on technical grounds, relating to the manner in which the measure had been legislatively handled. Temporarily, the question of its inherent constitutionality was left unanswered and the government moved to reintroduce it in Parliament, though in amended form. In the interim, the government felt it could still achieve many of its objectives through an ancillary agency, the Petroleum and Minerals Company of Australia, incorporated in the ACT and thereby out of state reach, which it had created some months earlier. Even this agency and its work were, however, a matter of legal contention.[8] Whatever the eventual judicial renderings on the Seas and Submerged Lands and PMA Acts, the states felt confident that they could variously thwart the government by exercising their own on-shore powers.

Another area of difficulty for the Whitlam government was in its efforts to ratify a number of international conventions, especially under the International Labour Organization (ILO), and to have them implemented as law in Australia. As we saw earlier, the subject-matter of these conventions was wide. The government was not only eager to insure what it thought to be better and more humane conditions in Australia but to demonstrate its attractive credentials abroad, for instance in the area of anti-discrimination. Whitlam felt that earlier governments had been very remiss in accepting obligations under international conventions and that the states were themselves to blame for being unresponsive. We are reminded of his 1970 remark that "In international relations, for which the Federal Government bears responsibility—for example the International Labour Organisation, maritime and human rights conventions—the States stagnate and obstruct."[9] As Bruce Juddery relates, Whitlam indicated that he would prefer to follow earlier procedural precedents in such matters. Where an international convention seemed to require domestic implementation, he would seek agreement of the states and of the federal Parliament. "But he need not do so—if Section 51 (xxix) [federal power in external affairs] meets his government's expectations."[10] Said Lionel Murphy, when he was Attorney-General:

> While judgments of the High Court have made it clear that the Australian Parliament cannot, by mere agreement with another country, take to itself the power to legislate on the subject matter of the agreement, I venture to say it is inconceivable that the High Court would call into question the bona fides of successive Governments in voting for ratifying and implementing the International Convention on Civil and Political Rights."[11]

The states did in fact show some skittishness about consenting to such proposals put before them. Deputy Liberal leader Phillip Lynch summarized one side of the argument. The L–CP did not believe that conventions should be ratified unless all states had formally agreed. Moreover, "a convention should not be ratified if any point of conflict exists between the law and practice, in any jurisdiction, of the provisions of the convention". The liberal use of the external affairs power to circumvent normal federal–state jurisdictional boundaries was impermissible.[12]

Again, as with the Seas and Submerged Lands and PMA legislation, the argument about international conventions underscored some of the obstacles facing a Labor government intent on pursuing indicated external policy objectives. Political considerations, differences in substantive philosophy, differing versions of what was or was not a proper level of centralist direction in Australia and divergent constitutional emphases intruded.

We now need to identify the structural sources of decision-making within the federal government. We begin with a negative: The principal source of decision-making is *not* Parliament. McMahon expressed it well:

> The conduct of foreign policy is essentially a function of the Executive. It is the Government which must be responsible for formulating policy and for carrying it through on a day to day basis. This is a responsibility which the Executive cannot and should not abdicate. To have an erosion of the Executive's responsibility for foreign policy would be to abandon an approach which has been accepted in the past by governments of all parties and which is a tried and tested part of our constitutional practice.[13]

Furthermore, "Executive control over external policy has been strengthened in Australia by a general tradition of cabinet domination, and by decades of national development during which foreign-policy questions were quite remote to the community at large, and received slight official attention."[14] To this can be added such factors as the relatively small number of members in the two chambers of Parliament, the relatively low interest in the subject on the part of most parliamentarians, and the small number of parliamentary sitting days and the very minor part of Parliament's business occupied by legislation bearing on external affairs. Treaties and other international agreements are an executive prerogative and Parliament need not even be consulted, though Parliament must approve non-self-implementing treaties.

What contributions to external policy-making did Parliament provide during Labor's term of office? Formally, it did a good deal. It gave legislative approval to the budgetary requirements of various departments, such as Foreign Affairs and Defence, and passed various Bills, such as those that implemented international conventions and provided for an increased federal role in resource management and exploitation. Apart from occasional amendments it chose to accept, the government's measures had no difficulty in being approved in the ALP-controlled House. The Senate, however, was a different matter, since at no time did Labor enjoy a majority there and the opposition in the House was often able to rely on the Senate to distract the government's policies. The government's situation was especially troublesome until mid-1974, because of the presence of five DLP senators, whose party was extremely critical of government external policy. While an adverse vote in the Senate could not topple the government, it could delay or defeat government legislation. The Seas and Submerged Lands legislation passed Parliament, but in conspicuously amended form. The PMA legislation passed the House, but was defeated in the Senate. It became one of the hooks on which the government hung its rationale for calling a double dissolution and contributed to the convening of a joint sitting of Parliament at which the PMA Bill and other stalled government measures were finally approved. With the High Court's invalidation of the PMA Act, on grounds of its faulty legislative handling, the government proceeded to resubmit a PMA Bill to Parliament. First, however, the government rewrote the PMA legislation, to meet some of the criticisms levelled against it by the opposition and by the mining industry. Senate opposition thereby affected the PMA legislation in three ways. Firstly, it considerably delayed its passage. Secondly, the fact that the government had committed a technical error, because it used Senate obstruction as a reason for calling a double dissolution and then a joint sitting, brought on High Court invalidation. Thirdly, delays in getting the PMA legislatively and constitutionally secured, and a wish to make it more palatable to the parliamentary opposition, caused the government to amend some of its more contentious features. The Labor government was dismissed by the Governor-General shortly after the amended version of the PMA legislation was introduced in Parliament.

The government's displeasure with the Senate was not, of course, limited to that chamber's intrusions into external policy subjects. In a rather special way, however, the government resorted to a "foreign policy instrument" by creating a vacancy in the Senate, in the hope of having a loyal Labor senator step in. This was the celebrated Gair affair. To general astonishment, Whitlam appointed Queensland DLP senator Vincent Gair to be Ambassador to Ireland, and Gair accepted. Victorian DLP senator Frank McManus insisted that he had been previously approached by a Labor minister, Morrison, with an unmistakable, authoritative offer of the ambassadorship to the Vatican if he, McManus, would resign from the Senate. McManus held to his story, despite government denials.[15] At any rate, the Gair appointment infuriated the opposition, and Snedden in particular. He described it as "the most shameful act ever perpetrated by an Australian Government",[16] and his anger with the Whitlam government probably had a bearing on his willingness to force a parliamentary impasse from which a double dissolution could (and did) arise.

Even when the House of the Senate were not in a position to force changes in government external policy, the non-Labor parties were able to use the parliamentary forum to berate the government. This is a common function of parliamentary oppositions. In theory, at least, opposition spokesmanship is presumed to serve a public expositional and educational role, to arouse attention and possibly to gain electoral sympathy. Skilfully executed, such spokesmanship could also cause a government to decide that excessively adverse publicity required some policy adaptation. It is likely, for instance, that frequent and sharp opposition criticism entered into government calculations on various defence policy decisions. For instance, shortly before the 1974 double dissolution, it refused the Soviet request for a space-science facility in Australia and hurried along announcement of new capital defence expenditures.

The opposition carried out its parliamentary attacks in various contexts. Some were familiar, such as seizing opportunity during foreign and defence policy debates, at question time and during adjournments. As we saw, the opposition's first motion of censure against the new government was based on a criticism of its defence policy movements. Moreover, as time went on, Snedden and Peacock in particular began to resort to a technique Whitlam himself had developed while in opposition. Numerous, often searching questions on external policy subjects were placed on notice. The replies provided ammunition with which to attack, for instance on the Baltic states recognition issue. When Fraser became Liberal leader, the tempo of attack intensified. Fraser not only challenged the merit of government policies but seemed especially eager to portray Whitlam and some of his colleagues as having offended Australia's parliamentary and other institutions. One instance was over the alleged irregularities surrounding Connor's and Cairns' efforts to obtain petrodollar loans for resource projects. Another was during the 1975 controversy over cables and letters sent to the two Vietnams. On that occasion, Fraser opened his remarks on a censure motion by charging that Whitlam had "misled the Parliament knowingly and deliberately. He took this course because he was not prepared to speak plainly to the Australian people of, his policies and his bias towards communist North Vietnam."[17] In the Senate, opposition parties frequently used their numbers to assail aspects of government defence under-preparedness, of flirtations with wrong-headed causes, and the like.

To an extent, Parliament also served as a base from which the government's own supporters, or collections of parliamentarians, were able to bring pressure or criticism upon the government. We will reserve until later an assessment of the ALP parliamentary caucus as an influence on policy outputs. But it should be noticed here that Labor members formed loose groups that urged some course of action upon the government. Petitions were signed, urging the government to withhold diplomatic recognition of the post-Allende régime in Chile, to consider a tougher line against South Africa, to take a more direct hand in helping to stabilize conditions in strife-torn East Timor in 1975 and at large to support closer relations with the PRG in Vietnam before the Thieu régime fell. There also was a "Friends of Israel" group within caucus, which overall was more explicitly well-disposed towards the Israeli cause in the Middle Eastern conflict than it believed the government to be, and some quite sharp questions were put to Whitlam in the House by some of his own party followers. There also were bipartisan collections of parliamentarians who were concerned about such matters as Portuguese Timor. The amnesty group, as we saw, extracted a pledge from Whitlam to raise the issue of political rights in countries he would be visiting, such as Indonesia and the Soviet Union. Perhaps the urging was unnecessary, but it likely strengthened Whitlam's resolve to put the matter clearly in his conversations with foreign leaders.

Parliament also had an institutionalized mechanism to deal with external policy, namely parliamentary committees. When the L–CP left office, there was a Joint (House and Senate) Committee on Foreign Affairs and of much more recent vintage, in the Senate, a Standing Committee on Foreign Affairs and Defence and a Select Committee on Foreign Ownership and Control. The new government widened the scope of the joint committee to "Foreign Affairs and Defence" and, for instance, increased its ability to call witnesses and papers and to draw upon necessary research staff and facilities.[18] Whitlam seemed genuinely interested in having this committee serve a useful educational function for its parliamentary members, as well as providing competent reports from time to time. Understandably, however, like his predecessors, he could not countenance a role for the joint committee, or for any parliamentary committee, that would undermine the government's own prerogatives. For nearly two years, the joint committee was preoccupied with the Omega study. As we saw, the government's reference of this subject to the joint committee was heavily political in inspiration. It was a gambit to temporize on Omega, to forestall party efforts to proscribe the installation while the committee had Omega under advisement. Of course, once the committee had reported, the government still had the problem of reconciling a favourable committee report (though with most Labor members indicating dissent) with a need to satisfy the party as such that Omega could properly be endorsed.

On the Senate side, the Select Committee on Foreign Ownership and Control was disbanded and in 1975, replaced by a new Standing Committee on National Development and Ownership and Control of Australian Resources. The Senate Standing Committee on Foreign Affairs and Defence proceeded to move into a number of sensitive areas, such as the role of Australia and the United Nations in the affairs of Australian territories, with special focus on the Cocos Islands. Then, quite suddenly, before the committee had completed its investigations, the government announced its intention to assert Australian authority in the Cocos more emphatically, through a move such as "buying up" the islands from the Clunies-Ross family. Indeed, it is a step that only a few months before had been rejected by officials as an option. The government's treatment of the committee was construed as cavalier, even contemptuous,[19] though the committee shortly thereafter came to essentially the same conclusion as had the government.[20] This committee also conducted an inquiry into the capabilities of the Australian Army. T. B. Millar wrote as follows:

> Not having control of the Senate, the Government felt that the Standing Committee there was deliberately trying to embarrass it; the first reference was on the role and capacity of the Army. The Government therefore prevented the Senate Committee from getting access to the classified information that would have enabled it to produce a more convincing report.

Moreover, regarding both the joint and Senate committees, Millar observed that under Labor they had fallen on hard times:

> Most A.L.P. members interested in foreign affairs were in the Ministry. The Government had its own experts on foreign affairs and defence, and saw no mileage in increasing the capacity of its own backbenchers or the Opposition to propose initiatives or ask embarrassing questions.[21]

Only in a most remote sense could it be said that, because of their weight and value, parliamentary committee reports influenced policy outputs under the Labor government.

The effective external policy locus of decision-making rested with the executive—the government. But Cabinet collectively was not the prime mover. That honour belonged to the Prime Minister. Australian political and international circumstances, and Whitlam's own qualities, were responsible.

Whitlam's interests had consistently been pointed at foreign rather than domestic affairs. He had been his party's foreign policy spokesman when in opposition. When elected to government, Whitlam already possessed a wealth of overseas experience and personal contacts, sharpened by historical learning, a retentive and agile mind and a gift for expression. His decision to assume the Foreign Affairs portfolio personally was inspired by several considerations, other than interest in the field. He had concluded that, under L–CP governments, the "superficiality" of foreign policy decisions had in part arisen "from the separation of the *de facto* External Affairs Minister—that is, the Prime Minister—from the professional advisers".[22] Since it was *desirable* for the Prime Minister to wield a commanding role in foreign policy, Whitlam's answer was to merge the two functions. A second consideration was the state of his party. The ALP had a disputatious tradition. When in opposition, first as deputy leader and then as leader, Whitlam had experienced strife with elements within the ALP, often over his foreign policy views. To foreclose the possibility of conflict between himself as Prime Minister and a separate Foreign Minister, to keep control over a fractious party, to insure that his conceptions of foreign policy would prevail, he found merit in assuming the portfolio himself. Labor entered office determined to chart new and important courses in foreign policy after years in frustrating opposition. Direct control over Australia's foreign policy, which was seen to involve a creative rather than a largely managerial role, was especially vital.

Whitlam surrendered the Foreign Affairs portfolio to Willesee less than a year after Labor's election. Willesee was a trusted, dependable and hard-working colleague and much of the detail in the portfolio could be taken off Whitlam's shoulders. Willesee could not be classified as a "yes man", and as Foreign Minister, he did take many decisions alone. But by force of his interest and temperament it was possible for Whitlam to remain the overarching figure. His foreign policy role was accentuated by his style. He flourished on high-level diplomacy: numerous overseas trips, visits with heads of government, painting with broad strokes. His forays into such diplomacy, much remarked upon, perhaps were "a representation of what Gough Whitlam believes international affairs are all about—relations and co-operations. It is capital R relations and capital C co-operation."[23] Activism, personal diplomacy and big ideas could be interpreted as not only putting Australia on the map more prominently but as means towards expounding its interests and principles directly and forcefully. Others saw it less as statesmanship than as a substitution of style for substance, and even as pursuit of ego gratification. Critics carped at Whitlam's flair for foreign travel as wasteful and as a distortion of priorities. Peacock complained in February 1975 that in two years of office, Whitlam had made eleven overseas journeys. He had spent at least 130 days outside the country, while Parliament during this period had sat for only approximately 143 days.[24] The *Sydney Morning Herald's* own acid comment was that "If Mr Whitlam really is planning more absences, he is elevating self-indulgence into an almost Shakesperean self-destructive flaw."[25]

There is no doubt that Whitlam left a substantial stamp on Labor's foreign policy. The strengths and the weaknesses of that foreign policy could in a way be traced to the dualism in Whitlam's own approach to the subject: "He is a realist who wants to be seen as an idealist; a pragmatist who decks himself out in principles."[26] The big decisions were made either on his own initiative or with his personal concurrence. Some decisions, such as on the Baltic states, were taken independently. Others, such as on South Africa's membership in the United Nations, were taken in the face of serious misgivings on the part of senior colleagues. Most were taken without prior Cabinet consultation.

An important reason why the Whitlam system worked reasonably well was that most of the Prime Minister's immediate colleagues, such as Willesee and Barnard, shared Whitlam's views about the general directions and the more specific features of Australia's external policies. As a group, Connor apart, they were more cautious than Whitlam. Even Cairns, in the handling of his specific portfolio responsibilities, was in degree less taken by idealism than Whitlam. Cairns was more committed to protectionism and, as Overseas Trade Minister, less eager to pursue trade sanctions against South Africa. Ministers such as Willesee, Barnard and Morrison, while having minds of their own, fitted well the roles of lieutenants rather than co-captains. The main exception to the rule of Whitlam's pre-eminence in external policy was Connor. Connor was a tough and determined man, knowledgeable in the resources field, and he commanded considerable admiration within the party. We have seen that he was much more interested in what Australia could in practice achieve for itself in minerals and energy than in global resource diplomacy questions. Whitlam was not very interested in the detail of this quite technical subject, but by temperament approached it from an international/foreign policy standpoint. Hence it was possible for the two men to coexist and at times to reflect seemingly different viewpoints. The merits of the positions aside, it was understandable that, on the resources aspects of external policy, political critics and the business community complained about what they saw as the government's inconsistency.

Connor's domination over resource policy eventually receded and then ended. In mid-October 1975, Whitlam forced Connor's resignation as Minister for Minerals and Energy, on grounds that Connor had earlier not fully apprised Parliament of his role in the search for massive overseas loans. Decline in Connor's influence had been evident earlier. His overall reputation and his standing in the party had slipped. This was due to his persistent inflexibility and his failure to provide detailed answers to questions and more detailed guidelines for his policies. Nor did his involvement in the loans affair enhance his standing with his colleagues. In August, a resources committee was created within Cabinet. It was composed of the Prime Minister, the Deputy Prime Minister, the Treasurer, the Minister for Foreign Affairs and Connor, as Minister for Minerals and Energy. Within the committee, Whitlam, Crean, Hayden and Willesee all took a more flexible view than Connor. Hayden, as Treasurer, was given responsibility over foreign investment policy. The various liberalized foreign investment steps in the last few months of Labor's time in office grew out of resource committee deliberations, with Connor being consistently overridden. Although these decisions were essentially collegiate, they represented a correction of what previously had often been (in the form of an entrenched Connor) a voice dissident to Whitlam.[27]

Whitlam's relations with minsiters who spoke or acted out of turn on matters unrelated to their portfolios were another matter. When Nixon resumed the bombing of North Vietnam very shortly after Labor was elected, Whitlam decided not to comment publicly, but Cairns, Cameron and Uren proceeded to make rude and barbed comments. Whitlam was plainly displeased and made it known that there would be no more statements on foreign policy except from himself, as Foreign Minister. But extramural remarks by ministers, often in clash with or in overstatement of government policy, did not stop. Cairns was the most persistent offender, but there were others as well. For instance, Health Minister Dr Doug Everingham urged a boycott of French imports in protest against nuclear testing, while Environment Minister Dr Moss Cass urged the recognition of the PRG.[28] Cairns, as we have seen, in 1974 became President of the Congress for International Co-operation and Disarmament, whose platform included a non-aligned Australian foreign policy, removal of all foreign bases from Australia and recognition of the PRG.

With one notable exception, Whitlam's efforts to contain outspoken ministers were not overly successful. At the April 1974 Cabinet meeting, Whitlam was very firm. At least for the duration of the forthcoming electoral campaign, ministers were to adhere strictly to the subject of their respective portfolios. Labor's continuation in office was at stake. The party had to speak with a single authoritative voice, especially in external affairs. The appeal worked. Independent ministerial expressions did carry effects. It took longer and became more difficult for Washington and the new government in Canberra to adjust to one another and raised unease in some South-East Asian capitals; not just in Saigon or Pnom Penh. It spurred the opposition and other critics to incriminate the government in two ways: that it was divided and unable to operate coherently, and that it contained extremist elements whose influence over policy could not be discounted. It was even claimed that some extramural ministerial statements were privately countenanced by Whitlam, who wanted to turn left, to set the climate for a leftward turn, but who politically was unable to overexpose himself in this way. Hence the *News Weekly's* charge that

> Mr Whitlam appointed Dr Cairns Minister of Overseas Trade but permitted him effectively to write and execute the Whitlam government's foreign policy, indistinguishable from that of any Communist state—except in the shifts of timing and emphasis, which are necessary in a country which must occasionally go to elections.[29]

Even allowing for editorial hyperbole, a claim such as this was insupportable. Cairns' outspokenness on foreign policy issues did give inspiration to the left, in and outside of the ALP. Perhaps on occasion, though indirectly, it caused more moderate ministers such as Whitlam to graduate their policies. In truth, we need to recall the large amount of pluralism in the ALP, the sense of principled commitment on the part of many of its members and the weak tradition of collective responsibility in Australian Cabinets, as illustrated by Liberal and Country Party ministerial disagreements during non-Labor administration federally, and in state practice as well. Labor's practice of electing Cabinet members prevented Whitlam from picking and choosing (or dismissing) ministers at will. Even had he had the power, he still would have needed to take party caucus feelings and shadings of opinion into account in constructing a government. When Labor came to power, Cairns topped the ministerial election poll in caucus. Indeed, Cairns' 1974 election by caucus to the deputy leadership in preference to Barnard did not dominantly turn on a left–right alignment. It was reaction by left and moderate caucus members alike against what was viewed as Whitlam's overbearing, over-independent manner as Prime Minister and as party leader, on both foreign and domestic issues. Cairns was seen as a partial counterweight to Whitlam, sufficiently independent and wedded to party principles and collegiality. When in 1975, Whitlam removed Cairns from the ministry for the latter's presentation of his involvement in the petrodollar search, Cairns did not submit gracefully. His removal had to be confirmed by caucus and, although he fell short, Cairns polled well in caucus in his bid to gain re-election as a minister. Had he succeeded, Whitlam's political position would have been exceedingly difficult.

An inference to be drawn from what has been said so far is that Cabinet collectively did not meaningfully contribute to external policy decision-making. Without exception, this view was reinforced by every minister interviewed by the author. Lloyd and Reid observed that

> Foreign affairs policy was almost completely outside the scrutiny of Cabinet. Some minor administrative items were referred to Cabinet ... Otherwise, the convention that foreign affairs was the exclusive preserve of the Prime Minister and the Foreign Minister was strictly followed. Cabinet was not even given the regular "tour d'horizon" by the Foreign Minister—a procedure common in other Westminster-emulating Cabinet systems ... Major statements on foreign affairs by the Prime Minister ... were usually heard by Cabinet Ministers for the first time when they were delivered to the Parliament.[30]

The present author feels that while Lloyd and Read correctly downgraded the role of Cabinet, they somewhat overstated the position, especially if defence is included under "foreign affairs". For instance, in mid-1973, Cabinet succeeded in setting the proposed defence vote lower than Barnard would have wished. In 1974, it considered the impending announcement of new defence equipment outlays. In 1975, it dealt with, and by majority vote ruled against, permission to allow a PLO delegation into Australia, and later that year it discussed and approved slightly stronger Australian trade-related measures against South Africa. What stands out is the *circumstances* in which Cabinet reviewed external policy. When Cabinet did discuss the subject, the usual circumstance was that it was taking note of what the Prime Minister and/or the Foreign Minister were doing or were about to do. This was more a ratifying than a "decision-making" function. One minister interviewed by the author said that when Cabinet did address itself to foreign affairs, most of the time was devoted to congratulating or querying a minister on a decision already taken. When on a rare occasion the preferred position of the responsible minister was altered or defeated, one of two considerations applied. One was when an external policy decision entailed the commitment of substantial funds that Cabinet members felt could more appropriately be spent on domestic priorities. This was illustrated by the 1973 decision on defence spending. The other factor involved issues of direct, even acute political concern to the party. This was explicitly illustrated by the January 1975 decision on the PLO. Cabinet was closely divided and in this case the pro-admission position of Whitlam, Willesee and Cameron was overriden. Granted, among Cabinet ministers there were some strong feelings about the substantive merits of allowing or disallowing a PLO visit. But among the majority for disallowing there also was sentiment that, on the eve of Terrigal, already deep *party* divisions on the issue would be further exacerbated if PLO people were allowed to come. Potentially grave political consequences could follow.[31] In any event, a few months later, Whitlam personally decided to allow a visit by a PLO member. This at minimum contravened the spirit of the earlier Cabinet decision; furthermore, as Hawke suggested, it is unlikely that Whitlam's personal decision would have been sustained had Cabinet been consulted and allowed to decide freely. It is also tempting to speculate on whether, had it been consulted and allowed to decide, Cabinet as a whole would have countenanced the Connor and Cairns ventures to obtain huge petrodollar loans. As it was, authorization for these efforts was given without publicity by a very small knot of ministers. When these activities came to light, there was criticism in various quarters, including among Labor ministers and backbenchers, of their secrecy and the highly exclusive nature of authorization, in addition to their substantive dubiousness.

There were understandable reasons for Cabinet's general ineffectiveness in shaping external policy. One was the relative lack of interest among Cabinet members at large, compounded by the unwieldy character of Cabinet itself—twenty-seven members and the lack of a more workable inner ministry. A second, perhaps dominant reason was Whitlam's own personalized style of conducting foreign policy. This not only referred to his indifference about careful Cabinet consultation but to his aversion to facing potentially discordant opinion, especially from those situated more to the left than he stood, or from those who objected to what they thought to be his circumvention of standing party policy.

The Prime Minister gave early signs of his approach to the uses (or non-uses) of Cabinet on the US defence installations issue. When Labor was elected, Whitlam created several Cabinet committees, one of which was on foreign affairs and defence, and which he personally chaired. The committee was to be a sort of screening mechanism for items later sent up to Cabinet at large. The committee met in late February 1973 to consider the draft of a statement on the US facilities, which Barnard, with Whitlam's approval, planned to announce publicly. Party feeling about the facilities, and especially the continuing secrecy that cloaked them, was rising. Contrary to previously set procedures, non-committee members of Cabinet were not advised of the meeting and therefore not given an opportunity to attend. We have seen that when the Barnard proposal came before caucus, there was widespread dissatisfaction. A caucus motion to refer the statement to Cabinet was supported by no less than ten Cabinet ministers, and some other ministers not in attendance would no doubt have backed it as well. The motion was endorsed by a majority of caucus members present, but technically failed. Whitlam was not interested in regarding the motion as having passed at least in spirit, remarking shortly afterwards that "I think there are more pressing matters for Cabinet to consider at this stage, as you'll see."[32]

The Cabinet committee on foreign and defence affairs did examine some matters of importance, but rarely, and essentially, in a forensic capacity. Two years after Labor's election, the author asked a senior minister, who had consistently been a member of the committee, about its work. To his recollection, he said, the committee had met only once, to discuss the North-west Cape renegotiation terms before the Barnard–Schlesinger agreement was executed. He remarked that committee members were very busy people. At any rate, the broad outlines of party policy were generally known, and honoured, by those ministers directly in charge of foreign and defence policy. There is no reason to believe the minister was being evasive in his replies. He could recall only *one* committee meeting. There in fact had been more, but they plainly had not been of sufficient importance to stick in his memory. The minister's explanations hardly added up to a characterization of the committee as a serious element in the external policy decision-making process. It was symptomatic of rising party, and Cabinet, concern about over-exclusive decision-making that, after the Connor and Cairns loan imbroglios, a special Cabinet committee on resources was established.

The external policy decisions taken by Australia's political élites were and are affected by the advice and pressures directed towards them. We will look at three basic sources of input: the bureaucracy, interest groups and the Labor Party itself. In our search for patterns, we will need to be mindful of the considerable difficulties associated with trying to draw causal connections between inputs and policy outcomes.

Formally, advice tendered to a government by officials is just that, namely advisory, but it nonetheless can be decisive in influencing ministerial judgements. It carries the weight of ostensibly non-partisan detachment, combined with high-level professionalism and often persuasive, knowledgeable argument. We will examine the adequacy of information available to external policy officialdom, the temper and commitments of the official/bureaucratic establishment, areas of intra-official tension and the means by which advice is transmitted to ministers. Finally, we will appraise the impact of official advice on decisions and their presentation.

How adequate were the informational and interpretative inputs available to those in the Canberra bureaucracy who counselled the Labor government? Firstly, a note on numbers. Within the Department of Foreign Affairs, personnel rose from 1 100 in 1962 to 2 200 in 1969 to 3 000 in 1972 to 4 700 in late 1974. The expansion was caused in part by the diversification of Australia's foreign policy involvements. For instance, greater attention was paid to the economic features of external policy. In part, it was brought on by an expansion of overseas missions and/or the scope of work performed within overseas establishments. Labor's considerable expansion of overseas missions placed some strain on adequate staffing of overseas posts and in some cases meant that only very small missions could be dispatched, or that heads of mission might need to carry double accreditation. Hence the Ambassador to China was also accredited to North Korea and the Ambassador to Sweden was additionally accredited to Finland and Norway. Indeed, personnel requirements for overseas postings continued to raise misgivings about the depletion of the home establishment (less than a quarter of all Foreign Affairs personnel) and its capacity to perform its own work.

The quality of Foreign Affairs officers posted overseas was generally high, reflecting the highly selective procedures used for recruiting people into the department. There were some problems. For example, while there was considerable Chinese language capability among those posted to Peking (including Ambassador FitzGerald), there was a shortage of Japanese language competence within the mission in Tokyo. Also, because of the rapid expansion of the department in the late 1960s and beyond, there was some shortage of experienced officers in the middle and upper ranges. The Labor government appointed some of the very best people available as heads of mission in the most important postings. This was illustrated by Richard Woolcott in Jakarta, K. C. O. Shann in Tokyo, Sir Patrick Shaw in Washington, Sir James Plimsoll in Moscow and Stephen FitzGerald in Peking.

We are led to ask to what extent the Labor government may have reached beyond the career Foreign Affairs service for diplomatic head of mission appointments. L–CP governments had made some political ambassadorial and high commissioner appointments. When Labor entered office, former Liberal ministers were serving as heads of missions in London, Tokyo and Wellington. All sooner or later stepped down, but were not pushed out by Labor. Perhaps the most successful of these Liberal appointees was Dame Annabelle Rankin, High Commissioner to New Zealand. It was under Labor, incidentally, that Australia acquired its first non-political, female head of mission— Ruth Dobson, appointed to Copenhagen. Labor made its own appointments from outside the career foreign service. The most blatant was Gair's, to Dublin. It was wholly political in inspiration. Gair lacked basic experience for an ambassadorial position. He prematurely replaced a highly respected career ambassador. Once on the job, his style and his overall performance left something to be desired. Sir Alexander Downer's replacement in London was a Labor politician, J. I. Armstrong. This was a patronage appointment, though that step was in keeping with long-standing Australian practice. Armstrong's replacement, Sir John Bunting, did not originate in Foreign Affairs. He was, however, an experienced and very senior public servant. Barnard's appointment to Stockholm was of course that of a non-career man, and a political reward. But it was not possible to quarrel with Barnard's qualifications, acquired in the Defence portfolio. Nor could there be much quarrel on these grounds with the appointment to New Delhi of the former academic and highly regarded journalist Bruce Grant. Indeed, despite many misgivings at the time within the Department of Foreign Affairs hierarchy, it was hard to fault the FitzGerald appointment. FitzGerald had at one time been an officer in the department. He was a respected academic Sinologist with an excellent grasp of Chinese. He had been to China with the Whitlam

party in 1971. Quite rightly, Whitlam believed that the inaugural appointment to Peking was something special: not just a competent
person was needed, but one whose thinking about China Whitlam
knew and generally shared. In late 1974, the government and the
Foreign Affairs Department agreed that, henceforth, much more
emphasis would be placed on the appointment of career officers as
consuls and consuls-general.[33]

Under the ALP, efforts were carried forward to widen the ambit of
Australia's own independently acquired sources of information and
assessment. Elaborate contacts with foreign, and especially American,
intelligence services were maintained, both in Australia and overseas,
and the flow of intelligence data from allied nations did not slacken.
Australia had for some time enjoyed a considerable communications
interception and decoding capability. When the DSD detachment was
removed from Singapore, it was not disbanded but rehoused in
Australia. ASIS, despite the extreme secretiveness surrounding it, had
always been a small-scale operation, over whose value Australian
professionals themselves disagreed. JIO was an intelligence-analysis
rather than an intelligence-gathering agency. It was administratively
under Defence, but successively had had senior Foreign Affairs officers as directors. It co-ordinated efforts of other (such as service-
based) intelligence agencies and reported its assessments to various
interested line departments and to ministers. In the present context,
we need to point out that JIO's staff of some 400 was varied. It included service as well as civilian personnel, a score of economists and
an occasional academic on secondment to it. Not only through intelligence channels but through increased and more effectively used,
regular overseas-posted personnel, Australia under Labor undertook
to widen its own independent sources of information. This was
designed to provide additional and if necessary corrective perspectives on what for so long had been conspicuous reliance on foreign,
and especially US and British, inputs. It also, as the government admitted, had a political/ideological component: to compensate for
what were felt to have been distorting infatuations with cold-war
preconceptions of the international order.[34] In fact, Australia continued to be in a position to influence other governments. Part of this
was in sharing its own data and assessments with friends and allies.
Part of it was through influences absorbed by South-East Asian,
Pacific, African and Caribbean diplomatic trainees. Part of it was
through dealings with foreign service officers of other countries,
notably New Zealanders, on secondment to Foreign Affairs in Canberra. All of this, of course, was apart from the ordinary network of official and political-level contacts in Australia and abroad.

It is equally helpful to look inside the major external affairs-related departments. Labor inherited a corps of public servants, most of whom had never known any political master save L–CP governments. The adjustment to a new Labor government was, however, achieved without undue difficulty. Some contingency plans had been drawn up before December 1972, to implement policies expected of a Labor government. For instance, the Defence Department made preparations for the doing away with conscription. When the initial two-man Whitlam–Barnard government made a host of decisions, Defence and Foreign Affairs proved helpfully responsive. Even before Labor came on, there had been considerable sentiment in Foreign Affairs that some foreign policy reorientations, such as recognition of China, were very much overdue. Collectively, the Department of Foreign Affairs under Labor could probably be best characterized as reasonably attuned to a Whitlam–Willesee reformist approach, but scornful of over-anxious or "radical" policies. One informant, while agreeing that the department's adjustment to the transition of government was generally carried off well, illustrated how traces of older habits die hard. His illustration was that departmental submissions for some time continued to speak in such terms as "China is no longer aggressive," rather than simply, "China is not aggressive." The department in many ways remained very well-disposed towards the United States and was eager that relations between the two countries not be allowed to suffer from untoward incidents.[35]

Within Defence, there also was considerable feeling about staying close to the US alliance, for example in keeping ANZUS viable and protecting the integrity of American defence facilities and generally about avoiding abrasive behaviour towards Washington.[36] The "forward defence" doctrine of Labor's predecessors had lost very considerable ground by 1975 and insinuations of a split on this subject between civilians and uniformed officers were seriously exaggerated. The strategic assessment prepared in the department in 1973 was somewhat more guarded in dealing with foreseeable threats to Australia than the tone of Barnard's speeches suggested, but the assessment had taken into account the new government's known predispositions about security issues. It is not true that Barnard had literally misrepresented the findings contained in the assessment. The preparation of the 1975 strategic assessment did occasion a measure of heartburn within the department. Independent checking broadly substantiated one commentator's allegations that Tange applied some influence to insure that the new report continue to project fairly favourable security conditions over a long span of years.[37] Much of the opinion within Defence was not, however, at all satisfied with the level of government commitment to authorized service personnel or with equipment, especially if the military had to regear to a continental defence doctrine. Morrison's 1975–76 budget promises of new capital equipment programmes were received as a welcome improvement.

Within major departments, the secretaries were men of strong will, but in general closely attached to their ministers. In Minerals and Energy, Sir Lenox Hewitt became intimately associated with Connor's prescriptions about foreign investment, mineral price negotiations, and government's role in resource search and exploitation, and so on. In Defence, Tange carried over from pre-Labor days. Especially on the reorganization of the department, he became an early and vigorous advocate of Barnard's objectives. Within his department, he was known for his definite, assertive manner. After Barnard stepped down in mid-1975, there was speculation that Tange and the new minister, Morrison, might not be able to get on especially well. On most indications, however, such anxieties seemed unfounded.

Renouf's appointment to Foreign Affairs was rather special. Sir Keith Waller's retirement a year after Labor took office had been entirely normal and voluntary. Renouf was a senior diplomat, personally selected for the job by Whitlam. Renouf was attractive because he suited Whitlam's notion that a more free-wheeling atmosphere was needed. Renouf had spent most of his career outside Canberra. He had executed assignments well, such as negotiating the recognition of Peking, and was known as a good "ideas" man. But it is not true that Renouf was chosen because he was thought to be some sort of apologist for Labor's preferred policies. The author understands that a generally favourable article he published on Evatt early in 1973 may actually have been a minus in Whitlam's eyes, since the Prime Minister genuinely desired an open-minded Foreign Affairs secretary.[38]

Once in charge, Renouf acquired a reputation for outspokenness. As we will see, he was not averse to chastizing other departments. He submitted himself to public interviews. He declared that Labor had properly freed itself of outworn stereotypes and that, if returned to office, the L–CP would probably retain 90 per cent of what Labor had done in foreign policy.[39] In April 1975, he publicly rebuked the opposition for holding to antiquated cold-war views and for having alleged that Australia under Labor had not done enough in playing a constructive role in the closing phases of the Vietnamese conflict. Fraser, in turn, rebuked Renouf for having violated canons of public service impartiality.

Renouf's justification of his remarks could, in context, be attributed to three factors: his own penchant for outspokenness, officially relaxed rules governing public servant utterances and the fact that he was restating the government's own known position, not a conflicting one. At all events, Renouf's criticism of the opposition was believed to enjoy wide support within Foreign Affairs.[40] Renouf's conception of a departmental secretary's role buttressed his candour. He said he believed in avoiding partisanship, but not political awareness. There was a danger that public servants could raise objectivity to a dogma and in so doing sacrifice ultimate effectiveness: "the Permanent Head must be capable of giving advice to his Minister and to the Government of a kind which demonstrates his recognition and appreciation of the political realities."[41]

Renouf in other ways demonstrated a flair for being something of a mover and a shaker. While he felt that lateral recruitment into the department was generally unwise, he favoured the introduction of some specialists in fields such as economics and law. This was in keeping with his view that the department should devote more attention to functional themes such as international and regional organizations, international economics and legal questions arising out of the law of the sea and other concerns. The department's structure was revamped to provide more functionally oriented divisions. A pair of academics and a journalist were brought in on secondment and business figures were desired as well. Young career officers were sent overseas on academic study-leave. The department's executive secretariat, whose origins lay in the L–CP period, was gingered up. Lying outside the normal structure, it was to provide forward planning, gadfly writing and rapid movement to assist individual sections with urgent problems.[42]

Renouf's outspokenness, and his drive to envigourate his department, leads us to consider interdepartmental relations. It is unexceptional to bureaucratic establishments that different departments, with different traditions, subject emphases and political clienteles, should at times hold differing perspectives, and indeed offer conflicting advice to ministers. This can be interpreted as desirable in the important sense that a kind of creative tension occurs, and the range of policy options available to governments will have been more critically assessed and enriched.

Simply because of its generality of concerns about Australia's overseas interests, it is not surprising that on a number of occasions Foreign Affairs should have urged a "bigger view" orientation than did more specialized departments. While not urging strong economic measures against South Africa, Foreign Affairs nonetheless did not, unlike Overseas Trade while Cairns was its minister, focus its thinking on Australia's profitable commercial ties with South Africa. Wherein Manufacturing Industry was eager to ply the Nomad on the international market, Foreign Affairs was more careful about sales to governments that could employ the aircraft for counter-guerrilla or sensitive war-theatre roles. Although it apparently did not file a formal submission on the subject, Defence in late 1974 and early 1975 seemed especially uneasy about the security implications of Portuguese Timor's political evolution. Foreign Affairs at first was more concerned about repercussions for the region and Australia's diplomatic image. Hence it was displeased when Whitlam originally appeared to place Timor's association with Indonesia ahead of the self-determination requirement and concentrated on pulling him back from his overstated, pro-Indonesian position. Increasingly, however, at least in its private counsel to the government, Foreign Affairs became emphatic about its preference for an Indonesian solution to the problem.

In some policy areas, Foreign Affairs' differences with other departments, or agencies, had jurisdictional as well as substantive overtones. We are particularly reminded of two conflict points, immigration and resource management. Foreign Affairs felt that Immigration (later Labour and Immigration) personnel were cautious, stuffy and above all at fault in providing proper opportunity for non-European migration to Australia. This was seen as flaunting the government's own anti-racialist commitments, we well as undermining Australia's credibility abroad, especially in Afro–Asia. In other words, this was seen as a *foreign policy* as much as an immigration issue. Foreign Affairs therefore wished to take over most visa-issuing responsibilities. Labour and Immigration resisted. It was willing to correct malpractices but not to relinquish its administrative prerogatives. An interdepartmental committee (IDC) tried, but failed, to resolve the dispute. The matter then went up to the Public Service Board, and eventually to Whitlam. Foreign Affairs was given control over passports. Labour and Immigration was to retain visa control, but a written agreement stipulated that in time it was to lose some of this to Foreign Affairs.[43]

The dispute over the content and management of resource policy was more critical. It involved a clash between Renouf, Connor and Hewitt of a quite fundamental character. Foreign Affairs objected to the Minerals and Energy approach on three grounds. There were substantive, foreign economic and diplomatic objections to what was seen as excessive economic nationalism. There was anxiety over the jostling of foreign government sensibilities by the Connor style of doing business. There was an allegedly over-independent, even secretive Connor and Hewitt style. This, it was said, bred disorganization and confusion and made it impossible for Foreign Affairs to know, and to explain to others, what really was happening in resource policy; Australia could not afford two resource policies. The unpublicized, abortive Connor quest for billions in petrodollar loans exacerbated conditions and brought Treasury into increased conflict with Minerals and Energy. One academic critic's illustration of problems included the following: Minerals and Energy's failure to consult Foreign Affairs on a decision not to allow Australia to participate in certain Organization for Economic Co-operation and Development energy deliberations; Minerals and Energy's refusal to supply adequate briefing materials to Cairns and Wriedt before their 1975 journey to the Middle East; Minerals and Energy's obstinacy in providing information on uranium and nuclear energy questions to JIO.[44] It is difficult to exaggerate the state of tension that existed between Foreign Affairs and Minerals and Energy. At one point, Renouf's sharply critical remarks of Connor over his uranium policy had to be papered over by a nominal apology. Key departments in Canberra were reacting not only in sorrow but in barely disguised anger. Communications between Foreign Affairs and Minerals and Energy for a time were virtually at a standstill. While Whitlam largely came around to the Renouf–Foreign Affairs version of much of resource policy, Connor for some time enjoyed a firm base. Differing departmental views in this area resulted less in creative tension than in mess. The merits of the positions aside, the spectacle of two departments and often separate ministers saying and doing different things about resource policy did Australia's interests little good.[45]

Was the system capable of accommodating sharply drawn interdepartmental disputes? To some extent, structural reform of interdepartmental relations was unnecessary, or simply beyond reasonable reach. For instance, because it had for so long been nearly moribund, the external relations and defence division of the Department of the Prime Minister and Cabinet did not have to be taken into serious account as a competitive force. When a new Secretary was brought in to the Prime Minister's Department, personal assurance was given to Foreign Affairs that no usurpation of its functions would take place. This pledge was generally honoured. However, when in 1975, the government announced its intention to create an Australia–Japan Foundation, in the face of apparently continuing misgivings within Foreign Affairs, administrative responsibility for it was lodged in the Prime Minister's Department, not Foreign Affairs itself. Although not a department, JIO provided inputs into the system, both to regular departments and at times directly to ministers. The prevailing view in Foreign Affairs of JIO's contributions was somewhere between neutral and mildly negative. JIO was thought to be a bit too abstract, insufficiently aimed at real and pressing concerns. It was even remarked in Foreign Affairs that material that it originally passed to JIO would sometimes return only slightly retouched by JIO. In other words, Foreign Affairs felt that in many respects *it* was best placed to prepare assessments in the form it liked them. Among other economically related departments, JIO was not taken very seriously, and even held suspect, because of its affiliation with the Department of Defence. Foreign Affairs was also displeased with the over-independent position enjoyed by ASIS over which it—Foreign Affairs—maintained nominal responsibility. Little structural tinkering was likely to disabuse one section of the bureaucratic establishment of biases about others.

A familiar mechanism for bringing departments together and for evolving collective viewpoints was the interdepartmental committee, or IDC. IDCs were generally convened on an *ad hoc* basis, the principal exception in the external area being the standing IDC on Japan, created in 1970. An IDC concept was no panacea for interdepartmental problems. One witness before the Royal Commission on Australian Government Administration recounted Foreign Affairs' efforts in early 1974 to establish a foreign economic policy committee to help co-ordinate and implement government policy in this realm. It was to draw expertise from Overseas Trade, Minerals and Energy, and Treasury. "Regrettably [these] other departments and their ministers saw this as a takeover bid and refused to co-operate.[46] Testimony before the Royal Commission by Hewitt and Renouf mirrored the gulf separating their reactions to IDCs. Hewitt took exception to the way in which some departments, such as Foreign Affairs, used IDCs to intrude on the prerogatives of others. Renouf took exception to the way in which IDCs produced reports that simply reflected the lowest common denominator of agreement.[47] Members of various departments would have agreed with Renouf's conclusion that interdepartmental dialogue was handicapped "by entrenched attitudes which are ... out of date and which create a situation tending to weaken the Government's effectiveness".[48]

Despite feeling that IDCs had only limited value, Renouf argued that Foreign Affairs should at least have the right to convene, chair and service IDCs whenever a need to co-ordinate policies with a major foreign affairs content arose. He also wanted Foreign Affairs to be consulted when any IDC within the bureaucracy was considering a subject with some international implications. His most controversial proposal was that Foreign Affairs be given the *central* role of co-ordinating and controlling Australia's foreign relations, a theme spelled out in some detail in his department's submission to the Royal Commission on Australian Government and Administration.[49] As expected, this proposal was widely scorned in other departments, on grounds of its lack of necessity, its impracticality, or because it was seen as unvarnished aggrandizement by Foreign Affairs. By the second half of 1975, however, Foreign Affairs could take comfort from a

few developments. A special Cabinet committee on resources was established. While this was a ministerial rather than an official body, its
function of co-ordinating priorities in the minerals and energy area
was in part designed to provide an open channel for departmental inputs, among the more important being from Foreign Affairs.[50]
Secondly, displeasure in ministerial circles with Hewitt's handling of
Minerals and Energy's relations with other departments, and other
considerations, may have prompted his replacement as Secretary by a
person of superior consensual skills, James Scully, previously Deputy
Secretary of Overseas Trade.

We now examine the links between official sources of advice and
political ministers. There is no cut-and-dried model of how and when
official advice was brought to ministerial attention. In some instances, and especially in Labor's earlier months, governmental decisions were taken without a prior departmental input. For instance,
there was no submission from Defence before the combat-troop pul-
lout from Singapore was announced. On those occasions when there
were advisory inputs, they did not necessarily entail a formal brief or
submission, but perhaps only conversation between a minister and
the departmental secretary. Officially prepared papers supplied to
ministers could vary from what essentially were inventories of the
variables and the pros and cons related to particular policy options to
overview assessments of some wider topic, such as JIO contributed
from time to time, or the strategic basis reports. At one time, Foreign
Affairs considered issuing "green papers", basically informal think-
pieces about what policies *might* be considered and why. This was rejected by Willesee, on grounds that it would be a breach of what
otherwise would be confidential advice. It could lead to misunderstandings over the differences between speculations about what
might be policy and what policy was actually becoming or actually
was.[51]

The initiative for providing advisory inputs at times lay with a
department or one of its senior members, and at times was at the request of ministers. Examples of the former practice were the idea that
Australia seek observer status at conferences of non-aligned nations,
the idea for putting forward Willesee's candidacy for the Presidency
of the UN General Assembly and the idea that Whitlam's Vietnam·
message to Nixon include mention of organizing Indonesia and Japan
to oppose American bombing.

The manner in which Foreign Affairs submissions were channelled
was itself instructive, since it underscored the department's recognition of Whitlam's ongoing interest and role in foreign affairs. After
Willesee became Foreign Minister, his office received all Foreign Affairs submissions. On key matters, the submission was also sent to

Whitlam, or the submission to Willesee contained a note suggesting that Whitlam be kept advised, or Whitlam's personal advisers were informally briefed on what was going to Willesee. Moreover, Foreign Affairs would occasionally "store up" papers for Whitlam, anticipating those periods when he, in Willesee's absence, would serve as acting Foreign Minister. Another form of Foreign Affairs "sensitivity" related to its interest in the political repercussions of external policy movements. Prior to mid-1974, the typical form of Foreign Affairs advice to ministers disregarded the domestic political dimension, though Waller had at one time apparently undertaken some minor experimentation. In any event, the Baltic states decision in mid-1974, its substantive value aside, imposed serious political embarrassment on the government. After that, Foreign Affairs concluded that while Willesee and Whitlam had their own sources of political advice, the department would on its part do a bit more in this area. Formal submissions still essentially overlooked political calculations, but the department took on some informal responsibility for flagging politically sensitive issues *vis-à-vis* ministers or their aides.

Ministers did not necessarily receive external policy advice from only one department or agency, or indeed solely from public servants as such. Two points in particular should be made. One is that Foreign Affairs enjoyed a certain procedurally institutionalized increment of influence with Whitlam not shared by other substantive departments. Prior to question time in the House, Whitlam underwent briefings. Foreign Affairs handled foreign policy subjects and the Prime Minister's Department all other subjects.

Secondly, we need to notice the role of personal ministerial advisers serving with the Prime Minister, the Foreign Minister and the Defence Minister. As a group, these aides were bright, young and politically alert, often coming from backgrounds in departments such as Foreign Affairs and Defence. In part, they were gatekeepers, placed between the departments and their respective ministers. They would read and screen departmental submissions for their ministers, provide their own comments to ministers and otherwise perform various facilitating and liaison tasks. The author's inquiries indicated that within departments, these aides were not resented for shielding ministers from departmental advice, nor accused of trying to play the role of grey eminences. There was some departmental feeling that personal advisers could, however, have been more effective in supplying clearer feedback to departments. At any rate, with perhaps one or two individual adviser exceptions, personal aides as a group did not actually shape external policy outputs. Advisers drafted speeches, alerted ministers to possible inconsistencies between professed goals and pending policy movements and offered advice as such, but on specifics rather than on general policy. Their concern with anticipating the party political or electoral implications of external policy appeared to have been sporadic. Occasionally, after a policy step had been taken (e.g. the Baltic states) or when a messy situation was in progress (e.g. Ermolenko), some of them became involved in trying to limit adverse public opinion fall-out. We saw earlier that, when a personal adviser alerted him to what was happening, Whitlam cancelled Australia's participation in a forthcoming SEATO naval exercise, since some broad diplomatic considerations were at stake. Against Foreign Affairs advice, Whitlam, in 1973, met with Cambodian Prince Sihanouk in Peking. His principal adviser, Peter Wilenski, had urged him to have the meeting. But so had Ambassador FitzGerald, and it is unlikely that Whitlam would have moved against the advice of both the department and FitzGerald, apart from what Wilenski might have recommended.

Finally, we need to raise the difficult question of actual official influence on external policy outputs and presentation. Ministers undertake policies for many reasons, which often cannot be isolated one from another. They react to official advice, but that advice, as we have emphasized, is not always consistent. They are susceptible to media criticism, to interest group appeals, to pressures from within their party, to the entreaties of fellow ministers and to electoral considerations. They approach decision-making choices with particular sets of predispositions. They not only make rational, so-called cost-benefit calculations, but are also susceptible to intuitive and gut-reaction judgements.

It is unexceptional that Labor ministers, like L–CP ministers before them and ministers in other political systems, over time both accepted and rejected official advice. Whitlam's guiding views on resource diplomacy were reinforced by Foreign Affairs advice. Whitlam and Willesee, in 1974 and early 1975, agreed with Foreign Affairs advice not to recognize the PRG. Whitlam and Barnard accepted the Defence and JIO view that the integrity of American defence installations should be preserved. Whitlam and Willesee followed Foreign Affairs' thinking favouring admission of a PLO delegation, but were overriden by Cabinet, and in this sense departmental advice at least temporarily was not translated into policy. When in September 1974, Whitlam left the distinct impression with the Indonesians that Australia would prefer that East Timor come under their aegis, he apparently went against JIO warnings, or perhaps those warnings had not reached him. At all events, he then gradually, in line with Foreign Affairs advice, softened his public position. Then, again with Foreign Affairs encouragement, his position became more firmly committed to countenancing an Indonesian takeover.

Whitlam, in 1973, rejected an IDC recommendation against undertaking a treaty with Japan. The following year, he was entirely dissatisfied with a "no recommendation" Foreign Affairs submission on South Africa's membership in the United Nations and made up his own mind—to change Australia's traditional posture.

The foregoing listing is obviously only illustrative, and no pretence of comprehensive knowledge of the character of departmental advice, ministerially accepted or rejected, is being made. All the same, it may be helpful to conjecture about patterns, if any. Overall, key ministers and their departments were generally operating on similar frequencies and ministers and their departmental secretaries were generally on close terms—Whitlam/Willesee and Renouf, Barnard and Tange, Connor and Hewitt. This general harmony was partially attributable to recognition within these departments of what at large a new Labor government, or its ministers, were disposed towards. The major contours of Labor's external policy objectives were not resisted, nor were patently unacceptable major foreign policy options pressed upon ministers. In terms of tone, both Foreign Affairs and Defence were prepared to adapt to changes from earlier L–CP practices, but the emphasis was on *adaptiveness* rather than a wish for radical turnabouts. Both departments, we have seen, continued to be closely attached to the American connection and valued their contacts with American officials.

On balance, perhaps Barnard was more susceptible to Tange's advice than Whitlam and Willesee were to Renouf's, but this in part may be because there were more, and more varied, substantive "foreign policy" than "defence' issues to be tackled. Others would say that Barnard was relatively susceptible to his department because he was easier to cultivate than were Whitlam or Willesee. One criticism, quickly raised on the left of the ALP early in the government's life, was—in Hartley's words—that Tange was running Australia's defence policy and Barnard "in a sense is too much a client of the Defence Department".[52] In another context, argument was made that Defence was able to drag its feet with impunity in producing appropriate implementing proposals following on the continental defence doctrine embodied in the 1973 strategic basis assessment. From this example and others, one academic commentator concluded that "By the end of Mr Barnard's tenure, Sir Arthur's [Tange's] dominance was absolute."[53] Another academic observer, writing from a quite different vantage-point, faulted the proposed defence reorganization scheme for divorcing the Defence Minister from ongoing intradepartmental policy debates. The reorganization plan, essentially put together in the department and endorsed by Barnard, was interpreted as an admission of ministerial weakness.[54] At least by inference, imputations of

Barnard's "weakness" *vis-à-vis* the Defence Department would not be inconsistent with an impression that Barnard, more than Whitlam or Willesee, was reliant on personal aide advice.

Analytically, the bureaucracy could be defined as a source or sources of interest expression impinging on the decision-making process. We turn now to essentially non-institutionalized but overt sources of interest expression. The familiar view is that group interests in Australia have had relatively little impact on external policy outputs. The executive enjoyed considerable autonomy in foreign affairs. Party discipline in Parliament was cohesive. The public ascribed relatively low salience to external affairs. On particular issues, the activity of a particular group interest would often be countervailed by another group seeking different outcomes. The influence of some groups was circumscribed by the image in which they had been painted by their detractors—cranks, fanatics, troglodytes, subversives, and the like.[55]

With Labor in office, the level of public and specialized group interest in external affairs was both stimulated and constrained. The previous extended debate over Vietnam, conscription and threats to Australia's security had spurred public consciousness, organized protest and counter-argument. However, the removal of Vietnam and conscription as deeply contentious issues, and government claims that threats to Australia were unlikely, could be interpreted as depressants of interest and of controversy. But Labor prided itself on being an activist and reformist government and thereby kindled interest in the new policy directions it undertook. As a government representing a party with broad, idealistic and often organizationally prescribed objectives and policies, it laid itself open to especially close scrutiny by those who wished to insure that ALP commitments were being honoured. We will wish to identify some major categories of interest groups, to appraise their methods and to speculate on their impact on external policy outputs and presentation.

We first glance at ethnic groups as a source of group expression. Overall, "ethnic" politics have not been a significant foreign policy factor in Australia. This had been due to Australia's relative homogeneity, even after the influx of non-Anglo-Saxon migrants after the Second World War, and to the fact that most external issues do not directly lend themselves to ethnic controversy as such. Under Labor, however, there were two major exceptions to this rule and perhaps were harbingers of more conspicuous ethnic overtones in the country's external policy debate.

One instance related to the government's *de jure* recognition of Soviet sovereignty over the Baltic states. Prior to the decision, spokesmen of the ethnic Baltic community tried to dissuade Whitlam from any such step, and they thought they had succeeded. When the admission of the step came, the Baltic community was shocked and galvanized into action. The decision was believed wrong on its merits and to have been a repudiation of promises given. The incensed Baltic community condemned the decision in newspaper advertisements, parliamentarians were petitioned and protest marches and demonstrations were staged.[56] When in New York later in 1974, Whitlam was picketed by Americans of Baltic extraction who had taken cues from their Australian brethren. The government did not change its policy. Indeed, the policy was virtually beyond reach, since the complaints were lodged after the fact. But the Baltic protest was not entirely without effect. There were about 25 000 Latvians, mostly migrants, in Australia, and a smaller number of Lithuanians and Estonians. That was small as an electoral bloc, and most who were enfranchised were L–CP voters anyway. But there is evidence that many Australians of Baltic origin then moved a step beyond being L–CP-voting supporters, to volunteering themselves as workers for the L–CP cause. Moreover, the after-the-fact Baltic agitation contributed to intra-Labor criticism of Whitlam. The policy was wrong, being a denial of principles of self-determination, and it had been taken in such a private, even secretive way. This riled party members who believed in open and collective government. Indirectly, the strenuous Baltic community protest probably stimulated the ALP, as a party, to take more of its own initiatives to anticipate and if possible influence future government policy decisions, such as on Portuguese Timor, PRG recognition and the Middle East. Within the Department of Foreign Affairs, as we noticed, political fall-out from the Baltic states decision encouraged more attention to alerting ministers of potential political ramifications of foreign policy decisions.

The other ethnic group seriously offended by Labor government policies was Australian Jews. The Australian Jewish community numbers about 75 000. Typically, Jews have voted Labor. But in the present instance, most were offended by what they thought was Labor's uneven-handed approach to Middle Eastern affairs generally, and then, more specifically, they opposed the entry of PLO spokesmen into Australia. Their leadership sought, and received, interviews with Whitlam. Like the Baltic people, they used advertisements and letters to newspapers to explain their position. Their ability to keep their position publicly visible and to gather non-Jewish supporters was considerable. Unlike the Baltic issue, the Middle Eastern question was long-term and multifaceted. Middle Eastern developments were quite important to Australia's interests, while the Baltic states were marginal. The Middle East issue also had considerable emotive content, in view of the Jews' plight under the Nazis and the vision of

Israel attempting to survive as a Jewish homeland state amidst
hostile Arab neighbours. There were some articulate Jews within the
ALP, including in Parliament. There were many non-Jews in the
party, Hawke among the most notable, who were vociferously pro-
Israeli. It therefore was not difficult for Australian Jews to enlist non-
Jews as allies in substantial lobbying efforts. For instance, an
Australian Council of Concern was formed by prominent Australians
to promote the cause of Jews in Arab countries. Massive advertisements with captions such as "Keep the P.L.O. Terrorists Out" were
purchased, and often included a remarkable array of signatories who
on most foreign policy issues were deeply divided among
themselves.[57] A number of ALP caucus members associated
themselves with the Friends of Israel group.

In the 1974 election, Labor lost some of the money traditionally
donated to it by the Jewish community, but lost relatively few Jewish
votes. The Jewish campaign on behalf of particular policy orientations was at best partially successful. The government's "even-
handed" Middle Eastern diplomacy was not changed and the original
ban on PLO visitors was quickly rescinded. But, especially in the way
Jewish publicity fortified the resolve of ALP members who were
positively disposed, there were effects. Relatedly, added incentive was
given to the government to follow and to explain at considerable
length policies that it hoped would not be misconstrued as leaning
against Israel. It is arguable that the very close January 1975 Cabinet
decision not to invite a PLO delegation—a most rare manifestation of
collective Cabinet decision-making—may well have been tilted by the
Jewish community's own efforts.

Another category of group expression related to the exposition of
humanitarian interests and causes. Some of these manifestations
were of long standing and had counterparts in a number of other
countires; for example, campaigns designed to encourage government
efforts towards relief of world hunger. Some were more explicitly
oriented towards particular aspects of Australian external policy. Occasionally, church and lay groups threw themselves into campaigns to
readjust policies regarded as morally untenable. Here we can particularly mention the efforts of the Australian Council of Churches
and the Roman Catholic Church's Justice and Peace Commission to
attack racialism in South Africa and Rhodesia. Obviously, numbers of
individual Protestant and Catholic laymen and clergymen either
cared little about this issue or took a different programmatic position.
To some extent, religiously based bodies such as these did common
cause with secular, even politically radical groups that also wished for
more vigorous Australian action, such as cutting air services, discon-
tinuing all trade-commission activities and even shutting off trade

with South Africa. It was extremely difficult for the government to disregard lobbying efforts by church-based bodies. Their patina of respectability made it hard to dismiss them as cranky malcontents. A number of clerics had cut their political teeth in the earlier Vietnam and conscription resistance movements, issues on which their views had coincided with those of the Labor Party. By attacking immorality and racialism, the church bodies could figuratively be said to have been on the side of the angels, and also on the side of ALP idealism, in these matters. Their representations were heard, and their campaign, together with that of lay-group lobbies, helped, by steps, to move the government towards tightening its posture, as for instance expressed by Willesee's letter of advice to Australian companies operating in South Africa, curtailment of trade-commissioner services in South Africa and the imposition of closer surveillance of travel agency and airline behaviour regarding the facilitation of travel to Rhodesia.[58]

We now consider the radical movement as an interest category in its own right. As we suggested earlier, the movement was heterogeneous in membership, issue emphasis and tactics. Some of its principal leadership elements were concerned that followers tended to be of two types: old-line veteran radicals, many over fifty years of age, and young people, often persons at universities or some somewhat older who had worked in Vietnam moratorium campaigns and the like. *Rapport* between these two generational groups was at times fragile and it was admitted that the disappearance of really emotional controversies such as Vietnam and conscription made it more difficult to keep people consistently interested in peace and reform causes. To counteract such problems, efforts were launched to promote involvement of people in radical movement causes through locally based community mechanisms. Effort was also made to enhance co-ordination among separate radical organizations through what was named the National Peace Liaison Committee and to give radical action more focus. Among targets selected were under-development, political and social liberation, anti-racialism and the struggle against the arms race.[59]

A composite analysis of radical/peace movement influence on Labor policy needs to take several ingredients into account. Perhaps the most significant is that the causes or policies espoused by the movement were being directed at a party of government that, overall, was considerably more attracted to reformist objectives than the L–CP had been. There is no evidence that L–CP government policies on Vietnam had been attenuated by the protest movement. If anything, L–CP governments exploited the movement by characterizing it as simplistic and unpatriotic. They tried to win political capital by linking it with the ALP, especially when demonstrations, and con-frontations with the authorities, were involved. During Labor's term in office, a number of party figures, both organizational and parliamentary, were not only sympathetic to the radical movement but associated themselves with it in one form or another. Cairns, for one, was convenor of the National Peace Liaison Committee and became President of CIDC. Other things being equal, the protest/radical movement's influence on a Labor government was predictably greater than over L–CP governments.

The radical movement was not, moreover, really isolated in its advocacy of various causes. For instance, its complaints against continuing links with South Africa were paralleled within some church groups that otherwise were not associated with most of the familiar radical causes. The radical movement's advocacy of self-determination in Portuguese Timor was, albeit from a different perspective, shared by a host of people on both sides of Parliament and within the community. In addition, on some controversies, such as opposition to established American defence facilities in Australia, or to the construction of an Omega station, a body of serious academic and technical literature served to buttress the movement's arguments.

The radical movement, or at least some of its adherents acting independently, resorted to a wide range of tactics—some crude, some highly stylized and sophisticated. Shortage of funds and an underlying suspicion of conventional media outlets limited large-scale advertising publicity. But the general public, and occasional political élite viewers, could not, for instance, escape graffiti work. The leadership of the Australian Union of Students promoted various protest causes and, as we noticed earlier, the content of university student newspapers was disproportionately left/radical in orientation. There were occasional street demonstrations, marches and the May 1974 pilgrimage from eastern states to the North-West-Cape signal-station. Some radical group members opted for more colourful action, such as public burnings of American flags and the display of Eureka flags as a symbol of revolt. We saw earlier that one esoteric faction, centred on South Australia, was suspected of having fomented industrial sabotage within foreign-owned plants. On balance, the publicity campaigns of the movement probably carried some substantive effect, beyond inspiring believers and outraging disbelievers. Some converts were won to the side of programmes or causes being advocated, for instance among tertiary students, but even there mass student opinion was not especially tractable and from roughly mid-1974 onwards, a more explicit, conservative impulse began to coalesce at universities and colleges of advanced education. In 1974, AUS-sponsored resolutions that denounced Israel and endorsed the Palestinian cause were widely repudiated in campus referenda.[60] Still, it was on an AUS invitation of persons from the General Union of Palestinian Students that, in 1975, PLO-related persons first began to visit Australia.

More specifically, however, what of policy impacts? The radical movement's campaigns may have carried effects in two ways. Much of the promotion was not just in terms of being for or against particular policies, but was unhesitatingly critical of the Whitlam government for its alleged betrayal of progressive principles and of authoritative party policy itself. The message was heard in party circles and for some party members served to reinforce their criticism of the government line. Relatedly, the radical movement undertook some successful lobbying among ALP parliamentarians. On Vietnamese issues, and especially relative to Australia's attitude towards the PRG, it helped to bring Labor parliamentarians together and presented them with considerable data and arguments. Recent visitors to PRG-controlled areas of South Vietnam made themselves available. A petition supporting a number of PRG proposals for settlement in Vietnam and attacking the Thieu régime was eventually signed by a clear majority of caucus members. This in turn helped to inspire ALP conference delegates at Terrigal to support a resolution that urged diplomatic recognition of the PRG. We recall that such a resolution actually passed, but in the course of procedural confusion was ruled to have been superseded by a compromise resolution that invited the PRG to seek an information office in Australia. Whitlam and Willesee felt compelled to accept the compromise. They would have preferred no party strictures at all to the ministerial leadership on this subject. Radical movement exploitation of the Labor government's "arrogance" and the movement's assistance in pulling Labor parliamentarians together on Vietnamese issues probably affected what happened later at Terrigal.[61]

Bodies representing a particular set of identifiable interests or causes represent our final category of group-interest expression. There were a great many of such groups, differing greatly in size, visibility, access to decision-makers or those around them and, of course, in degree of influence. For instance, environmentalists tried to persuade unions to impose a ban on the mining and processing of uranium, pending a full-scale assessment of the environmental impact of uranium exploitation. Commercial interests, on the other hand, sought through general publicity and contacts with official and political figures to obtain a relaxation of government policy in the energy and minerals field. As we saw earlier, efforts were mounted to counter anti-foreign investment sentiment. The Returned Services League (RSL) was pleased with Labor's improvement of service personnel conditions, but not with defence policy and the nation's preparedness. The RSL found Barnard fully accessible, but not sympathetic to criticisms of defence policy.[62] The RSL was stunned when Morrison told it that it had indulged in scaremongering and in wild and irresponsible outbursts.[63] Various other groups interested in strengthening Australia's defences took up missionary work in this field. In mid-1975, for example, a group of civilians and retired senior military officers founded a sort of defence think-tank body, the Australian Defence Conference.[64]

In the interest of focus, we will stress the trade-union impact on Labor's policies and behaviour in external affairs. We of course cannot assume that the expressions or actions of particular unions or their leaders were always, or even often, representative of the generality of unions or of the rank-and-file. Nor can we assume that trade-union behaviour would necessarily have been markedly different under a L–CP government. All the same, we cannot overlook the special ALP/trade-union relationship, as expressed in the party's organizational network, its reliance on a strong trade-union vote and its general sympathy for trade-union and unionists' causes.

Much of the access to the Labor government, and the potential for influence over government policy, lay in the closeness of party–union ties and in the considerable overlap in membership and leadership. This was so even when party–union élites spoke for themselves rather than for unions. Hartley and Hawke were unionists as well as members of the ALP Federal Executive. Hartley was a Federal Conference delegate, while Hawke, who was both ACTU and Party President, in his latter capacity presided over Federal Conferences. The relative stature and influence of both was thereby enhanced. While the two often disagreed, neither could be disregarded. Hawke was fervently pro-Israeli and firmly opposed a PLO visit. He openly attacked what the government chose to describe as an even-handed Middle Eastern policy and at one time considered resigning his party presidency over these differences. Hartley deeply angered Whitlam by moving on his own initiative to arrange a PLO delegation visit, since Whitlam would have preferred to have proceeded in the manner and timing of his own choosing. Hartley then exacerbated the picture by intimating that failure to bring PLO people in could strain Australia's commercial relations with Arab states. The ensuing national and intra-party furore brought about the sharply divided Cabinet decision not to invite PLO visitors at that time.

The party–union nexus was demonstrated with special prominence when the government's externally related policies touched on worker interests. Hawke indicated that on some issues such as tariffs and immigration policy, in which both government and the unions had a considerable interest, his personal understanding of Labor's thinking "has made it easier to get a broad understanding and some degree of acceptance within the industrial movement of important government decisions in these areas".[65] All the same, we have seen that the ACTU complicated the government's efforts to bring in Filipino automobile workers. We also noticed the very stiff trade-union criticisms of government tariff policy, criticisms that had an effect on the series of protectionist measures imposed by the government, especially on goods from Asian countries. We also noticed the trade-union outcry against the domestic employment implications of the government's defence procurement practices. Stern trade-union representations were directed towards Barnard and others. The matter reached Cabinet. A joint government–union committee was formed to explore ways to avoid retrenchments. The government's objective of achieving maximum economies in the defence field was somewhat eroded, for various expedients were introduced to keep Australians working on defence-related projects.[66] These union pressures also had the effect of stimulating government efforts to obtain the best possible offset agreements when foreign equipment-purchase contracts were negotiated. Indirectly, such pressures helped to sustain a local defence production capability. The unions' arguments about defence production and employment apparently contributed to Barnard's ability to persuade Cabinet colleagues to accept an increased defence budget in 1974.

Because of their pervasiveness within the nation's commercial and industrial life, the unions' resort to industrial action in pursuit of policy objectives could not be lightly dismissed. In some instances, threats were made. In others, they were carried out.

One instance of a union threat related to Omega. Even before the Wheeldon Committee's report, a "Stop Omega" campaign had lobbied unions, asking them to threaten, or if needed carry out, black bans against the construction of such a facility.[67] Some union leaders who opposed Omega were independently disposed to urge such bans. The government's own very cautious, delaying approach to Omega could well have been influenced by such prospects.

In late 1973, a ban on most shipments to Chile was imposed by politically militant maritime unions. Then, in early 1975, the unions resisted what promised to be a lucrative wheat sale to Chile. Wheat farmers were furious, and the opposition was delighted to exploit any Labor "capitulation" of its governmental responsibilities to outside, and especially radical, interests. The government would have preferred the sale to proceed, but, as we have seen, advised the Wheat Board that attempts to ship the wheat could lead to industrial disputes on the waterfront. It felt that a potentially ugly confrontation with unions was inadvisable and its leverage for arguing the case for consummating the deal was weakened by the international circumstances surrounding the issue. The "humanitarianism" implicit in a sale of food grain had to be balanced against the Labor government's professed disdain for repressive, "anti-humanitarian" régimes, as ruled in post-Allende Chile.[68]

More dramatic, and contentious, were bans imposed against the United States and France. When US interdiction against North Vietnam was resumed shortly after Labor came to office, resentful maritime unions declared a ban on American shipping and expressed threats of further retaliation against American companies, goods and airlines. Whitlam appreciated the sentiment behind the ban, but not the tactics or the foreseeable consequences. He did not feel the ban would force a change of policy in Washington. He was concerned about counter-productive economic results for Australia, especially since a counter-ban on Australian shipping was started by American unions. He felt the union action could jeopardize his government's efforts to adjust Australia's foreign policy without estranging the Americans. He was not oblivious to the political damage the L–CP could inflict if his government could not or would not successfully intervene. He was aware that the ban was backed by only a fraction of the industrial movement and that the ACTU as such opposed it. But he was reluctant to risk an open confrontation with the militant unions and to stake his own prestige, or that of his government, on what could have been an unsuccessful intervention. Also it was difficult for him to challenge the unions without coming down hard on three of his highly outspoken, newly appointed ministers, without risking a major intra-party row. Instead, it was Hawke who interceded with the unions. His intervention, plus the cessation of American bombing, helped to lift the ban.[69] The episode was an example of union ability to defy and to embarrass the Labor government. It also was an example of how union leaders could help to bail out the government. While Hawke opposed the boycott, his negative views on US bombing policy were unquestioned. This, plus his combined party and union status, facilitated his intermediary role and the dispute's settlement.

Later in 1973, the ACTU imposed a ban on French goods and communications, in protest against France's nuclear-testing programme in the Pacific. Whitlam was opposed to the ban at large, feeling that it would be ineffective and could rebound against Australia's commercial interests. He was especially eager to avoid postal and telecommunications bans, since they would contravene Australia's international commitments and could prejudice Australia's legal case before the International Court of Justice. On this issue, Whitlam and Hawke found themselves on opposite sides. A personal meeting between the two men resolved nothing. The ACTU leadership was fully committed to a comprehensive boycott, and Hawke indicated that the unions were not tools of the government. Although the boycott was by no means air-tight, it dragged on for some months. When it was suspended later in 1973, it was less through any government pleas than because of the ACTU's view that circumstances had changed, among them the end of the current series of French tests and the prospect of subsequent tests being conducted underground. Moreover, as argued by the President of the International Confederation of Free Trade Unions, whose collective policy had been to boycott France, the boycotts had not had any influence on policy taken in Paris.[70] In late October 1975, the principal maritime and waterfront unions launched a ban against Indonesian shipping, in protest against Jakarta's Portuguese Timor policy. The Whitlam government was *de facto* following a different line; its removal from office occurred before government–union frictions had a chance to become worrisome.

Our narrative of interest-group activity suggests several conclusions. Firstly, much of the influence of group pressure was quite indirect, largely in the form of generating publicity for particular causes and conditioning the climate in which government policy was formulated and presented. Secondly, group influence stood a better chance of affecting policy outputs, or at least the style and tempo of policy presentation, if it represented courses or objectives towards which there already was a temperamental or political disposition within the government. Thirdly, influence was enhanced to the degree that a particular movement or group interest enjoyed access to the government or to the ALP, rather than simply working around the margins. Finally, as indicated by the trade-union example, a mass-based structure within the political system, with independent means of exerting leverage, was exceptionally well placed to assert itself on external policy issues. At times, the party–union connection promoted the course of action preferred by the government. At other times, the connection helped little, or indeed hampered the government. We need to stress that many of the interest-group activities pursued during Labor's tenure would probably have taken place under a L–CP government. But official responsiveness would have differed, as would have the partisan atmosphere in which government reactions to interest-group expressions were received in the political marketplace.

We turn finally to the contributions of Labor as a party to the external policy-making process. There were forces that buffered the government from party intrusion, and those which worked opposite. Government immunity from effective party intrusion was strengthened by the traditions of executive authority in external affairs. It was strengthened by the fact that the Prime Minister himself not only involved himself deeply in external affairs but that he leaned towards a personal, authority-concentrating role. Men such as Willesee and Barnard, and to a degree Morrison, were in turn close to Whitlam, rather than enjoying independent party-power bases. Moreover, Whitlam and his close ministerial associates were aware of the electoral damage that ostensible government over-indulgence of party whims and pressures could carry. We should also remember that even within élite Labor Party structures, foreign affairs were not held in consistent and high interest.

On the other side of the coin, the key factor was that, by explicit direction of its constitution, the final and authoritative source of Labor policy was the party conference. The Federal Executive was authorized to interpret and otherwise supervise policy between conferences. The federal parliamentary caucus was entitled to determine policy not covered by conference decisions and to deal with parliamentary tactics. Because of the system of caucus election of ministers and various practical considerations, it was very difficult for a Labor Prime Minister to discipline ministerial colleagues. Many party members were deeply imbued with the tradition of authoritative, collectively taken ALP decision. If ministers in a Labor government were believed to be seriously flaunting party policy, or to be circumventing conventional guidelines of party collegiality, a strong reaction could be expected. Within a party strongly influenced by idealism and by a measure of ideological commitment, criticism and attempts at correction of allegedly diluted or overly "pragmatic" ministerial policies could likewise be expected. And, as a Labor minister himself once remarked, "The thing to note about Labour Party foreign policy, and indeed about any aspect of the Party's policy, is that it is an endless, open debate."[71] This process of ongoing dialogue has implied that party policy has seldom been neatly settled or has been reasonably comfortable for Labor's various wings and persuasions. By no means were all intra-party differences over external policy divisible into "left" and "right" categories. Many, however, did have that inflection, and it usually was the group supporting the more adventurous or "left" persuasion that was most vocal and eager to impose itself on the government, when it found the government too timid or too devious to its liking.

We have noted a number of examples when party figures attacked the government and took views dissimilar to it. While they may have earned rebukes from Whitlam or others, there were few practical means by which the leadership could neutralize them. We recall Cairns' unauthorized remarks about foreign policy and Senator

Brown's attack on Green and the American presence in Australia. Hartley, in early 1973, accused Barnard of being under Tange's thumb and of swallowing American strategic attitudes. ALP Federal President T. J. Burns wired Hartley. He warned that such attacks on the government were causing grave concern and urged that if any criticisms were to be expressed, they should fall "within the confines of the party organization you represent". Hartley's reply was a gesture to abide, but he denounced efforts at stifling opposing points of view.[72] Thereafter, both in and outside party organs, Hartley continued to berate the government on a wide range of issues.

Some of the sharpest exchanges in party circles were over Middle Eastern policy and much of the debate was carried out in the form of personal spokesmanship. Hartley was sympathetic to the Palestinian cause and drew Whitlam's ire for his allegedly personal diplomacy in trying to get a PLO delegation into Australia. Hawke was stoutly pro-Israeli and openly decried what he believed to be the government's *un*even-handed diplomacy. He said that he was not really challenging government policy, since neither Cabinet nor caucus had dealt with it, and Labor's platform called for even-handedness—which was Hawke's professed wish. In fact, Hartley's and Hawke's stature and visibility in the party made their voices count for a great deal and compounded the government's problems in dealing with delicate Middle Eastern affairs in what it defined to be a sensible way.

Under the Labor government, the Federal Executive led a fairly placid existence; the action was in conference. It was on the Middle East that the executive almost, but not quite, was brought into prominent play. In early 1974, Hawke wished to bring Middle Eastern policy before the executive, to discuss what he felt to be the government's uneven-handed (and therefore in breach of party policy) approach. Some executive members wanted the controversy ventilated and if possible settled in the executive. Others were afraid of running it into formal party channels. In the event, on the motion to consider the Middle East, the executive deadlocked 8 to 8 and the motion was lost. One commentator wrote that the tied vote "prevented the Middle East issue from becoming a greater source of party controversy by leaving both Mr Whitlam and Mr Hawke able to continue espousing their respective policies".[73] Against this stood the interpretation that nothing was settled, and salvos from different sides did not abate.

The ALP caucus only very rarely, in its corporate capacity, undertook initiatives on foreign and defence policy. The first time was in early 1973. Then, we recall, caucus members of various persuasions were annoyed by government secretiveness over the American defence facilities and caucus directed that the entire issue be placed before Cabinet for further consideration. The motion was declared lost on a technicality. Whitlam refused to go to Cabinet and government policy remained unaffected. Later in the year, a group of nearly sixty caucus members eventually signed a petition asking the government to withhold recognition of the new Chilean régime. But the government had just managed to beat the caucus signatories to the punch by announcing that it would extend recognition. Caucus gave *post hoc* approval to the decision, 45 to 24. It was faced by an accomplished fact. Some who resented the decision voted to support the Prime Minister, because of his reported appeal that a caucus rebuff would damage his international standing and the party's standing within Australia.[74] A 1975 caucus appeal to ministers to examine more stringent measures against South Africa conceivably helped to bring about the decision to close one consulate. But this step was in itself extremely marginal. In any event, senior ministers had themselves been edging towards additional measures and probably needed no prompting from caucus. Later in the year, in the midst of commotion in Portuguese Timor, caucus adopted a motion urging Whitlam not to sanction Indonesian intervention. This motion had no effect on Whitlam's substantive position, though it may in some degree have made him more cautious in his public pronouncements.

The infrequency with which caucus became involved in trying to give a foreign policy lead to the government, or indeed with which it registered any success, was partially attributable to the government's own style of behaviour and partially to factors symptomatic of caucus' own condition. In external policy, the government simply preferred to operate with minimum caucus involvement. That protected its policies from unwanted challenge and possible change, and purportedly avoided the embarrassing public washing of party linen. The government also invoked claims of executive independence in foreign affairs. The government was helped by standing party rules, which referred to ministers themselves bringing an agenda before caucus; most agenda items pertained to legislation, not executive actions, one of the domains of which was external affairs. Thus when external affairs subjects were brought before caucus, it usually was in a rapporteurial, after-the-fact context.

The author's inquiries disclosed that caucus members themselves ascribed little viability to the institution. Terms such as "fragile" and "impotent" were applied to the caucus' role in external affairs. Most party parliamentarians were more interested in domestic than in foreign affairs, and they perceived domestic affairs as far more critical electorally. To an extent, there was deference to a government led by an imposing and persuasive man. There also was almost no input to caucus from its own foreign affairs and defence committee. It met very rarely, usually suffered from sparse attendance and contributed next to nothing by way of reports for caucus at large to deliberate upon. In March 1975, some caucus committee members visited Portuguese Timor and then carried back their impressions. But this was a most exceptional event, and in the last resort, with little if any impact on policy. The Friends of Israel group in caucus was an informal collection, not caucus by another name. While it took an interest in Middle Eastern affairs and in Israel's cause, its influence on the government was nominal. To the government's pro-Israeli critics, policy was somewhat less than even-handed, and the ultimate decision to admit a PLO visitor, regrettable. Rather, it was individual parliamentarians who, through questions in Parliament or through other channels, occasionally placed ministers on the defensive. This fell short of causing shifts in policy, though it extracted elaborate justifications.

As of mid-1974, however, there was somewhat more movement in caucus, though the evidence is mild and in respects inferential. Starting in late 1974, individual caucus members took a closer look at the East Timor situation. A year later, acting on what was the unusual occurrence of advice rendered by its foreign affairs and defence committee, caucus petitioned Whitlam to follow a more positive and in particular Indonesian restraining posture relative to Timor.[75] Also, and outwardly impressively, 66 of the then 96 caucus members, including 14 ministers, Barnard and Morrison among them, signed a petition that condemned the Thieu régime in South Vietnam and in effect supported the legitimate status of the PRG. This, however, was an action of a majority of caucus members, not a corporate caucus action *per se*. It was not directly addressed to the Australian government, asking it to do this or that. Moreover, the bringing together of the signatories had not really so much been a spontaneous caucus move as a response to organizing efforts mounted by Australian radical groups.

Their personal convictions aside, it can also be argued that this kind of activity among caucus members also grew out of frustration with the government's closed and often unpopular way of doing business, in external affairs and otherwise. Most caucus members had been shaken by the Gair appointment. Later many were shaken by the Baltic states decision, both in its substance and in the way it was done, then by the Ermolenko incident, and then by Whitlam's expressions on Indonesia's role in East Timor. The election of Cairns in mid-1974 as deputy leader was, as we suggested before, less a case of applause for leftist sentiment than a wish to have a deputy leader who would be more sensitive about caucus feelings and who presumably would more vocally safeguard the party platform. Wheeldon's election at that time to a Cabinet vacancy can in degree also be so construed.[76] Admiration for someone willing to stand up to senior

ministers may have played a part in Berinson's election to the
vacancy opened by Cairns' removal in July 1975. Crean's election to
the deputy leadership at that time was of a man widely popular in the
party who, less than a year before, had humiliatingly been sacked as
Treasurer by Whitlam. The Berinson and Crean elections came in the
aftermath of the Connor and Cairns loan-raising controversy. At Terrigal, Berinson had defied Connor's ideas and methods. On his election as deputy leader, Crean criticized Connor's efforts to raise huge
loans for mineral and energy projects and urged more *collective*
decision-making in Cabinet and in caucus.[77] In other words, caucus
appeared to be groping for some corrective to its relative impotence
under a powerful Prime Minister. Its complaints about being slighted
were varied, but they included government actions in the field of
foreign policy.

Government external policy received far more challenge in conference than it did in caucus. Conference was, after all, the
authoritative policy body. It was composed of delegates proportionately more concerned about external affairs than was caucus, and
conference contained proportionately more people of party stature
and of outspokenness. While it included both backbench and
ministerial parliamentarians, as a body it was not as politically
obligated or subject to manipulation by government ministers. There
was a certain amount of situational restraint imposed on the 1973
and 1975 conferences. In 1973, there still was an aura of good feeling
that carried over from the sweet victory of a few months earlier, a
victory prominently attributed to Whitlam's efforts. In 1975, there
was a measure of unease that another election might soon be forced
by the opposition, and the government's already low fortunes could
be aggravated in the event of a devisive conference. All the same,
both at Surfers Paradise and at Terrigal, there was an undercurrent of
dissatisfaction with government external policy. Some of it typified a
wish that policy be carried out differently, more dramatically or
radically. Some of it was displeasure over what was felt to be improper circumvention of party positions. The people objecting were,
after all, those authorized to frame party policy.

At both conferences, Whitlam invoked the mandate thesis in
defence of government policy on the US installations. His argument
was that, on major issues, the party could not impose its will on the
government unless an equivalent policy pledge had been extended in
the preceding general election. Some delegates were persuaded, while
others believed the mandate thesis to be a subterfuge. At both conferences, Whitlam was able to blunt attacks on the US installations,
but at Surfers Paradise, found it necessary to accede to a resolution
that required *party* endorsement before Omega could be built. At

Surfers Paradise, a pro-PRG resolution was lost. At Terrigal, however, a resolution urging recognition of the PRG actually was passed, against Whitlam's opposition. It was superseded by another motion only because of the procedural confusion then prevailing on the conference floor. The motion adopted was not intrinsically to Whitlam's liking, but it was the best deal he could hope for, and he accepted it, opening the prospect of a PRG information office in Australia.

Conference was one, albeit one of the more important, of many sources of pressure and influence operating on the making, execution and presentation of external policy under the Labor government. The government also needed to weigh the electoral consequences of its behaviour in external policy. So did the opposition, both in how it attacked the government and in the alternatives it offered. This is the subject of our final chapter.

NOTES

1. For recent treatments, see H.S. Albinski, "Foreign Policy", in *Public Policy in Australia*, ed. R. Forward (Melbourne: Cheshire, 1974), pp. 15–54; T.B. Millar, "The Making of Australian Foreign Policy" (AIIA conference paper, Adelaide, June 1974); and J.W. Knight, "Aspects of the Foreign Policy Decision-Making Process" (APSA conference paper, Canberra, July 1975).
2. On aspects of federal power in external affairs, see C. Howard, "The External Affairs Power of the Commonwealth", *Melbourne University Law Review*, 8 (August 1971): 193–214, and his *Australian Federal Constitutional Law* (Sydney: Law Book Co., 2nd edn, 1972), pp. 422–66; G. Sawer, "Australian Constitutional Law in Relation to International Relations and International Law", in *International Law in Australia*, ed. D.P. O'Connell (Sydney: Law Book Co., 1966), pp. 33–51; W.A. Wynes, *Legislative, Executive and Judicial Powers in Australia* (Sydney: Law Book Co., 4th edn, 1970), pp. 118–218, 281–85; P.H. Lane, *The Australian Federal System: With United States Analogues* (Sydney: Law Book Co., 1972), pp. 71–97, 135–54; and R.D. Lumb and K.W. Ryan, *The Constitution of the Commonwealth of Australia Annotated* (Sydney: Butterworths, 1974), pp. 145–53.
3. See the summary of state reactions by F. Cranston, *Canberra Times*, 4 July 1974.
4. G. Negus, *Australian Financial Review*, 21 August 1974.
5. See B. Toohey, *Australian Financial Review*, 20 February 1975.
6. See the review by J. McIlwraith, *Australian Financial Review*, 29 May 1974.
7. Cited in *Australian Financial Review*, 10 November 1975.
8. See *Australian*, 26 June 1975.
9. *Australian [Commonwealth] Parliamentary Debates, (APD)*, House of Representatives (HR) (2 June 1970), p. 2722. Also see his UN Human Rights Day remarks of 10 December 1973, cited in *Australian Foreign Affairs Record (AFAR)* 44 (December 1973): 867.
10. B. Juddery, *At the Centre: The Australian Bureaucracy in the 1970s* (Melbourne: Cheshire, 1974), pp. 174–75.
11. L. Murphy, article in *Sydney Morning Herald*, 22 March 1974. Also see the remarks of S.D. Ross, *Sydney Morning Herald*, 5 May 1973.
12. *APD*, HR (15 May 1973), p. 2102. See support for the nonelastic use of the external affairs power in such matters by Sir Robert Menzies, article in *Sydney Morning Herald*, 15 March 1974. Also see the remarks of Senator I. Greenwood, *APD*, Senate (15 May 1975), p. 1516.
13. *APD*, HR (19 March 1970), p. 700.

318   *Australian External Policy under Labor*

14. Albinski, "Foreign Policy", p. 19. More generally, see J.D.B. Miller, "The Role of the Australian Parliament in Foreign Policy", *Parliamentarian* 50 (January 1969): 1–6; and H.S. Albinski, *Politics and Foreign Policy in Australia: The Impact of Vietnam and Conscription*, (Durham, N.C.: Duke University Press, 1970), pp. 19–22.
15. For McManus' charges, see *Australian*, 3 April 1974. For an account of the approach, which belittles McManus' allegations, see L. Oakes and D. Solomon, *Grab for Power: Election '74* (Melbourne: Cheshire, 1974), pp. 24–25.
16. *Sydney Morning Herald*, 3 April 1974.
17. *APD*, HR (13 May 1975), p. 2112.
18. For descriptions of the committee's authority, see Whitlam, *APD*, HR (15 March 1973), pp. 625–27 and 18 July 1974, pp. 387–88. Also see C.J. Lloyd and G.S. Reid, *Out of the Wilderness: The Return of Labor* (Melbourne: Cassell, 1974), pp. 172–73.
19. See F. Cranston, *Canberra Times*, 3 September 1975 and Melbourne *Age*, 4 September 1975.
20. See *Canberra Times*, 1 October 1975.
21. Millar, "Making of Australian Foreign Policy", p. 14.
22. E.G. Whitlam, "Beyond Vietnam—Australia's Regional Responsibility" in AIIA, North Queensland branch, *Australia's Foreign Policy in the Seventies* (?Townsville: 1968), p.24.
23. R. Haupt, *Australian Financial Review*, 29 April 1975.
24. *APD*, HR (11 February 1975), p. 75.
25. *Sydney Morning Herald*, 21 January 1975. For a critical analysis of Whitlam's style, see in particular O. Harries, "Mr Whitlam and Australian Foreign Policy", *Quadrant* 17 (July–August 1973), pp. 55–64.
26. C. Burns, Melbourne *Age*, 30 April 1975.
27. On Connor's fall, see T. O'Leary, *Canberra Times*, 15 October 1975. On the work of the Cabinet resources committee, see P. Kelly, *Australian*, 29 September 1975; and B. Toohey, *Australian Financial Review*, 23 October 1975.
28. On Everingham, see *Australian*, 24 April 1973. On Cass, see *Sydney Morning Herald*, 22 March 1974.
29. *News Weekly*, 5 June 1974.
30. Lloyd and Reid, *Out of the Wilderness*, pp. 133–34.
31. See in particular M. MacCallum's assessment, *Nation-Review*, 31 January 1975.
32. Whitlam, press conference of 13 March 1973, transcript, p. 3.
33. See *Australian*, 3 September 1974.
34. See D. Willesee (untitled AIIA conference paper, Adelaide, June 1974), pp. 3–4.
35. For an earlier indictment of conservative thinking in External Affairs/Foreign Affairs, see G. Clark, "Between Two Worlds: The Radicalization of a Conservative", *Meanjin Quarterly* 33 (June 1974): 117–27. For Clark's later thoughts, see his "The Australian Department of Foreign Affairs—What's Wrong with Our Diplomats", *Australian Quarterly* 47 (June 1975), pp. 21–35.
36. For instance, see the previously confidential memorandum of Sir Arthur Tange of 25 January 1973, *Nation-Review*, 28 June 1974.
37. See A. Clark, *National Times*, 26 May 1975. Also see Barnard's rebuttal, *APD*, HR (27 May 1975), p. 2831; and Clark's rejoinder, *National Times*, 2 June 1975.
38. See Renouf's Evatt article, *Bulletin*, 6 January 1973; M. Walsh's charge of partiality, *Australian Financial Review*, 27 July 1973; and Renouf's rejoinder, *Australian Financial Review*, 14 August 1973.
39. For example, his interview with P. Kelly, *Australian*, 4 May 1974.
40. On the controversy, see Melbourne *Age* and *Australian* of 11 and 12 April 1975. See Renouf's speech, in *AFAR* 46 (April 1975): 180–83.
41. Renouf, statement of 12 February 1975 before Royal Commission on Australian Government Administration, in *AFAR* 46 (February 1975): 73.
42. On Renouf's departmental views and actions, see his interview with G. Davidson, *Canberra Times*, 4 January 1974; and with K. Randall and A. Ramsey, *New Accent*, 16 August 1974; Renouf's 21 November 1974 Canberra address, transcript; *Submission by the Department of Foreign Affairs to the Royal Commission on Australian Government Administration* (Canberra: 1974); C. Crouch, *Sydney Morning Herald*, 17 April 1974; and B. Juddery, *Canberra Times*, 19 March 1975. For an analysis of departmental operations under the L–CP, see F.A. Mediansky, "The Department of External Affairs and the Foreign Policy Process", *Public Administration* (December 1969), pp. 278–93.

43. For some commentaries, see A. Clark, *National Times,* 24 June 1974; and J. Edwards, *National Times,* 24 February 1975; S. Simson, *Australian Financial Review,* 20 June and 20 August 1974; and M. Steketee, *Australian,* 13 September 1974.
44. See A. Farran, "Foreign Policy and Resources: Problems Arising from a Disintegrated Decision-Making Process" (APSA conference paper, Canberra, July 1975), esp. pp. 7–12.
45. For commentaries, see B. Murray, *Australian,* 12 October 1974; L. Oakes, Melbourne *Sun News-Pictorial,* 12 October 1974; R. Haupt, *Australian Financial Review,* 28 April 1975; and J. Jost and C. Burns, Melbourne *Age,* 24 May 1975.
46. Testimony of D.M. Connolly, MHR, cited in *Australian,* 25 February 1975.
47. See a summary of these differences in *Australian,* 20 February 1975.
48. Renouf, 12 February 1975 Royal Commission testimony, in *AFAR* 46 (April 1975), p. 71.
49. See Department of Foreign Affairs *Submission,* Part IV, esp. pp. 36–47.
50. See B. Toohey, *Australian Financial Review,* 2 September 1975; and P. Kelly, *Australian,* 29 September 1975.
51. On "green papers", see Renouf's interview with K. Randall and A. Ramsey, *New Accent,* 16 August 1974; A. Clark, *National Times,* 10 June 1974; and *Rydge's,* September 1974.
52. Cited in *Sydney Morning Herald,* 6 March 1973. For some analyses, see A. Reid, *Bulletin,* 3 March 1973; and D. Armstrong, *Australian,* 8 March 1973.
53. D.J. Ball, "Political Constraints on Defence and Foreign Policy Making" (APSA conference paper, Canberra, July 1975), p.11.
54. T.B. Millar, *Canberra Times,* 4 July 1975.
55. For analyses of interest-group impact, especially under the L–CP, see D. Altman, "Internal Political Pressures on Australian Policy", in *Foreign Policy for Australia: Choices for the Seventies,* ed. G. McCarthy (Sydney: Angus and Robertson, 1973), pp. 97–112; Albinski, *Politics and Foreign Policy in Australia,* pp. 101–62; and Albinski, "Foreign Policy", pp. 38–42.
56. For typical advertisements, see *Sydney Morning Herald,* 8 August 1974, *Australian,* 5 September 1974 and *Canberra Times,* 17 September 1974. Also see the summary in E. Dunsdorfs, *The Baltic Dilemma: The Case of the De Jure Recognition by Australia of the Incorporation of the Baltic States into the Soviet Union* (New York: Robert Speller, 1975), pp. 230–56.
57. For example, see Melbourne *Age,* 14 June 1975.
58. For the ACC/Justice and Peace Commission viewpoint, see the memorandum of 1 August 1974 issued by the Joint Secretariat on Action for World Development.
59. See AICD (NSW), *Press Statement,* 11 July 1974.
60. For examples of university student reaction to the AUS motion, see the account in *Lot's Wife* (Monash University), 25 March 1974. For later AUS leadership efforts, see P. Samuel, *Bulletin,* 8 March 1975. Also see D. Altman, "A Secular Democratic Palestine: A New Litmus Test for the Left", *Politics* 10 (November 1975): 169–77.
61. On lobbying of parliamentarians, see Australia–Indo-China Society, *Newsletter,* August 1974 and November 1974. On the Labor petition, see *Tribune,* 19 November 1974 and *Nation-Review,* 13 December 1974.
62. See W. Crouch, *Sydney Morning Herald,* 25 April 1974.
63. See *Australian,* 28 October 1975.
64. See *Australian,* 30 June and 1 July 1975.
65. Interview in *New Accent,* 8 March 1974.
66. For a review of the politics of this issue, see N. Swancott, *Australian Financial Review,* 16 July 1974.
67. For example, see *Australian,* 15 August 1973; and J. Jukes, *Australian,* 22 July 1974.
68. For summaries, see *Sydney Morning Herald,* 16 January 1975; Sydney *Sun,* 15 February 1975; and S. Simson, *Australian Financial Review,* 24 April 1975.
69. For summaries, see *Australian,* 10 January 1973; P. Terry, *Australian,* 4 January 1973; and J. Hurst, *Australian,* 5 January 1973.
70. See the remarks of Donald MacDonald, ICFTU president, *Australian,* 28 August 1973. For summaries, see D. Solomon, *Canberra Times,* 16 May 1973, and *Direct Action,* 24 May 1973.
71. K.E. Beazley, "Labour and Foreign Policy", *Australian Outlook* 20 (August 1966): 129.

72. See *Australian*, 6 March 1973.
73. J. Edwards, *Australian*, 15 February 1974. Also see *Sydney Morning Herald*, 15 February 1974 and *Bulletin*, 23 February 1974.
74. See Melbourne *Age*, 11 and 18 October, 1973.
75. See Melbourne *Age*, 27 and 28 August and 3 September 1975.
76. On Cairns' views about caucus upgrading, see P. Kelly, *Australian*, 14 June 1974. On Wheeldon's views of a minister's role, see M. Steketee, *Australian*, 11 June 1974. On the role of caucus generally, see P. Waller, "Caucus Control of Cabinet: Myth or Reality?", *Public Administration* 33 (December 1974): 300-6.
77. Melbourne *Age*, 15 July 1975 Also see the assessment by R. Haupt, *Australian Financial Review*, 15 July 1975.

⑨ Electoral Politics and External Policy

The previous chapter considered the contributions of various institutional and group influences on the shaping, content and presentation of external policy. We now concentrate on the interplay between electoral politics and external policy. After a brief introduction, our analysis will be divided into broadly chronological sections—before, during and after the 1974 electoral campaign.[1]

Following Labor's victory in December 1972, the L–CP had to adjust itself to an unfamiliar opposition status. In a variety of policy areas, including foreign affairs and defence, it had to evolve a style of spokesmanship that could provide meaningful counterpoint to Labor's policies, elicit popular sympathy and, if possible, contribute to early retrieval of office.

Part of an opposition's problem, especially in external affairs, is adequate access to information. In some instances, an opposition s access to sensitive and otherwise classified material can help to avoid uninformed public debate capable of compromising national interests. Access to a range of data and informed interpretations from knowledgeable and expert sources can sharpen the thrust of opposition criticisms of government policy and improve the soundness and persuasiveness of its own alternative positions. Such access can, in turn, enhance the electoral credibility of an opposition.

As we suggested earlier, nearly all of the top external policy spokesmen on the opposition side were men who not only had a distinct personal interest in the subject but who had enjoyed ministerial experience. For the Liberals, this included Bowen and then Peacock, Forbes and then Killen, and certainly Fraser. Snedden was perhaps the least-versed in the area, though he made serious efforts to educate himself. On the Country Party side, Anthony had long been expert in matters of overseas trade, while Sinclair had kept up a close, ongoing interest in defence questions particularly.

Shortly after the change of government, Snedden accepted an invitation to be briefed on the nature of the American defence installations. And, as Barnard explained later in 1973, "in contrast to the difficulties that I laboured under in opposition, I have made sure that the Shadow Minister for Defence, Dr Forbes, has access to intelligence material on which the strategic assessments are based. I don't want an alternative Government to base its policies on false premises."[2] Moreover, the Labor government did not discourage the access of opposition spokesmen, or of opposition caucus committees, to officials for purpose of background briefings and the like.[3] While Labor's policy on information to the opposition was more generous than the L–CP had followed when in government, it nonetheless fell short of what it might have been in a more trust-oriented political party system, especially where external policy differences were less sharply drawn and debated. In New Zealand, for example, National Party opposition leaders Marshall and Muldoon had the option to read cables if they chose, an option unavailable to the Australian opposition.

In Australia, opposition external affairs spokesmen consulted with departmental officials and, by and large, were satisifed with what they were given. Their access was only in part attributable to the government's formal acquiescence in this practice. It also related to the ability of opposition spokesmen to cultivate the personal contacts they had developed over time, especially when they served in government. A particularly good example was Forbes, who had served as Minister for the Army, and whose contacts among serving officers were especially close. In 1975, the opposition was visibly upset with Renouf after he had publicly chided the opposition for unfounded criticism of the government's Indo-China policy. On good evidence, however, it appears that after this incident, opposition access to Renouf, or to his department, did not suffer. From time to time, through various leaks, opposition spokesmen came into possession of non-public or classified information that normally would not have been available to them. Because of such revelations, the opposition more acutely placed the government on the defensive and may have scored some political points. One incident, in 1974, referred to the government's refusal to grant asylum to an East European diplomat. Another, in 1975, referred to the implications of differently worded messages destined for Hanoi and Saigon.

Nevertheless, both before and after Snedden's fall, opposition foreign affairs and defence spokesmen lacked adequate personal staff support. John Knight, a personal aide to Snedden who concentrated on foreign policy and who maintained close liaison with Peacock, corrected for this somewhat. It was in recognition of the relative weakness of adequate professionally based inputs that, in mid-1974, occasional closed seminars with international relations specialists were initiated by opposition external affairs spokesmen. After Fraser became leader, two academics were engaged in an honourary capacity as advisers on foreign policy. Opposition spokesmen also made increased use of the foreign affairs legislative research service personnel in the Parliamentary Library. During the first Whitlam government, the two opposition parties had maintained separate parliamentary committees devoted to external affairs. The creation of a joint capstone committee in 1974 may have had some effect on improving inter-party liaison and serving as an educational and consensus-building mechanism. But opposition parliamentary committees were not effective in providing meaningful input to leaders and spokesmen. Some useful input and political ammunition was available to opposition members of the several parliamentary standing and select committees that dealt with external subjects. In political terms, for example, it was possible for opposition spokesmen to point to the misgivings expressed about the state of the Australian Army by the Senate Standing Committee on Foreign Affairs and Defence. This added an element of respectability to L–CP criticisms of government defence policy.

Between the 1972 and 1974 elections, the opposition parties began to show signs that they were appreciative of the new political circumstances in which they found themselves. Some of the analysis raised earlier in Chapter 3 is in point here. The new spokesmen—Snedden, Forbes and, as of the latter part of 1973, Peacock—sought answers to what might have been faulty in traditional L–CP policy and to make adjustments that would be rational, politically palatable and, if possible, electorally viable. Indeed, as individuals, Snedden, Peacock and Forbes, and especially the former two, were on balance programmatically more pliable than their respective predecessors–McMahon, Bowen and Fairbairn.

A second element in the Liberal equation was that the Labor government was undertaking foreign and defence policy decisions that, in varying degrees, the Liberals regarded as desirable, or difficult or impossible to reverse, or electorally popular. For all three reasons, for example, the Liberals were unprepared to promise reintroduction of conscription except under extraordinary circumstances, though they had waged the 1972 campaign on the promise of having it foreseeably retained. During this period, at appropriately spaced intervals, Snedden announced his support for some key Labor decisions, such as recognition of China and the reconstitution of SEATO.

Thirdly, what emerged as formal opposition foreign policy, but somewhat less so in defence policy, was not a hodge-podge of ideas hastily slapped together under electoral pressure. After Bowen's departure and for nearly half a year before the double dissolution, systematic attention was given to a new external policy platform. This was done under the aegis of the Liberal Joint Standing Committee on Federal Policy, and especially through its subcommittee on defence and foreign affairs. The subcommittee, chaired by Peacock, included political, organizational and expert/academic personnel, who as a group reflected reasonably progressive and realistic sentiments. For electoral as well as other reasons, the group was persuaded that the party would need to project a positive, not just a reactive or negative image. It was agreed that "(a) statements on foreign policy should not put the Party in the position of always opposing the Government, and (b) equally statements should not "paint the Party into a policy corner" at this stage."[4]

What seemed to be the opposition's electorally promising external affairs targets during the first Whitlam government? There was a good deal of rhetoric and motion. We have seen that, in part to give publicity to its anti-government criticisms, the opposition's first censure motion in the newly assembled House was over defence policy. In the Senate, partially through DLP efforts, motions of urgency on foreign and defence topics were happily joined by Liberal and Country Party senators. A large number of press releases came off the presses of opposition spokesmen. There of course was substantive criticism of specific Labor policies. On the other hand, a number of Labor's decisions were either popular with the public (e.g. the ending of conscription), or seemed to be part of a general international trend (e.g. recognition of China), or complemented L–CP policy (e.g. maintenance of ANZUS and the preservation of American defence facilities). Although the opposition hardly operated as a smooth, well-integrated force of criticism, there were some patterns of attack that began to settle into place. At large, they were focused more on the mood and style of Labor than on specific policy judgements.

Liberal Party strategists had by the end of 1973 identified several areas in which criticism was being or should continue to be made. One was *misdirection*, meaning that tried and valued connections were being frayed at the expense of new, untried and possibly dangerous flirtations. Another was *irresponsibility*, meaning failure to honour pledges, allegedly as in the case of the Singapore troop commitment. Another criticism was over *contempt for the conventions of diplomacy*, meaning Whitlam's allegedly over-personalized, bumptious style of conducting international business. A further complaint was over *double standards*, meaning that solemn professions of even-handedness were flawed in practice; for instance, in Middle Eastern policy, or on the different reactions to French and Chinese nuclear testing.

Another was *uncertainty*, meaning that Labor faltered and sputtered rather than being direct, as on the confusion over retaining logistical troops in Singapore, and also meaning that party and union pressures were forcing the government into backing and filling. A final criticism was over *lack of nerve in controlling intemperate ministers*, a number of whom, Cairns in particular, were with relative impunity able to make personal and embarrassing remarks on external subjects. The imputation was that in some respects Whitlam was leading a rabble, not a disciplined government.[5]

The opposition was able to take some comfort from public-opinion surveys conducted during the first Whitlam government. By the close of that period, a large majority of voters agreed that there had been noticeable changes in external policy under Labor. On specifics, however, the public mood was guarded. An early poll showed that stronger ties with China and Japan were endorsed, but there was disquiet that this was being achieved at the cost of more traditional friendships.[6] In late 1973, the public was about evenly divided on whether Australia had become too friendly with China.[7] In 1974, virtually on campaign eve, a majority of the public desired closer relations with the United States and Britain than had transpired under Labor and 41 per cent desired an improvement of relations with South Africa.[8] French nuclear testing in the Pacific was roundly denounced, but so were union boycotts of French firms,[9] something Whitlam had been unable to prevent. When it was disclosed that the Soviets wanted a space-science facility in Australia, the public was more than 2 to 1 opposed.[10] Moreover, shortly before the double dissolution, the political situation in Western Australia seemed especially inauspicious for the Labor government. Not only had the state Labor government just lost office, but state government ALP figures in Western Australia insisted that the Whitlam government's restrictive resource and foreign investment policies had helped to bring about the defeat.[11]

Most of the first Whitlam government's external orientations and major policy steps had been foreshadowed when Labor was still in opposition and in the 1972 campaign debate. Much of what it did in office was more than a perfunctory honouring of promises; it was a matter of conviction. It is therefore unlikely that, at least in calendar year 1973, Labor's major policy steps were noticeably influenced by calculations of electoral gain or loss. Although the Senate was throughout Labor's term of office in non-Labor hands, it was not until late in 1973 that serious thought was given to the prospect that Senate obstruction of government programmes would precipitate a double dissolution and a very early election. With no early election in clear sight, Labor's incentive to calculate the electoral repercussions of its policies was relatively low. If, however, there was an exception to the rule that Labor was not much affected by electoral considerations, that may have been its policy towards the American alliance, and the defence installations in particular. This is not to say that ministers such as Whitlam and Barnard did not actually favour the positions they assumed. It is to say that they probably also were persuaded that policies the opposition could neatly portray as anti-American would have deep, long-term and electorally damaging consequences for the ALP. Critics on Whitlam's left were often less gentle in their assessments. One critic identified two major domestic objectives of the government's foreign policy:

> On the one hand, it must please a broadly conservative population and meet the demands of dominant economic interests. It does this by pursuing essentially conservative policies. On the other hand, a Labor government has to give satisfaction to some of the more radical elements within the A.L.P., and this is achieved by the cultivation of a highly personalized and assertive style in the conduct of foreign policy.[12]

At all events, before the 1974 campaign actually got under way, three sets of favourable developments appeared to have crystallized, all indicating Labor's ability to withstand electoral damage from opposition criticism of its external policies. One dealt with movements on the international scene. The second related to the government's own capacity to build insulation around itself. The third referred to the comparative spokesmanship abilities of the two major party leaders.

By April–May 1974, various developments in international politics had dampened the opposition's political opportunities to exploit external affairs. Overall, relations with Asian countries, aligned and non-aligned, were probably better than they had been at any point under the Whitlam government. There were no more dramatic, argumentative scenes such as Whitlam had had with Lee in 1973. Australia's status prompted Labor spokesmen to cultivate the image of a nation standing ten feet tall: "The Australian flag now flies higher in Asia and around the Pacific than it ever has previously," leaving the opposition, and its criticisms, "completely out of touch with .international affairs".[13] The Prime Minister's previous controversial remarks about the desirability of "bringing down" racist régimes in Africa, about condoning revolutionary movements and his characterization of Rhodesian and South African leaders as being as bad as Hitler were largely set aside. The controversy was also partially deactivated by the success of the anti-rightist coup in Portugal in late April 1974.

The government's vulnerability to electoral castigation was, even more conspicuously, reduced by the course of actual Canberra-

Washington relations. For instance, by the latter part of 1973, all SEATO members, including the United States, acceded to the organization's reconstruction along Australia's preferred, largely non-military lines. It was no longer necessary for Labor to condemn SEATO as "moribund", or "irrelevant" or "provocative", or to spar with Washington over presumed obligations owed to Thailand's defence. The opposition complained that Labor was vitiating the US alliance through its misgivings over American facilities at Diego Garcia. The government's appeal to Moscow, as well as to Washington, to observe restraint in the Indian Ocean slightly overcame this criticism. During the campaign, Labor's position was cushioned by the British Labour government's reassessment of defence policy and by lack of great enthusiasm about the Diego Garcia project. Even in America, the project was under close scrutiny and counsels were divided. Controversy over the status of the North-West Cape signal-station was amicably resolved at the opening of 1974 with Barnard's visit to Washington. America kept what it wanted. Barnard went home with a package of symbolically important concessions in his pocket, as well as promises of better consultations and of the transfer of two American monitoring stations to Australia. From a domestic politics standpoint, the Barnard mission was a great success. Claims were made that the alliance had not only been protected but even enhanced. Overall, to the unnerving of opposition spokesmen, the government could advertise that "There is a basic accord in outlook between Americans and Australians which makes possible a working relationship on this [mutual respect] basis".[14]

So too in other matters, large and small, the Labor government pictured itself as a responsible international actor, operating parallel to, or at least not in conflict with, American policy. Australia's professed even-handedness in dealing with the 1973 Middle Eastern conflict, which included avoiding offence to Arab states, was pictured as having spared the nation from an oil boycott and as having complemented Washington's efforts at preserving *détente* between the super-powers.[15] While the international oil squeeze was still in progress, Transport Minister Jones continued to urge acceptance of Omega, a project desired by the United States. One of his arguments was that the facility would result in considerable savings of bunkering fuel to ships in Australia's regular trade.[16] *Détente*, Labor spokesmen increasingly stressed, was the American way and the Australian government's way. Borrowing an old L–CP•device, Labor cloaked itself in pro-Americanism. We are reminded of Willesee's remarks, make in April 1974, that "The reason we have been able to retreat from the cold war situation is that the intelligent people of this world, the Dr Kissingers, realize that there is no future for us but there will be destruction for all of us if this [crisis] situation goes on" [17]

As an election became more imminent, the Whitlam government took steps to minimize political fall-out. Some of this was done through the finessing of policy, while some was aimed at keeping the ALP as free as possible from imputations of recklessness and disorderliness.

The Soviet request for a joint space-science facility in Australia, revealed less than two months before the double dissolution, was an example of Labor's caution. The Americans and the Australian Defence and Foreign Affairs Departments strongly advised against the facility. The government at first temporized, saying that it was taking its time to study the matter. Then, on 10 April, in a terse announcement, the Soviet request was rejected. Even apart from political considerations, it is unlikely that approval would eventually have been forthcoming. But there is little doubt that the impending election expedited the decision. We recall Willesee's comment, made on 1 April, that the examination of the proposal would proceed "from a scientific point of view, from a political point of view and in the context of the Indian Ocean" [18] Internal evidence corroborates the weight of the political factor applied in reaching a speedy decision. Such evidence also supports the view that the government's 9 April announcement of new capital outlays for military equipment was hastened by politics.

To protect its flanks, Labor also needed to polish its image as a responsible and cohesive government, not constantly buffeted by "outside" interests and its own headstrong ministers. Hawke for the time being suspended his campaign against the government's Middle Eastern policy. In early 1974, there were no embarrassing union boycotts against America, France or anyone else. The Omega station decision was in abeyance, pending a report from the Wheeldon committee. Labor strategists were gratified that there was relatively little noise and demonstration in the streets. Rightly or wrongly, such manifestations could have rubbed off on to the Labor Party, especially if some of its more prominent figures had been taking part. There was one exception to this tranquil atmosphere. This was the long march to the North-West Cape in May, sponsored by the Campaign Against Foreign Military Bases in Australia. The government was uneasy over it, even though the protest challenged prevailing Labor as well as L–CP policy on the station's retention.

The most direct action taken by Whitlam to shield his party from opposition barbs related to the extracurricular expressions of ministers. We saw that several times in the past Whitlam had tried to impress on ministers that they should not speak out of turn, but he had not been successful. At the 7 April Cabinet meeting, he made still another very forceful presentation. At least for the duration of the forthcoming campaign, ministers were to adhere rigidly to the subject of their respective portfolios. Labor's continuation in office was at stake, and single-voice, responsible spokesmanship, especially in external affairs, was imperative.

There was a third factor that helped to insulate Labor from electorally damaging external policy criticisms: the relative credibility of the two party leaders as foreign policy expositors. In breadth of experience and visibility, Whitlam plainly outranked Snedden. Efforts were made in opposition quarters to narrow the disparity. As part of the "making of the alternative Prime Minister" image, Snedden spoke on external subjects with increased frequency, both in the House and outside, and issued a large number of press releases under his name. He also, first in mid-1973 and then in early 1974, undertook overseas tours, concentrating on Asian capitals, including Tokyo and Peking. All the same, Whitlam's overseas journeys were far more frequent, more prominently reported, and of course carried the weight of committing Australia to decisions in a way that Snedden could not. There was a rather half-hearted opposition effort to neutralize the partisan benefits accruing to the ALP from the Prime Minister's journeys, in the claim that his uncommonly frequent absences from home had produced neglect and delay in domestic programmes.[19] But that particular criticism never took off and was not later employed as an electoral argument.

Snedden's own overseas trips were not accident-free. His mid-1973 trip was partially overshadowed in Australia by publicity given to Labor's Federal Conference proceedings. In 1974, he had to share the limelight with Whitlam, who was also travelling in South-East Asia, and Snedden found it prudent to curtail his itinerary.[20] Moreover, the "Snedden, the statesman" image did not quite come off. On his return home from the 1973 trip, his friends as well as critics were startled by the report—which he claimed was distorted—that he wanted Japan to undertake a major expansion of its military contributions.[21] His comments on China were generally unexceptional, and his assessment of China's view of Australian trade with Taiwan drew a fiercely deflating retort from Cairns. Snedden's remarks, Cairns argued, showed him to be "either unbelievably ignorant or he's pulling the public's leg". The Snedden performance was a "farce played by a ham actor—Billie the Kidder", who as "the synthetic Marco Polo of Liberal foreign policy has trouble living up to his new image".[22] Six months later, Snedden's visit to South-East Asia persuaded him that Australian relations with states in the region had severely deteriorated, especially because of the troop pull-out from Singapore.

Actually, Whitlam's own visit to South-East Asia was, on its part, a major personal as well as diplomatic success. Much of the earlier tension between him and Lee had been dissipated. Singapore made no effort to urge a reversal of Australia's troop removal, and in fact Lee construed Snedden's offer to negotiate a return of the troops as designed for Australian political consumption.[23]

We now deal with the 1974 electoral campaign itself. In setting the stage, we first need to consider in some detail the considerations that persuaded strategists in both major party groups to downplay foreign and defence issues.

The first consideration derives from much of our earlier discussion. Both party groups sensed the presence of electorally negative or doubtful features in their respective external policy records or positions. The opposition felt that recent international developments and Labor's own, often pragmatic moves partially neutralized prospects for a strong and successful attack. Snedden was mismatched with Whitlam on foreign policy. The Liberals had produced refurbished foreign and defence policy documents, but the new trend was not well tested. The Liberals' overall adaptation on foreign policy issues had, at all events, brought the party closer to Labor, and the opposition did not wish to waste gains made towards the building of a "reformist" party image by indulging in hot and heavy attacks. On its part, Labor read the results of opinion polls. The public heart and mind had not been fully won over. Popular thinking seemed to be cautious, even somewhat critical of a number of policy results under Labor administration.

A second factor was that both major party groups thought they recognized clues in the 1972 and preceding elections and incorporated this reasoning into their decisions on the electoral applications of external issues in 1974. To the L–CP, confusion in the 1972 campaign seemed to suggest that the opposition must now choose a game plan and abide by it, and that external issues had been shown to have lost much of their electoral potency for the anti-Labor forces. The lessons drawn by Labor from 1972 in designing its 1974 campaign were quite revealing. Party strategists concluded that a sublimation of external affairs had apparently worked in 1972 and therefore deserved similar treatment in 1974. All the same, the party was also persuaded that, at least since 1949, foreign and defence policies had tended to be electoral assets for the L–CP and liabilities for Labor. Therefore, rather than invite trouble, it was thought best to handle the subject circumspectly rather than, for instance, advertising the Labor government's own foreign policy accomplishments or Whitlam's personal involvement in such accomplishments. Regarding conclusions drawn from 1972 by both party groups, it should be remembered that between the 1972 and 1974 House elections there had been no intervening Senate election at which to test hunches of this sort. There had been only one House by-election, in Parramatta, NSW, won by the Liberals with an increased majority. There, at all events, external issues were almost wholly bypassed by the candidates and a very local issue (the siting of an airport) conspicuously intruded.

Party interest in stressing external issues was also depressed by readings that indicated that such issues lacked electoral drawing-power. The various survey research organizations as of 1972 and onwards into the 1974 campaign reported that foreign/defence policy was far down the list of significantly regarded issues. In 1972 and then moving into the 1974 campaign, only about 7 per cent of the electorate ranked this as the prime national issue. There seemed to be no appreciable difference between opinions collected throughout Australia at large and in marginal electorates. The Labor Party did not commission independent surveys prior to the 1974 election, but the Liberals did, over a period of some months, and were given much the same reading about low issue salience for external subjects. Survey data consistently showed that L–CP voters were twice as likely as their Labor voting counterparts to construe foreign/defence policies as electorally salient. Thus from an L–CP standpoint, ALP supporters, as a group, were not especially suitable targets for external policy publicity. Then, too, a survey published in early April 1974 disclosed that while far more voters were favourably disposed towards raising spending for "overseas relations" (to be read: ALP activism in foreign affairs?) than desired cut-backs, an increased defence budget (a potential L–CP electoral plank) was favoured by very, very few. Only 2 per cent desired much more, and 6 per cent a bit more defence spending, while 9 per cent wished for a bit less and 34 per cent wanted much less than the incumbent Labor government itself was then spending.[24] ALP strategists saw young members of the electorate as generally supportive of Labor external policies, but this group was expected to vote disproportionately pro-labor in any event.

There was one jarring event that nearly led Labor to switch to heavier emphasis on external issues. Early in the formal campaign, a university-based poll in the Labor-held Melbourne suburban seats of Diamond Valley and Casey described "swinging" voters as leaning distinctly towards the opposition. So much so that a national trend of equivalent magnitude would foreshadow defeat for the Whitlam government. A feature of the findings was that swinging voters in the two seats appeared to hold inordinately salient feelings about external policies. At first, the Melbourne survey perplexed people in the ALP. But before demoralization (and a possible shift of issue emphasis towards foreign/defence policy) could set in, party operatives examined the methodological basis of the poll and found it faulty. They reassured the party that it was not in electoral jeopardy or pursuing wrong-headed strategy.

Another element that helped to downgrade external issues in 1974 was major party perceptions of minor parties. Consider the DLP, which in the past had made a heavy and even shrill contribution to campaign dialogues. Early in 1974, Snedden sought out Santamaria's views on defence policy, given Santamaria's closeness to the DLP. The personal recollections of the two men differ somewhat. The upshot, however, was that Snedden, and the Liberals, decided to discount the DLP. The Liberals did not adjust their external policies to court DLP second preferences. They did not, with their "reformed" image in mind, wish to be associated with a hard-line party. At any rate, by the time the 1974 campaign opened, the DLP was in disarray and a declining electoral force. It had been thrown into confusion by the Gair affair, was severely short of funds, was scrambling to avert submersion by associating itself with the Country Party in Queensland and in Western Australia, was flustered by its failure to reach accommodation with the Liberals over Senate slates, was confined to Victoria in presenting its own House candidates and was otherwise left behind as, with the arrival of the 1974 campaign, the external policies of the major parties gradually converged.

To the extent that the Australia Party's role was noticed by either Liberal or ALP strategists, its earlier, progressive, white-collar and independent voter appeal on foreign policy was discounted. In part, this was because the major parties did not stand on fundamentally different platforms. In part, because the Australia Party in 1974 moved to a position more striking for its romance than for its electoral captivation: non-alignment, cancellation of all defence treaties and foreign military installations and the conversion of Australia into what was poetically described as the "Samarkand of the South Seas".[25] Nor did independent or mini-party candidates pose any problems for the major parties. As was written with a stroke of understatement, "The Indian Ocean Peace Zone party is not seriously expected to capture the blue-ribbon Liberal seat of Curtin in the forthcoming federal election".[26]

Perhaps the foremost situational constraint respecting the uses of external issues by the major parties was the character of the impending campaign itself. Both Whitlam and Snedden, and their strategy advisers, became convinced that issue *focus*, not diffusion, was the key to electoral success. In the first place, the campaign was to be very brief. It had not been known until very late that there would be a double dissolution and a House election at all. Secondly, within an unusually brief time-frame, the parties were confronted with the difficult and unfamiliar tasks of actually waging campaigns in three directions simultaneously: the House election, an election for the entire Senate, and four constitutional referenda on which the ALP and the L–CP assumed opposite and partisan positions. Hence focus and simplicity .in issue presentation was adopted on both sides. To Snedden, this meant hammering a clear, understandable, pocket-book issue: inflation. To Whitlam, it meant indicting the opposition for frustrating progressive measures, and attacking the foreign economic presence in Australia. Eventually, Whitlam came into more direct clash with Snedden over inflation and economic conditions generally.

The actual application of external issues in the 1974 campaign can be analysed by considering the extent of their use, the degree of major party efforts at policy differentiation and the tangential introduction of external policy issues.

The opening shots of the campaign, fired by party leaders in their policy speeches, gave some indication of what the subject-matter preoccupation was to be. In the published versions of their addresses, Whitlam's remarks on foreign and defence policies occupied 2½ of a total 39 pages; Snedden's 1 of 13 pages. Anthony's policy speech had no foreign or defence policy content, though it was identified as a supplement to Snedden's, which was a joint statement of the Liberal and Country Parties.[27] Moreover, sections on foreign affairs and defence in the small book (136 pages) of policy papers issued by the L–CP were revealing, insofar as they made no attack on, or even mentioned, the external policy record of the Labor government.[28] Signs such as these were consistent with the strategic design of the two party groups. Snedden was to seize the initiative, concentrating on inflation. It was hoped that, while he would not relinquish this initiative, his interspersed remarks on other issues would be elaborated upon in "follow-up" speeches by his front-bench colleagues. Labor strategy called for three stylistic phases: (i) attack the opposition for Senate obstruction of vital government programmes, i.e. "Go Ahead"; (ii) discredit the opposition as still being "men of the past"; (iii) stress Whitlam's qualities over Snedden's, i.e. "Whitlam—he's so much better." Programmatically, Senate-obstructed legislation and the good life made possible under Labor were to be highlighted. Whitlam's early concentration on the drawbacks of foreign economic influence was in a way his choice, but still consistent with an issue focus and an external policy avoidance approach.

The electoral use of principal external policy spokesmen casts further light on campaign strategy. An examination of listed movements by government ministers in the three weeks preceding 18 May disclosed that Willesee and Barnard each spent about two-thirds of his time campaigning in his home (and indeed under-populated) state. This was arranged because the two men were felt to be personally popular on home ground and therefore electoral assets in Western Australia and Tasmania respectively. Also, given the downgrading of foreign and defence policy, their spokesmanship was not required for nation-wide campaigning. On the Liberal side, efforts at establishing a format for shadow Cabinet member movements were not well concerted. In the event, Peacock did travel a fair amount beyond his home state of Victoria, but Forbes largely confined himself to his own home state, South Australia.

Prepared electoral speeches by party leaders, and their replies to press conference or television questions, never indicated that external policies were regarded as superior or even equivalent to domestic issues (if Labor's foreign economic influence theme is construed as essentially domestic), though the L–CP was more inclined to mention them than was Labor. Snedden delivered one speech on foreign policy as such, midway through the campaign. External issues were virtually overlooked in the leaders' widely covered speeches before the National Press Club in Canberra during the final week of campaigning, and their closing campaign remarks were similarly domestically oriented. In terms of public speeches, perhaps the most outspoken person on external topics among the L–CP leadership was the one with the least national visibility, Country Party deputy leader Sinclair, and his remarks were aimed more at defence than at foreign policy. Willesee and Barnard, of course, continued to issue statements in their official capacities, and a number of these releases had political content or inspiration. Forbes' and Peacock's offices issued a great many press releases, but many of these were either ignored or given only cursory attention in the media, in part because the campaign turned so prominently around the party leaders—who themselves were concentrating on domestic issues. The original Liberal plan for a harmonized "follow-up" campaign of various themes that were first to be broached by Snedden never really materialized. Into the last week of the campaign, with signs abroad that the Liberals were going to lose, Snedden diversified his campaigning to an extent. But the shot tended to scatter and, in the event, external policy subjects never took hold.

Consistent with presentations made by spokesmen, party advertising also de-emphasized external subjects, though here and there, especially under local or private auspices, both pro- and anti-government material was inserted in newspapers. This was most prominently done in Queensland, on the anti-Labor side. When the major parties used the media or other publicity outlets on these themes, the intent was usually incidental to publicizing foreign and defence policy *per se*. Thus the Labor poster that recalled that it was L–CP politicians who had originally been associated with the introduction of conscription—and that predicted that they would do so again and send conscripts back to Asia—was simply one aspect of ongoing ALP strategy to assail the "men of the past". When the Liberals countered with newspaper advertisements that they had no intentions of this sort, it was to set the record straight and to help dispel a "men of the past" image. The ALP produced a set of co-ordinated film-clips for television screening. Whitlam was to be shown as a statesman figure: delivering aspects of his policy speech, then in the company of the Queen, Nixon, Mao, etc. The idea was not to inject foreign policy into the campaign, but to tie in with the Whitlam-is-better-than-Snedden theme of the closing phase of the campaign. For several reasons, the advertisement was found expendable and was not broadcast.

In the interests of perspective, it is helpful to illustrate some of the outward exceptions to the generalization that external policies were muffled by both sides in the campaign. The first question is whether Western Australia, where some believed security consciousness to have been especially prominent, was an exception to the rule. We saw earlier that Liberal Premier Court was on particularly poor terms with Whitlam. Court and his colleagues portrayed federal Labor as impervious to Western Australia's security requirements. During the electoral campaign, the government made certain pacifying gestures, such as requesting of Moscow that Soviet whalers, even in international waters, avoid hunting in traditional Australian catch areas, and the government announced the transfer of an RAN hydrographic survey vessel to a Western Australian base. Perhaps Barnard's 9 April announcement of intended military hardware purchases, so far as it had political content, had some bearing on assuaging Western Australian feelings. Interviewed in Perth in May, Whitlam himself made that inference.[29] One motive for having Willesee operate in Western Australia was to permit him, as required, to counter arguments hostile to Labor's defence policies. The federal Liberals made some effort to exploit Western Australian defence concerns, but by no means systematically. Snedden delivered his only major external policy speech in Western Australia, not in the suburbs of Melbourne or Sydney, and the party promised to accelerate construction at Cockburn Sound, to flesh out coastal patrols and defence capacity in the region generally and to maintain support for the upgrading of American facilities at Diego Garcia.[30]

The Christmas Island controversy underlined Labor's efforts to decompress foreign and defence policy issues in Western Australia and elsewhere. It also illustrated the opposition's intention to focus on inflation and related domestic issues, but to allow latitude for external policy attacks. There were press reports that Whitlam and Lee had secretly agreed in principle to the transfer of Australian-held Christmas Island to Singapore. There was a chorus of outcries from the opposition, accusing the government of further compromising security interests in the Indian Ocean area, further denigrating Western Australia's security and of planning to part with phosphate-rich property, a further demonstration of Labor's disdain for the man on the land. Peacock, Forbes and Sinclair (but not Snedden personally) expressed criticism and the L–CP attack did not subside until polling-day.[31] Liberal politicians in Western Australia were vocal as well and the controversy had quite considerable publicity in Perth.

What did the opposition hope to gain from its Christmas Island criticisms? In the first place, the author is persuaded from internal evidence that part of the quick and emphatic *Liberal* Party criticism had nothing to do with berating Labor. It was designed to emphasize the Liberal Party's concern for the phosphate deposits on the island— of interest to rural Western Australians—and thereby to upstage the Country Party, against whom (as well as against Labor) the Liberals were competing in some Western Australian federal seats. In the context of opposition–Labor electoral competition, L–CP criticism really was a case of taking advantage of a windfall. The attack was left to lieutenants rather than L–CP leaders, and at all events Christmas Island could not be considered as a methodical gambit for drawing defence issues into the campaign spotlight. Labor treated the controversy in accordance with governing party strategy. Whitlam issued an indignantly worded denial of any agreements or negotiations for transfer of the island's sovereignty. Opposition imputations to the contrary were branded as falsehoods and as revealing commentary on the L–CP's flagging electoral fortunes.[32] The chosen tactic was to deny once and flatly: to suppress the issue and to avoid its possible proliferation into a broader debate over external policy.

Unlike Christmas Island, Labor found it politically imprudent to dismiss by terse retort criticisms levelled against its attitude towards Middle Eastern problems. We have seen that there was much disquiet within the ALP itself, notably on Hawke's part. The opposition had been imputing non-even-handedness to the government. Jewish interests exerted themselves to bring about change in official attitude. Labor was somewhat concerned that, in a tight election, the loss of Jewish votes in a few key seats (such as Philip in New South Wales) could be critical. It also wished to neutralize criticism that it was hypocritical in its professions of even-handedness. It worked hard to minimize any electoral fall-out. Willesee and Whitlam produced a flurry of statements. These explained the government's position, denied charges of partiality and counter-attacked the opposition for allegedly dismal, partisan attempts to pursue "sectionalism" and for contradicting its own basic Middle Eastern position, claimed by Labor to have been no different from its own.[33] The Department of Foreign Affairs undertook to provide personalized answers to critical newspaper editorials and letters from prominent individuals. Members of the Prime Minister's staff worked in Melbourne and Sydney to dispel Jewish disquiet, while Hawke tried to play down the impact of the rift between himself and Whitlam and castigated the opposition for shameless electioneering.[34] In the meantime, it was necessary to avoid the appearance of bending over backwards, since Australia's Arab community was beginning to assert itself.

We now ask whether the major parties tried to portray external policies as substantively congruent or divergent. However one might objectively view the content of party external policies, and apart from whether the parties consciously emphasized or de-emphasized external policy differences, most commentators regarded the policies as basically similar. For instance, referring to "a new composite figure, Gill Sneddlam", the *National Times* remarked that

> the Liberals have abandoned the thought of reviving the "Red Bogey", endorsed Labor's "equal partner" line on relations with America, retained the even-handed Middle East policy and supported Labor's China, Taiwan and North Vietnamese initiatives ... In defence, the Liberals have swung over to support the Labor line on American bases, and in all but one area—regional defence arrangement—the two policies are utterly compatible.[35]

The Melbourne *Age*, pleased that the L–CP was no longer tormenting the electorate with "atavistic fears of phantom foreign hordes", was also relieved by the "new pragmatism" that had largely replaced "the old anti-imperialist dogmatism which used to dominate much of Labor's thinking on foreign policy".[36] Thus by the very nature of external policy reception in the media, public concern over such subjects during the electoral campaign was diluted.

Country Party leaders, while broaching defence preparedness and the US alliance, largely overlooked foreign policy themes as such. On his rare excursions into foreign policy, Anthony conveyed a mixed attitude. While stressing continuing dangers to Australia from communist sources, he accepted Labor's close involvement with Third World and socialist nations.[37] For the Liberals, Snedden did, to be sure, try to draw defence policy distinctions on a number of occasions. But when on a few occasions he drew distinctions with Labor's foreign policy, he tended to stress *situational* or *stylistic* material rather than embroidering larger, thematic pictures. Hence he struck out at Labor's alleged non-even-handedness on the Middle East and against the "double standard" response towards French and Chinese nuclear testing. He criticized a run-down in US–Australian relations and Labor's lack of enthusiasm for the Diego Garcia project.[38] It fell on Peacock to serve as protagonist for the wider dimensions of L–CP external policies. Among his numerous press releases and public remarks could be found a reasonably coherent exposition of his party's outlook. However, it should be remembered that media coverage of foreign policy generally, and of remarks by party lieutenants as opposed to leaders, was weak. In the face of these obstacles to getting a reasonable hearing, Peacock insisted upon "the very significant differences between the Liberal and Country Parties' position and that of the Australian Labor Party".[39] The only other Liberal spokesman known to have tried his hand at presenting a broad-ranging analysis of ALP–opposition external policy was Fraser; interestingly, he did this in an address before a Jewish audience.[40] Speakers' notes issued by the Liberals to candidates and others provided suggestions on how to distinguish between party external policies,[41] but such material was not widely used among rank-and-file campaigners.

Labor was committed to disengaging external affairs from the election. It sought to do so not simply by striving to avoid the subject but by searching for opportunities to allege that there was little to debate, since government and opposition policies had largely become convergent. Several days before the party speeches were delivered, a television interview programme held between Peacock and Willesee turned into a non-event. The former tried to open channels for substantive foreign policy discussion and to assert real inter-party differences, while the latter dodged and minimized confrontation.[42] Commenting on the L–CP platform, the Foreign Minister "welcomed the acceptance by the Opposition of nearly all the foreign policy initiative taken by the Whitlam Government ... Imitation is the sincerest form of flattery."[43] In his policy speech, Whitlam flatly announced that "Australia now has basically a bipartisan foreign policy."[44] And so Labor proceeded almost across most of the campaign.

As an electoral issue, defence proved more difficult for Labor to subdue than did foreign policy, since the opposition made defence one of its more explicit, though subsidiary, campaign themes. Labor was relieved, however, that the attack upon it was not more sustained or more penetrating. Party strategists had been genuinely worried that an all-out and well-co-ordinated L–CP offensive over defence policy could have cost Labor a close election.

We are already familiar with L–CP criticisms of Labor's defence policy. These included the threat climate, the state of *détente*, officer resignations, a run-down in personnel, equipment and spending, and so on. Forbes set the mood: The Australian people would regard eleventh-hour decisions as "the panic reactions of a group of men frightened by the electoral consequences of failing to do anything".[45]

The L–CP's defence policy attack failed to secure a hold for several reasons. Firstly, the issue was never given anything approximating the attention lavished on inflation and surrounding domestic matters. This was consistent with established party strategy guidelines. Secondly, in April and May 1974, a threat-requires-response argument was difficult to sustain. Vietnam was at last over, no security alarms were ringing around Australia's shores and there was a certain reticence in Liberal ranks to preach a heavy "military" theme at a point when the party was working to shed its "men of the past" image. Thirdly, the L–CP found itself in a bind of its own making. It was difficult to elevate inflation to premier-issue rank, to argue for budgetary austerity (and a $600 million cut-back in federal spending), while simultaneously promising to perform expensive wonders for the nation's defence. This, in part, blocked the L–CP from conspicuously differentiating itself from Labor on defence upgrading. Matters became much worse for the opposition when, on 3 May, Anthony acknowledged that due to a combination of financial constraints and lack of immediate international danger, an L–CP government would not quickly move to exceed Labor's level of defence spending.[46] To Labor's delight, fresh ground for bipartisanship in external policies had been discovered. Barnard hurried to remark that Anthony had apparently accepted the ALP's strategic assessment.[47] Had Anthony attended the late-April L–CP strategy session, at which these matters had been discussed, he might not have said what he did and thereby not handed Labor a splendid gift.

Concurrently, the government tried to demonstrate that it was diligent about defence. A new capital equipment programme was announced and so were promises to unionists that redundancy in defence industries would be strenuously resisted. A string of material improvements for service personnel was announced. Apart from their inherent merit, such measures were also tailored to mollify concerns about defence neglect, and in part were directed at service personnel themselves. In 1974, Labor conceded that most of the service vote, which now included no reluctant conscripts, would favour the opposition. But even a few service votes changed might carry some electoral advantage. One illustration of this was a letter written by a minister, Kep Enderby, on behalf of himself and Labor's candidate for the newly created second Australian Capital Territory federal seat. On official Parliament stationery and addressed to the numerous service personnel living in the Canberra area, it was a recitation of good deeds performed by Labor on behalf of members of the armed forces and a frank appeal for electoral support: "There is much to be done, and a vote for the Whitlam Government on 18th May will be a vote for the continuation and expansion of these initiatives and programmes."[48]

By asserting that there were no outstanding inter-party divisions over defence policy, and by deeds that pictured Labor as not selling out on defence, the government went about detaching defence issues from the electoral campaign. The overall result was not especially pleasing to the L–CP and was overtly depressing to persons and groups holding pronounced views on defence policy. Santamaria sensed that bipartisanship in both defence and foreign policy had arrived in Australia, "the liberals having adopted the essence of the policies fastened on Labor by Dr Cairns and the Left". To him: "Among all Australian parties, the DLP alone gives Australia's defencelessness its correct priority ... there is no other way of keeping Australia's defences alive than by keeping the DLP strong in the Senate."[49] The DLP's external policy platform was indeed non-imitative of allegedly "identikit" Liberals and Laborites. But there were signs that its principal Senate candidates recognized that a campaign hung on vivid external policy presentation was not the wisest strategy. Back in 1973, Senator Jack Kane had already concluded that defence and foreign policy issues had by and large become electorally defused and had thereby caused defections among previous DLP supporters.[50] In the course of his bid to retain his New South Wales seat, Kane publicized non-external subjects, such as the abolition of death duties. Victorian Senator Frank McManus was less disposed to jettison external policy. At a press conference, he mournfully remarked: "If the D.L.P. is to be unpopular for insisting that our Defence Policies be such that we could contribute to our own defence and be able to assist our allies, rather than be 'free loaders', then the D.L.P. is prepared to be unpopular."[51] Still, McManus' election material followed a "Vote Mac Back" rather than a party political, DLP theme, and the emphasis was on his record and the need for an independent Senate voice, not on external affairs spokesmanship as such.

A word is finally in order about ancillary manipulations of external policy themes by the parties, i.e. how such themes may have been mated with other features of electioneering.

The L–CP might have chosen to confront Labor on its credibility as a government: radical influences upon it, ministerial disunity, unplugged security leaks, and so on. In fact, it did very little in this direction. One very important reason was that the April–May period was quite tranquil for Labor as a party and as a government. No major protest manifestations occurred to upset public sensibilities. The

marchers to the North-West Cape did skirmish with police and residents, but their cause, as we have seen, was anti-Labor as well as anti-
L–CP. At all events, the marchers did not reach their destination until
just after polling had been completed. No new security breaches
cropped up between 1 April and 18 May. Then, too, Whitlam's
schoolmaster lecture to his ministers paid off. There were no
noticeable ministerial indiscretions on external policy matters. During the campaign, Whitlam tried to dismiss the importance of the
matter. He squelched an interview question on whether out-of-turn
ministerial comments might not have been unhelpful to his government by retorting, "Well, to use an Americanism. Crap!"[52] The most
independent external policy remarks from a prominent ALP figure
came from Wheeldon—not then a minister—who urged the
severance of Australian defence ties with America and the dismantl-
ing of US facilities.[53]

Labor's efforts to insulate itself from criticisms of stylistic fault in
its handling of external affairs created some frustrations within the
L–CP. Peacock, for instance, on several occasions tried to draw out
and entrap Labor by accusing it of concealing its policies, and he invited outspoken ministers such as Cairns and Uren to "put their case
directly to the people–for approval or rejection".[54] The bait was not
taken. Still, the Liberals were not especially eager to precipitate an
electoral slugfest in this area. The party had prepared dossiers on
Cairns and others, but the material was hardly used. Men such as
Snedden and Peacock were not temperamentally disposed to urge a
personalized "boots and all" campaign. This was in keeping with the
party's decision not to deviate much from an inflation issue emphasis
and with organizational advice that, if Labor counter-attacked heavily, Snedden could not in substance or in style match the Prime
Minister in an exchange over external policy. Also the opposition
may have been reluctant to encourage ripostes in kind from Labor
about party unity and the like, since Snedden and Anthony were
themselves divided on several key issues during the campaign.

If, however, in 1974, the L–CP was unable or unwilling to resort to
tactics of emotive ridicule of Labor's credibility, Labor found an
emotionally serviceable tool with which to beat the opposition. Much
of Labor's campaigning, especially in the earlier stages, was targeted
against the foreign economic presence in Australia. For some months
prior to the campaign, and then during it, various ministers pictured
the issue in highly picturesque terms. A number of imputations were
levelled against foreign financial underwriting of the opposition, and
both Connor and Whitlam, in the midst of the electoral campaign,
told audiences (in remarkably similar, perhaps orchestrated
phraseology) that Australian independence, which in war foreign

arms could not conquer, foreign money was now threatening to conquer. Whitlam predicted that this might be the Australians' last chance to choose to conserve their independent economic inheritance "for our children and our children's children".[55]

Labor's treatment of foreign economic issues was viewed by a number of observers as transparent but probably profitable electioneering, and also as a contradiction of ALP professions, of being a party of social healers. As the *Australian Financial Review* editorialized, "The ploy is obviously to work foreign ownership, the multinationals and the mining companies into some new kind of foreign demon for which all red-blooded Australians can work up an understandable loathing."[56] The opposition also took umbrage. Anthony, for instance, issued a special statement entitled "No Place for Hatred in Australia", in which he argued that the only legitimate fears were fears of Labor's erroneous domestic and external policies; here was a contrived, "old political tactic of a government in trouble—give the people a foreign enemy to hate".[57]

Labor's attack is relevant not just because it was directed at "foreign" interests but because of a certain interface between ALP foreign economic attitudes and policies, and foreign policy more explicitly. In 1974, Labor was reluctant to debate foreign policy, but was not averse to permitting electoral windfalls that might result if emotional presentations about the foreign economic presence could remind the electorate of the government's pursuit of independence and national dignity in foreign affairs. Some ministerial remarks during the campaign attempted to draw that connection[58] and were consistent with the government's perceptions of the meaning, relationship and handling of issues.

We now examine the interplay between electoral politics and external policy following the May 1974 election. For a number of months after the election, the author inquired of a number of Labor and opposition politicians and organizational people whether, from an electoral standpoint, they felt their side had given about the right emphasis to external policies during the campaign. The answers were preponderantly in the affirmative. The dominant explanation was simply that the public was known to have been far more concerned about socio-economic issues. Post-election survey data tended to confirm, or at least not to contradict, that the vast majority of voters had not been influenced by external policy considerations. A privately conducted Country Party survey of over 700 respondents in various rural electorates uncovered only one person who said that defence policy considerations had pre-eminently influenced his vote; no one alluded to foreign policy. On election day itself, the McNair organization polled 346 voters in six swinging Sydney electorates. Pre-election data were largely confirmed. Labor was thought to have had the better programme on overseas-controlled Australian resources, the L–CP on defence policy. It was also confirmed that more Liberal than Labor voters felt that *among* the issues guiding their vote were superior foreign and defence policies. Within the survey group were thirty-six persons who changed their vote to Labor in 1974 from non-Labor in 1972. Among these, four persons, or 11 per cent, listed as *a* reason for their switch a better Labor foreign policy stance, and one listed the abolition of conscription. No one listed control over the foreign economic presence. While the 11 per cent figure seems high, the sample was very small and therefore statistically fragile. Moreover, multiple reasons for change of vote were given, preventing the isolation of the foreign/defence policy variable.[59] Inferential evidence suggests that, despite disgruntlement over government Middle Eastern policy, very few Jews of usual ALP allegiance actually shifted to the L–CP.

What evidence, if any, could political strategists on either side adduce that after May 1974 the electorate might have given particular reception to various external policy issues? On the basis of available survey data, the opposition could take somewhat more comfort than the government. For instance, twice as many people disapproved of the Baltic states decision as approved of it; even normally Labor supporters were about evenly divided.[60] Also there were strong majorities among both L–CP and ALP voters to keep South Africa in the United Nations, although in the Security Council the Labor government voted against South Africa.[61] Early in 1975, there was overwhelming endorsement by both L–CP and Labor supporters for a neutral Australian position on the Middle East—an avowed government attitude. But there also was very strong Labor and L–CP voter resistance to allowing a PLO delegation to enter Australia.[62] This was the original, but not eventual, government position. In September 1975, though a very large part of the public (44 per cent) was undecided, persons favouring an independent Portuguese Timor outnumbered those who would have wished it to be part of Indonesia by more than a two-to-one margin.[63] Connor's efforts to raise billions of petrodollars were disapproved of by a very considerable proportion of the electorate.[64] Perhaps most disconcerting to Labor was a poll taken in 1975, as the Thieu régime in South Vietnam was collapsing. Two out of three persons (58 per cent versus 29 per cent) believed Australia was likely to be menaced by another country within the following decade. The 58 per cent figure was 4 per cent more than had expressed a similar opinion in 1970, when the L–CP was in office and the Vietnam War was in full swing. In 1975, Labor supporters were themselves about equally divided on the foreseeability of a menace to the country.[65]

For some time after May 1974, electoral opportunities to test public receptivity to external issues were few, and at all events represented extremely imperfect barometers. There were state elections in Queensland and South Australia, but their state nature could not be adequately compared to federal campaigns. In Queensland, in December 1974, the incumbent non-Labor government was swept back into office. Bjelke-Petersen tried to tar the state ALP opposition with the sins of the Whitlam government in Canberra and made a number of pointed attacks on federal Labor's alleged flirtations with communist nations.[66] But the Premier's attack on federal Labor, and on Whitlam, was wholesale, far exceeding external policy complaints. The weakness of the state Labor Party at that time, plus other considerations, greatly overshadowed any impact the allusions to foreign affairs might have had on the electoral outcome. Bjelke-Petersen later entered into a dispute with the Whitlam government by threatening to block further Queensland coal sales to Japan, unless Japan bought Queensland beef. This kind of excursion into state "resource diplomacy" was, if anything, an acute embarrassment to the L–CP opposition in Canberra, which itself had been accusing Connor and others of excessive international arm-twisting.[67] At the July 1975 South Australian election, the incumbent Dunstan Labor government was returned with a reduced majority, but Liberal Party fortunes slipped even more drastically. In any event, the use of federal external policy issues was almost zero.[68] In June 1975, there was a federal by-election in Barnard's former Tasmanian seat of Bass, and was carried by the Liberals on a massive anti-Labor swing. Whitlam and Fraser both campaigned in Bass. External issues were not entirely absent, but decidedly secondary, even tertiary. There was some discussion of Omega, especially since Tasmania was one potential site for it, but the overall effect was ambiguous. Some independent Tasmanian unions declared that they would black-ban construction work on an Omega station, and environmentalists were also upset by the prospect of a facility. But there were signs of people eager to have an Omega familiy nearby, to stimulate the local economy.[69]

After the 1974 election, the federal opposition was not inactive in building a case against the government, a case that hopefully could sooner or later bring some electoral pay-off. Some of the criticisms were highly situational, designed to exploit Labor's existing public relations or intra-party troubles. One such issue was the Prime Minister's lengthy European trip in December 1974 and January 1975, during which some of his remarks and his actions received a poor reception in the Australian press and within Labor Party quarters as well. Hence Peacock's stab that there were "many Australians, not least in the Australian Labor Party, who believe the

Prime Minister would be better employed cutting back on expenditure and applying himself to Australia's future."[70] When he returned, Whitlam made a special report to the nation. It was to serve a double purpose: to explain the accomplishments of his mission as such and to counter the political fall-out caused by criticisms of the trip. The opposition was pleased to watch the ALP tear at itself over issues such as the PLO visit and to hear Whitlam admit that "Mr Hawke and Mr Hartley have been responsible, as much as anyone, for exacerbating divisions in Australia on the Middle East."[71]

Two, and to a degree overlapping, phases of the opposition's efforts to mount a general attack on government external policy were detectable. The L–CP felt that its external policy issue emphasis in the context of the 1974 campaign had been reasonably appropriate. It also understood that there were few signs that the electorate's concern over external subjects had measurably increased. All the same, the judgement as of mid-1974 was to intensify foreign policy criticism and to offer a clearer appearance of Labor–L–CP differences. Little electoral mileage could be realized by the opposition if the *impression* of Labor–L–CP policy similarly continued to be widespread. Large issues such as conscription, China, the status of American defence installations and the Singapore troop commitment had by then for most intents and purposes been settled. In the second half of 1974, there were no comparably large issues to be controverted, apart from the ongoing dispute over resource and foreign investment policy. But the opposition felt that the government's handling of individually lesser issues could be tied together and subjected to overall criticism for being clumsy, irresponsible and variously inconsistent with Labor's own professions. The opposition was in this way amassing foreign policy criticisms not just to say that Labor had been wrong on X, Y or Z, but to impugn its credit as a party of government, a credit already suffering some decline over economic performance. It also hoped to pin a good deal of blame on Whitlam personally, in part to narrow the public-image gulf between him and Snedden.

We have already dwelled on the kinds of issues over which the opposition attacked and some of the rationales it presented. There had been the Gair affair (a personal Whitlam decision of "political immorality"). There was the Ermolenko case ("deprivation of human rights" and "uneven-handedness" in favour of communist régimes). There was the South African vote at the United Nations (denial of the principle of universal membership in the world body). And, of course, there were the Baltic states. The opposition played up this decision as a biased, pro-Soviet action and slapped at Labor's rhetoric about the virtues of self-determination. Particular efforts were made to show that ethnic minorities in Australia were contemptuously treated by the government. Snedden's remarks before a Latvian audience pointed up the electoral uses to which the L–CP put the Baltic decision:

> It was an action taken in direct contradiction of Mr Whitlam's own undertakings given to you. There can be no clearer words. The words I remember were these: that the Labor Government in office would pursue the same policy as its predecessor Government, the Liberal Country Party. That undertaking was given. You were entitled to rely on it. Some of you may even have been misled into voting for them—relying on that undertaking. But now the reality of the unreliability of any word given by Labor is clear ... It is a sad reflection on the chaos that is now the Labor Government's foreign policy. Surely they have enough trouble in economic/domestic terms. Why make such a mess of our foreign policy.[72]

Foreign policy was at least tangentially tied to Snedden's own fall from the Liberal leadership in March 1975. Snedden had originally played a useful accommodating role for a party badly shaken by its 1972 defeat. The L–CP had made a respectable showing in a losing cause in 1974, but Snedden's substantial inability to match Whitlam's commanding political personality was upsetting. Not long after the election and the ensuing joint parliamentary sitting, there were signs that the opposition, via the Senate, might try to force another early election. But Snedden was seen as much the same decent yet pedestrian figure he had been before. His parliamentary performances were interpreted by party colleagues as undistinguished. Peacock was conducting most of the party offensive in foreign policy. In this area, Snedden was seen as particularly ineffective in challenging a government, or a Prime Minister, whose external policies seemed to invite crisp, aggressive spokesmanship from an alternative L–CP Prime Minister. Malcolm Fraser beat Snedden in a leadership spill for a number of reasons. But among those who voted for him were Liberals who felt he would be much more electorally credible, and marketable, when attacking Whitlam on the Prime Minister's own special field of interest, namely external policy. Fraser had at one time been Minister for Defence. While in opposition, he had maintained a close interest in external policy and had spoken on it in various settings. In foreign and defence policy, he was known to be rather more tough-minded, or conservative, than Snedden had been. Some Liberals found this appealing. Shortly after Fraser's election, a commentator related reactions he attributed to some Liberals. "Suddenly we feel thirty years younger," one said. Another averred that "We never feel more secure than when we feel threatened, and never more at peace than when we are at war." A third was purported to have remarked that "Nothing exciting ever seemed to happen with Snedden. No red manaces, no yellow perils. Only money, money, money. Even Peacock, with all his charisma, couldn't whip up a fair dinkum threat from the North."[73] Even after allowing for hyperbole and figures of speech, there seemed to be a mood abroad in Liberal ranks that welcomed Fraser as a substitute for Snedden in external policy spokesmanship.

Following Fraser's election to the leadership, the intensity of L–CP external policy criticism did in fact rise. In part, as foreseen, this was because of Fraser's own interest in the field and his wish to give the subject more attention. In part, it was because Fraser held a somewhat more agitated view of world trends than Snedden had. In part, it was attributable to salient international events such as the fall of Indo-China to communism and violent disorders in Timor. Such events were seen as confirmation that Australia was living in an unstable and threatening region, and that Labor was too complacent or misguided to do whatever was needed. Moreover, under Fraser, the opposition consciously enlarged on the strategy, begun in 1974, that called for impugning the veracity, credit and overall competence of the government in the course of L–CP attacks on the substance of policies. In 1974, issues such as the Baltic states, Ermolenko and the South African UN vote had served to build this kind of case. During Fraser's leadership, the issues that presented such opportunities seemed more fundamental or capable of being more publicly sensationalized. Hence regarding the government's handling of its Vietnamese diplomacy, or of the Connor and Cairns efforts to raise petrodollar loans, the opposition assailed Labor for misleading Parliament and the public, for its underhandedness, for its stark lack of integrity, and so on. Regarding Vietnamese refugees, the opposition tried to picture Labor as weak, vacilating, over-sensitive to communist régime reactions, and in the last resort, callous towards victims of war and dislocation.

The opposition also revived the technique of trying to discredit the government by discrediting a controversial minister. Cairns had long been a L–CP target, for what were regarded as his outrageous pronouncements on foreign policy and his ability to defy Whitlam's injunctions about extramural ministerial remarks. But the political value of criticisms against Cairns had been somewhat elusive, since Cairns' remarks often did not reflect the government's own more moderate thinking. Connor was different. He had long been the butt of opposition criticism. In his case, since his views were very often actual government policies, the wrongness of his views, and the gracelessness of his style, could more easily be used to indict the government as such. By mid-1975, Connor's, and therefore, the government's, political vulnerability was more exploitable in the aftermath of the loan episode. Cairns had been sacked, but Connor remained and was defended by Whitlam. For Anthony, "The continued survival of the Minister for Minerals and Energy in the Ministry must remain one of the greatest mysteries surrounding the Whitlam Government." He could not understand why, in addition to wrecking the mining industry, alienating foreign countries and irritating various officials and departments in Canberra, Connor "is allowed slowly to wreck the Labor Party".[74] When Whitlam sacked Connor in October, the opposition's reaction was that this was more than a vindication of its misgivings about Connor and his methods. It also provided a basis for redoubling attacks on the government's credibility and rationale for holding up Labor's budget in the Senate. Fraser said that, "The Opposition in the Senate has acted to bring about an election—in accordance with Constitutional practice—because the Government has lost the confidence of the people. Its sordid scandals have caught up with it—the Prime Minister and his Government can no longer evade responsibility."[75]

The opposition was not itself free from intra-élite problems. Peacock was somewhat less intense, more modulated in his views and words than were the two coalition party leaders. Hence in August 1975, apparent;y with Fraser's support but against the grain of Peacock's thinking, Anthony raised a communist takeover vision of events in Timor and urged the establishment of an Australian presence there.[76] There also were some press imputations that the new opposition policy statements on foreign policy and on defence, issued in October, had involved serious differences among party élites. It was said that Fraser had caused substantive rewritings in what Peacock and Killen had desired in their respective papers.[77] This impression is believed to be misleading. The author understands that the original drafts of these papers were authored by academics and then, with guidance and consent from Peacock and Killen, were refined by the opposition's Policy Co-ordinating Committee. Fraser's hand was not obtrusive and no meaningful modifications were apparently "imposed" by him. A good test lies in the policy documents themselves. While the foreign affairs and defence statements reflected many of the opposition's familiar differences with Labor, they were couched in essentially cautious and pragmatic terms.[78] The L–CP's foreign investment statement,[79] prepared by Lynch and his staff, was closely tied to the Canadian model and was remarkably close to the position Labor had reached by the closing months of its tenure.

Government spokesmen, apart from exploiting any discord they noticed in opposition ranks, rebutted charges of error or duplicity in external affairs in two ways. They pictured the government as applying a sober and intelligent approach to difficult problems, and pictured the L–CP, especially under the more pungent, Fraser-style of criticism, as cynical and opportunistically unworthy. Also they tried to portray the opposition as unreconstructed crisis-mongers, men who had taken Australia into the mire of Vietnam and who now had the effrontery to speak of honour.

How much of this party political sparring seemed applicable to building foundations on which electoral advantage could be laid? In the second half of 1975, knowledgeable persons on both political sides were inclined to think much as they had in 1974, that for the electorate, economic and other domestic issues continued to overshadow external policy. Therefore the parties were not counting on substituting questionable issue emphasis priorities. As one L–CP figure expressed it:

> Unless there is unexpected resurgence of communist activity in southeast Asia, it seems unlikely to expect that Foreign Affairs or Defence will assume any substantial electoral prominence. It is quite remarkable how quickly the communist takeover of all of Vietnam has ebbed from public prominence. This is very regrettable as the Red devils are very active at the moment in Malaysia.[80]

However, there was some guarded feeling that, in the large sense, events ranging from the fall of Into-China to turmoil on Timor may have restored some of the respectability of anti-communist sentiment. Perhaps one small evidence of this was the previously cited 1975 survey, which indicated that two out of three Australians believed the country would face an external menace within the next decade.

In any event, much of the 1975 inter-party debate, on external affairs and otherwise, was conducted in an atmosphere that indicated the possibility that the opposition might try to force an early election. That in itself placed a premium on the sharpening of opposition attacks on all policy fronts and helped to explain the explicit coupling of imputations of irresponsible government with imputations of improper policies. It also tempted speculation that some of the Labor government's policy movements may in part have been designed to neutralize opposition external policy criticisms that could be expected to arise in an electoral campaign. There was the fairly extensive shopping-list of military capital equipment announced in the 1975–6 budget and the government's rapid moves towards a major relaxation of policies governing foreign investment.

The prospect of some kind of early election arose when the opposition used its numbers in the Senate to block Labor's budget. On 11 November, the deadlock was broken by the Governor-General, Sir John Kerr, who argued that the provision of supply was paramount. Whitlam's commission was withdrawn. The L–CP was to allow Labor's budget to pass. A double dissolution was called, with elections scheduled for 13 December. In the meantime, Fraser was to head a caretaker L–CP government, which was not entitled to undertake new policy initiatives.

The 1975 electoral campaign is essentially beyond the scope of this study, insofar as Labor was no longer the government after 11 November. Some comments are, however, in order, to complete the transition from Labor in power to the election in December of a Fraser government that was swept to office with an unprecedented majority in the House and full control over the Senate.

Survey data collected during the campaign showed that only about 1 per cent regarded foreign and defence policy as the single most important national issue,[81] though between 13 and 16 per cent ranked "defence" as one of the three most personally important issues.[82] As in the past, non-Labor voters were proportionately more interested in foreign and defence issues than were Labor supporters. Some special circumstances were noticeable. In Victoria, for instance, Jews went out of their way to promote the defeat of Hartley, who had been placed on the ALP's Senate ballot.[83]

The low salience of external issues in the 1975 campaign was considerably influenced by the climate generated by the political crisis of the time. The L–CP operated a low-key campaign, focusing on Labor's economic mismanagement and more generally on its lack of credit as a party of efficient and upright government. These had been the ostensible opposition rationales for obstructing the budget and forcing an election. Labor had been caught by surprise by the Governor-General's action. It was furious with what it construed as Kerr's constitutionally unjustifiable intervention and possible collusion with Fraser. Hence, for the first part of his campaign, Whitlam hammered on the theme that Labor had been cheated of the right to govern, since its control over the House had remained intact. Only later did Whitlam shift more to a defence of his government's economic policies and a challenge of L–CP alternatives.

While the atmosphere was not conducive to the exposition of a wide range of issues, it was, at least on Labor's part, conducive to some highly emotional imputations. Shortly after Labor's dismissal, Cairns exhorted a political rally, arguing that, "The Liberal and Country Party, with the help of the multi-national companies and the CIA, is spending $1 million in television and advertising. We will answer them with one million people."[84] Shortly before the campaign ended, as Labor's electoral prospects were fading, Whitlam told a television interviewer that while he would not assert that there had been CIA involvement in his dismissal, "I wouldn't blankly refute the possibility."[85] Imputations such as these were perhaps understandable in the heat of Labor's anger, frustration and dismay over what had happened. Their veracity is another matter. They were not substantiated, and of course were firmly denied by both American and L–CP sources. On balance, for reasons we discussed earlier about the

American position in and attitude towards Australia, and towards Labor particularly, their plausibility is questionable.

When substantive external issues did appear in the 1975 campaign, they more often than not were presented in a hit-and-miss and unedifying manner. L–CP spokesmen, for instance, said that Labor had sanctioned aggression by its Baltic states decision, had followed a pro-Soviet policy in the 'Middle East, and that Hartley's place on the Senate ballot was a sign of further Labor betrayal of Israel's interest.[86] The ALP, with its preoccupation with recent domestic Australian political events, tried to tie some external issues to the crisis. For instance, Morrison warned that Fraser's obsession with austerity could lead to defence cutbacks under an L–CP government and thereby endanger Australia's security.[87] On his part, Whitlam suggested that with Australia distracted by an election forced by the L–CP, Indonesia may have been given incentive to intervene full scale in Timor.[88]

Electoral considerations were, of course, only one, and a not always easily distinguishable influence upon the mosaic of Australian external policy. Historical legacies, party conceptions and dispositions, the roles played by key personalities, the peculiarities of Australia's political structures, the host of advisory inputs and of group pressures and, above all, unfolding international developments also contributed to what became the substance and the stylistic conduct and presentation of external policy. A change of government in 1972 had brought some new definitions, directions and methods. These were greeted by boasts of great achievements and by condemnations of outrageous bungling. Taken in perspective, Labor's record and performance can probably be characterized as adaptive. There were real shifts of emphasis in both substance and style from what had been done under L–CP governments, but continuity was preserved in the basic outlines of Australia's external policy.

As in any open society, openly expressed disagreements over assumptions, programmes and priorities remained. On occasions, these differences were embittered. Much more often, especially in the government–opposition dialogue, beneath the layer of rhetoric and political·posturing was noticeable inter-party consensus on Australia's interests, and even on the means of their achievement. Australia had not achieved and was not likely to achieve bipartisanship in external affairs. During the period of Labor government, however, both the ALP and the L–CP made adjustments, resulting in a measure of convergence between the two sides. Changing international realities played their part in this process. So did the reversal of roles that took place in December 1972. We recall Bruce Grant's comment, mentioned earlier in this book, that, with reference to foreign policy, by

1972 both the L–CP government and the ALP opposition had, in different ways, become irresponsible. After twenty-three years, the L–CP no longer understood the role of an opposition, while Labor had lost sight of the obligations of power.[89] The two party groups were not transformed by their experience after December 1972, but they were sobered by it.

NOTES

1. Portions of this chapter are drawn from the author's "The Role of Foreign Policy in Australian Electoral Politics: Some Explanations and Speculations", *Australian Outlook* 28 (August 1974):118–41. Thanks for permission to use the material are expressed to Dr (now Professor) Peter Boyce, editor of the *Australian Outlook*, a publication of the Australian Institute of International Affairs.
2. L. Barnard, address in Perth of 29 October 1973, transcript, p. 9.
3. The government's position was outlined by Willesee in *Commonwealth [Australian]Parliamentary Debates (APD)* Senate (8 April 1975), pp. 761–62.
4. Derived from non-attributable source . On aspects of Liberal foreign policy making and presentation, see J. Knight, "Foreign Policy Development in Opposition: 1972–1975", *Dyason House Papers* 1 (March 1975): 5–8.
5. Derived from non-attributable source.
6. *Australian*, 15 March 1973 (ANOP).
7. Melbourne *Age*, 24 December 1973 (ASRB).
8. *Australian*, 25 March 1974 (ANOP).
9. *Australian*, 30 June 1973 (ANOP).
10. *Morgan Gallup Polls*, no. 93 (1974).
11. See remarks by ex-Premier Tonkin, cited in *Sydney Morning Herald*, 3 April 1974. Also see A. Thomas, *Canberra Times*, 13 April 1974.
12. J. Camilleri, "In Search of a Foreign Policy", *Arena*, nos. 32–33 (1973), pp. 78–79.
13. J.M. Riordan, *APD*, HR (7 March 1974), p. 191.
14. Barnard, address in Washington of 4 January 1974, Department of Defence, *Press Release*, no. 200/74 (5 January 1974)
15. For instance, see M. Walsh's appraisal, *Australian Financial Review*, 22 November 1973.
16. *Canberra Times*, 6 February 1974.
17. *APD*, Senate (3 April 1974), p. 630.
18. Willesee interview of 1 April 1974, in Department of Foreign Affairs memorandum.
19. See Lynch's criticism, *Sydney Morning Herald*, 25 February 1974.
20. For representative appraisals of the two visits, see J. Jost, Melbourne *Age*, 12 January 1974; B. Wilson, Melbourne *Herald*, 22 January 1974; and D. Solomon, *Canberra Times*, 19 February 1974.
21. See Melbourne *Age*, 6 July 1973; and B. Toohey, *Australian Financial Review*, 13 July 1973.
22. For Snedden's remarks, see his *Press Statement* of 2 July 1973, release no. 73/100; and the account in *Sydney Daily Telegraph*, 17 July 1973. On Cairns, see his statement of 17 July 1973, parliamentary press office memorandum.
23. See D. Solomon, *Canberra Times*, 8 February 1974; P. Kelly, *Australian* 15 February 1974; B. Johns, *Sydney Morning Herald*, 16 February 1974; and B. Toohey, *Canberra Times*, 9 May 1974.
24. Melbourne *Age*, 8 April 1974 (ASRB)
25. See summary of the Australia Party platform, *Sydney Morning Herald*, 29 April 1974.
26. J. Henderson, *Nation-Review*, 19 April 1974.
27. *Australian Labor Party: Policy Speech*, Whitlam, 29 April 1974; *Federal Election 1974: Opening Speech*, Snedden, 30 April 1974; and *Policy Speech: 1974 Federal Election*, Anthony, 2 May 1974.

28. Liberal Party of Australia, *The Way Ahead with a Liberal Country Party Government* (Canberra: 1974); foreign affairs on pp. 11–17, defence on pp. 18–22.
29. Radio talkback interview, Perth, 2 May 1974, transcript. Also see Whitlam's reassuring remarks to Court of 7 May 1974, reproduced under the aegis of the Minister for Foreign Affairs, 12 May 1974.
30. For instance, see Snedden's speech at Balga (WA) of 7 May 1974, *Press Release* no. 74/75 (n.d.); and his press conference in Perth of 9 May 1974, transcript.
31. For Peacock's initial attack, see his *Press Release* 12 May 1974. For summaries of other criticisms, see *Australian*, 14 May 1974.
32. See especially Melbourne *Age*, 14 May 1974.
33. For instance, Willesee's statement of 8 and 9 May 1974, in Department of Foreign Affairs, *News Release*, nos. M69, M69 (as amended) and M70 (n.d.); and Whitlam, reported in Melbourne *Age*, 17 May 1974.
34. On Hawke, see Melbourne *Age*, 13 May 1974.
35. *National Times*, 29 April 1974.
36. Melbourne *Age*, 7 May 1974.
37. *Sydney Morning Herald*, 26 April 1974: and *Canberra Times*, 4 May 1974.
38. For a major statement in which Snedden attempted to summarize inter-party differences generally, see his speech at Coolangatta of 1 May 1974, *Press Release*, no. 74/66 (n.d.)
39. Peacock, *News Release*, 9 May 1974.
40. Fraser, notes of remarks of 5 May 1974 in Melbourne, *Press Statement*.
41. See Liberal Party of Australia, Federal Secretariat, *Research Notes: Federal Election Speakers' Notes*, no. 1 (22 April 1974). pp. 18–19; no. 2 (26 April 1974), pp. 1–6; and no. 4(7 May 1974), pp. 3–7.
42. ABC interview with R. Carlton, 24 April 1974, transcript.
43. Department of Foreign Affairs. *Press Release*, 23 April 1974.
44. ALP, *Policy Speech*, p. 35.
45. Forbes, *APD*, HR (9 April 1974), p. 1243.
46. *Australian*, 4 May 1974.
47. See Barnard's press statement of 3 May 1974, *Press Release*, no. 263/74 (n.d.).
48. Enderby, letter to "Dear Sir or Madam" of 19 April 1974, text.
49. B.A. Santamaria, "Point of View" commentary, *News Weekly*, 15 May 1974.
50. See P. Samuel's story, *Bulletin*, 6 October 1973.
51. McManus, Sydney press conference of 6 May 1974, press statement issued by his office, Parliament House.
52. Brisbane press conference of 6 May 1974, transcript.
53. *Sydney Morning Herald*, 26 April 1974.
54. Peacock's *News Release*, 3 May 1974. Also see his *News Releases*, 28 April and 1 and 5 May 1974.
55. *Canberra Times*, 3 May 1974. For Connor's remarks, see *Australian* 7 May 1974. On Labor's foreign investment strategy, see L. Oakes and D. Solomon, *Grab for Power: Election '74* (Melbourne: Cheshire 1974), pp. 342–43.
56. *Australian Financial Review*, 6 May 1974. For similar passages, see B. Johns, *Sydney Morning Herald*, 26 April 1974; and B. Juddery, *Canberra Times*, 8 May 1974.
57. Anthony, *Media Release*, 17 April 1074
58. Notably by Morrison. See his speech to the AIIA, Townsville, 30 April 1974, *Release* from the office of the Minister for Science. Also see Connor's observations issued under the aegis of the Ministry of Minerals and Energy, 18[?] April 1974.
59. *McNair Poll*, 18 May 1974.
60. *Morgan Gallup Polls*, no. 161 (1974).
61. *Morgan Gallup Polls*, no. 167 (1974).
62. Melbourne *Herald*, 4 March 1975 (AIPO).
63. *Morgan Gallup Polls*, sheet for nos. 234, 267, 270–5, 277–8 and 281–2 (1975).
64. *Morgan Gallup Polls*, no. 261 (1975).
65. *Morgan Gallup Polls*, no. 216 (1975).
66. See H. Lunn's review, *Australian*, 6 December 1974; and more generally on the Queensland election, M.N.B. Cribb, "Australian Political Chronicle Queensland", *Australian Journal of Politics and History*, 21 (April 1975): 73–75.
67. See B. Toohey, *Australian Financial Review*, 18 February 1975.

68. For summaries of the South Australian campaign, see B. Juddery, *Canberra Times*, 4 and 7 July 1974; D. Armstrong, *Australian*, 10 July 1975; and T. Colebatch, Melbourne *Age*, 14 July 1975.
69. See A. Downie's assessment, *Nation-Review*, 4 July 1975.
70. Peacock, *Media Release*, 2 January 1975.
71. Whitlam press conference of 29 January 1975, in *Australian*, 30 January 1975.
72. Snedden, address of 8 September 1974, transcript. p. 3.
73. Cited by D. Kennedy, *Nation-Review*, 4 April 1975.
74. Anthony, *Media Release*, 11 July 1975.
75. Fraser's *Press Release* (23 October 1975), p. 1. Also see Killen, *APD*, HR (14 October 1975), pp. 2070–71.
76. For summaries of this rift in opposition ranks, see R. Haupt, *Australian Financial Review*, 29 August 1975; and C. Burns, Melbourne *Age*, 30 August 1975. For Anthony's position, see transcript of his radio interview in his *Media Release* (28 August 1975).
77. See especially M. MacCallum, *Nation-Review*, 22 August and 10 October 1975.
78. Liberal and National Country Parties, *Foreign Policy* (Canberra: Liberal Party Federal Secretariat, 1975); and *Defence Policy* (Canberra: Liberal Party Federal Secretariat, 1975). See assessments of the "moderation" of Liberal foreign policy in C. Burns, Melbourne *Age*, 7 October 1975; and in A. Clark, *National Times*, 13 October 1975.
79. Liberal and National Country Parties, *Foreign Investment Policy* (Canberra: Liberal Party Federal Secretariat, 1975).
80. Derived from non-attributable source.
81. Melbourne *Age*, 4 and 11 December 1975 (ASRB).
82. *Morgan Gallup Polls*, sheets for nos. 307–8 and nos. 311–20 (1975).
83. On Jewish reactions, see E. Wynhausen, *National Times*, 1 March 1976. For the reaction of the ethnic press to the election, see V. Basile, Melbourne *Age*; 10 December 1975.
84. Melbourne *Age*, 13 November 1975.
85. TDT television interview report in Melbourne *Age*, 10 December 1975.
86. For instance, Fraser, Melbourne *Age*, 1 December 1975; and Peacock, Melbourne *Age*, 3 December 1975.
87. *Canberra Times*, 3 December 1975.
88. See Melbourne *Age*, 8 and 11 December 1975; and the commentary in *Australian*, 8 December 1975.
89. B. Grant, "Labor and the World", in *Labor in Power: What is the Difference?*, Victorian Fabian Society Pamphlet no. 22 (Melbourne: 1972), pp. 11–13.

Bibliography

The following select bibliography is confined to secondary sources. Book material, apart from a very few basic sources on the L–CP period, is limited to titles published in the 1970s. Periodical articles and brief monographic items emphasize the period of the Labor government as such. The titles selected for this bibliography cover a wide range of subject-matter and reflect various political perspectives. Readers interested in greater bibliographic depth will find more exhaustive references in footnote citations.

There are some particularly helpful official publications, especially relating to government actions and pronouncements. These include *Hansard*, the *Australian Government Digest* for 1973 and 1974, the *Australian Government Weekly Digest* for 1975, the *Australian Foreign Affairs Record*, the Department of Foreign Affairs *Backgrounder* from the latter part of 1975, and various departmental and ministerial releases. Australian external policy developments (as well as political events generally) are summarized in the *Australian Journal of Politics and History* and in the *Australian Quarterly*.

Aitchison, R., ed., *Looking at the Liberals* (Melbourne: Cheshire, 1974).
———, *Thanks to the Yanks?* (Melbourne: Sun Books, 1972).
Albinski, H.S., *Australian Policies and Attitudes Toward China* (Princeton: Princeton University Press, 1965).
———, "Foreign Policy", in *Public Policy in Australia*, ed. R. Forward (Melbourne: Cheshire, 1974), pp. 15–54.
———, *Politics and Foreign Policy in Australia: The Impact of Vietnam and Conscription* (Durham: Duke University Press, 1970).
———, "The Role of Foreign Policy in Australian Electoral Politics: Some Explanations and Speculations", *Australian Outlook* 28 (August 1974): 118–41.
Altman, D., "A Secular Democratic Palestine: A New Litmus Test for the Left", *Politics* 10 (November 1975): 169–77.
Arndt, H.W., "The Economics of the Loan Affair", *Quadrant* 19 (September 1975): 11–15.
Ball, D., "American Bases in Australia: The Strategic Implications", *Current Affairs Bulletin* 51 (March 1975): 4–17.
——— and Babbage, R.E., "The Australian Aircraft Industry: A Defence Point of View", *Australian Quarterly* 47 (June 1975): 62–78.
Bambrick, S., "Australian Resource Development: Some Long Term Issues", *Dyason House Papers* 2 (October 1975): 4–8.
———, *The Changing Relationship: The Australian Government and the Mining Industry*, M Series, no. 42 (Sydney: Committee for Economic Development of Australia, 1975).
Beddie, B.D., ed., *Advance Australia—Where?* (Melbourne: Oxford University Press, 1975).
Bell, H., "Australian Government Policy in Relation to Foreign Investment", *Australian Quarterly* 48 (March 1976): 44–58.
Bruns, G., "Restricting Foreign Investment in Australia", *Round Table* no. 251 (July 1973): 391–401.

Bull, H., "Australia's Involvement in an Independent Papua-New Guinea", *World Review* 13 (March 1974): 1–18.

Camilleri, J.A., "In Search of a Foreign Policy", *Arena* nos. 32–3 (1973): 65–79.

——, *An Introduction to Australian Foreign Policy* (Brisbane: Jacaranda, 1973).

Castles, A.C., *Australia and the United Nations* (Melbourne: Longman, 1973).

Catley, R. and McFarlane, B., *From Tweedledum to Tweedledee: The New Labor Government in Australia* (Sydney: ANZ Book Co., 1974).

Clark, C., ed., *Australian Foreign Policy: Towards a Reassessment* (Melbourne: Cassell, 1973).

——, "Labor's Policy at the United Nations", *Australia's Neighbours*, 4th Series, no. 89 (February–March 1974): 4–8.

Clark, G., "The Australian Department of Foreign Affairs: What's Wrong with Our Diplomats", *Australian Quarterly* 47 (June 1975): 21–35.

——, "Between Two Worlds: The Radicalization of a Conservative", *Meanjin Quarterly* 33 (June 1974): 117–27.

Collins, H., "Australian Foreign Policy in the Era of Détente", *Australian Quarterly* 29 (August 1975): 133–48.

Cook, W.C., Holmes, F.W. and Robinson, A.D., eds., *New Zealand–Australia Cooperation: Proceedings and Papers* (Wellington: Department of University Extension, Victoria University of Wellington, 1974).

Cranston, R., "Foreign Investment Restrictions: Defending Economic Sovereignty in Canada and Australia", *Harvard International Law Journal* 14 (Spring 1973): 345–67.

Dalton, J., "Foreign Policy and Domestic Politics in Australia", *Dyason House Papers* 2 (October 1975): 1–4.

Dunsdorfs, E., *The Baltic Dilemma: The Case of the DeJure Recognition by Australia of the Incorporation of the Baltic States into the Soviet Union* (New York: Robert Speller, 1975).

Eldridge, P.J., "Australia's Relations with Indonesia: An Alternative Approach", *Australian Outlook* 29 (April 1975): 34–52.

Farran, A., "The Freeth Experiment", *Australian Outlook* 26 (April 1972): 46–58.

FitzGerald, S., *Talking with China: The Australian Labor Party Visit and Peking's Foreign Policy*, Contemporary China Papers, no. 4 (Canberra: Australian National University Press, 1972).

Fox, L., *Australia Taken Over?* (Potts Point, NSW: published by the author, 1974).

Goldsworthy, D., "Australia and Africa: New Relationships?", *Australian Quarterly* 45 (December 1973): 58–72.

——, "The Whitlam Government's African Policy", *Dyason House Papers* 1 (January 1975): 1–5.

Grant, B., *The Crisis of Loyalty: A Study of Australian Foreign Policy* (Sydney: Angus & Robertson, 2nd ed, 1973).

—— and Whitlam, E.G., "Labor to Power: What is the Difference?", pamphlet no. 22 (Melbourne: Victorian Fabian Society, 1972).

Greenwood, G., ed., *Approaches to Asia: Australian Postwar Policies and Attitudes* (Sydney: McGraw-Hill, 1974).

—— and Harper, N., eds., *Australia in World Affairs, 1966–1970* (Melbourne: Cheshire, 1974).

Griffin, J., ed., *A Foreign Policy for an Independent New Guinea* (Sydney: Angus & Robertson, 1974).

Hamel-Green, M., "Conscription and Legitimacy 1964–1972", *Melbourne Journal of Politics* 7 (1974–5): 3–16.

Harries, O., "Australia's Foreign Policy Under Whitlam", *Orbis* 19 (Fall 1975): 1090–1101.

——, "Mr Whitlam and Australian Foreign Policy", *Quadrant* 17 (July–August 1973): 55–64.

Hastings, P., "Timor, Indonesia, and Australia", *World Review* 14 (July 1975): 3–15.

——, "The Timor Problem–I", *Australian Outlook* 29 (April 1975): 18–33.

Hogan, W.P., "Australian Economic Policy Opportunities in Asia and the Pacific", *Australian Outlook* 28 (April 1974): 15–23.

Howard, C., "The External Power of the Commonwealth", *Melbourne University Law Review* 8 (August 1971): 193–214.

Hudson, W.J., *Australia and the Colonial Question at the United Nations* (Sydney: Sydney University Press, 1970).

——, ed., *New Guinea Empire: Australia's Colonial Experience* (Melbourne: Cassell, 1974).
Hughes, C.A., "The Rational Voter and Australian Foreign Policy", *Australian Outlook* 24 (April 1970): 5–16.
Hutton, D., "The Omega Navigational System: Friendly Lighthouse, or Nuclear Target?", *Current Affairs Bulletin* 52 (May 1976): 26–30.
King, P., "Wither Whitlam?", *International Journal* 29 (Summer 1974): 422–40.
Knight, J., "Australia and Proposals for Regional Consultation and Co-operation in the Asian and Pacific Area", *Australian Outlook* 28 (December 1974): 259–73.
——, "Foreign Policy Development in Opposition: 1972–1975", *Dyason House Papers* 1 (March 1975): 5–8.
Lloyd, C.J. and Reid, G.S. *Out of the Wilderness: The Return of Labor* (Melbourne: Cassell, 1974).
McCarthy, G., ed., *Foreign Policy for Australia: Choices for the Seventies* (Sydney: Angus & Robertson, 1973).
——, *The Great Big Australian Takeover Book* (Sydney: Angus & Robertson, 1973).
McFarlane, B., "A Neo-Colonial Policy for the Pacific Rim", *Arena* nos. 32–3 (1973): 29–34.
McGavin, R.J., "Australian and Canadian Involvement in the Japanese and American Energy Crisis", *Australia's Neighbours*, 4th Series, no. 84 (February–March 1973): 1–5.
Mackie, J.A.C., "Australia's Relations with Indonesia: Principles and Policies,–I", *Australian Outlook* 28 (April 1974): 3–14.
——, "Australia's Relations with Indonesia: Principles and Policies, II", *Australian Outlook* 28 (August 1974): 168–78.
McLaren, J., ed., *Towards a New Australia* (Melbourne: Cheshire, 1972).
Macmahon Ball, W., "The Foreign Policy of the Whitlam Government", *Australia's Neighbours*, 4th Series, no. 90 (April–June 1974): 1–4.
Mediansky, F.A., "Now Here is Our Foreign Policy", *Current Affairs Bulletin* 49 (September 1972): 98–112.
Mench, P., "After Independence ... Australian Military Involvement?", *New Guinea and Australia, the Pacific and South-East Asia* 9 (January 1975): 42–54.
Mendelsohn, O., *Australia's Foreign Aid: The Perceptions of Parliamentarians* (Canberra: Parliament of Australia. Parliamentary Library, 1973).
Millar, T.B., *Australia's Defence* (Melbourne: Melbourne University Press, 2nd ed, 1969).
——*Australia's Foreign Policy* (Sydney: Angus & Robertson, 1968).
——, "Defence Under Labor", *Current Affairs Bulletin* 52 (December 1975): 4–18.
——, *Foreign Policy: Some Australian Reflections* (Melbourne: Georgian House, 1972).
Miller, J.D.B., "Australian Foreign Policy: Constraints and Opportunities—I", *International Affairs* 50 (April 1974): 229–41.
——, "Australian Foreign Policy: Constraints and Opportunities—II", *International Affairs* 50 (July 1974): 425–38.
——, ed., *Australia's Economic Relations* (Sydney: Angus & Robertson with McGraw-Hill, 1974).
Murphy, D., "New Nationalism or New Internationalism, Australian Foreign Policy 1973–74", *World Review* 13 (October 1974): 14–22.
Noone, B., *Australian Economic Ties with South Africa* (Carlton, Vic.: Australian Union of Students, 1973).
O'Brien, P., "The Ermolenko Affair", *Quadrant* 18 (July–August 1974): 16–24.
O'Connell, D.P., ed., *International Law in Australia* (Sydney: Law Book Co., 1966).
O'Neill, R., ed., *The Strategic Nuclear Balance: An Australian Perspective* (Canberra: Australian National University Press for the Strategic and Defence Studies Centre, Australian National University, 1975).
Peacock, A., "An Alternative Foreign Policy for Australia", *World Review* 13 (July 1974): 3–11.
Pettit, D., ed., *Selected Readings in Australian Foreign Policy* (Melbourne: Sorrett, 1973).
Renouf, A., "New Challenges in Foreign Policy Administration", *Australian Outlook* 28 (August 1974): 109–17.
Richardson, J.L., "Australian Foreign Policy Under the Labor Government", *Cooperation and Conflict* 9, no. 1 (1974): 9–18.
Rivett, K., "Non-White Migration: A Turning Point?", *Australia's Neighbours*, 4th Series, no. 87 (September–October 1973): 1–4.

Roberts, N.S., "Foreign Policy and Australian General Elections", *World Review* 12 (July 1973): 22–30.

Robertson, J.R., "Are Western Australians Worth Defending?", *Australian Outlook* 28 (April 1974): 57–70.

Santamaria, B.A., "The First Six Months", *Current Affairs Bulletin* 50 (July 1973): 8–11.

Scott, R. and Richardson J., eds., *The First Thousand Days of Labor*, vol. 1: *Public Policy and Interest Groups and International Relations* (Canberra: Canberra College of Advanced Education, 1975).

Sharman, G.C., "The Australian States and External Affairs: An Explanatory Note", *Australian Outlook* 27 (December 1973): 307–18.

Shaw, L., ed., *The Shape of the Labor Régime* (Canberra: Harp Books, 1974).

Siracusa, J.M., "Ambassador Marshall Green, America, and Australia: The Making of a New Relationship", *World Review* 14 (October 1975): 17–25.

Skully, M.T., "Australia's Trade Potential with the Centrally Planned Economy Countries", *Australian Outlook* 29 (December 1975): 341–48.

Smith, H., "Internal Conflict in an Independent Papua New Guinea: Problems of Australian Involvement", *Australian Outlook* 28 (August 1974): 160–67.

Stevens, F.S., ed., *Racism: The Australian Experience. A Study of Race Prejudice in Australia*, vol. 3: *Colonialism* (Sydney: ANZ Book Co., 1972).

Stock, R.L., "Labor's External Policy: A Businessman's View", *Dyason House Papers* 1 (March 1975): 1–5.

Stockwin, J.A.A., "Australia's Relations with Japan: Complementarity and Strain", *Round Table* no. 258 (April 1974): 149–58.

Stop Omega Research Group, *Omega, Poseidon, and the Arms Race: Why Omega is an Aggressive War Base*, Occasional Paper, no. 5 (Sydney: Association for International Co-operation and Disarmament, 1974).

Suter, K.D., "The Australian Government's Policy on Recognition and Diplomatic Relations", *Australian Quarterly* 47 (September 1975): 67–79.

United Service 28 (October 1974): *passim*.

Verrier, J., "Priorities in Papua New. Guinea's Evolving Foreign Policy: Some Legacies and Lessons of History", *Australian Outlook* 28 (December 1974): 290–307.

Waller, P., "Caucus Control of Cabinet: Myth or Reality?", *Public Administration* 33 (December 1974): 300–306.

Warner, G., "The Foreign Policy of the Australian Labor Government", in *The International Yearbook of Foreign Policy Analysis*, ed. P. Jones (London: Croom Helm, 1974), vol. 1, pp. 155–79.

Watt, A., *The Evolution of Australian Foreign Policy 1938–1965* (London: Cambridge University Press, 1967).

Whitlam, E.G., "Australian Foreign Policy: New Directions, New Definitions", 24th Roy Milne Lecture, Brisbane (Melbourne: Australian Institute of International Affairs, 1973).

Withers, G., *Conscription: Necessity and Justice. The Case for an All Volunteer Army* (Sydney: Angus & Robertson, 1972).

Witton, R., "Australia and Apartheid: The Ties that Bind", *Australian Quarterly* 45 (June 1973): 18–31.

Index